Hot Questrists
After The English Renaissance

✽

Essays on Shakespeare
and His Contemporaries

✽

The Editorial Committee

YUKIO KATO, University of Tsukuba
AKIKO KUSUNOKI, Tokyo Woman's Christian University
YOICHI OHASHI, University of Tokyo
HIROSHI OZAWA, Kwansei Gakuin University

Hot Questrists After the English Renaissance

Essays on Shakespeare and His Contemporaries

In Commemoration of
the Thirty-fifth Anniversary of
The Shakespeare Society of Japan

Editor-in-Chief

Yasunari Takahashi

AMS Press, Inc.
New York

Library of Congress Cataloging-in-Publication Data

Hot Questrists after the English Renaissance: essays on Shakespeare and his contemporaries : in commemoration of the thirty-fifth annivesary of the Shakespeare Society of Japan / editor-in-chief, Yasunari Takahashi
    (AMS Studies in the Renaissance; no. 37)
    Includes bibliographical references and index.
    ISBN 0-404-62337-9 (alk. paper)
    1. English literature—Early modern, 1500-1700—History and criticism. 2. Shakespeare, William, 1564-1616—Criticism and interpretation. 3. Shakespeare, William, 1564-1616—Contemporaries. 4. Renaissance—England. I.Takahashi, Yasunari, 1932- II. Series.
PR423. H68 2000
822.3'3 —dc21　　　　　　　　　　　　　　　　99-59710

All AMS Books are printed on acid-free paper that meets the guidelines for performance and durability of the Committee on Production Guidelines for Book Longevity of the Council on Library Resources.

Copyright © 2000 by AMS Press, Inc.
All rights reserved

AMS Press, Inc.
56 East 13th Street
New York, NY 10003-4686
U.S.A.

MANUFACTURED IN THE UNITED STATES OF AMERICA

Contents

Foreword
    Yasuo Tamaizumi   vii

Introduction
    Yasunari Takahashi   1

Falling Backward and Broken Maidenhead:
Language of Sexuality in *Romeo and Juliet*
    Soji Iwasaki   5

Diagnosing Male Jealousy: Woman as Man's Symptom in
The Merry Wives of Windsor, Othello, The Winter's Tale and
Cymbeline
    Yoko Takakuwa   19

The Wonder of the Virgin Queen:
Through Early Colonial Discourse on Virginia
    Emi Hamana   37

The Taming of the Shrewd Critics
Who Talk Wild of *The Wild-Goose Chase*
    Shoichiro Kawai   53

Creating the Female Self:
Margaret Cavendish's Authorial Voice and Fictional Selves
    Mami Adachi   69

    *   *   *

Dialogue in *Romeo and Juliet*
    Tetsuo Kishi   89

"Those Are Pearls That Were His Eyes":
Shakespeare's Holographic Imagination
    Mitsuru Kamachi   101

Coriolanus and the Body of Satan
    Koichi Muranushi   115

The Bee Emblem in *The Rape of Lucrece*
  MISAKO MATSUDA   131

Overlapping Exits and Entrances in Shakespeare's Plays
  MARIKO ICHIKAWA   145

                    *   *   *

Theories of Nature and Political Legitimation:
Two Orestes Plays in English Renaissance Drama
  AYA MIMURA   167

The First and the Second Parts of *Henry IV*:
Some Thoughts on the Origins of Shakespearean Gentleness
  SHIGEKI TAKADA   183

"Remember Saint Crispin": Narrating the Nation in *Henry V*
  TED MOTOHASHI   197

Tamburlaine's Prophetic Oratory and
Protestant Militarism in the 1580s
  ARATA IDE   215

On the Margins of a Civilization:
The Representation of the Scythians in Elizabethan Texts
  ATSUHIKO HIROTA   237

The Masque of Queens: Between Sight and Sound
  YUMIKO YAMADA   255

Contextualizing Shakespeare:
The Renaissance Debate on the Nature of Slavery
  SERGIO MAZZARELLI   269

Notes on Contributors   289

Index   293

Foreword

> How many ages hence
> Shall this our lofty scene be acted over,
> In states unborn and accents yet unknown.
> *(Julius Cæsar, 3. 1.)*

SO SPEAKS CASSIUS immediately after the assassination of Caesar, still "signed in thy [i.e. Caesar's] spoil, and crimson'd in thy lethe," and to this Brutus responds, "How many times shall Caesar bleed in sport." These famous utterances in which Shakespeare makes fun of his own profession tell us how self-conscious a dramatist he was. As historical personages, Cassius and Brutus must have known Britain very well, when they acted this "lofty scene" in 44 B. C., though they hardly imagined this "scene" would be enacted more than one thousand five hundred years later in an English "accent." But it is not obvious Shakespeare knew the "state" of Japan at any point in his life. Shakespeare the great reader read William Strachey's letter describing the disaster of the Virginia voyage of 1609 in manuscript, when he worked over *The Tempest*, but it was not until 1625 when he had been dead about ten years that the letter appeared in printed form in *Purchas his Pilgrimes* where various voyages to Japan were related. There is no certainty, either, of his ever seeing or reading Barnabe Barnes's *The Devil's Charter* (1607), a play in which the name of Japan was first referred to on the English stage.

The prophecy that Shakespeare put into the mouths of Cassius and Brutus has come true even in Japan, and ever since about 1840, when Shakespeare's name was first known to Japanese readership through the re-translation of an English book from Dutch, his drama has given much stimulus to Japanese literature and drama. There are more than thirty translations including two complete ones, and also many adaptations including Kabuki scripts in the Meiji period, films like Kurosawa's *Kumonosu-jo* (*Throne of Blood*), and the recent Kyogen play,

Foreword

The Braggart Samurai; Ninagawa's *Macbeth* and Suzuki's *Tale of Lear* have appealed tremendously to world-wide audiences. It is hardly an exaggeration to say that Shakespearean drama has been acclimatised and become a cultural asset of Japan.

In the academic field, however, this assimilative impulse meant that Japan was for some time content to be an "import" country, without making substantive contributions to the development of Shakespeare studies in the world. There were important early studies, but they were written in Japanese for the Japanese. As was the case with classical studies in Renaissance Europe, the chief concern of our predecessors in studying foreign things and ideas was to enrich our own culture, and extend what Spenser called "the kingdome of oure owne language."

Now, as the world shrinks and our personal contacts with various scholars around the world increase, the situation is very different. When the Fifth World Shakespeare Congress was held in Tokyo in 1991, many Japanese scholars were looking beyond a domestic market and were eager to make their thoughts and ideas available in English. In accordance with this welcome change, the Shakespeare Society of Japan, which has hitherto been publishing its memorial studies in Japanese every five years since its fifteenth anniversary, decided to publish this thirty-fifth anniversary volume in English.

I hope this book will be appreciated by many readers all over the world, and will contribute to the development of future Shakespeare studies.

Yasuo Tamaizumi
President
The Shakespeare Society of Japan

Introduction

Yasunari Takahashi

A CENTURY, ALMOST to the year, has elapsed since an anonymous critic wrote in a literary journal in Tokyo:

> Today there are some among younger generations who do talk of Shakespeare, but their voices do not as yet possess sufficient authenticity to command respect. If one aspires to specialize in the study of Shakespeare's drama, one must start by doing one's utmost to master the English language; otherwise one is doomed to miserable failure. Ah, the difficulty of studying Shakespeare on this far-off island in the East![1]

The jeremiad would be a pointer to the fact that Shakespeare's name was becoming one of the fashionable passwords among would-be intellectuals in *fin-de-siècle* Japan, thirty years after the Meiji Restoration. His works indeed had been very much in evidence in the world of journalism and entertainment. By 1896, one could have seen or read adapted and partial versions of such plays as *Julius Caesar*, *The Merchant of Venice*, *Romeo and Juliet*, *As You Like It*, *Hamlet*, and *King Lear*. More than one translation of the "To be or not to be" soliloquy had made Hamlet a cult figure for sophisticated literary-minded youths. But the wailing critic was so far right that the reception of Shakespeare in the form of seriously faithful translation, let alone in the field of critical and academic studies, had to come much later than adaptations and performances.

The greatest figure in the history of Shakespeare translations and studies during the hundred years that followed is undoubtedly Shoyo Tsubouchi (1859-1935). It is just possible that the critic quoted above was none other he; it is tempting to conjecture that he came to realize the necessity of "serious" translation upon seeing an adapted performance of *Othello* in 1903, produced by the notoriously talented actor-manager, Otojiro Kawakami, which might have well looked abominably clever and irresponsible to him.[2] Be that as it may, Tsubouchi was certainly the one who played the vital roles of translator, director, and producer in the 1911 *Hamlet*, a historic production in which characters and locations were named as in the original for the first time, with a translation as faithful and an acting style as realistically Western as one could reasonably hope for at the time.

Tsubouchi then assigned himself the superhuman labour of translating the whole canon single-handed. It was completed in 1928, but he continued revising the text until his death. The same year saw the publication of his scholarly work, *Notes on the Study of Shakespeare*. This solid, all-round, and remarkably up-to-date introduction, together with the first fully comprehensive study of the dramatist in Japan, Takeshi Saito's *Shakespeare: His Life and Art* (1916), paved the way for a countless number of essays and books on Shakespeare and related subjects to be produced over the ensuing eighty years.

It is true that some of them were written in English, but it is a relatively recent phenomenon that Japanese scholars have started publishing in English. In this context, we acknowledge with pleasure that a fresh impetus for "internationalization" was engendered by the Fifth World Shakespeare Congress in Tokyo in 1991, hosted by the Shakespeare Society of Japan. In presenting here a volume of critical studies to international readership to commemorate the thirty-fifth anniversary of the (new) Shakespeare Society of Japan re-founded in 1961, we also remember, with some emotion, that Tsubouchi was elected the Honorary President of the (old) Shakespeare Society of Japan when it was founded in 1930.

Looking at the table of contents of this volume, the reader may wonder at one thing: the absence of "Japanese" themes. Such themes, it should be stressed, were not excluded by the editorial committee when it made a call for papers to the members of our Society, so that the result as we see it now is purely accidental and, in that sense, surprising to ourselves. By a hindsight, however, there is a sense in which this could have been predicted. "Japanese" themes or perspectives have for some time been—are now being and will continue to be—given quite a lot of attention. There was a seminar on "Acting and Language in Shakespeare and the Eastern Theatre" at the 1991 Congress, which later grew into a book.[3] This was followed by a seminar on "Shakespeare Performances in Japan" at the Sixth Congress in Los Angeles in 1996, which again expects publication[4] but may be preceded by another

Introduction 3

project on a similar subject.⁵ On the other hand, the recently published *Hamlet and Japan* has a section dedicated to a group of essays focusing on the Japanese reception of the play.⁶ Far from there being anything wrong about this tendency, we the Japanese scholars are only glad of the attention paid to our culture as well as of the chances it affords us of joining or sometimes leading the discussions. Although it should be added that all of the above-mentioned projects include non-Japanese contributors, it seems natural that a Japanese scholar should feel it incumbent on him or her to explore the significances of Shakespeare's impact on Japanese culture.

And yet it would be equally natural that one should resist the assumption that this is a recognized territory of one's own beyond which one is not supposed to venture. One has a desire to go boundary-free in terms of themes. While the truth is one must willy-nilly have a multi-layered awareness of one's cultural roots, one cannot avoid taking up the challenge from outside, or responding to the urge within, to engage in discussions of critical problematics at international level—which is exactly what this collection of essays is about.

The seventeen essays wrestling with Shakespeare and his contemporaries are divided into three groups. The first group contains those dealing with what might be termed the "woman question" in a broad sense of the phrase. The subjects range from the language of sexuality in *Romeo and Juliet* to male jealousy in *Othello* and other plays, from the icon of Elizabeth I to the re-valuations of Fletcher and Cavendish. The second section consists of five papers, three of which are concerned with various aspects of theatrical experiences: the nature of dialogue in *Romeo and Juliet*, the manifold effects of Shakespeare's imagination, and the way exits and entrances overlap in Shakespeare's plays. The other two are an emblematic study of *The Rape of Lucrece* and an exploration of the Satanic imagery in *Coriolanus* respectively. The last group of essays are more or less of historicising and politicising orientation. The political implications of two neglected Orestes plays are diagnosed, and Marlowe figures as the subject of two papers, one discussing him in relation to Protestant militarism and the other deciphering the representation of the Scythians in Elizabethan texts. *Henry IV* offers an occasion to one writer to consider the idea of Shakespearean gentleness while the nationalistic strain of *Henry V* is stressed by another. An analysis of Jonson's masque is followed by a paper (the author happens to be the only non-Japanese contributor) which concludes the volume with an examination of the Renaissance debate on slavery.

None of these essays make recourse to explicitly "comparative" or "Japanologist" perspectives, aspiring as they do to join the republic of academic studies and maintain dialogues with their international colleagues. Whether they have the power to survive initial reactions of those readers who may have expected to find something "Japanese" is not, of course, for us to say. We can only hope that present-day Japanese scholarship as represented here will have gone some way towards pacifying the ghost of our anonymous ancestral critic.

On behalf of the Shakespeare Society of Japan and the editorial committee, I wish to thank Professor Graham Bradshaw who kindly accepted, and executed with admirable conscientiousness and perceptiveness, the task of reading and commenting on all the essays. Without his cooperation, the book would not have been what it is. Our profound gratitude must go to Professor Yuji Kaneko for the enormous labour he has undertaken in preparing camera-ready copy with so much good will and expertise. We are also deeply indebted to Professor John Manning who, by rigorously going over the whole draft, saved us from many an error.

Notes

1. Anonymous, "Sheikusupia kenkyuka ni atau" [A Message to Students of Shakespeare], *Teikoku Bungaku* [*The Imperial Literature*] 2, 1 (Tokyo: January 10, 1896). See *Sheikusupia Kenkyu Shiryo Shusei* [*The Collected Shakespeare Studies in Japan*] vol. 1, ed. Takashi Sasaki (Tokyo: Nihon Tosho Center, 1997) p. 130.

2. See Harue Tsutsumi, *Seigeki Muro Wasero* [*Tragedy of Muro Wasero*] (first performed in Tokyo, 1995), a play in which Tsubouchi is shown attending the first performance of Kawakami's adapted *Othello*.

3. Minoru Fujita and Leonard Pronko, ed. *Shakespeare East and West* (Surrey: Curzon Press, 1996).

4. John Gillies, Ian Carruthers and Ryuta Minami, ed. *Performing Shakespeare in Japan* (Cambridge: Cambridge Univ. Press, forthcoming).

5. Takashi Sasayama, Ronnie Mulryne and Margaret Shewring, ed. *Shakespeare and the Japanese Stage* (Cambridge: Cambridge Univ. Press, 1998).

6. Yoshiko Uéno, ed. *Hamlet and Japan* (New York: AMS Press, 1995). See also Tetsuo Kishi and Graham Bradshaw, *Shekespeare in Japan* (London: Athlone Press, forthcoming) and Yoshiko Kawachi, ed. *Japanese Studies in Shakespeare and His Contemporaries* (Cranbury, N. J.: The Assocated Univ. Presses, 1998).

Falling Backward and Broken Maidenhead: Language of Sexuality in *Romeo and Juliet*

Soji Iwasaki

1

IN *ROMEO AND JULIET*, two contrasting female types are found in Lady Capulet and the Nurse, a cold and distant woman of a privileged family and a warm and intimate woman of a profession sometimes considered demeaning. Rosaline, another cold and distant woman, is no more than Romeo's portrayal of the forever unavailable Petrarchan lady who "has sworn that she will still live chaste" (1. 1. 217).[1] The anti-Petrarchan woman of open sexuality that Mercutio imagines, "That she were, O that she were / An open et cetera" (2. 1. 37-38), is a specimen of the Nurse type, but only a piece of male phantasy. Juliet, the central figure of the play, is a compound of the two contrasting types, socially constructed between her natural mother, cold and distant, and her surrogate mother, warm and close.

The Nurse is a very physical presence. When she first appears on the stage, she says to Lady Capulet,

> Now, by my maidenhead at twelve year old,
> I bade her come. What, lamb! what ladybird!
> God forbid! (1. 3. 2-4)

The word "maidenhead," echoing Sampson's sexual joke on "the heads of the maids" and "maidenheads" in 1. 1 (22-26), suggests the Nurse's sense of her own bodily existence. In the ensuing conversation the Nurse mentions her teeth—"I'll lay fourteen of my teeth—/ And yet, to my teen be it spoken, I have but four—/ She's not fourteen" (1. 3. 13-15). She further refers to other parts of her body, again of sexual significance, "my dug" (27) and "the nipple / Of my dug" (31-32). Later in 2. 5 she complains of her aching "back" (50) and "bones" (63), and in 2.4 she says, "Every part of me quivers" (157-58), possibly with sexual implication. As a wet-nurse, she nursed Juliet till she was weaned at the age of three, a rather late weaning. To Juliet the Nurse is intimate and affectionate, perhaps more so than her natural mother, and the Nurse's concept of love is always bodily and sexual. When Juliet expects to see Paris at the masque, she says to her, "seek happy nights to happy days" (1. 3. 106); when Romeo has been banished from Verona she even advises Juliet to obey Capulet and marry Paris, saying, "Your first [husband] is dead, or 'twere as good he were / As living here and you no use of him" (3. 5. 225-26).

As a woman of the privileged class Lady Capulet apparently values the conventional womanly virtues of chastity, obedience, and reticence. When she first tells her daughter about Paris as a possible bridegroom, of primary importance is the social aspect of the match. Her outlook is revealed in her speech in 1. 3 where the book metaphor is elaborated. She develops the metaphor using so many words related to a book—"volume," "writ," "pen," "content," "margent"—and further she says,

> This precious book of love, this unbound lover,
> To beautify him, only lacks a cover.
> . . . That book in many's eyes doth share the glory
> That in gold clasps locks in the golden story;
> So shall you share all that he doth possess,
> By having him making yourself no less.   (1. 3. 88-95)

In the book-metaphor here, a bachelor is not a competent individual, he is yet "unbound." When covered with a wife, he is beautified, the golden story being locked in gold "clasps." Marriage is a patriarchal institution binding man and wife in a socially established contract, which is metaphorically a clasp-bound book. The content of the book should be a "golden" story and the clasps "gold", the repeated words "gold" and "golden" emphasizing the concept of wealth and social status. This elitist view is in contrast to the Nurse's idea of marriage, marriage as a bodily conjugation; at the word "marriage" she instantly imagines conjugation and conception. At Lady Capulet's "By having him making yourself no less," she cries, "No less! Nay, bigger; women grow by men."

When Lady Capulet asks her daughter "[C]an you like of Paris' love?" Juliet's reaction is that of a girl of the privileged society:

> I'll look to like, if looking liking move;
> But no more deep will I endart mine eye
> Than your consent gives strength to make it fly.   (98-100)

The tone of her speech, its rhetorical sophistication, the metaphoric figure (looking compared to shooting a dart, with an association of Cupid's darts), and the rhyming couplet—all are imitations of her mother's way of speaking. In the later balcony scene Juliet's speech is more simple and plain, for there Juliet is Juliet in her natural self, but in this earlier scene she is practically contained or learning to conform to the conventional elitist culture.

Juliet's body is sexually mature, her humour being sanguine. Her "unmann'd" blood makes her blush quite often (2. 2. 86; 2. 5. 70; 3. 2. 14), and as with the coy mistress in Marvell's poem, her "willing [animal] Soul transpires / At every pore with instant Fires."[2] In the Capulets' ball scene (1. 5) she readily responds to Romeo's wooing, letting him kiss her on the lips in a very short space of time (1. 5. 93-106). In Juliet two types of women exist, a chaste maid of a privileged family and an innocent active girl who tends to be free from the social decorum of the higher classes. Juliet's desire is bound by patriarchal definition and regulation; the two forms of female desire, desire of natural and inevitable sexual growth and desire as an act of obedience to custom and precedent, are contained in the body of Juliet.

In Juliet's enculturation from her infancy through girlhood to marriageability, weaning is the earliest hardship to suffer. In a society in which wet-nursing is institutionalized, the physical interdependence of nurse and baby is greater than that of natural mother and child. In Juliet's case "Lady Capulet's absence from the scene of weaning should be taken as emblematic of her physical, hence emotional withdrawal from Juliet."[3] Juliet's weaning is something of a rite of passage, the baby is separated from her breast mother and enters a new phase of life. For the child the shock can be seismic.

Indeed, Juliet's weaning happened on the day of the memorable earthquake.

> 'Tis since the earthquake now eleven years;
> And she was wean'd—I never shall forget it—
> Of all the days of the year, upon that day;

> For I had then laid wormwood to my dug,
> Sitting in the sun under the dove-house wall;
> My lord and you were then at Mantua.
> Nay, I do bear a brain. But, as I said,
> When it did taste the wormwood on the nipple
> Of my dug, and felt it bitter, pretty fool,
> To see it tetchy, and fall out with the dug!
> Shake, quoth the dove-house. 'Twas no need, I trow,
> To bid me trudge. (1. 3. 24-35)

Only the day before, the toddling Juliet fell and hurt her head. The Nurse's husband, now dead, saw Juliet fall on her face and made a joke of it:

> 'Yea,' quoth he, 'dost thou fall upon thy face?
> Thou wilt fall backward when thou hast more wit,
> Wilt thou not, Jule?' and by my holidam,
> The pretty wretch left crying and said, 'Ay'. (1. 3. 42-45)

In the perspective of the whole play, we can understand that Juliet's separation from her breast mother prefigures her later separation from her social mother, and her falling on her face presages her falling backward in her bridal bed. The earthquake may have as sexual a significance as Juliet's falling, for "Every part of me quivers" says the Nurse in 2. 4 (157-58) with a sexual overtone. To the Nurse the breast and the sexual organ are the most significant parts of a woman's body; and to Juliet as well, the breast is a crucially significant part of her body, for she will plunge Romeo's dagger into her breast and "die" in ecstasy. The successive experiences Juliet had on her weaning day and before, falling, weaning and earthquake, comprise her bodily and psychic traumas, and, through their correspondences with the later falling, separation and temporary interment, they have a central significance to the meaning of the whole tragedy of sexuality. Thematically, as Gail Kern Paster aptly points out, "The [Nurse's] husband's witticism consists in constructing the two falls antithetically—forward replaced by backward, accident replaced by purpose and design, fear replaced by desire, broken forehead replaced by broken maidenhead."[4] *Romeo and Juliet* is a tragedy of the loss of maidenhead.

2

In his *Impersonations* (1996) Stephen Orgel quotes from Thomas Wright's *The Passions of the Mind in General* (1604): "a personable body is often linked with a pestilent soul; a valiant Captain in the field for the most part is infected with an effeminate affection at home."[5] Orgel says, "lust effeminates, makes men incapable of manly pursuits: hence the pervasive antithesis of love and war."[6] In *Romeo and Juliet* the antithesis of love and hate, or sexuality and violence, is clear, and Romeo, who has just been married to Juliet in passionate love, finds himself unmanned before Tybalt's attack:

> O sweet Juliet,
> Thy beauty hath made me effeminate,
> And in my temper softened valor's steel!   (3. 1. 110-12)

In the balcony scene (2. 2) before this, Romeo is already emasculated by desire. Here Juliet "is the sun" dominating him; she is masculine standing high on the balcony.

> O, speak again, bright angel, for thou art
> As glorious to this night, being o'er my head,
> As is a winged messenger of heaven
> Unto the white-upturned wond'ring eyes
> Of mortals that fall back to gaze on him,
> When he bestrides the lazy-pacing clouds
> And sails upon the bosom of the air.   (2. 2. 26-32)

Juliet is in a higher position and is like an angel who "bestrides the lazy-pacing clouds," in contrast to Cleopatra wishfully imagining how happy the horse would feel "to bear the weight of Antony" (*Antony and Cleopatra*, 1. 5. 21). Romeo, on the other hand, *"falls back* to gaze on *him,"* a reversal of gender positions, which reminds us of the Nurse's repeated references to the infant Juliet's "falling backward." But an irony is that it is Romeo, not Juliet, who first falls backward. Romeo is effeminate, Juliet masculine. Desire has changed him from masculinity to effeminacy.

Romeo is effeminated by his desire for Juliet; his transformation is confirmed when he consents to Juliet's request:

> Deny thy father and refuse thy name;
> Or, if thou wilt not, be but sworn my love,
> And I'll no longer be a Capulet.   (2. 2. 34-36)

When Juliet says, "Romeo, doff thy name; and for thy name ... Take all myself," Romeo steps out into her view and says, "I take thee at thy word: / Call me but love and I'll be new baptiz'd; / Henceforth I never will be Romeo" (49-51). Now Romeo is no Romeo, he is love itself, or he has identified himself with Love by lending his eyes to the blind God. When Juliet asks, "By whose direction found'st thou out this place?" Romeo answers:

> By love, that first did prompt me to enquire;
> He *lent* me *counsel*, and I lent him eyes.
> I am no pilot; yet, wert thou as far
> As that vast *shore* wash'd with the farthest sea,
> I should *adventure* for such *merchandise*.   (2. 2. 80-84; italics added)

Many of the words Romeo uses here have sexual overtones. According to Rubinstein, "(Ad)venture" means "copulate." Referring to this passage Rubinstein says, "Romeo says love 'lent me counsel'—LENT (yielded sexually) COUNSEL (a bawd's advice)—and, were Juliet on a far-away 'shore' (SHORE, brothel), he would still 'adventure for such merchandise' (i.e. that which is bought and sold)."[7] The implication here is that Love/Cupid is a bawd giving Romeo advice for an adventure with a prostitute in a brothel. We are reminded of the Nurse's call for Juliet, "What lamb! what ladybird!" (1. 3. 3) ("lamb" and "ladybird" both being words capable of meaning "whore"[8]) and of Mercutio's reference to the Nurse as "A bawd, a bawd, a bawd!" (2. 4. 127). Love in Romeo now is not an ever-unfulfilled desire for an absent lady of chastity; it is physical and erotic.

In her brief courtship Juliet is forthright about her desires:

> ... but farewell compliment!
> Dost thou love me? I know thou wilt say ay,
> And I will take thy word; yet, if thou swear'st,
> Thou mayst prove false; at lovers' perjuries
> They say Jove laughs. O gentle Romeo,
> If thou dost love, pronounce it faithfully.
> Or, if thou think'st I am too quickly won,
> I'll frown, and be perverse, and say thee nay,
> So thou wilt woo; but else, not for the world.   (2. 2. 89-97)

She does not want Romeo to "swear" his love but just wants him to "pronounce it faithfully." Juliet in love with Romeo is free from those figures of speech of a lady of the upper classes, and from that pretended perversity and frown of a "coy mistress" or a Petrarchan lady. And Romeo, under Juliet's initiative, comes to assume the same simplicity. Theirs is a natural love, bodily desire for sexual union and pleasure. When the time comes for the lovers to part and Romeo says, "O, wilt thou leave me so unsatisfied?" Juliet knows what "satisfaction" Romeo wants. But she is so much the daughter of Lady Capulet that she refuses to give it to him before marriage.

Romeo has grown out of his "artificial" (1. 1. 140) love of Rosaline and into the natural desire for Juliet. But it is not only that. He also changes from a member of the feudal patriarchal family of Montague to a romantic lover—a modern individualist. He was "new baptiz'd," did "deny his father" and "doff his name." Juliet and he have now been liberated from their familial bondage and also from the artificial/rhetorical language of love in the dominant patriarchal society. The emergent modern individualism and romantic love in the lovers is what Cedric Watts affirms in his discussion of the "sexual politics" of the play. From a feminist-political viewpoint Watts examines the contemporary changing attitudes to arranged marriage and romantic love and, criticising the more "patriarchal" readings of Lawrence Stone and others, associates the play with the "romantic" attitudes of emergent modern individualism.[9]

Thus Juliet's language in the balcony scene is not that rhetorical way of speaking she adopted in the conversation with her mother. The language of "books", or of patriarchal bondage, has been thrown away and the lovers now speak the language of sexuality. The most natural way of expressing desire is to utter the name of the person one loves; Viola says she would cry out "Olivia!" and "make the babbling gossip of the air [*i.e.* Echo]" cry again (*Twelfth Night*, 1. 5. 227-29). Juliet in this play did cry out her lover's name: "O Romeo, Romeo, wherefore art thou Romeo?" and still she would do so but that

> Bondage is hoarse, and may not speak aloud;
> Else would I tear the cave where Echo lies,
> And make her airy tongue more hoarse than mine.
> With repetition of my Romeo's name.   (2. 2. 160-63)

Juliet's speech here is full of sexual connotations. "Tongue" and "ears"

(167) may be words of ordinary conversation, but they may at the same time be words of sexuality: according to Rubinstein, "tongue" means "penis; clitoris" and "ear" vagina.[10] Rubinstein further says:

> (1) Juliet would tear Echo's cave (*valcava*: a hollow cave, used by Boccaccio for 'a womans quaint [cunt]'—F). She would *tear* out and use Echo's TONGUE (clitoris) as the clapper (tongue—F & H) of a bell, to recall Romeo. (2) *Abrocare*: to become hoarse, to fart (F)—another of Sh's gibes at the airy, insubstantial quality of this 'too sudden' love.[11]

What I should like to add here is that "tear" reminds us of Marvell's lines:

> Let us roll all our Strength, and all
> Our sweetness, up into one Ball:
> And *tear* our *Pleasures* with rough *strife*,
> Thorough the Iron *gates* of Life.
> Thus, though we cannot make our Sun
> Stand still, yet we will make him run. (Italics added)[12]

Eric Partridge in *Shakespeare's Bawdy* explicates: "Strive. To struggle amorously";[13] "pleasure and pleasures. Sexual pleasure; pleasures of sexual intimacy. *R.& J.*, II. iii. 160-64"[14]; "gate GAIT. The vulva."[15] In this poem of Marvell's, sexual meaning is clear, and when we compare Juliet's "Bondage is hoarse" speech with Marvell's "tear our pleasures with rough strife, / Thorough the iron gates of life," *Romeo*'s "tear the cave where Echo lies" is understood as meaning "tear the maidenhead," and we thus know that the maidenhead-motif continues.

"Bondage" here has a remote echo of the book-metaphor in Lady Capulet' speech in 1.3; there Paris was an "unbound lover" (88), implying that marriage is the patriarchal bondage which binds man and wife in gold clasps. Once Romeo also was talking in book metaphors, using such "bookish" words as "note" and "read" (1. 1. 235-36), but now he is liberated through the natural love he experienced with Juliet and says,

> Love goes toward love as school-boys from their books. (2. 2. 156)

Thus the lovers leave the patriarchal bondage "toward love," that is, love between two individuals who "look" at each other so that "passion lends them power." "Looks" liberate the lovers from "books."

Passion is what liberates Romeo and Juliet from the "book" of patriarchal bondage, the "book" of Petrarchan love conventions by which Romeo kissed Juliet at their first meeting (1. 5. 112), and "the book of arithmetic" (3. 1. 98-99) by which Tybalt wielded his long sword. Those books are now discarded.

3

Along with the language of sexuality, there is the language of life-and-death running throughout the play. The two languages are closely intertwined, or rather interfused. The Chorus's words in the Prologue, "star-crossed lovers" and "their death-marked love," presage the play's motif of 'Liebestod,' or love unified with death. And the pun of "the heads of the maids" and "maidenhead" in the opening scene proves to be of central importance, for in this pun the two themes, of killing and of loving, overlap and the two languages are interfused. The key image in this context is that of a dagger, and the three outstanding dagger sequences are first the scene where the street brawl involves Benvolio, Tybalt, Montague and Capulet (1. 1), the middle scene where Mercutio's violent death is followed by Tybalt's (3. 1), and finally the churchyard scene where Juliet pierces her breast with Romeo's dagger (5. 3).

In the last catastrophic scene, Juliet takes up Romeo's dagger and kills herself, saying,

> O happy dagger!
> This is thy sheath; there rust, and let me die.   (5. 3. 168-69)

What happens in this scene is that Juliet first sips the remains of the poison Romeo left in the vial, the poison recalling the "wormwood" the infant Juliet tasted on the Nurse's nipple in 1. 3 as well as the "distilled liquor" (4. 1. 94) the Friar provided and Juliet drank the day before her proposed marriage to Paris. Then she thrusts Romeo's dagger into her own breast. To the infant Juliet the Nurse's breast was the locus where she tasted delights *and* the bitter wormwood, and now her own breast is where she attains her death, death as the end of her bodily existence and as her sexual ecstasy. She has now "more wit" and "falls backward," and the fall this time means physical death as well as sexual ecstasy. In the sexual language of the play the "dagger" stands for penis and the "sheath" vagina. The words "happy dagger" and "die" mean the lovers' sexual consummation, the actualization of Friar Lawrence's unintentional prediction: "these violent delights have violent ends, / And in their triumph die; like fire and powder, / Which, as they kiss, *consume*" (2. 6. 9-11); the words "in their triumph die" and "consume" belong to the language of sexuality and that of life-and-death.

A problem, however, remains with the word "rust" in this passage. The phrasing of "This is thy sheath . . . and let me die" is consistent in its sexual implication, but "rust" does not so properly fit the context. Q1 reads:

> O happy dagger thou shalt end my fear,
> Rest in my bosome, thus I come to thee.

"Rest" is the word repeatedly used in this play, with a sexual overtone. We recall the Nurse's sexual joke in 4. 5:

> The County Paris hath set up his *rest*; that you shall *rest* but little.
> (4. 5. 6).

C. T. Onions, based on *OED* (Rest, sb. 2, 6), explains the word "rest" as: "at primero, the stakes kept in reserve, which were agreed upon at the beginning of the game, and upon the loss of which the game terminated,"[16] and Onions further says that "set up one's rest" figuratively means "to be resolved or determined" (cf. *OED*, Rest, sb. 2, 7. c). Thus what the Nurse means by "The County Paris hath set up his *rest* . . . " is that Paris is determined to be so active in the bridal bed that Juliet will have little rest or sleep. Another instance of the word "rest" occurs in the graveyard scene, where Romeo, finding Juliet's body in suspended animation, says,

> Ah, dear Juliet,
> Why art thou yet so fair? . . .
> . . . Here, here will I remain
> With worms that are thy chambermaids. O, here
> Will I set up my everlasting *rest* . . . .   (5. 3. 101-10)

Romeo's "here / Will I set up my everlasting rest" echoes the Nurse's joke on that Paris who "hath set up his rest." The word "rest," however, means more than Onions notes. *OED*, Rest, sb. 3, 2. goes:

> In mediaeval armour, a contrivance fixed to the right side of the

cuirass to receive the butt-end of the lance when couched for the charge, and to prevent it from being driven back upon impact . . .

and, probably based on this, Rubinstein says that "rest" means "Erect penis in its desired place of rest."[17] Reading this way, both Paris's "rest" and Romeo's "everlasting rest" are clearly recognizable as belonging to the language of sexuality.

Thus the original Q1 reading "rest," it seems to me, should be restored in place of the generally accepted "rust," and the sexual overtone of the dagger-sheath metaphor will be confirmed. Looking back to 2.4, Mercutio's comment on Tybalt's fencing, "*Rest* me his minim rest, one, two, and the third in your bosom" (2. 4. 22), might be taken as an ominous prediction of what the mortal dagger will do in the third and final dagger scene.

The language of sexuality in *Romeo and Juliet* is interfused with the language of life-and-death. Here "death" means physical decay and "sexual ecstsy"; the death-bringing poison is "quick" (= living; life-giving); and "eternal rest" means "restful death" *and* "eternally erect penis." The grave in *Romeo and Juliet* is "a fine and private place" (as in Marvell's poem) for lovers to embrace, but here the lovers are in death. In his last speech Romeo says, "Death is amorous" with Juliet, and this is more or less a recapitulation of the many references to Death as bridegroom in the play. In fact the association of "Death and the Virgin" is an outstanding motif in *Romeo*, and this erotic and bizarre image of amorous Death lying with a maid is a variation on a traditional German *topos* of "the encounter between the Maiden and Death."[18]

The image of Death as bridegroom identifies Romeo with Death. Romeo who was "new baptiz'd" as Love/Cupid in the earlier part of the play (2. 2) now lies with Juliet on their death/marriage bed. It is not that Romeo mutates from Love to Death but he is concurrently Love *and* Death, or it may otherwise be said that "Death is amorous" in him; and such an association of Love and Death was a commonplace in books of emblems and prose narratives in Shakespeare's England.

Geoffrey Whitney's *A Choice of Emblemes* (1586) and Henry Peacham's *Minerva Britanna* (1612) have each an emblem on 'Cupid and Death.' The shorter version of the two, Peacham's "*De Morte, et Cupidine*" goes:

> DEATH meeting once, with *CVPID* in an Inne,
> Where roome was scant, togeither both they lay.
> Both wearie, (for they roving both had beene,)
> Now on the morrow when they should away,

> *CVPID* Death's quiver at his back had throwne,
>   And *DEATH* tooke *CVPIDS*, thinking it his owne.
> By this o're-sight, it shortly came to passe,
> That young men died, who readie were to wed:
> And age did revell with his bonny-lasse,
> Composing girlonds for his hoarie head:
>   Invert not Nature, oh ye Powers twaine,
>   Giue *CVPID'S* dartes, and *DEATH* take thine againe.[19]

Here, Cupid and Death exchange functions, Death killing the younger and Cupid the older, and this is what is happening in the play *Romeo and Juliet*. At the end of the play young people like Mercutio, Tybalt, Paris, and of course Romeo and Juliet are all dead, while the aged people, Montague, Capulet and Lady Capulet, Escalus, Friar Lawrence and the Nurse are still alive, heading for a reconciliation. This is, as it were, a play of the triumph of Love armed with Death's darts; or it may better be called a play of the phallic dagger's violation of "the gates of life." Coppélia Kahn aptly says, "The blood-spattered entrance to [the Capulets'] tomb that has been figured as a womb recalls both a defloration or initiation into sexuality, and a birth."[20] The life-and-death irony and the womb-tomb metaphor coming into one focus, the patriarchal language of "books" is thus replaced by the Shakespearean language of sexuality.

Notes

The present essay was originally written for the seminar on "Languages of Gender and Sexuality" conducted by Professor Coppélia Kahn at the International Shakespeare Conference at Stratford-upon-Avon in August, 1996 and was read and commented on by the seminar participants. The author expresses his thanks to the people concerned.

1. All quotations from Shakespeare are from *William Shakespeare: The Complete Works*, ed. Peter Alexander (London and Glasgow: Collins, 1951).
2. Andrew Marvell, "To his Coy Mistress," ll. 35-36; Marvell, *The Letters and Poems*, ed. H. M. Margoliouth, revised by Pierre Legouis with the collaboration of E. E. Duncan-Jones (Oxford: Oxford UP, 1971), p.28.
3. Gail Kern Paster, *The Body Embarrassed: Drama and the Disciplines of Shame in Early Modern England* (Ithaca, NY: Cornell Univ. Press, 1993), p. 225.
4. Paster, p. 226.
5. Thomas Wright, *The Passions of the Mind in General* (1604), ed. W.W. Newbold (New York: Garland, 1986), p. 237; cited in Stephen Orgel, *Impersonations: The*

Performance of Gender in Shakespeare's England (Cambridge: Cambridge Univ. Press, 1996), p. 25.

6. Orgel, p. 25.

7. Frankie Rubinstein, *A Dictionary of Shakespeare's Sexual Puns and Their Significance* (New York: St. Martin's Press, 1995), p. 5.

8. Gordon Williams, *A Dictionary of Sexual Language and Imagery in Shakespearean and Stuart Literature* (London and Atlantic Highlands, NJ: Athlone Press, 1994), pp. 779, 776. For "ladybird" see Rubinstein, p. 143.

9. Watts says, "Protestantism, the Humanistic tradition and middle-class individualism tended to place a higher valuation than had Catholicism on mutual marital love, so marriage could increasingly be seen as the goal of a passionate relationship." Cedric Watts, *Romeo and Juliet (Harvester New Critical Introductions* series) (Hemel Hempstead, Hertfordshire: Harvester Wheatsheaf, 1991), p. 99. Dympna C. Callaghan in her materialist study of *Romeo and Juliet* argues that the play provided an ideological model for the modern idea of romantic married love. Callaghan, "The Ideology of Romantic Love: The Case of *Romeo and Juliet,*" in Dympna C. Callaghan, Lorraine Helms and Jyotsna Singh, *The Weyward Sisters: Shakespeare and Feminist Politics* (Oxford: Blackwell, 1994), pp. 59-101.

10. Rubinstein, pp. 278, 85. Gordon Williams also defines "tongue" as "penis-analogue," though he explains "ears" not as vagina but as of phallic significance, saying, "The dog's way of lifting and drooping its ears according to mood provides an obvious analogy with the penis." Williams, p. 429.

11. Rubinstein, p. 86.

12. Marvell, "To his Coy Mistress," ll. 41-46; *Letters and Poems,* p. 28.

13. Eric Partridge, *Shakespeare's Bawdy: A Literary and Psychological Essay and a Comprehensive Glossary* (London: Routledge and Kegan Paul, 1947; 1955), p. 196.

14. Partridge, p.167.

15. Partridge, p.119. Williams defines "gate" as "vagina," and "pleasure" "sensual gratification." Williams, pp. 585, 1055.

16. C.T. Onions, *Shakespearean Glossary* (London: Oxford Univ. Press, 1953), p. 183; under 'rest sb. 2'.

17. Rubinstein, p. 219.

18. François Laroque, "Tradition and Subversion in *Romeo and Juliet,*" in *Shakespeare's* Romeo and Juliet: *Text, Context, and Interpretation,* ed. Jay L. Halio (Newark: Univ. of Delaware Press, 1995), p. 31. Cf. Erwin Panofsky, *The Life and Art of Albrecht Dürer* (Princeton Univ. Press, 1955), fig. 93.

19. Henry Peacham, *Minerva Britanna* (1612), ed. John Horden (Menston, Yorkshire: Scolar Press, 1973), p. 172. Cf. Geoffrey Whitney, *A Choice of Emblemes* (1586), ed. J. Horden (Scolar Press, 1969), p. 132.

20. Coppélia Kahn, *Man's Estate: Masculine Identity in Shakespeare* (Berkeley: Univ. of California Press, 1981), p. 101.

Diagnosing Male Jealousy: Woman as Man's Symptom in *The Merry Wives of Windsor, Othello, The Winter's Tale* and *Cymbeline*

YOKO TAKAKUWA

1

PSYCHOANALYTICALLY, A WOMAN is a symptom of man.[1] Although Shakespeare lived three hundred years before psychoanalysis was invented and four hundred years before deconstruction, surprisingly the work of Jacques Lacan and Jacques Derrida can illuminate aspects of Shakespeare's plays. But perhaps it is not so surprising after all, since Sigmund Freud himself owed a great deal to literature, including the "Oedipus" complex itself.[2]

I realise, of course, that some critics tend too easily to label both psychoanalysis and deconstruction as "non-historical" or "a-historical" and solely to emphasise the anachronism of reading Shakespeare's "historical" texts in the light of current theory, without fully taking account of the important possibilities of theory. In my view, however, we need theory, because theory provides us with the methodological framework and thus, the radical strategy of reading both the text and the cultural system we inhabit.

If even after four hundred years, we still today read Shakespeare again and again, moreover, we read neither in order to re(dis)cover the lost past as the historical truth, nor to reaffirm the universal truth as the master-narrative of history. Our knowledge of "history" is, to a large extent, constituted in and through how we read historical documents or texts. We cannot read from anywhere other than the present, and what we identify is the difference of the past.

And since we read from the present, we are surely entitled to use whatever instruments the present offers. I read Shakespeare, because

Shakespeare's plays make me consider the problems of subjectivity, gender, sexuality, desire, love, marriage or the family in their historical difference. What I find in the plays is to some extent motivated by the existence of these problems in modern culture. At the same time, the perspective offered by the analysis of a remote historical culture can throw new light on our understanding of our own.

Othello, The Winter's Tale, Cymbeline and *The Merry Wives of Windsor* dramatise and diagnose the husband's jealousy as the symptom of a man caught up in the labyrinthine web of the meanings of "woman" for him.[3] Male jealousy comes from the ambivalence of his desire for and fear of "woman," who remains radically other than he is, and thus demonstrates the impossibility of possessing her internal "truth" as his property. Jealousy, according to Derrida, is "all desire for possession, guarding, property, exclusivity, nonsubstitution."[4] Othello is anxious to unveil and possess the *hidden* truth of Desdemona behind her "seeming." Leontes and Posthumus are jealous of what they imagine they see *and* know. Ford and Falstaff desire to possess "woman" in and outside marriage. Although Ford's worry about his wife's faithfulness to him seems to contrast with Falstaff's disregard of the chastity so highly valued by patriarchy, both Falstaff's conceited wooing and Ford's jealous distrust of his wife originate in their misogynous idea of "woman" in love/lust. In this essay, I propose to examine Falstaff's wooing and Ford's jealousy as man's symptom, diagnosed in their relations with the "merry" wives, along with a comparative analysis of jealous husbands in Shakespeare.

2

Othello fears that Cassio usurps what he possesses. Leontes suspects that Polixenes possesses his property. Posthumus is enraged by Iachimo's appropriation of what he owns. Yet all these husbands' suspicions are illusory. On the other hand, Ford's cuckold phobia is not utterly imaginary, since Falstaff aspires to what Ford possesses. Although Mrs. Ford, displeased by "whale" Falstaff's love letter, says that she has "an eye to make difference of men's liking" (2. 1. 54-55), Ford devalues his wife's "eye." Ford assumes that "woman" in love/lust may desire any "man." Falstaff comically surpasses the conventional definition of a seductive lover. At the same time, this singularity of Falstaff as "cuckolder" makes *The Merry Wives of Windsor* unique among

Shakespeare's plays.

In his letters, Falstaff rationalises why he loves Mrs. Page and/or Mrs. Ford: they are "not young," they are "merry" and they "love sack" (6-8). What he loves best is the wives' economic power or, more precisely, their rule of their husbands' purses as Elizabethan middle-class wives. He attempts to appropriate the middle class in Windsor, which seems to promise him the fulfilment of his desire to possess "woman," money and enjoyment. In other words, Falstaff is jealous of the Windsor middle-class men, who seem to have what he does not have and wants. That is why Falstaff shows excessive contempt for Ford, insultingly calling him cuckold, whose wife and money he wants to possess. Falstaff is driven by the desire for possession.

The *merry* wives are the signifier "woman" as over-invested by Falstaff with the un-repressed meanings of enjoyment (mirth, money, drinking and *jouissance*). As a result, in a counter-transference relation, the "loving" Falstaff imagines the wives—his objects of desire themselves—desire him as his *own* property.

> I can construe the action of her familiar style, and the hardest voice of her behaviour, to be Englished rightly, is "I am Sir John Falstaff's." (1. 3. 42-45)

As Pistol puts it, Falstaff "translates" Mrs. Ford's "will—out of honesty into English" (46-47): he formulates in words the desire he attributes to her. He also interprets Mrs. Page's "most judicious oeillades" and "the appetite of her eye" as "greedy intention" (55-63). The gaze imagined by Falstaff in the absence of the wives' desire motivates his wooing. In effect, Falstaff translates his own desire constituted in fantasy into "English" (language).

The wives take their revenge on Falstaff with "a fine-baited delay" (2. 1. 92)—by way of deferring and differing his desire.[5] Falstaff disguised as Herne with a buck's head personifies not only the object of the wives' hunt,[6] but also a speaking animal, urged on by his uncontrollable drives and entrapped in the web of the un-conscious meanings of "woman" as enjoyment. As seen in the "twin-brother" version of his love letters to the wives (69), Falstaff does not recognise women singularly. His identification of women as a whole with love/lust parodies the totalising patriarchal account of "woman."

3

When Mrs. Page receives Falstaff's "love" letter, she recalls and checks her attitudes towards Falstaff concerning her "mirth." Ford disguised as Brook doubts whether in other places Mrs. Ford, who appears "honest" to him, "enlargeth her mirth so far that there is shrewd construction made of her" (2. 2. 214-16). Why is "mirth" as merriment or laughter connected with female transgression? It is the *merry* wives' sense of humour that endows them with a subversive power, by making a joke of the seemingly fixed meaning of "husband" or "wife."[7] They decide to punish Falstaff of their own will, without consulting their husbands, and claim to be "the ministers" (4. 2. 206) in their revenge. At the same time, they enjoy their hunting of Falstaff as *lawful* merriment.[8]

Meanwhile, the wives are very careful about "the warrant of womanhood" (193-94). They know that their chastity as "wives" is the condition of their female power. The undecidability of meaning in their slogan that "wives *may be* merry *and yet* honest *too*" (96; my emphasis), however, displaces the single position of "woman" defined by patriarchy. With their wit and sense of humour, the merry wives jest at men's belief in the feminine masquerade of "Still swine" (98).

Cymbeline believes in his second wife's feminine masquerade. She confesses, however, that she "never lov'd" her husband but "Abhorr'd [his] person," and she was "wife to [his] place" (5. 5. 37-40). Cymbeline asks, "Who is't can read a woman?" (48):

> Mine eyes
> Were not in fault, for she was beautiful:
> Mine ears that heard her flattery, nor my heart
> That thought her like her seeming. (62-65)

Cymbeline's wife's disclosure overthrows his reliance upon the gaze ("eyes") and the speech ("ears") constitutive of his knowledge. Cymbeline, a subject of knowledge, is reluctant to admit his "fault" in *misreading* (the truth of) "a woman" behind her "seeming." And yet he cannot but acknowledge his "folly" (67) as a careless reader too dependent on the conventional meaning of womanliness and thus incompetent to read between the lines of the "feminine" representation.

Conversely, denying Leontes' accusation against her as "adulteress" and "traitor" in *The Winter's Tale*, Hermione refuses the performance of feminine tears: "I am not prone to weeping, as our sex / Commonly are" (2. 1. 108-09). Her patience is a refusal of the feminine masquerade. Meanwhile, one of the *merry* wives in Shakespeare, Paulina resists Leontes' control of power-knowledge in a different way. Calling Paulina "A mankind witch" (2. 3. 67) and "A callat / Of boundless tongue" (90-91), Leontes blames Antigonus for being unable to silence and control his wife. Paulina wishes that Leontes too did "dread" his wife (80), for Leontes evidently underestimates his wife's equality and singularity, treating her as if she were his property. Paulina repudiates Leontes' truth claims, based on his sovereign rights, as madness and his "own weak-hing'd-fancy" (118).

Another *merry* wife, Emilia in *Othello*, calls into question the meaning of "the wrong" for women (adultery) and the right/wrong distinction as reproduced relatively in the changeable register of power:

> Why, the wrong is but a wrong i' th' world; and having the world for your labour, 'tis a wrong in your own world, and you might quickly make it right. (4. 3. 79-81)

She defies a dissymmetrical power relation between husband and wife, in which the meaning of right or wrong is defined and delimited, and maintains wives' equal rights with their husbands (92-95). Although Iago charges Emilia to "charm [her] tongue" (5. 2. 179) to prevent her from revealing his "villainy," she insists on speaking: "'Tis proper I obey him—but not now" (193). Iago stabs her to death but she still demands to speak as she thinks. Emilia's desire to "speak true" (248) on behalf of the slain, silenced Desdemona exposes Iago's lie, Othello's blind belief in Iago's words and his claims to the truth of Desdemona as non-sense made up in the male-oriented mode of discourse. Her "unwomanly" eloquence unfolds both her resistance to the "proper" place (propriety) of female silent subjection and her challenge to a hom(m)ology of meaning and truth.

From different perspectives from their husbands', the *merry* wives jest and laugh at male imaginary mastery of power-knowledge and displace the female subject(ed)-position in the patriarchal system of signification. They claim to speak of their own will, either for resistance or as a challenge to the existing ideological meaning of "woman," and affirm the singularity of each woman as man's equal.

4

Ford's deep distrust of his "wife with herself" comes from his irrepressible anxiety about her unknown otherness.

> I will rather trust a Fleming with my butter, Parson Hugh the Welsh man with my cheese, an Irishman with my aqua-vitæ bottle, or a thief to walk my ambling gelding, than my wife with herself. Then she plots, then she ruminates, then she devises; and what they think in their hearts they may effect, they will break their hearts but they will effect. (2. 2. 290-97)

His inconsistent lapse from "she" (his wife) into "they" (the wives or women as a whole) shows his fear of "feminine" otherness and transgression. In order to rationalise his jealousy and justify himself, he develops the logic of sexual identity by way of the dialectics of binary opposition between "we" as "simple" innocent men, who "know nothing," and "they" as designing, insidious women. When suspicious Ford sees Mrs. Page with Falstaff's page, therefore, he believes that he detects "them," Mrs. Ford and Mrs. Page, plotting together and sharing "damnation" as "revolted wives" (3. 2. 35). Thus he decides to take Falstaff,

> then torture [his] wife, pluck the borrowed veil of modesty from the so-seeming Mistress Page, divulge Page himself for a secure and wilful Actæon. (35-39)

Taking for granted his mastery of the gaze, Ford is anxious to unveil the *hidden* "truth" of the "so-seeming" feminine other and to disclose Page's, not his, unmanned identity as a cuckold. Ironically, however, in spite of their confidence in the mode of male power-knowledge, both Falstaff and Ford come to curse the wives as unruly objects of desire and demonise them.

Similarly, jealous Posthumus first starts his speech by attributing every vice to "the woman's part" (2. 4. 174-78). He too then turns "she" into the totalised "they":

> All faults that name, nay, that hell knows, why, hers
> In part, or all: but rather all. For even to vice
> They are not constant, but are changing still. (179-81)

His speech ends with his curse on "them," whom "The very devils cannot plague ... better" (186). Unable to place "inconstant, changing" women on his map of knowledge, Posthumus puts women *beyond* the devils—as the transcendental signifier of "vice"—and demonises them.

The witch of Brainford in *The Merry Wives of Windsor* is another signifier of female "vice." Ford calls the old woman of Brainford "witch" and "quean" (4. 2. 158) and identifies witchcraft with lechery as female sexual transgression. In place of his wife, whose adultery he suspects, he curses the old woman of Brainford, whose trickery is beyond "our" knowledge, and instead of *torturing* his wife, he beats "the witch" with a cudgel.[9]

> We are simple men; we do not know what's brought to pass under the profession of fortune-telling. She works by charms, by spells, by th' figure, and such daubery as this is, beyond our element; we know nothing. (160-64)

Ford's disgust at the witch and his hysterical attempt to exorcise "her" from his house reveals his unconscious fear of unknown, unknowable "feminine" otherness: "Out of my door, you witch, you rag, you baggage, you polecat, you runnion, out, out!" (170-72). The possibility of witchcraft as impossible knowledge disquiets "man" as the subject of (the desire for) knowledge.

Falstaff disguised as the old woman of Brainford, moreover, upsets Ford's attempt to exclude the "feminine" negative other as an external contaminating cause from the inside of his house, for this ostensibly "feminine" other is the self-claimed "masculine" Falstaff, who boasts his attractiveness as man, and whom Ford paradoxically acknowledges masculine enough to be his wife's lover in place of himself. As a parody of the bearded witches in *Macbeth*, furthermore, Falstaff's female disguise causes male anxiety about the indeterminacy of the gender of the witch, who inhabits the confines of the meanings of masculinity and femininity. Evans thinks that "the 'oman is a witch indeed" and he does not like it "when a 'oman has a great peard" (179-80). His uneasiness about the bearded woman/witch echoes Banquo's alarmed question to the witches,

> you should be women,
> And yet your beards forbid me to interpret
> That you are. (1. 3. 45-47)[10]

The witchcraft motif runs all through Brabantio's accusation against Othello of having "enchanted" Desdemona by "magic" (1. 2. 63, 65). When Brabantio defines Desdemona as "a maid so tender, fair and happy, / So opposite to marriage" (66-67), he believes that he *possesses* his daughter as the object of his knowledge as well as his own property. Thus he denounces Othello as a thief and a magician: "She is abused, stolen from me and corrupted / By spells and medicines" (1. 3. 61-62). Othello testifies that his speech is the only "witchcraft" he has used (170). Brabantio is obliged to realise his mastery of the gaze and power-knowledge as "a father" delusive and find the insidious other in his *own* daughter. He warns Othello of Desdemona's potential betrayal of her husband and the necessity for him to master the gaze:

> Look to her, Moor, if thou hast eyes to see:
> She has deceived her father, and may thee.   (293-94)

Iago also describes Desdemona as the deceptive, unknown other in terms of a witchcraft associated with lechery:[11]

> She that so young could give out such a seeming
> To seal her father's eyes up, close as oak —
> He thought 'twas witchcraft.   (3.3.212-14)

He insinuates that Desdemona's "seeming" blinds not only her father's eyes but also her husband's and makes Othello more uneasy about the inability of man *seeing* his wife's internal truth (or non-truth?) underneath her "seeming."

Male jealousy demonstrates the impossibility of "man," as the subject of the desire to know, *possessing* "woman" as his own and proper object of knowledge. Thus "the philosopher behaves *like* a jealous husband."[12] In *Spurs: Nietzsche's Styles*, Derrida argues that the male philosopher-historian wants to get at the truth of "woman" behind her feminine veil or appearance. Unable to possess the truth of "woman" in its immediacy, without distance, he regards "woman" as the register of non-truth. The inaccessibility of "woman" as the object of knowledge suspends philosophical truth claims.[13] The idea of "woman" does not exist in its ideality beyond the (hi)story of the metaphysics of presence. "This is why metaphysics, which is jealous," Derrida says, "will never be able to account, in its language, the language of presence, for jealousy."[14]

5

Cuckold phobia reaffirms men's own awareness of the uncertainty of the patriarchal symbolic identification of the woman with the "house," attaching her to values of habitation, the hearth, the private life or the inside.[15] Ford's jealousy shows the strength of his sense of economy rather than of his love for his wife. Derrida presents the concept of "economy," which etymologically means "household management," in terms of the law of the family, the house and possession, and the sense of property and propriety.[16] Despite his profound distrust of "feminine" otherness and fear of transgression from the inside of his house, Ford needs "woman" in order to reproduce the family and circulate the proper name, property and propriety in the patriarchal economy. Unlike the Pages, however, the Fords' marriage does not reproduce the *proper* form of the family without children. In a patriarchal society, Ford's "failure" to be a father occasions him anxiety about his male identity and desire for possession, and makes him more jealous.

In a fit of jealousy—at the moment of a crisis in his male identity—Ford tries to retrieve his identity and be *proper* to himself by calling his proper name "Master Ford" (3. 5. 130-34). It is "Terms! Names!" that constitutes symbolic identity.[17] After Falstaff abusively calls Ford "cuckold," Ford bursts with anger about "the hell of *having* a false woman" (2. 2. 280-85; my emphasis). His strong sense of economy or husbandry concerning his "bed," "coffers" (money), "reputation" (his proper name or identity) and wife as properties, is related to his excessive jealousy as the desire to possess. Let us remember his distrustful speech about Mrs. Ford. He is always concerned about his *own* properties (*my* butter, cheese, aqua-vitæ bottle, ambling gelding and wife) and the possibility of his properties being expropriated. In spite of his constant anxiety, however, Ford declares that he trusts a thief rather than his wife.

"Feminine" otherness suspends male desire for his own proper(ty) in the economy (house) of the patriarchal family. Leontes longs for the forever lost time without women when he was "unbreech'd" (1. 2. 155), and Polixenes also narrates his and Leontes' boyhood's "innocent" friendship before female "Temptations" (77). So Hermione says to Polixenes, "Of this make no conclusion, lest you say / Your queen and I are devils" (81-82). Again, while men need women to circulate their proper(ty), they fear (and yet are attracted to) the otherness of women as "devils," who undermine the category of the same as "twinn'd lambs" (67).

Consequently, the more jealous Leontes is, the more anxious he is to prove "the specular, imaginal, or speculative circulation of the proper, of one's own proper(ty)" in the mirror of his son Mamillius.[18]

> Thou want'st a rough pash and the shoots that I have
> To be full like me: yet they say we are
> Almost as like as eggs; women say so,
> (That will say any thing): but were they false
> As o'er-dy'd blacks, as wind, as waters; false
> As dice are to be wish'd by one that fixes
> No bourn 'twixt his and mine, yet were it true
> To say this boy were like me.   (128-35)

In order to substantiate his paternity as an origin(al) and his son's legitimacy as "a copy out of [his]" (122), Leontes must unwillingly *cite* and *summon* what "they false" women say about them, which he mistrusts and yet depends on. Leontes' contradictory *citation* brings to light male anxiety about the uncertainty of his identity or propriety as "father" or "husband" in the patriarchal family system.

The imaginary cuckold, Leontes thinks that he plays "so disgrac'd a part" (188). He finds "comfort" in the *fact* that not only he but "many a man" is a cuckold, who "little thinks [his wife] has been sluic'd in 's absence," and whose "pond" (his wife's sexuality) is "fish'd" (expropriated) by "his next neighbour" (190-96):

> nay, there's comfort in't,
> Whiles other men have gates, and those gates open'd,
> As mine, against their will.   (196-98)

He tries to adjust his "disgrac'd part" as "man" by equating himself with "the tenth of mankind" (199), despite his sovereign position as "a king." Here we find male homosocial desire underlying his "comfort." Along with sexual imagery associated with the female body, moreover, the notions of sluice and gate undermine the illusory enclosure of the family home as the inside or one's own proper(ty). Notwithstanding male homosocial desire, it is other men who disrupt husbands' imaginary mastery of their proper(ty).

Iago is also obsessed by the idea (of economy) that his properties, his "seat" and "night-cap" (2. 1. 294, 305), are expropriated by Othello and Cassio due to his wife's adultery. Jealous Iago's narrative order is incoherent. His contradictory definitions of Othello "of a constant, loving, noble nature" (287) and "the lusty Moor" (293) suggest his madness. And yet, by taking his "revenge" on Othello, Iago wants to be "evened with" Othello (297) in the equivocal male rivalry relation (underlain by homosocial desire). His jealousy infects Othello and causes him alarm for his husband-ry concerning his property and propriety. Othello finds himself "abused" and curses marriage, by which men can legally call their wives "ours," but whose institutional frame does not enable men to control female desire ("their appetites") or keep his property ("a corner in the thing I love") from appropriation "For others' uses" (3. 3. 271-77). Iago maintains that marriage does not guarantee a man the possession of his wife and bed (her sexuality) as his own property:

> Think every bearded fellow that's but yoked
> May draw with you. There's millions now alive
> That nightly lie in those unproper beds
> Which they dare swear peculiar. (4. 1. 66-69)

Cuckold phobia related to a sense of economy reaffirms the fear of finding his properties and his identity as "man" or "husband" itself, not "peculiar" (proper), but "unproper" and capable of substitution by another bearded fellow.

When Iago says, "I never found a man that knew how to love himself" (1. 3. 314-15), moreover, he un-consciously confesses his profound hatred for his male fellows and, above all, for himself. While a jealous man is urged on by his insatiable desire to possess (either "woman," money or enjoyment as his property and propriety), he is also afraid of his "failure" to prove himself *properly* "a man." Male jealousy discloses man's own distrust or hatred for himself, who cannot but be *other* than "man" ought to be.

6

Hermione's eloquent "seduction" of Polixenes into a longer stay makes Leontes jealous. Iago is jealous of Othello's seductive speech, with which he won Desdemona's love, and blames it for evoking "violence": "with what violence she first loved the Moor, but for bragging and telling her fantastical lies" (2. 1. 220-21). Speech induces "violent" effects in the subject, retroactively modifying its subject-position in the symbolic. Referring to the lie, the mistake and ambiguity of speech, Lacan says that speech introduces "what isn't" as well as "what is."[19] It is other men's, Iago's or Iachimo's, speech that causes the husband's jealousy. Their jealous speech, driven by the desire to possess, leads Othello or Posthumus to suspect the certainty of their proprietary rights as "husband."

Even more than his description of Imogen's bedchamber and presentation of material proof (her bracelet), Iachimo's account of Imogen's body (a mole under her breast) and of his desire stirred up by it convinces Posthumus that his wife committed adultery and makes him jealous. Imaging himself a cuckold, Posthumus swears vengeance on her for restraining his "lawful pleasure" under the pretence of chastity (2. 4. 161). His rage as "husband" is that of the proprietor, who finds his properties (wife and bed) and propriety (his legal marital rights) expropriated. The bestial imagery of his account of Imogen as "colted" (133) and "mounted" (169) contrasts with the image of their romantic love. Othello, infected by Iago's jealousy as a form of madness, also starts using animal imagery: "toad" (3. 3. 274), "aspics" (453), "Goats and monkeys" (4. 1. 263), "foul toads" (4. 2. 62) and "summer flies" (67). Excessive jealousy monster-ises "man."

Cymbeline ends by reaffirming Imogen's honour as a chaste wife and celebrating their marriage based on true love. We have to bear in mind, however, that the evidence of Imogen's adultery, Posthumus' jealousy and the reconfirmation of Imogen's chastity all depend on what Iachimo says and whether Posthumus takes Iachimo's word for it. Posthumus' easy lapse into excessive jealousy caused by Iachimo's speech reveals the vulnerability of the marriage system, sustained by a contract between husband and wife in the name of "true love." As promises, marriage vows, husband or wife's legal rights and their love are all guaranteed only in and by language. Posthumus' sexual jealousy or uncontrollable desire, moreover, brings into relief the difficulty of circumscribing and domesticating desire as "lawful pleasure" within the institutional frame of the marriage system. An excess of desire always already subsists as the disruptive power in the marriage, whose purpose is to confer and confirm the stability of love and maintain the family on behalf of the project of patriarchy.

It is Othello himself who strains Iago's speech "To grosser issues" (3. 3. 223), translates it into more "poisonous" meaning through his imagination and frames "Dangerous conceits" in his mind. Iago detects Othello already changed with his "poison":

> Dangerous conceits are in their natures poisons
> Which at the first are scarce found to distaste
> But with a little art upon the blood
> Burn like the mines of sulphur.   (329-32)

Iago knows from his own *experience* how "the thought whereof / Doth like a poisonous mineral gnaw [his] inwards" (2. 1. 294-95). Othello cries, "Nature would not invest herself in such shadowing passion without some instruction. It is not words that shakes me thus!" (4. 1. 39-42). It is "words" or speech, however, that produce "such shadowing passion"—such meanings as suspicion, jealousy, fury, desire, love, honour or symbolic identity itself. Speech, as Lacan puts it, is "the founding medium of the intersubjective relation, and what retroactively modifies the two subjects. It is speech which, literally, creates what installs them in that dimension of being . . . ."[20]

Jealous Othello asks Desdemona, "Why, what art thou?," and she replies, "Your wife, my lord: your true and loyal wife" (4. 2. 34-35). Her "true" answer cannot yet satisfy his insatiable desire to see and know her "truth" *behind* her "seeming."

7

Jealous husbands take for granted the mastery of the gaze, which they believe enables them to see and know their wives' *hidden* "female desire" behind the feminine veil. Posthumus imagines that he sees Imogen's unchaste body *beyond* Iachimo's speech. Leontes thinks that he witnesses in Hermione's treatment of Polixenes a hospitality that is "Too hot, too hot" (1. 2. 108). He then imagines that he *finds* "affection" unite with "something":

> Affection! thy intention stabs the centre:
> Thou dost make possible things not so held,
> Communicat'st with dreams; —how can this be?—
> With what's unreal thou coactive art,
> And fellow'st nothing: then 'tis very credent
> Thou may'st co-join with something; and thou dost,
> (And that beyond commission) and I find it,
> (And that to the infection of my brains
> And hard'ning of my brows).   (138-46)

"I find it," and yet he cannot articulate what is the "something" that infects his brains and cuckolds himself. Both Posthumus and Leontes are convinced of their wives' adultery by what they imagine they see. But indeed they see what they cannot see and what is not there.[21] "In every analysis of the intersubjective relation," Lacan explains, "what is essential is not what is there, what is seen. What structures it is what is not there." The absence of Imogen's body and the "something" that remains inarticulate in Leontes' speech—what is neither there nor present—constitute their jealousy.

Othello is similarly propelled by the desire to see and know what can never be presented—by "a possible theatre."[22] He asks Iago, "Show me thy thought" (3. 3. 119), and thinks that "This honest creature doubtless / Sees and knows more—much more—than he unfolds" (246-47). Iago's "thought" or lie is precisely "what is not present" until introduced by his speech. In the process of unveiling "the truth" of Desdemona's adultery, Othello first asserts, "I'll see before I doubt, when I doubt, prove" (193), and asks Iago to give him "the ocular proof" (363). Iago produces a handkerchief and Cassio's erotic dream of sleeping with Desdemona as "visual" proofs. "Now do I see 'tis true" (447). Othello thinks that Iago's "ocular proof" convinces him of what he sees but, in effect, he sees what is not there—what he cannot see. Iago's or Iachimo's forged visual proofs disrupt the husband's imaginary mastery of the gaze and knowledge taken for granted in the patriarchal economy of the truth-system.

Likewise, Ford is overpowered by "the devil" (3. 3. 199)—by "the imaginations of [his] own heart" (4. 2. 143-44), which exists "nowhere else but in [his] brain" (146). "Jealousy always comes from the night of the unconscious, the unknown, the other," writes Derrida:

> Pure sight relieves all jealousy. Not seeing what one sees, seeing what one cannot see and who cannot present himself, that is the jealous operation. Jealousy always has to do with some trace, never with perception. Seen since *Sa*, thought of the trace will then be a jealous (finite, filial, servile, ignorant, lying, poetic) thought.[23]

Unknown, unknowable otherness—the impossibility of possessing "woman" as the object of his knowledge—makes "man" jealous of her imperceptible truth *hidden* behind her veil. Othello, Leontes, Posthumus and Ford are all driven by the unconscious, the unknown and the other—"thought of the trace" seen in the other scene. That is why "jealous souls," as Emilia explains, "are not ever jealous for the cause,"

> But jealous for they're jealous. It is a monster
> Begot upon itself, born on itself.   (3. 4. 159-62)

The monstrosity of jealousy as "the green-eyed monster" (3. 3. 168), moreover, discloses the split in the subject urged on by the drive for its own proper, for the heterogeneity of the very drive undermines the subject's "authorial" intention to be proper to itself. An excess of jealousy monster-ises "man" as a self-claimed autonomous, rational subject. When the "horn-mad" Ford invites Page, Shallow, Evans and Caius to his house, saying, "I will show you a monster" (3. 2. 74), he means Falstaff by "a monster," but he comes to show another monster *inside* himself. Shallow acknowledges the irreducible alterity of the uncontrollable drive in men, regardless of their social identities (2. 3. 43-45). The heterogeneity of the unconscious other subsists *inside* man himself as irreducible alterity. The logic of identity based on dialectical binarism is always already subject to deconstruction, owing to the fragile border between proper/other, inside/outside, masculine/feminine.

8

A husband's jealousy exposes the fragility of the institutional frame of marriage. Jealous husbands are propelled by the uncontrollable, destructive drive. Ford wants to "torture" his wife. Leontes and Posthumus wish to kill their "beloved" others. Othello, still attracted by the sleeping Desdemona's beauty, predicts in order to justify himself in slaying her: "Yet she must die, else she'll betray more men" (5. 2. 6). The insatiable desire to overrule "feminine" otherness and dissolve a distance between him and his other underlies these husbands' excessive desire for their own proper(ty)—and their fear of impropriety.

The Merry Wives of Windsor ends with Ford's declaration of the reconsummation of his marriage: "he to-night shall lie with Mistress Ford" (5. 5. 242). I wonder how much confidence this "happy" ending generates, in view of the ambivalence of desire for and fear of the other as other.

Notes

I am grateful to Catherine Belsey for her incisive comments on an earlier version of this essay. Part of this paper on *The Merry Wives of Windsor* was first given at the 34th Annual Shakespeare Conference on 21 October 1995.

1. Jacques Lacan, "Seminar of 21 January 1975," in *Feminine Sexuality: Jacques Lacan and the École Freudienne*, ed. Juliet Mitchell and Jacqueline Rose, trans. Jacqueline Rose (London: Macmillan, 1982), p. 168.
2. Among his many references to literature, for example, Freud acknowledges that "[t]wo scenes from Shakespeare" helped him to pose and solve a problem in "The Theme of the Three Caskets," in *The Penguin Freud Library*, vol. 14: *Art and Literature*, ed. Albert Dickson, trans. James Strachey (London: Penguin, 1985), pp. 233-47. Hoffmann's "The Sand-Man" also illuminates his way of reading "The 'Uncanny'", in *Art and Literature*, pp. 335-76.
3. All references are to the Arden Shakespeare: *Cymbeline*, ed. J. M. Nosworthy (London: Methuen, 1955); *The Merry Wives of Windsor*, ed. H. J. Oliver (London: Methuen, 1971); *Othello*, ed. E. A. J. Honigmann (Surrey: Thomas Nelson and Sons Ltd, 1997); *The Winter's Tale*, ed. J. H. P. Pafford (London: Methuen, 1963).
4. Jacques Derrida, "At This Very Moment in This Work Here I Am," trans. Ruben Berezdivin, in *Re-Reading Levinas*, ed. Robert Bernasconi and Simon Critchley (London: Athlone Press, 1991), p. 46.
5. "Differentiating," as Derrida would call it in "Differance," in *Speech and Phenomena and Other Essays on Husserl's Theory of Signs*, trans. David B. Allison (Evanston, IL: Northwestern Univ. Press, 1973), pp. 129-60.
6. Falstaff in this disguise believes himself to be "Herne the hunter" and "a woodman" (5. 5. 26-27), who pursues women as a desiring subject. Despite his first intention to give his horns as a phallic symbol to the wives' husbands as the symbol of cuckoldry, however, his horns are deprived (castrated) by the children in fairies' disguise. Coppélia Kahn, in "'The Savage Yoke': Cuckoldry and Marriage," in *Man's Estate: Masculine Identity in Shakespeare* (Berkeley: Univ. of California Press, 1981), pp. 119-50, points out a resemblance between the mockery of the "cuckolder" Falstaff's horns and of the cuckold's horns, which represent both the phallic symbol and the symbol of unmanned virility (and thus male anxiety about an uncertain masculinity). Conversely, in Japanese medieval folk tales and Noh drama, it is not a jealous man but woman who turns into an ogress with horns. This cultural difference denaturalises the Western notion of horns as the phallic symbol.
7. For example, Mrs. Page makes a jest about the idea(l) of "wife," who is expected (especially, by her present husband) to be constant to her only husband even after his death:

> *Ford* I think, if your husbands were dead, you two would marry.

Mrs. Page Be sure of that—two other husbands. (3. 2. 12-14)

The "merry" wives' (widows'?) friendship forms their alliance not only towards their mutual enemy, Falstaff, but also towards their husbands' mastery of meaning as the authors of the rightful meaning of "wife." Mrs. Page's joke makes Ford more uneasy about his "rights" as a husband.

As Mistress Quickly describes Mrs. Page's free-willed, "happy" domestic life, in addition, Mrs. Page chooses Caius before Slender for her future son-in-law against her husband's will. "My husband will not rejoice so much at the abuse of Falstaff as he will chafe at the Doctor's marrying my daughter," she maintains, "but 'tis no matter: better a little chiding than a great deal of heart-break" (5. 3. 6-10). Her plan based on the mother's "rights" is, however, further ironically upset by her daughter Anne's free-willed choice of her marriage partner. In the seeming homogeneous space of the family, the wife's or the child's other consciousness evinces the heterogeneity of the other and overthrows the hierarchical relations between husband and wife or between parents and children.

8. Falstaff embodies an amoral outlaw in *Henry IV* and *Henry V*. When Falstaff hears that Hal becomes king, he brags that "the laws of England are at my commandment" (5. 3. 132-33) in *Henry IV, Part II*, the Arden Shakespeare, ed. A. R. Humphreys (London: Methuen, 1966). Henry V must relegate Falstaff to prove himself to be "a king" who validates the law and upholds the socio-symbolic order. The Windsor community likewise needs to make "public sport" (4. 4. 14) of Falstaff as the enemy who tries to encroach on the socio-symbolic order. Falstaff must be "publicly shamed" (4. 3. 207-08) for his attempt at class, marital or sexual transgression.

9. Nancy Cotton, in "Castrating (W)itches: Impotence and Magic in *The Merry Wives of Windsor*," *Shakespeare Quarterly*, 38 (1987), 322, notes that "Ford's unconscious identification of wife and witch suggests that he equates the witch's spells with the wife's power to cuckold or 'unman' him."

10. *Macbeth*, the Arden Shakespeare, ed. Kenneth Muir (London: Methuen, 1951).

11. Iago further defines Desdemona's choice of her husband, who is different from "her own clime, complexion and degree," as "most rank, / Foul disproportion, thoughts unnatural" (3. 3. 232-37). Iago's emphasis on all the sexual, cultural, racial, rank and age differences between Othello and Desdemona drives Othello to despair of dissolving a distance between himself and his wife, who seems to remain radically other than he is.

12. Peggy Kamuf, "Introduction: Reading Between the Blinds," in *A Derrida Reader: Between the Blinds*, ed. Peggy Kamuf (Hemel Hempstead: Harvester Wheatsheaf, 1991), p. xl.

13. Jacques Derrida, *Spurs: Nietzsche's Styles*, trans. Barbara Harlow (Chicago: Univ. of Chicago Press, 1979).

14. Jacques Derrida, *Glas*, trans. John P. Leavey, Jr., and Richard Rand (Lincoln: Univ. of Nebraska Press, 1986), p. 134.

15. Jacques Derrida, "Voice II," trans. Verena Andermatt Conley, in *Points*... :

Interviews, 1974-1994, ed. Elizabeth Weber (Stanford: Stanford Univ. Press, 1995), p. 170.

16. Derrida, *Glas*, p. 133.

17. Ford's disgust at a (female) witch makes a strange contrast with his choice of the (male) devil's name before "cuckold" for himself.

> Terms! Names! Amaimon sounds well; Lucifer, well; Barbason, well; yet they are devils' additions, the names of fiends. But cuckold? Wittol? Cuckold! The devil himself hath not such a name...
> Fie, fie, fie; cuckold, cuckold, cuckold! (2. 2. 285-89, 301-02)

But he himself repeats the name "cuckold," which frames his jealousy in his brain and a sense of being a cuckold. "The form in which language is expressed itself defines subjectivity," as Lacan explains in *Écrits: A Selection*, trans. Alan Sheridan (London: Tavistock, 1977), p. 85. Ford traps himself in the (self-conscious) prison house of language.

18. Derrida, *Glas*, p. 134.

19. Jacques Lacan, *The Seminar of Jacques Lacan, Book I: Freud's Papers on Technique*, ed. Jacques-Alain Miller, trans. John Forrester (Cambridge: Cambridge Univ. Press, 1988), pp. 228-29.

20. Lacan, *Freud's Papers on Technique*, p. 274.

21. Lacan, *Freud's Papers on Technique*, p. 224.

22. "Jealousy is always excessive," says Derrida, "because it is busy with a past that will never have been present and so can never be presented nor allow any hope for presentation, the presently presenting. One is never jealous in front of a present scene—even the worst imaginable—nor a future one, at least insofar as it would be big with a possible theatre" (*Glas*, p. 134).

23. Derrida, *Glas*, p. 215.

The Wonder of the Virgin Queen:
Through Early Colonial Discourse on Virginia

EMI HAMANA

> This shall be for me sufficient, that a marble stone shall declare that a queen, having reigned such a time, died a virgin. —— Elizabeth I, 10 February 1559.

ELIZABETH I WAS acutely aware of the vulnerability of her royal power owing to the problematic circumstances of the establishment of the Tudor dynasty, a series of unhappy experiences in her childhood, and a long series of difficult domestic and foreign affairs, as well as for other reasons. She manipulated her self-representations in order to mask this, to maintain the national order by reinforcing her power, to evade the threats of resistance and rebellion by her male subjects, and to attract her people's hearts and eyes. She might also have been acutely aware of specularity as a human condition—the fact that a human being is an image to others and furthermore, that the subject can look at itself only as an image outside itself; she might have wished to exploit this. As has been shown by many scholars, the image of the Virgin Queen in particular, although intended to elicit wonder, is in fact one of the most contradictory representations she fashioned.

The idea of virginity is multivalent. It can represent "chastity," physical or spiritual, or both; in terms of the Early Modern Western colonial discourse it can represent "a land that is neither invaded nor conquered by Christendom"; it can represent "maternity," "mercy," or "fertility," especially in connection with the Virgin Mary. It represents a variety of things according to context. However, most of the best work on the Queen's virginity is concerned with her appropriation and manipulations of the image of the Virgin Mary.[1]

In the 1580s when past the age of procreation and faced with perpetual virginity, the Queen fashioned for herself an Anglican version of the Virgin Mother. This representation proved, for the most part, a success, and proves her great sense of political tactics. But no matter how splendidly it worked, it could not overcome a fundamental limitation, namely, that the Virgin Mary gave birth, but the Virgin Queen did not, even though she declared she was married to England, implying she was mother of her nation. It was indeed her central mystery that despite several possible love affairs and marriage proposals, ranging from those by Philip II of Spain to those of Francis, Duke of Alençon, she remained unmarried, neither producing an heir nor ensuring the successor her people desired to secure national stability. Because of this condition, Elizabeth had to manipulate a variety of supplementary notions to fill the image of the Virgin Queen and her reign with dignity. Most scholars have judged that she juggled extremely difficult roles adeptly. The purpose of this paper, however, is to rethink the representation of the Queen through the early colonial discourse on Virginia, during her reign and after her death, collected in Richard Hakluyt's *Principal Navigations, Voyages, Traffiques and Discoveries of the English Nation* (1599) and Samuel Purchas's *Hakluytus Posthumus, or Purchas His Pilgrimes* (1625).

*

Peter Hulme has discussed in his influential book, *Colonial Encounters: Europe and the Native Caribbean, 1492-1797*, how the representation of virginity was evoked in colonial discourse.[2] Louis Montrose and Stephen Orgel, among others, have also interestingly discussed the subject.[3] However, these writers have mainly been concerned with Walter Ralegh's *Discoverie of Guiana* (1596) and the early seventeenth-century colonial materials, a fact which is understandable. Ralegh planned, invested in, and actually sent his men with settlers to Virginia more than five times, in 1584, 1585, 1586, 1587, and 1590, the last voyage being financed by a company set up to relieve and develop his colony. The colony was finally lost. Nobody knows exactly what happened to the more than one-hundred settlers (including women and children—one of whom was Virginia Dare, the first English person born in North America) who stayed on Roanoke Island and who became "the Lost Colonists" of Modern American history.[4]

Ralegh's enterprise in Virginia proved a costly failure. By contrast, his *Discoverie of Guiana* remains a work of great value. It constitutes an early adventure book on South America and a fantasy of El Dorado; it is also an essay on the policies of colonization, although the venture was a failure as he found no abundant gold. Early seventeenth-century Virginian colonial materials are dramatic with their "hero" in Captain John Smith and "heroine" in the legendary Indian princess, Pocahontas.[5] The colonial discourse during 1584-93 is also overshadowed by the English defeat of the Spanish Armada in 1588. I would like, here, to focus on the early colonial materials, collected in Hakluyt's *Principal Navigations*.[6] These have been neglected by scholars. I would also like to connect them to the Virgin Queen as a source of wonder.

The Queen and Lord Burghley, her long-trusted prime minister, are believed to have harboured negative attitudes towards expansionism, with the notorious exception of Ireland. However, on 25 March 1584 the Queen issued a patent entitling Ralegh to occupy in the name of the Crown of England such lands as he might discover. A part of the patent is often quoted: "to discover, search, finde out, and view such remote, heathen and barbarous lands, countreis, and territories, not actually possessed of any Christian prince, nor inhabited by Christian people." In fact, the patent is lengthy, and mentions not only "journeis of discoverie" but "journeis of conquest."[7] In 1578 the Queen issued a similar patent to Humphrey Gilbert, Ralegh's stepbrother, containing words such as "occupy," "inhabit," and "rule," although omitting "conquest."[8] (Gilbert's voyage ended in shipwreck in 1583.) Richard Hakluyt the Elder wrote "Inducements to the Liking of the Voyage Intended towards Virginia . . ." in 1585, probably requested and directed by Ralegh; he employed the word "conquer," proposing a tripartite reason for colonization, "to plant Christian religion," "to traffic," and "to conquer."[9] The Queen's patent of 1584 anticipated this reason and it is of great note that she employed the term "conquest" in her patent to Ralegh, while also demanding that he conduct exploration and colonization peacefully. Although she has been considered a pacifist, the Queen was active in the Early Modern Western ambition for conquest of the New World.[10]

After Ralegh obtained the patent, two barks, commanded by Philip Amadas and Arthur Barlowe, sailed for North America, going by the way of the West Indies, and reaching their destination early in July. On the 13th, on what are now the North Carolina Outer Banks, they took formal possession of the land for Queen Elizabeth; and by implication of all that lay to north or south for a distance of 600 miles in either direction, which was not already in European hands. The English made friendly contact with the Algonkian Indians, and were taken to their village at the north-west end of Roanoke Island, where they learnt something of the country and the Indian way of life. They left the coast in August, taking two Indians as interpreters, and returned to England about the middle of September. On 6 January 1585 Ralegh was knighted; the Queen allowed him to use the name Virginia (instead of Wingandacoa) for the land recently discovered, and named him governor.[11]

The crux concerns the name of "Virginia" proposed by Ralegh and permitted by the Queen. Its unusualness as a toponym is clearer when we compare it, say, with "New Albion," which Francis Drake gave to the west coast of America when he succeeded in the first English circumnavigation of 1577-80. Why did the Queen, by then over fifty years of age, allow the name of Virginia to be used, rather than the many plausible alternatives, such as Eliza, Astraea, Gloriana, Tudoria, or New England? Hulme states, "Virginia had difficulty maintaining the coherence and integrity that its name had hopefully suggested."[12] Phillipa Berry writes, "by naming the first colony in America Virginia, he attempted to assert the identity of the English queen and the New World through which he hoped to define himself."[13] In connection with Ralegh's infamous passage in *The Discoverie of Guiana*, Montrose writes that when he "describes the northeast interior of South America as a virgin, the rhetorical motive is not an homage to the queen but rather a provocation to her masculine subjects . . . . it is as if the queen's naming of Virginia elicits Ralegh's metaphor of Guiana's fragile maidenhead."[14] Jeffrey Knapp discusses the sexually dangerous analogy between Elizabeth and Virginia in Hakluyt's passage dedicated to Ralegh (1587).[15] Each critic's comments on the name are valid and suggestive in their own way. What matters here, however, is to understand that Virginia had extremely troubling significations as the name for a colony.

It was conventional to regard a land as a woman, especially a virgin in the Western discourse of exploration. Note also that the word "virgin" is gendered; both sexes can be virgins but it is accepted, usually, as a female or passive quality. When explorers "discovered" land, they gave it a name related to virginity, or else they took it implicitly as "virgin land." For example, Columbus discovered a group of about 100 small islands, the West Indies, in 1493 and named them the Virgin Islands after the martyr St. Ursula and her 11,000 virgins. There are also many "virgin straits" in expeditionary records. Men invaded those places often with difficulty to find navigable passages, reserves of precious metal, or to plant Christianity, or just to conquer. Explorers of the Age of the Great Voyages made a number of reports on both coasts of North and South America in which they told of hard struggles to find places to penetrate safely into a virgin land. This is also a feature of records of early explorations in Virginia. The trope of land as a virgin was employed by male voyagers (and voyeurs?) in colonial discourse and as such it disturbingly evokes stereotypical images of female body and genitalia, sexual intercourse, and rape. (In this connection, homoerotic elements are also pervasive in colonial discourse, but it is beyond the scope of this paper to explore them.)

When Ralegh proposed the name of Virginia for a land in North America, in all probability he wished to imply by wordplay an honour to the Queen, but also to suggest that no matter how unsoiled it might be, a virgin land is called such to invite men to invade and conquer it. While on the one hand he asked the Queen, as a loyal subject, to maintain her virginity to refuse foreign invasion at home, on the other he asked her, as a vigorous expansionist, to allow her subjects to invade and conquer a virgin land overseas. The Queen was confronted with the double demand of maintaining her national virginity and of conquering virgin land. There was bound to be a tension in the representation of her virginity and colonial discourse. The boundary between the Queen and virgin land is not fixed in masculine colonial discourse: the Queen might be permanently displaced into the status of virgin land and as a virgin might be brought under the rule of her masculine subjects' fantasy and desire. We may assume that even knowing all of Ralegh's implications, she allowed him to use the name of Virginia. She might have hoped to turn his provocation to her own advantage.

In *The Discoverie of Guiana* (1596), Ralegh mentions that the Queen's virginity, representing as it does chastity and virtue, fills indigenous people with admiration, in contrast to the Spanish king's inhumanity.

Representations of the Virgin Queen presumably began to be fashioned in the early 1580s. Those who went to Virginia during 1584-90 made mentions of the Queen to the indigenous people; however, in the materials I have read, mainly in Hakluyt's *Principal Navigations*, they never mention her virginity. It is even unknown whether the natives knew that the Queen of England across the ocean had named their land

Virginia. No more than a few could have known it through local interpreters. Ralph Lane wrote in 1585-86 that two groups were willing to subject themselves to "the great Weroanza of England,"[16] but we do not know what exactly he told them about the Queen.

The Virginia Colony Ralegh planned ended in failure during Elizabeth's reign. Although voyagers at the early stages of the enterprise often said it was like a wonderland of the Golden Age, and abundant in natural resources, in fact it yielded no gold or silver, and soon proved difficult for the English to inhabit, with its severe winter, stormy seas, and food shortages. There was also the problem of relations with the natives, for even when these were good, the colonists often suffered attacks and complained of "conspiracies." Fifteen settlers were attacked by the natives on Roanoke Island in 1586, and two were killed, leaving thirteen to escape by boat, but nobody knows what happened to them later;[17] the following year saw the tragedy of "the Lost Colonists." Ralegh was unable to send relief. Virginia Colony disappeared, presenting us with a paradise lost. When John White went to Roanoke Island in 1590, he found the habitations deserted, which he felt an awful and macabre sight.[18] Virginia was an untamable land. It was, we might add, sterile like the aging Queen.

*

Soon after the failure of his colonial enterprise in Virginia, Ralegh was disgraced by his clandestine marriage to Elizabeth Throckmorton in 1592. In 1595, however, he obtained a patent for an expedition to Guiana, South America, hoping by this to restore himself in the Queen's favour and win honour by finding El Dorado, a fabulous city of gold in the interior of South America; in 1596 Ralegh published *The Discoverie of the Large, Rich, and Bewtiful Empyre of Guiana, with a relation of the great and Golden Citie of Manoa (which the Spanyards call El Dorado) And of the Provinces of Emeria, Arromaia, Amapaia, and other Countries, with their rivers, adjoyning*. In the book whenever he met indigenous people, he proclaimed to them the Queen's virtue and greatness. He also referred with admiration to her virginity.[19] At the close, however, he suddenly wrote:

> To conclude, Guiana is a Countrey that hath yet her Maydenheade, never sackt, turned, nor wrought, the face of the earth hath not beene torne, nor the vertue and salt of the soyle spent by manurance, the graves have not beene opened for gold, the mines

not broken with sledges, nor their Images puld down out of their temples.[20]

Stephen Greenblatt commented on this passage in his early book, *Sir Walter Ralegh: The Renaissance Man and His Roles*. He found "a note of regret and dread running counter to the dominant assertion," that is, "the conquest of Guiana":

> The images of the virgin land and of an earth whose face has not yet been torn by the plough recalls Ovid's description of the Golden Age . . . .This is the landscape of wish-fulfillment, the unspoiled world of man's imagination, and its image subverts the ethic of empire and aggressive capitalism.[21]

Ralegh's mind is divided; Guiana is at once a virgin land to be conquered and a place to be kept unspoiled.

Certainly there is a peculiar tone here, suggestive of Ralegh's internal divisions in his whole discourse on Guiana. Once we take into account the history of his enterprise in Virginia, however, Greenblatt's account seems insufficient. As Ralegh's apology indicates,[22] he bore in mind the bitter experience of being unable to relieve the settlers on Roanoke Island in 1587; it was inscribed in his mind as a trauma. Furthermore, Ralegh had a series of upsets during 1587-96, in great losses of money and people, his downfall at Court, sundry disappointments, and his unsatisfied desire for conquest. He enlarged the El Dorado fantasy during these repressive years. I read his discourse on Guiana's maidenhead as a symptom, that is, as a subjective phenomenon which erupts to represent an unconscious conflict; it reveals the ambition for conquest of a virgin land while compensating for the sense of guilt and failure. Ralegh's masculine desires and aggressions are offset by his ambivalent stance between hopes of possessing the fantasy and an unwillingness to destroy it.

In the end of the book Ralegh wrote that if the Queen conquered the empire of Guiana, her honour would be known to all the world: "the name of a virgin, which is not only able to defend her own territories and her neighbors, but also to invade and conquer so great Empires and so far removed."[23] Still, his conclusion about the conquest of Guiana is indecent. The trope of a virgin land had been firmly established in colonial discourse. The description of the virgin as an object of rape is, to our regret, also familiar in Elizabethan poetry and drama. Ralegh's phallic discourse might therefore not deserve either special accusation or defense. We are, nevertheless, amazed at the historical fact that virginity, or rather the metaphorical rape of a virgin, is described so openly in the very book intended to be read by the Virgin Queen. We cannot but be amazed at the extent to which this kind of discourse was circulating.

The Discoverie of Guiana is a historically unique text in which coexist an image of a virgin imagined as the object of rape and conquest by a phallic colonial discourse, and the representation of Queen Elizabeth, the object of admiration as a chaste and invulnerable maid. I would like to consider this subject under the term of the "wonder" of the Virgin Queen.

*

We have been looking at the representation of the Virgin Queen from a particular viewpoint, namely, that of colonial discourse on Virginia used by the men sent mainly by Ralegh. We have noted that the discourse on her virginity was, curiously, absent in this period. However, the Queen was always present by the very fact that the land was named Virginia. Let us recall another familiar idea of "the king's two bodies" in order to understand the inherent tension in the representation of the Virgin Queen. The King or Queen was supposed to possess a body physical, visible and mortal, as an individual, and a body politic, invisible and immortal, as a national unit. The Queen, endowed with two bodies, had especially to represent the immortal body politic for the sake of the nation. The trope of a virgin land evoked in colonial discourse, however, resulted in the emphasis on the physical body. As the connection between the representation of a virgin and the title of a queen was tenuous, there was always a danger of this separation occurring; in the masculine fantasy the Queen might be pulled down into the role of ordinary virgin. This problem, and the wonder, that is, the marvellous or extraordinary fact that the Queen managed to reign, despite everything, are drastically shown in Ralegh's *Discoverie of Guiana*. It may also be pointed out that soon after the Queen's death, Virginian natives fell victim to the English desire for conquest, under James I, though also known for his pacifism; when the sovereign turned male, Virginia was "raped" as we shall discuss later.

In colonial discourse, a "discovered" land is routinely imagined and described as if it were a female. Through repetition, the Virgin Queen is also evoked as a site of desire. The representation of the female body in colonial discourse functions, basically, to provoke masculine desire. This phallic discourse tries to define woman as body so as to hold the mastery of women by men, as well as maintaining the fiction of male sexuality premised on this mastery. The Queen was forced to put herself into an odd condition that as sovereign, she allowed the phallic discourse of conquest to prevail, and as a desiring subject, to identify herself with masculine desire. Furthermore, the colonial discourse of this age acquired a new inflection through the sovereign's being female. Masculine colonial discourses on early Virginia, and especially Ralegh's *Discoverie of Guiana*, not only assumed female sexuality, which a virgin shared, as the object of male desire, but actually affirmed and celebrated it. No matter how real the violence exercised might have been, the idea of a virgin land in America remained as a fantasy produced by English colonialism. As such, it was able to represent abundance, strength, chastity, savagery, vulnerability, sterility, or whatever the English masculine subjects hoped. It became the object of colonization precisely because it was marvelous.

The overdetermined representation of virginity invites a variety of meanings and responses. The complex representation of Elizabeth's virginity as well as her enigmatic personality refuses a straight analysis and a single, final interpretation. This complexity is her unique source of continuing amazement.

*

Let us turn to the colonial discourse on Virginia after the Queen's death, as collected in Purchas's *Hakluytus Posthumous, or Purchas His Pilgrimes* (1625). Although this work preserves some records of early voyages otherwise unknown, it has been criticized by many scholars, New Historicist and post-colonialist, and others. It is of great interest to explore the work precisely because Purchas's intensely patriotic and colonialist position is problematic. He inherited many of the manuscripts of Richard Hakluyt, who died in 1616, and published his bulky work, compiled many from these and other accounts of voyages.[24]

Early colonial discourses on Virginia in Hakluyt's and Purchas's works share the trope of "discovered" land as virgin. There are, however, crucial differences. Although voyagers to the New World themselves did not refer to the Virgin Queen and neither did Hakluyt, Purchas mentioned her as such many times. This might be the result of the notion gaining currency after the Queen's death. More importantly, Purchas appropriates the term for the sake of English colonialism. During the Queen's reign, Virginia was, in fact, Ralegh's colony. The contemporary plantation of Virginia, located to the north of Ralegh's, was a grand national project promoted by James I. Purchas quoted part of the first patent granted by the King on 10 April 1606 at the beginning of his section entitled "English Plantations, Discoveries, Acts, and Occurrents, in Virginia and Summer Llands since the Yeere 1606 Till 1624." While James's patent shared fundamental features in common with Elizabeth's of 1584, it was couched in a more provocative discourse because his nation had since launched into the age of full-scale colonialism. James declared:

> We greatly commending and graciously accepting of their desires to the furtherance of so Noble a worke, which may by the providence of Almightie God hereafter tend to the glorie of his Divine Majestie, in propagating of Christian Religion, to such people as yet live in darknesse, miserable ignorance of the true knowledge and worship of God, and may in time bring the Infidels and Savages (living in those parts) to humane civilitie and to a settled and quiet government . . . .[25]

This discourse presents the core of Western colonialism as it remained for centuries; Europeans had absolute confidence in their superiority over the people of the New World, as well as over various cultural others, based on the conviction that their religion was true and that only their civilization ranged from civility and writing through navigational and military technology to good government.

Purchas took this conviction to its extreme. Examining early modern ethnographic discourse, William M. Hamlin explores the ways in which Renaissance ideas of savagery and civility evolved during the sixteenth and early seventeenth centuries. He writes:

> The Puritan celebrant of English colonization, Samuel Purchas, perfectly exemplifies this Manichean opposition when he asks, early in the seventeenth century, "Can a Leopard change his spots? Can a Savage remayning a Savage be civil? Were not wee our selves made and not borne civil in our Progenitors dayes? and were not Caesars Britaines as brutish as Virginians?"[26]

This opposition of mutual exclusion did not hold, as Hamlin states, and yet Purchas tried to maintain it throughout his work. Purchas rendered "arguments for Virginian plantation, as being honorable" in terms of religion, humanity, profit, "manifold necessities of these times" and scores of other reasons. On the other hand he asserted the English right to the possession of the land by evoking Elizabeth I as its legitimate godmother: "for Virginia . . . it received that name from our Virgin-Mother, Great Elizabeth."[27]

Purchas devoutly hoped that the English nation would grow into a great empire, expanding its territories overseas; in this context he adored Elizabeth I because of the English defeat of the Armada during her reign—a miraculous event which had encouraged the nation for years. Most of South America had then been held by Spain, but by 1609, when James I granted a new charter to the London Virginia Company, Spain's imperial power was temporarily abating; yet the Dutch and French were sending expeditions to North America. Many other impending geopolitical conflicts were emerging in the New World. Under these circumstances, in all probability Purchas represented Jacobean English colonists' shared passionate desires. They wanted to possess the land of Virginia by all means to secure a firm foothold for their development in North America, and because of this desire they regarded its natives as savages; the land was filled with wonder and marvels just as its godmother was, but its natives were barbarous. Through recourse to the familiar trope of land as a virgin, Purchas declared that Virginia should be married to the English rather than raped by savages:

> But looke upon Virginia; view her lovely lookes (howsoever like a modest Virgin she is now vailed with wild Coverts and shadie Woods, expecting rather ravishment then Mariage from her Native Savages) survay her Heavens, Elements, Situation . . . . her Virgin portion nothing empaired, nay not yet improoved, in Natures best Legacies . . . . she is worth the wooing and loves of the best Husband.[28]

Although the English would, we should say, ravish Virginia soon enough, in Purchas's perverse rhetoric of conquest they would woo and marry Virginia. He then concludes his argument for the English plantation of Virginia in praises of Queen Elizabeth as well as of King James and God.[29]

In his colonial discourse on Virginia, as Purchas appropriated the wonder of the representation of the Virgin Queen, he also took on its inherent tension. Of the greatest interest, however, is the relation between England and Spain in his discourse. In the final chapter of his *Marvelous Possessions: The Wonder of the New World*, Stephen Greenblatt treats the subject of "the marvelous as a sign of the eyewitness's surprising recognition of the other in himself, himself in the other." Bernal Díaz del Castillo had served under Cortés in the campaign against the Aztecs; many years later he wrote a lengthy narrative, *The Conquest of New Mexico*, first printed in 1632. In Díaz's discourse on the Aztecs, "wonder is, in effect, at war with itself"; on the one hand, this provoked an uneasy perception of the similarity between Spanish and Aztec practices, religious and otherwise. He blocked this perception because "the marvelous," "the radical other" should remain different for the sake of the Spanish enterprise of marvelous possession. Díaz's discourse thus oscillated between identification and difference under the sign of wonder.[30] He was confronted with the critical recognition of Spaniards themselves in the other of the New World, even though he did not wholly acknowledge this.

Purchas was not an eyewitness of the English plantation of Virginia. But, like Díaz, he evidently had an uneasy perception of identification, not with Virginian natives, the proper object of wonder in Western colonial discourse, but rather with the Spaniards. Purchas discoursed on Virginia after the massacre of 1622 in which indigenous people rebelled against the English aggression and killed more than five hundred settlers. Although he was an eager expansionist like Hakluyt and Ralegh, Purchas preached "a middle path," that is, moderate colonization, considering also the *via media* which was the foundation of the Church of England established during Elizabeth's reign:

> I have read more stories of them [Savages] then perhaps any man, and finde that a cruel mercy in awing Savages to feare us is better then that mercifull cruelty.... Smith & Newport may by their examples teach the just course to be taken with such: the one breeding awe and dread without Spanish or Panike terror....[31]

While admiring the Queen towards the end of his discourse on Virginia, Purchas condemned Spaniards for "a most lamentable disaster" incurred by their "perfidious treachery" in 1567. Breaking certain articles concluded between England and Spain, he wrote, Spaniards as-worst of all, a hundred and fourteen men were exposed to "the mercy of cruell elements, crueller Savages, cruellest Spaniards, who exercised in the Inquisition with bondage, rackes, whips, fire, famishment, & plurima mortis imago, what the other had spared . . . ."[32]

For all this condemnation, Purchas envied Spain as he mentioned "the Castilian greatnesse," the contemporary greatest empire that "grew from an almost nothing out of the Moorish deluge" by a series of discoveries and conquests all over the world.[33] In fact, Spain, the most advanced colonizer, was a wonder and marvelous example for England. Purchas tried drastically to objectify and demonize Spain, stressing the radical difference between Catholic Spain and Protestant England, precisely because he hoped to conceal the fact that his nation had the same desire for conquest as the Spanish. Seen in this light, an Anglican version of the Virgin Mother Purchas appropriated could have a troubling impact since it evoked all those brutal acts done by Spaniards in the name of their "Great Lady," in the New World as well as elsewhere.

Elizabeth I fashioned and manipulated the representation of the Virgin Queen, which was filled with wonder, contradiction, and complexity. After her death, Purchas appropriated this for English colonialism in his discourse on Virginia. Through her own manipulation and Purchas's appropriation, the representation of the Virgin Queen ironically appears to become, exactly, an image in tune neither with her historical reality, nor with her identity. Through these exploitations of specularity as a human condition, the Queen represents the specularity itself. This surprising wonder of the Virgin Queen will invite our further speculation.

Notes

1. Some of the recent works on the subject of Elizabeth I and the Virgin Mary are: Peter McClure and Robin Headlam Wells, "Elizabeth I as a second Virgin Mary," *Renaissance Studies*, 4: 1 (1990): 38-70; Helen Hackett, *Virgin Mother, Maiden Queen: Elizabeth I and the Cult of the Virgin Mary* (London: Macmillan, 1995). See also John N. King, "Queen Elizabeth I: Representations of the Virgin Queen," *Renaissance Quarterly*, 47: 1 (1990) 30-74. King discusses the cult of Elizabeth I from various perspectives.

2. Peter Hulme, *Colonial Encounters* (London and New York: Routledge, 1986), pp. 136-73.

3. Louis Montrose, "The Works of Gender in the Discourse of Discovery,"

Representations, 33 (Winter, 1991) 1-41. Stephen Greenblatt, ed., *New World Encounters* (Berkeley: Univ. of California Press, 1993), pp. 177-217. Stephen Orgel, "Gendering the Crown," in Margaret de Grazia, Maureen Quilligan and Peter Stallybrass, ed. *Subject and Object in Renaissance Culture* (Cambridge: Cambridge Univ. Press, 1996), pp. 133-65.

    4. In *Trade, Plunder and Settlement: Maritime Enterprise and the Genesis of the British Empire, 1480-1630* (Cambridge: Cambridge Univ. Press, 1984). However, Kenneth R. Andrews writes, "It was only later, about 1610, that William Strachey, himself a reliable authority, acquired what he regarded as sufficient evidence that some of the colonists had lived for over twenty years with the Chesapeake tribe until, at or shortly before Christopher Newport's arrival in Chesapeake Bay in the spring of 1607, they were massacred along with all that tribe on the orders of the great Indian chief Powhatan" (p. 309).

    5. If we hope to find a heroic figure in early Virginia, he could possibly be Francis Drake, who brought supplies and offered a ship for colonists' use on Roanoke Island in 1586. Ralph Lane was moved by his generosity and kindness. See Richard Hakluyt, *The Principal Navigations, Voyages, Traffiques and Discoveries of the English Nation* (London, 1599; Glasgow: MacLehose, 1903-05), 12vols, vol. 8 (1904), pp. 342-45. Of course, Drake is the hero of the defeat of the Armada. We can also find a prototype of Pocahontas, wife of an Indian king's brother who welcomed the Englishmen and protected them on Roanoke Island. See "The first voyage made to the coasts to America, with two barks, where in were Captaines M. Philip Amadas, and M. Arthur Barlowe, who discovered part of the Countrey now called Virginia, Anno 1584," in Hakluyt, *The Principal Navigations*, pp. 304-06.

    6. Materials collected in Hakluyt's *Principal Navigations* must be read with caution as some are of doubtful accuracy, both historical and geographical. In this connection, Andrews writes, "Barlowe's record of the voyage, vigorously edited for publicity purposes after his return, provides nearly all we know about this expedition, and for that very reason deserves to be treated with some caution" (*Trade, Plunder and Settlement*, p. 201).

    7. "The letters patents by the Queenes Majestie to M. Walter Ralegh, now Knight, for the discovering and planting of new lands and Countries, to continue the space of 6. yeeres and no more," in Hakluyt, *The Principal Navigations*, p. 293.

    8. "The Letters Patents graunted by her Majestie to Sir Humfrey Gilbert knight, for inhabiting and planting of our people in America," in Hakluyt, *The Principal Navigations*, pp. 17-23.

    9. Hakluyt, "Inducements to the Liking of the Voyage Intended towards Virginia . . . ," in Louis B. Wright, ed., *The Elizabethans' America: A Collection of Early Reports by Englishmen on the New World* (London: Edward Arnold, 1965), p. 31. It reads as: "The ends of this voyage are these: 1. To plant Christian religion. 2. To traffic. 3. To conquer. Or, to do all three. To plant Christian religion without conquest will be hard. Traffic easily followeth conquest; conquest is not easy. Traffic without conquest seemeth possible and not uneasy. What is

to be done is the question."

10. The evaluation of Elizabeth's foreign policies varies according to the age and each person's political position. For a negative view, see, for example, Wallace T. MacCaffrey, *Elizabeth I: War and Politics 1588-1603* (Princeton: Princeton Univ. Press, 1992), esp. pp. 556-57. MacCaffrey attempts to demystify the Queen almost malignantly, reminding us of Walter Raleigh's criticism of her in his "English Voyages of the Sixteenth Century," in Hakluyt, *The Principal Navigations*, vol. 12, esp. p. 42. She did not take the aggressive policies most expansionists hoped, but this is not because she was stingy as some critics state, nor because she was concerned only with England and Ireland, but is possibly because she had a larger view of politico-military conditions in Europe. At any rate, it is evaluated highly from today's postcolonial perspective that Elizabethan England was not an aggressive colonialist nor imperialist country, unlike some other European states. See also Andrews, *Trade, Plunder and Settlement*: "Elizabeth was certainly not a Chatham or a Churchill—and fortunately not. There were others who hoped and argued for more aggressive policies at sea—Hawkins, Drake, Ralegh, Essex, for example—but none of these was in a position to see the war as a whole with knowledge and understanding that Elizabeth possessed" (p. 236).

11. David B. Quinn and Alison M. Quinn, ed. *Virginia Voyages from Hakluyt* (London: Oxford Univ. Press, 1973). See esp. Chronology of Virginia Voyages, pp. xx-xxv. Regarding the word "Wingandacoa," see Wright, ed., *The Elizabethans' America*: "The meaning of this word has never been satisfactorily determined; but it is clear that the English were mistaken in taking it for the name of the country" (p. 288, n. 6).

12. Hulme, p. 139.

13. *Of Chastity and Power: Elizabethan Literature and the Unmarried Queen* (London and New York: Routledge, 1989), pp. 148-49.

14. Montrose, p. 188.

15. *An Empire Nowhere: England, America, and Literature from* Utopia *to* The Tempest (Berkeley: Univ. of California Press, 1992), p. 149.

16. Lane's letter to Hakluyt, in Hakluyt, *The Principal Navigations*, vol. 8, p. 336.

17. "The fourth voyage made to Virginia with three ships, in the yere 1587," in Hakluyt, *The Principal Navigations*, pp. 394-95. The English violence should also be remembered, for example, in "The third voyage to Virginia made by a ship sent in the yeere 1586," in Hakluyt, *The Principal Navigations*: we read "and for feare they should be left behind they left all things confusedly, as if they had bene chased from thence by a mighty army: and no doubt so they were; for the hand of God came upon them for the cruelty and outrages committed by some of them against the native inhabitants of that countrey" (p. 347).

18. "The fifth voyage to Virginia made by master John White in the yeere 1590," in Hakluyt, *The Principal Navigations*, pp. 414-18.

19. Ralegh, *The Discoverie of the Large, Rich and Bewtiful Empyre of Guiana* (London, 1596; Amsterdam : Theatrum Orbis Terrarum, 1968). "I made them un-

derstand that I was the servant of a Queen, who was the great *Casique* of the north, and a virgin, and had more *Casiqui* under her then there were trees in their land" (Ralegh, *The Discoverie*, p. 7). Some of the original spellings are modernized by the present writer.

20. Ralegh, *The Discoverie*, p. 96. The theme of virginity is echoed later in the play *Eastward Ho!* (1605), by George Chapman, Ben Jonson, and John Marston; Captain Seagull, commander of the ship that is to go to Virginia, says, "Virginia longs till we share the rest of her maidenhead" (cited in Wright, ed., *The Elizabethans' America*, p. 154).

21. Greenblatt, *Sir Walter Ralegh* (New Haven and London: Yale Univ. Press, 1973), p. 113.

22. Ralegh, *The Discoverie*, p. 5. In this connection, Purchas records a brief note of 1602: "Samuel Mace of Weimouth, a very sufficient Mariner, an honest sober man, who had beene at Virginia twice before, was employed thither by Sir Walter Raleigh, to finde those people which were left there in the yeere 1587. To whose succor he hath sent five severall times at his owne charges" (*Purchas His Pilgrimes*, London,1625; Glasgow; MacLehose, 1905-7; New York: AMS Press, 1965, vol. 18, p. 321). It is hard to determine the credibility of this note as elsewhere since Purchas is infamous for his incorrect compilation and carelessness of facts.

23. Ralegh, *The Discoverie*, p. 101.

24. The original work was published in 4 vols. and its fine reprint was in 20 vols. in 1905-7. The volumes directly related to the subject of this paper are 16, 18, and 19.

25. *Purchas His Pilgrimes*, vol. 18, p. 400.

26. *The Image of America in Montaigne, Spenser, and Shakespeare: Renaissance Ethnography and Literary Reflection* (New York: St. Martin's Press, 1995), pp. 30-31.

27. *Purchas His Pilgrimes*, vol. 19, p. 226.

28. *Purchas His Pilgrimes*, vol. 19, p. 242.

29. *Purchas His Pilgrimes*, vol. 19, pp. 258-67.

30. *Marvelous Possessions* (Oxford: Oxford Univ. Press, 1991), esp. pp. 128-51 and also p. 25. Greenblatt finds in Montaigne a sophisticated version of wonder, the "recovery of the critical and humanizing power of the marvelous" (p. 25). Purchas was not a Montaigne. However, Greenblatt mentions Purchas as one of a few Renaissance writers who partially acknowledged the value of colonial documents written by people of "meane qualitie" (p. 146).

31. *Purchas His Pilgrimes*, vol. 18, p. 497.

32. *Purchas His Pilgrimes*, vol. 19, p. 263.

33. *Purchas His Pilgrimes*, vol. 19, p. 239.

The Taming of the Shrewd Critics Who Talk Wild of *The Wild-Goose Chase*

SHOICHIRO KAWAI

WHY DID JOHN Fletcher's *The Wild-Goose Chase* (1621) achieve great popularity on the seventeenth-century stage? One could argue that the popularity of the play, as indeed that of the playwright, was as inflated and fleeting as the recent bubble economy in Japan. Shakespeare's collaborator and successor as leading playwright for the King's Men, Fletcher enjoyed an immense popularity on stage to such an extent that he was sometimes regarded as superior to Shakespeare.[1] His sophisticated and affected drama was quite influential not only in the Restoration period but also in the early eighteenth century.[2] According to Dryden, two "Beaumont and Fletcher" plays were performed for one of Shakespeare's or Jonson's during the Restoration.[3] However, in the eighteenth century, the decline of Fletcher's popularity on stage gradually lowered his critical worth, and the bracketing of Fletcher's name with Shakespeare's, a custom that lasted for a hundred and fifty years, had to be discarded.[4] Now Fletcher is no longer regarded as a member of an elite triumvirate with Shakespeare and Jonson, but has been demoted to the ranks of the lesser playwright, utterly obscured by many of his contemporaries.

Granted that the past popularity of *The Wild-Goose Chase* could be partly ascribed to Fletcher's "bubble" reputation, I would argue that the play is underestimated because of some misunderstandings. Many critics think that this play is about Mirabell, the wild-goose, being chased and caught by his betrothed Oriana, who is variously described as a "resourceful maiden," "the high-mettled" heroine, or "the emancipated young woman who ... indulge[s] her witty resource at the expense of the male sex."[5] Clifford Leech, who cannot confidently tell why the play was popular, writes: "the play was very popular before the Civil

War probably because there was then a greater novelty than later in the theatrical presentation of a woman as a relentless wooer."[6] I would argue contrarily. Oriana is not a high-mettled, relentless wooer but a helpless, dependent girl; the play is called *The Wild-Goose Chase* not because Oriana chases Mirabell; and the play was popular because it was a kind of Cinderella story climaxing in Oriana's amazing transformation from a pitiful, submissive girl into a fascinating lady, the theatricality of which must have been enhanced by the sensuality of the boy actor in the seventeenth century.

Who Chases The Wild Goose?

Let us begin with the title. Although many critics have written on *The Wild-Goose Chase*, no one, to my knowledge, has ever commented on the meaning of the title, probably because the phrase "wild-goose chase" is too common. Critics seem to take for granted the meaning of the phrase—"a foolish or hopeless and unproductive quest" (*The Concise Oxford English Dictionary*)—as it is used today.

Apparently it is based on this usage that *The Oxford Companion to English Literature* summarizes the main plot of the play as follows:

> Mirabell, the 'wild goose', a boastful Don Juan with an aversion to marriage, is 'chased' by Oriana, his betrothed, who tries various wiles to bring him to the altar. She feigns madness for love of him, but he sees through the pretence, and she finally traps him in the disguise of a rich Italian lady.[7]

In this context one can gather that Mirabell is called "the wild goose" because he is as unlikely to be caught, and that the play is called *The Wild-Goose Chase* because Oriana's attempts to catch him fail again and again so that she appears to be pursuing "a foolish or hopeless and unproductive quest."

However, the current meaning of "wild goose chase" was established in the eighteenth century and has nothing to do with its Elizabethan meaning. Since Samuel Johnson defined it in his dictionary as "a pursuit of something as unlikely to be caught as the wild goose" in 1755, we have lost the original, seventeenth-century definition, which was based on wild geese's peculiar behaviour that when a leading goose flies in a different direction, the whole flock follows it. According to *The Oxford English Dictionary*, it can be defined as:

> An erratic course taken or led by one person (or thing) and followed (or that may be followed) by another (or taken by a person in following his own inclinations or impulses).

It was also used to refer to a kind of horse-race, in which "two horses were started together, and whichever rider could get the lead, the other was obliged to follow him over whatever ground the foremost jockey chose to go."[8] When the eponymous character of Chapman's *Monsieur d'Olive* (1605) says, "drinke sacke, and / talke Satyre, and let our witts runne the wilde-goose chase" (1. 2. 108-9),[9] he means exactly the same thing as Mercutio in *Romeo and Juliet* (1594-96), who says to Romeo, "Nay, if our wits run the wild-goose chase, I am done" (2. 4. 71-2)[10]: namely, to have a kind of contest of wit, in which whoever makes a funny remark or joke first, others are obliged to respond to it by another witticism in a similar vein. In no instance in Renaissance drama does the phrase mean anything other than an eccentric sequence of events or actions.[11]

In *The Wild-Goose Chase* Mirabell is the leading wild goose who takes an erratic course, and the others are obliged to follow him. He tells his fellow gallants, Pinac and Bellure, to observe his trick of treating ladies and follow suit: "Come, go in Gentlemen, / There mark how I behave my self, and follow" (1. 2. 87-88). Thus when Pinac and Bellure woo Nantolet's "Aërie Daughters"—Lylia-Biancha and Rosalura respectively—they are following Mirabell's instructions; and Mirabell as supervisor observes "How they behave themselves" (2. 1. 211). Moreover, his eccentric tricks of deception are imitated also by the ladies during the course of the sex war. Just as Mirabell acts as instructor for the gallants, so Lugier the tutor to the "Aërie Daughters" instructs the ladies. Lugier declares, "Since he has begun with wit, let wit revenge it" (3. 1. 12). In other words, the play is full of wild geese following the leading wild goose Mirabell, engaged in a battle of wits begun by Mirabell. Mirabell is the wild goose because he is a fanciful person who delights in witty pranks. In the first quarto of Fletcher's *The Night Walker*, the only substantive edition of the play, the character "Wildbraine" is sometimes referred to as "Wildgoose," precisely because he acts as a kind of trickster to lead the witty plot.[12]

Whose Plot Was This?

This means that the play is not simply a war of the sexes between Mirabell and Oriana with two other pairs of lovers fighting subsidiary skirmishes. Rather, it is a war of wit fought under the direction of two commanders, Mirabell for the gallants and Lugier for the ladies. It is always Lugier who hatches counter-tricks against Mirabell's tricks.[13] Nantolet's daughters tell the audience how they are directed by Lugier. "We follow'd your directions, we did rarely," says Lylia-Biancha to Lugier, "We were Stately, Coy, Demure, Careless, Light, Giddy, / And plai'd at all points" (3. 1. 44-45). Rosalura also says that they kept their men always "up and down" and performed "ever those Behaviours [Lugier] read to [them]" (3. 1. 50-51). Fletcher emphasizes Lugier's directorship by introducing a scene (3.1) where the sisters try to act without Lugier's precepts and find it necessary to turn to him again. When Mirabell is finally tricked into marrying Oriana, who is disguised as an Italian lady, he knows that it is not Oriana's own trick. That is why he asks, "whose plot was this?" (5. 6. 81), and it is Lugier who admits it as his own.

The point is that the play is not about the witty Oriana who herself hatches various wiles to bring Mirabell to the altar, for all her tricks (except the feigned madness at the end of act 4) are prepared by Lugier, while Oriana is merely instructed by him. At the beginning of the play Oriana is confident, saying, "my mind tells me / That I, and onely I, must make [Mirabell] perfect" (1. 1. 153), but when she meets him and is told that he has no intention of marrying her, all she does is run away "weeping" (2. 1. 161). Seeing his sister slighted by Mirabell, the angered De Gard turns for help to Lugier the machinator, who has already begun giving directions for Lylia-Biancha and Rosalura. Lugier declares that he will be in charge of Oriana—"for this Gentlewoman / So please her, give me leave" (3. 1. 83-84)—and insists on his total command over her: "Ile doe my best, and faithfully deale for ye; / But then ye must be ruled" (3. 1. 86-87). Thus Oriana joins the "wild-goose chase" of witty skirmishes as late as in act 3 under the strict supervision of Lugier the strategist. In act 2, Lylia-Biancha and Rosalura mock their wooers Pinac and Bellure respectively as instructed by Lugier. In other words, the "wild-goose chase" has long been in progress when the helpless Oriana starts to follow the "chase." That is to say, while Lugier acts as commander for the two sisters and Mirabell for the two boys, Oriana is left alone, doing nothing until act 3. Before she comes under Lugier's care, the poor, whimpering Oriana is merely pitied by other characters. "Ne'r vex your self, nor grieve," Rosalura comforts her (2. 3. 1). Lugier expresses his sympathy to De Gard, "I pitty your poor Sister" (3. 1. 3).

There is nothing in the text that suggests that Oriana is a "resourceful maiden," "the high-mettled" heroine, or "the emancipated young woman" as some critics would make her. On the contrary, Oriana is presented as a type of woman who was considered "womanly" in a patriarchal society — shy, reserved, maudlin, helpless and dependent— a characterization that is the sine qua non of the play's overall design, in which the more pitiful Oriana is, the more effective her amazing metamorphosis into a fascinating lady in the last scene becomes.

Until this climactic scene, Fletcher takes great care to present her as quietly as possible. She is so reticent that throughout the play she speaks less than one third as much as the sprightly Lylia-Biancha. Most of her lines are spent when she confesses her love of Mirabell to her brother at the beginning of the play. In the following scene, when Mirabell first meets Lylia-Biancha and Rosalura, Oriana stands aside, silently watching them. For a hundred and fifty-five lines, Oriana observes them and all she says is "I fear not" (1. 3. 231). In act 2 when Rosalura surprises Bellure by her sudden demureness, Oriana acts like Rosalura's maid with her face concealed under a veil. Again, in this scene with Mirabell, she says no more than two lines: "Sure I have seen him, Lady" and "Sure he is crazed" (2. 3. 61, 69). All the while Rosalura vehemently accuses Mirabell for his sauciness, Oriana keeps silent, and even Mirabell does not recognize her. Thus, as a retiring, unenterprising girl, she is ready to resort to Lugier's "pity" (3. 1. 85) and to be transformed by him.

The Tame Oriana

Since the dismal Oriana's mutation into the captivatingly attractive lady comprises the climax of the play, one cannot overstate the fact that she is presented as anything but an emancipated woman until the last scene. How Fletcher intends Oriana's characterization may be seen from the fact that *The Wild-Goose Chase* is partly a remake of Fletcher's own *The Woman's Prize, or The Tamer Tamed*, a mock sequel to Shakespeare's *The Taming of the Shrew*. Petruchio, who tames Katherine the shrew in Shakespeare's play, is now a widower and tries to marry Maria, but Maria acts as another shrew, who sets out taming her husband. Supported by her bellicose female friends, she barricades her house against him and demands him to surrender. She says that unlike a "childish woman / That lives a prisoner to her husbands pleasure," she has her "own Noble will" which tells her that she is created not "for his use" but for his "fellowship" (1. 2. 13-39). Contrasted with this high-mettled Maria in the main plot is her timid younger sister Livia in the subplot, who is so shy and reserved that she is appalled at the idea of taming one's husband. However, when her father commands her to marry an old man, she turns to her sister for help, for Livia wants to marry her sweetheart Rowland. This gallant is so attitudinizing that he pretends not to care for her, but Livia succeeds, following the instructions of her friends, in tricking him into marrying her: she feigns a deathbed sickness, exactly the same trick that Oriana performs. This subplot is developed into the main plot of *The Wild-Goose Chase*: Mirabell is modelled on the gallant Rowland, Oriana on the helpless Livia, Lugier on the resourceful Tranio who helps Livia, and Lylia-Biancha on Byancha the madcap, friend to Maria. In both plays, after hilarious upheavals, the gallants are tricked into marriage and they show exactly the same attitude: Rowland says, "I have lost then, and Heaven knows I am glad ont" (5. 3. 36), while Mirabell's words are "I thank ye, I am pleas'd ye have deceived me; / And willingly I swallow it, and joy in't" (5. 6. 79-80). The similarity is significant because it suggests that the playwright's idea for Oriana's characterization is modelled on Livia's, who is bashful and helpless and does not know how to win her love until help is offered. Livia weeps (3. 4) as pitifully as Oriana (2. 1; 4. 3), and her tears motivate Tranio to help her, just as Oriana's tears goad De Gard and Lugier.

Oriana's Age

Oriana's helplessness and desperation can be confirmed also by the fact that her age is given as "eighteen" (2. 1. 143), while the ages of all the other characters are not specified. She is as old as the Jailer's daughter in *The Two Noble Kinsmen* (cf. 5. 2. 30), who is also desperate for love and must be supported by fatherly figures. A woman's age is all the more significant as a sign of characterization because female roles were acted by boy actors and because the age of marriage is remarkably low in Elizabethan drama. Juliet in *Romeo and Juliet* is thirteen going on fourteen. Fourteen is the earliest age for a girl to be regarded as a woman, and it is the age of marriage in William Rowley's *A Woman Never Vext* (1. 1. 498).[14] William Rowley writes that fifteen is "womans ripe age" just as twenty-one is for men (*The Maid in the Mill* 2. 1. 138).[15] Most Elizabethan heroines are aged fourteen,[16] fifteen,[17] and sixteen.[18] Seventeen is an age for an attractive wife in *The Tragedy of Valentinian* (1. 1.

20); nineteen is an age for a rich widow in *The Alchemist* (2. 6. 31),[19] and a twenty-year-old unmarried woman is a wonder in *Cupid's Revenge* (1. 1. 18). Although the average age of marriage for women during 1598-1619 was 20.5 in London and much higher in other parts of the country, it was considerably lower for dramatic characters.[20] Girls were sexually premature on stage: it was a cliché to joke about girls losing their maidenheads at the age of thirteen[21] or fourteen.[22] "Fifteen shall make a Mother of a Mayd" (*Cupid's Revenge* 1. 2. 32) and virginity at fifteen is considered a wonder.[23] A maidenhead of sixteen is joked about,[24] and "seventeen and upward" can be called "Nun, votarie, stale maidenhead" (*The Two Angry Women of Abington*, line 1492).[25]

Thus, when female characters in love are aged eighteen, it means that they have every reason to be eager for marriage. It is in this context that Mirabell ridicules Oriana's age: "thou art eighteen now, / And if thou hast thy Maiden-head yet extant, / Sure 'tis as big as Cods-head" (2. 1. 143-45). Oriana and the Jailor's daughter, both aged eighteen and denied a promised marriage, must have induced a sentimental pity in seventeenth-century audiences—the pity which is ideologically induced by a male-dominated society.

The Fashionable and Sexy Oriana

The climax of the play is Oriana's transformation into an Italian lady, the impact of which is emphasized repeatedly in the text. Voices of wonder are ubiquitous. When the metamorphosed Oriana appears on the upper stage, Rosalura "admire[s] her Presence" (5. 4. 3) and Lylia-Biancha declares, "she is the handsomest, / The rarest, and the newest to mine eie / That ever I saw yet" (5. 4. 44-46). Evidently it is her costume that makes her different. With "two Pinacles" on her head and "a bouncing Bum" (5. 4. 30, 35), the fashionable Oriana impresses herself on Mirabell. He is struck with wonder and avows that she appears "one of the sweetest, / The handsomest: the fayrest, in behaviour" (5. 5. 12-13).

The point is that Oriana, disguised as an Italian lady, is sexually attractive. The vulgar servant is sexually aroused and wishes "to have but one fling at her" (5. 4. 37). The lascivious Bellure says, "She is a lusty wench: and may allure a good man" (5. 6. 6). These speeches confirm that the transformed Oriana is not only fashionable but also voluptuous. Considering the virtuosity of seventeenth-century boy actors, it was possible that the boy actor who played Oriana acted in such a way that "she" looked sexually alluring. We know that in the 1632 revival the role was performed by Stephen Hammerton, and it is very likely that in the original 1621 production it was performed by Richard Sharp. It is conjectured that Sharp played amorous women like Hippolyta in *The Custom of the Country* (1620), Cleopatra in *The False One* (1620), and Erota in *The Laws of Candy* (1620). Although much has been said about boy actors' sexuality in general,[26] we should also pay more attention to the extent to which feminine sensuality could be represented on stage by boy actors.

Oriana's glamour is heightened by her singing. The bashful Oriana turns into a sensual beauty and succeeds in winning Mirabell's heart and no doubt in fascinating the audience. Critics wonder why the war of wit ends here, or why Mirabell agrees to marry Oriana after the identity of "the Italian lady" is revealed, but the answer is simple: it is because he now finds her "attractive." The Jacobean and Caroline audience who witnessed the gorgeous and sensual Oriana and heard her enchanting singing voice must have had every reason to differ from the modern view that "there is no more reason for [Mirabell's yielding] at that point than before."[27]

Actors' virtuosity always comprises a vital aspect of Fletcher's drama.[28] Nevertheless, the boy actor's sensuality is something we cannot infer from the text. In this sense, Taylor and Lowin's compliments to the reader in the Folio of *The Wild-Goose Chase* may sound a bit sarcastic: "Onely we wish, that you may have the same *kind Joy* in *Perusing* of it, as we had in the *Acting*" (sig. [A]2r).

The Background of A Cinderella Story

Fletcher's drama was extraordinarily popular with female spectators, because it represented "attractive" female characters—"attractive" in the sense that they were feminine and sexual, as perceived by a patriarchal society. In this aspect, his drama bears a resemblance to today's woman's magazines which tell women how to behave. What Lugier directs girls to assume is exactly the same kind of femininity that is acclaimed in those magazines.

Equivalents of today's woman's magazines existed in the seventeenth century and enjoyed great popularity. A cosmetic manual, Sir Hugh Platt's *Delightes for ladies, to adorne their persons, tables, closets, and distillatories* (1599), had a sixteenth edition in 1640; Gervase Markham's *The English Huswife* (1615) was revised for the fifth time in 1637; and

Dorothy Leigh's pamphlet on housekeeping, *The mothers blessing, or the godly counsaile of a gentle-woman* (1616), had a nineteenth edition in 1639. The popularity of these self-help pamphlets for women corresponds to the success of *The Wild-Goose Chase* in the seventeenth century.

Sandra Clark points out that in *The Wild-Goose Chase* "it is a male instructor who teaches the women their role-playing," suggesting that the seeming war of the sexes is actually the enactment of the roles fabricated by men's concepts of gender.[29] Lugier instructs the women to play those roles which are characterized by "womanliness as a code, learnt and socially constructed," as Clark puts it, while Mirabell instructs the boys to assume a faked manliness. Every role, whether it is the women's or the men's, is produced by "that 'vulnerable male ego' which Cyrus Hoy has discovered in Fletcherian romantic comedy."[30]

Behind the figure of Lugier the instructor, we may find the Fletcherian "male ego," which pervades his work. Fletcher delineates women as the object of men's sexual desire. That is why mothers do not usually appear in Fletcher's drama. Instead, fathers and brothers are always "protecting" pretty heroines. Thus, when Oriana succeeds in deceiving Mirabell into marriage in the last act, she is supported not only by Lugier and De Gard but also by Mirabell's father La-Castre (5. 1. 10) and the sisters' father Nantolet (5. 2. 61; 5. 6. 75).[31] De Gard seriously thinks of drawing his sword for his sister's honour (3. 1. 13), and the protected Oriana is totally submissive to male authority. When Lugier demands Oriana's obedience, she says, "In all, I vow to ye" (3. 1. 87). Her obedience is again repeated in her last line addressed to Mirabell, "I obey you, sir, in all" (5. 6. 88). Her total dependence on patriarchal authority presents an overall scheme of the play, in which she finds a way to transform herself to be sexually appealing to men's eye.

The patriarchal dominance in *The Wild-Goose Chase* characteristically belongs to the Jacobean period in which playwrights dramatized those female characters who struggle against constraints imposed by husbands, fathers, or brothers. Bianca in Middleton's *Women Beware Women* (1621) complains about being kept in the house (3. 2. 167-68), just as the Duchess in Webster's *The Duchess of Malfi* (1614) argues against her brother's will to have her "cas'd up, like a holy relic" (3. 2. 139).[32] Strong-willed women were continuously dramatized: Regan in the anonymous *King Leir* (1590), who is much fiercer than Shakespeare's Regan, Lady Macbeth in Shakespeare's *Macbeth* (1606), and Camiola in Massinger's

The Maid of Honour (1621).[33] It was also a time when heated controversy over women was crowned with two important pamphlets, *Hic Mulier: Or, The Man-Woman* and *Haec-Vir: Or The Womanish-Man*, both published in 1620.[34]

Fletcher was no doubt conscious of the movement, as is evident from *The Woman's Prize* (1611), in which Maria speaks like a female pamphleteer of the time:

> Tell me of due obedience? what's a husband?
> What are we married for, to carry sumpters?
> Are we not one peece with you, and as worthy
> Our own intentions, as you yours? . . .
> Take two small drops of water, equall weigh'd,
> Tell me which is the heaviest, and which ought
> First to discend in duty?   (3. 3. 97-103)

Modifying Adriana's "drop of water" speech in *The Comedy of Errors* (2. 2. 110-46), Fletcher poses as if he cares about the emancipation of women. The play ends happily, however, when Maria readily yields to her husband with a very condescending speech: "I have done my worst, and have my end, forgive me; / From this houre make me what you please" (5. 4. 45-46).

Fletcher is undoubtedly a male chauvinist, and his was a drama of loyalty or doctrinal obedience in all respects. In *The Sea Voyage* (1622), the Amazonian women first congratulate themselves on their freedom from male domination and make "oathes never to looke / On man, but as a monster" (2. 2. 207-08). Nevertheless, the play ends happily with married couples, with all enmity simply forgotten as if marriage dissolved the problem. In *Bonduca* (1613), Fletcher's sexism is more apparent. The honorable general Caratach expresses his contempt of the valiant conqueress Queen Bonduca as follows:

> Caratach. The woman fool . . .
>   . . .
> The divell, and his dam too, who bid you
> Meddle in mens affairs?
>   Bonduca.   I'll help all.
>   Caratach.   Home,
> Home and spin woman, spin, go spin, ye trifle.   (3. 5. 128-35)

Consequently Bonduca's sexual allure is made to dominate her martial attributes. Even her courage which she demonstrates in her suicide is comically transformed into sexual appeal, when Petillius the humorous Roman General falls in love with her at the sight of her brave death. In Fletcher's chauvinistic world, women are always subjugated and labelled as "the weaker sex." The heroine of "masculine" spirit in *The Humorous Lieutenant* (1619) weeps and says, "I confess, I am a foole, a woman" (1. 2. 30). Fletcher uses the phrase "to be a woman"—in such a way as "Go to, you are a woman," designating women's inferiority—the most frequently of all his contemporary dramatists.[35]

This makes one wonder why Fletcher's drama was immensely popular with female audiences, but then we have to remember that it was an age when women's subservience to men was considered a law of nature not to be transgressed. Fletcher patronizes women and writes plays in which a woman can be a happy Cinderella protected by men's chivalry, courtliness, and honour. Oriana wins insofar as she yields to male authority. Elizabeth Cary the viscountess of Falkland (1585-1639) dramatizes her own conflict with masculine authority in *The Tragedie of Mariam* (1613), the first English play known to be written by a woman. In the play, however, she has to assign the following proclamatory lines to a loose, degenerate woman:

> Why should such priviledge to men be given?
> Or given to them, why bard from women then?
> Are men then we in greater grace with heaven?
> Or cannot women hate as well as men?
> Ile be the custome-breaker: and beginne
> To shew my Sexe the way to freedomes doore,
> And with an offring will I purge my sinne.   (1. 4. 315-21)[36]

This is as vehement a protest as Shylock's against racism in *The Merchant of Venice* (3. 1. 59-65), and as determined a challenge as Posthumus's against the superficiality of the world—"To shame the guise o' the' world, I will begin / The fashion"—in *Cymbeline* (5. 1. 32-33). Such a voice, however, had to be subdued in the early seventeenth century. Her biographer, one of her daughters, tells us that Cary lived as an exceptionally submissive and obedient wife.[37] It is understandable that the heroine of the play, Mariam, is characterized as a modest, submissive woman, as if to represent Cary in her oppressed life, and speaks like Fletcher's Oriana. "Excuse too rash a judgment in a woman," says Marian, "My Sexe pleads pardon" (1. 4. 8-9).

Notes

I am grateful to Mr. Timothy Keenan for proofreading this paper.

1. In a commendatory verse in the 1647 Beaumont and Fletcher Folio, William Cartwright valued Fletcher's wit above Shakespeare's: "Shakespeare to thee was dull, whose best jest lyes / I'th Ladies questions, and the Fooles replyes" (sig. d2^v).
2. See Joseph W. Donohue, Jr., *Dramatic Character in the English Romantic Age* (Princeton, N. J.: Princeton Univ. Press, 1970), pp. 13-83.
3. John Dryden, *Of Dramatick Poesie* (1668), sig. H1.
4. Some began to criticize the bracketing of Fletcher with Shakespeare around 1750. See Peter Whalley, *An Enquiry into the Learning of Shakespeare* (1748; facsimile ed., New York: AMS, 1970), p. 11; William Dodd, *The Beauties of Shakespear: Regularly Selected from Each Play with a General Index Digesting them under Proper Heads* (1752), facsimile ed., 2 vols., gen. ed. Arthur Freeman, *Eighteenth Century Shakespeare*, nos. 8 and 9 (London: Frank Cass, 1971), vol. 1, p. xix.
5. Mary Cone, *Fletcher without Beaumont: A Study of the Independent Plays of John Fletcher*, Salzburg Studies in English Literature Under the Direction of Professor Erwin A. Stürzl, Jacobean Drama Studies 60 (Salzburg: Universität Salzburg, 1976), p. 108; William W. Appleton, *Beaumont and Fletcher: A Critical Study* (London: Allen & Unwin, 1956), p. 105.
6. Clifford Leech, *The John Fletcher Plays* (London: Chatto & Windus, 1962), p. 75.
7. *The Oxford Companion to English Literature*, ed. Margaret Drabble (Oxford: Oxford Univ. Press, 1985), p. 1067.
8. Dyce's definition, quoted in Alexander Schmidt, *Shakespeare Lexicon and Quotation Dictionary: A Complete Dictionary of All the English Words, Phrases and Constructions in the Works of the Poet*, 2 vols. (New York: Dover, 1971), vol. 2, p. 1367.
9. Quoted from *The Plays of George Chapman: The Comedies, A Critical Edition*, ed. Allan Holaday (Urbana: Univ. of Illinois Press, 1970).
10. Quoted from *The Riverside Shakespeare*, gen. ed. G. Blakemore Evans (Boston: Houghton Mifflin, 1974).
11. See Fletcher's *The Mad Lover* (1617; 2. 1. 102), Thomas Middleton's *The Mayor of Queenborough* (1615-20; 5. 1. 112), Fletcher's *The Pilgrim* (1621; 5. 1. 22), Middleton and Dekker's *The Spanish Gypsy* (1623; 1. 1. 322), Philip Massinger's *The Guardian* (1633; 5.2.11), Thomas Nabbes's *Tottenham Court* (1633-34; 2. 4. 37), Massinger's *A Very Woman* (1634; 1. 1. 286), and William Denny's *The Shepherds' Holiday* (1651; 391). All quotations from the Beaumont and Fletcher canon refer to *The Dramatic Works in the Beaumont and Fletcher Canon*, gen. ed. Fredson Bowers, 10 vols. (Cambridge: Cambridge Univ. Press, 1966 - 1996). For Massinger's works, references are made to *The Plays and Poems of Philip*

Massinger, 5 vols., ed. Philip Edwards and Colin Gibson (Oxford: Clarendon Press, 1976); for Middleton's works, to *The Works of Thomas Middleton*, 8 vols., ed. A. H. Bullen (London: Nimmo, 1885), unless otherwise noted. For *The Spanish Gypsy, Tottenham Court* and *The Shepherds' Holiday*, I refer to *English Verse Drama: The Full-Text Database*, CD-ROM edition (Cambridge: Chadwyck-Healey, 1995).

12. *The Night Walker*, 1. 2. 5; 1. 4. 36; 1. 6. 1; 1. 7. 22. See also *The Wild-Goose Chase*, 3. 1. 139-41, where Lylia-Biancha speaks jokingly of Mirabell's "pregnant brains."

13. See 4. 1. 1-2; 4. 2. 1-3; 5. 3. 7-28 and 5. 6. 81.

14. See Robert Dodsley, ed., *A Select Collection of Old English Plays*, 15 vols. (1744; 4th ed. revised by W. Carew Hazlitt, 1874-76; New York: Blom, 1964), vol. 12, p. 117; the line number is based on *English Verse Drama*, CD-ROM edition. Shakespeare in *Much Ado About Nothing* mentions that women from fourteen to thirty-five are interested in fashion (3. 3. 132-33). Hylas in Fletcher's *Monsieur Thomas* is interested in women "Of any age, from fourscore to fourteen" (4. 4. 32).

15. Quoted from *The Dramatic Works in the Beaumont and Fletcher Canon*, gen. ed. Fredson Bowers, vol. 9.

16. Cf. Fletcher's *The Women's Prize* 2. 4. 19; Fletcher, Field, and Massinger's *The Knight of Malta* 3.2.85; Fletcher's *The Humorous Lieutenant* 2. 3. 12; Fletcher and Massinger's *The Elder Brother* 1. 1. 52.

17. Cf. Dekker's *The First Part of The Honest Whore* 3.3.42 (*The Dramatic Works Thomas Dekker*, ed. Fredson Bowers, 4 vols. [Cambridge: Cambridge Univ. Press, 1953-68]); Fletcher and William Rowley's *The Maid in the Mill* 2.1.138; Fletcher's *Pilgrim* 1.1.34; James Shirley's *The Lady of Pleasure* 1. 1. 260 (Ronald Huebert, ed., The Revels Plays [Manchester: Manchester Univ. Press, 1986]); Fletcher's *The Humorous Lieutenant* 2. 3. 15 (cf. 5.2.21).

18. Cf. Thomas Heywood's *The First Part of the Fair Maid of the West* 5.1.74 (R. K. Turner Jr., ed., Regents Renaissance Drama Series [London: Arnold, 1968]); Fletcher and Massinger's *The Little French Lawyer* 5. 3. 47; Middleton's *Women Beware Women* 3. 2. 99 (J. R. Mulryne, ed., The Revels Plays [Manchester: Manchester Univ. Press, 1975]).

19. For Jonson's works, I refer to *Ben Jonson*, ed. C. H. Herford and Percy and Evelyn Simpson, 11 vols. (Oxford: Clarendon Press, 1925-53). *The Alchemist* is in vol. 5 (1937).

20. See Ann Jennalie Cook, *Making a Match: Courtship in Shakespeare and His Society* (Princeton: Princeton Univ. Press, 1991), p. 265.

21. Cf. The anonymous *Nobody and Somebody*, line 1995, the anonymous *The Honest Lawyer* 2. 1. 436, and H. Shirley's *The Martyred Soldier* 5. 1. 24. For these plays, I refer to *English Verse Drama*, CD-ROM edition.

22. Cf. Beaumont and Fletcher's *The Maid's Tragedy* 2. 1. 18.

23. Cf. Beaumont and Fletcher's *The Woman-Hater* 5. 2. 26, Massinger's *The Maid of Honour* 2. 2. 16, and the anonymous *The Partial Law* 2. 3. 38. For *The Partial Law*, I refer to *English Verse Drama*.

24. See Richard Brome's *Novella* in *The Dramatic Works of Richard Brome Con-

taining Fifteen Comedies Now First Collected in Three Volumes (1873; New York: AMS, 1966), p. 115. The line number is 1. 2. 173, according to *English Verse Drama*.

25. Quoted from *The Two Angry Women of Abington*, ed. Michael Jardine and John Simons (Nottingham: Nottingham Univ. Press, 1989).

26. See, for example, Stephen Orgel, "Nobody's Perfect," *South Atlantic Quarterly* 88 (1988), 7-29.

27. Clifford Leech, *The John Fletcher Plays*, p. 75.

28. For John Lowin in this play, see my "John Lowin as Iago," *Shakespeare Studies* (Tokyo) 30 (1996), 17-34.

29. Sandra Clark, *The Plays of Beaumont and Fletcher: Sexual Themes and Dramatic Representation* (New York: Harvester, 1994), p. 147.

30. Cyrus Hoy, "Fletcherian Romantic Comedy," *Research Opportunities in Renaissance Drama*, 27 (1984), 3, quoted by Clark, p. 147.

31. George Farquhar completely neglects this structure, when he writes an adaptation of *The Wild-Goose Chase*, entitled *The Inconstant* (1736). He seems to interpret the play as a sex war between Mirabell and Oriana with the subplot of subsidiary skirmishes by another two pairs of lovers. In order to contrast the main plot and the subplot, as he construes them, he blends the "Aërie Daughters" into one character, the "Mad-cap" Bisarre (sig. B1^r), and Pinac and Bellure into Captain Duretete. Consequently Mirabell is no longer the boys' commander and naturally the play loses the women's commander Lugier. So Farquhar's Oriana is a resourceful, high-mettled heroine, acting of her own accord. As a result, the whole point of the original play is lost. Namely, the play no longer offers the framework in which the ladies have to act as directed by men.

32. Quoted from *The Duchess of Malfi*, ed. John Russell Brown, The Revels Plays (Manchester: Manchester Univ. Press, 1974).

33. For *King Leir*, see *The History of King Leir*, Malone Society Reprints, (Oxford: The Malone Society, 1907), esp. 2371-76. Of course there are a lot more strong female characters, including Duchess of Gloucester in *2 Henry VI* (c. 1590), Franceschina in *Dutch Courtesan* (1605), Isabella in *The Insatiate Countess* (1607), and Vittoria in *The White Devil* (1612).

34. The controversy became heated with three women's angry responses in 1617 to Joseph Swetnam's pamphlet *Arraignment of Lewd, idle, froward and unconstant women* (1615), followed by a satirical comedy *Swetnam the Woman-hater, Arraigned by Women* (acted 1618). For bibliography, see Elizabeth H. Hageman, "Recent Studies in Women Writers of the English Renaissance" in *Women in the Renaissance: Selections from English Literary Renaissance*, ed. Kirby Farrell, Elizabeth H. Hageman, and Arthur F. Kinney (Amherst: Univ. of Massachusetts Press, 1988), pp. 228-309.

35. Fletcher repeats it in *Cupid's Revenge* (1608) 2. 3. 2-3, *The Woman's Prize* (1611) 3. 3. 93, 5. 1. 31, *The Scornful Lady* (1613) 4. 1. 169, *Valentinian* (1614) 3. 3. 36, *Wit Without Money* (1614) 3. 1. 28, *Monsieur Thomas* (1615) 1. 2. 137, *The Mad Lover* (1617) 1. 1. 198, *The Loyal Subject* (1618) 1. 2. 33, *The Little French Lawyer* (1619) 3. 4. 5, *Women Pleased* (1620) 5. 2. 64, *The Custom of the Country* (1620) 1. 1.

221, 4. 3. 24, *The Island Princess* (1621) 3. 1. 239, and *The Wild-Goose Chase* (1621) 3. 1. 300, 4. 1. 166. These are parts not penned by Beaumont or Massinger according to Cyrus Hoy, "The Shares of Fletcher and his Collaborators in the Beaumont and Fletcher Canon (I)-(VII)," *Studies in Bibliography* 8 (1956), 129-146; 9 (1957), 143-155; 11 (1958), 85-99; 12 (1959), 91-116; 13 (1960), 77-108; 14 (1961), 45-68; 15 (1962), 71-90.

36. Quoted from *The Tragedy of Mariam*, ed. A. C. Dunstan, The Malone Society Reprints (London: The Malone Society, 1992).

37. *The Lady Falkland: Her Life* (c. 1655), p. 14. See also Elaine V. Beilin, *Redeeming Eve: Women Writers of the English Renaissance* (Princeton: Princeton Univ. Press, 1987), pp. 157-76; Sandra K. Fischer, "Elizabeth Cary and Tyranny, Domestic and Religious" in *Silent But for the Word: Tudor Women as Patrons, Translators, and Writers of Religious Works*, ed. Margaret P. Hannay (Ohio: The Kent State Univ. Press, 1985), pp. 225-37. See also Hageman (cf. note 34), p. 278.

Creating the Female Self:
Margaret Cavendish's Authorial Voice and Fictional Selves

Mami Adachi

1

IN THE PROLIFIC works of Margaret Cavendish, Duchess of Newcastle (1623-1673), we repeatedly hear the distinctive voice of the female author delivering her manifesto of ambition:

> I confess my ambition is restless, and not ordinary, because it would have an extraordinary fame: and since all heroic actions, public employments, powerful governments, and eloquent pleadings, are denied our sex in this age, or at least would be condemned for want of custom, is the cause I write so much; for my ambition being restless, though rather busy than industrious, yet it hath made that little wit I have to run upon every subject I can think of, or is fit for me to write on.[1]

Boldly stating her desire for an "extraordinary fame"—for she is after all trumpeting her precarious entry into a public and textual space which had been established as a masculine preserve—Cavendish indicates that her prolific writing is a means of expressing her self.[2] She admits that she is channeling her ambition into the only outlet that is not denied to a female in her time and culture. Her writing is a substitute for what she would have liked to engage in, the traditionally male activities of "heroic actions, public employments, powerful governments, and eloquent pleadings." She hastily concedes that her restless ambition is "rather busy than industrious," and assumes a halfhearted modesty ("that little wit I have").

This excerpt is a typical instance of Margaret Cavendish's assertion of selfhood in her endeavour to realize her urge to establish her self by writing, which constitutes her bid for immortal fame. She adopts a curious, conciliatory and self-effacing tone, which disturbs rather than convinces the reader, precisely because she is exposing the contradictory social position in which her writing has placed her. In her awareness of the importance of her self, specifically a female self, she emphasizes the autonomous over the determined, giving wider scope to the possibilities of the self in its engagement with the world.[3]

2

Recently the work of Cavendish has been reassessed by scholars in various fields.[4] Feminist studies have made a seminal contribution in pinpointing the extents to which Margaret Cavendish has provided an example for subsequent feminist writers by becoming their precursor in her public avowal of her ambition to see her works in print and in her practice of publishing her works under her real name.[5] In this sense, Virginia Woolf's comments on Cavendish have set the way to a reappraisal of her works from the socio-feminist point of view in this century.[6] While exhibiting a potentially subversive political stance against patriarchal society and against monarchism on the one hand by referring to the non-subjection of women to any authority,[7] however, Cavendish has resisted attempts to see her as champion of her sex, her attitude to members of the same sex being notoriously ambiguous— she insists on the equality of the sexes and the need for female education while deploring the unenlightened and frivolous employments in which women are left to languish by men, at the same time implying that most women deserve their own plight.[8] Manifesting an elitism and marked lack of sympathy towards women of lower classes, though she sought to mark out for herself a fame that transcends time and place,[9] she is at the same time very much a product of her age and culture, a conservative and a member of the privileged class. Her ambivalent stance as author and fluctuating awareness of selfhood points towards a fundamental amorphousness that resists any straightforward modern categorization into pioneering feminist, Royalist reactionary, radical scientific virtuoso who promoted atomism and later vitalistic materialism, shy recluse or self-aggrandizing author. She is at once all and none of these.

The importance of biographical factors cannot be underestimated in any appraisal of Cavendish's conception of selfhood and her *oeuvre*.[10]

First, the Civil War changed the context of women's lives, since it forced women to assume new roles that broke with tradition such as defending their own castles and homes, acting as secret agents, or standing in for absent men in the capacities of managers and chief breadwinners. For examples to refer to, Cavendish had to look no further than those of her mother Elizabeth Lucas and her queen Henrietta Maria.[11] Moreover, since Cavendish was a Royalist loyal to the cause of a king without a kingdom, she had faced the overwhelming disruption and reversal of her environment in a tremendous upheaval that challenged the ideological foundation of her life. In a different way, her marriage to the supportive Duke of Newcastle, a leading Royalist peer and patron of arts and science,[12] shaped her career and stimulated her to discover a way of inventing a female self while providing the stimuli for her writing.[13] In this sense it could be argued that she was able to indulge in the creation of a female authorial voice precisely because she was privileged by a complicitous and benign patriarchy, which proved to be remarkably resilient despite the radical changes in society. Furthermore her enforced isolation in exile in Paris and Antwerp, a state that she voluntarily adhered to after the Restoration on her husband's estate, may be seen to have provided her with a private enclosure in which she revelled in imaginative freedom.[14]

Regarding the immediate context of her decision to publish her writings, a crucial occasion is her visit to interregnum England with her husband's brother Charles Cavendish to petition for her right to her husband's estate. Though her petition was a failure, she was exposed to the liberal air of interregnum London, where women sectarians, in particular the Levellers, preached and wrote tracts, while women petitioners represented their menfolk.[15] As Cavendish noted: "this Age hath produced many effeminate Writers, as well as Preachers, and many effeminate Rulers, as well as Actors,"[16] and this may well have encouraged her to find her "effeminate" voice and to publish her first book. Therefore it may be no coincidence that it was during her stay in England that she wrote her speculations on natural science, probably influenced by the interest of Charles Cavendish in contemporary discoveries in science and mathematics, and published them under the title of *Poems and Fancies*, followed by *Philosophical Fancies*.

However, living on the Continent at a moment in history when the scientific spirit imbued the intellectual life with new meaning, Cavendish must have been conscious of other women who were somehow able to surmount their at best tenuous positions in patriarchal society to establish the female self—Queen Christina of Sweden, for example, and Princess Elizabeth of Bohemia, both close correspondents with René Descartes.[17] Cavendish certainly knew Christina in person, since she and her husband William Cavendish entertained the queen and her entourage in Antwerp. Though there is no evidence that Cavendish discussed philosophy with Christina on this or any other occasion, acquaintance and familiarity with these remarkable women—impeccably aristocratic, highly educated, formidably intellectual, well able to seize the initiative and to hold their own on an equal footing with men—may have provided the inspiration for her perception of women and their abilities to create and sustain a female self.

Notwithstanding, Margaret Cavendish was more than aware of the considerable differences, differences that she refused to view as disadvantageous, between herself and these paragons of female learning. In the Introduction to *Loves Adventures* in *Playes* (1662) occurs the following exchange:

> *First Gentleman* . . . this Play was writ by a Lady, who on my Conscience hath neither Language, nor Learning, but what is native and naturall.
> *Second Gentleman* A woman write a Play!
> Out upon it, out upon it, for it cannot be good, besides you say she is a Lady, which is the likelyer to make the Play worse, a woman and a Lady to write a Play; fye, fye.

This excerpt points out the central issue of Margaret Cavendish as an author. She is a "Lady," with "neither Language, nor Learning, but what is native and naturall." Unlike the educated noblewomen of European circles[18] and even her contemporary Englishwomen,[19] Cavendish had a minimal education, spelled erratically all her life, was unable to communicate in Latin, Greek or any modern language other than her native English despite the considerable time she lived on the Continent. What access she had to learning was perforce through the medium of her husband, her husband's brother Charles Cavendish, and her own brother John Lucas. But this did not deter Margaret Cavendish in searching for a definitive authorial self. She sets about to justify the product of a singular woman who possesses nothing but "native and naturall" qualities.

In order to carve out a distinct authorial stance for herself and to place her ideas of selfhood in the context of her culture, Cavendish resorted to intricate and at times subversive strategies for circumventing the dichotomies between her self as the woman patriarchal society willed her to be and her self as writing woman. She consciously endeavours to cater to the readers' expectations by referring to the patriarchal discourse of the ideal author—male, learned, and prolific in several languages—only to subvert these expectations, stating that she is not such an author.[20] She employs several devices by which she seemingly effaces herself from the critical views of those that, like the Second Gentleman, she imagines will disapprove of her efforts. She is ready to face the possibility of her works being unread, yet would not "quit my pastime" since "they delight me."[21] "Pastime" the works may have been inasmuch as her motive in resuming her writing during the Interregnum was partly to take her mind off her childlessness and ill health. Aware of the benefits she reaped from her exceptionally privileged position, she is unstinting in her gratitude towards the complicity of her husband William Cavendish, stating that his praise gave her the confidence to publish her works:

> I cannot chuse but declare to the World how happy I and my works are in your Approvement, which makes me confident and resolute to put them to the Press . . .[22]

She enlists his help in some scenes of her plays and concedes him first place in poetry, insisting that she had not the art that he possessed:

> My Lord was pleased to illustrate my Playes with some Scenes of his own Wit, to which I have set his name, that my Readers may know which are his, as not to cozen them, in thinking they are mine; also Songs, to which my Lords name is set; for I being no Lyrick Poet, my Lord supplied that defect of my Brain with the superfluity of his own Brain; thus our wits join as in Matrimony, My Lords the Masculine, mine the Feminine Wit, which is no small glory to me, that we are Married, Souls, Bodies, and Brains, which is a treble marriage, united in one Love, which I hope is not in the power of Death to dissolve; for Souls may love, and Wit may live, though Bodies dye.[23]

As seen in this quotation, she is scrupulous in acknowledging which scenes and songs are written by William Cavendish, thus showing a heightened awareness of authorship even in collaboration, a departure from Elizabethan and Jacobean practices of collaboration in which collaborators often did not precisely identify their respective contributions. It should be noted here that collaboration involved an erasure of individual authorial voices—the ideal collaboration was a seamless whole, which precluded identification of authorship.[24] Set against this idea of erasure, Cavendish's insistence on identifying the contribution of her collaborator introduces the potentially revolutionary idea of distinct authorial voices that proclaimed instead of effaced their selves. Furthermore, the fact that this is a female-male collaboration, one of the few known as such in that period, validates her comparison of collaboration to a marriage of wits, making it into a far apter metaphor than in the case of a collaboration between two members of the same sex.[25] In this marital union, though she concedes to the superiority of her husband's "superfluity" of wit, Cavendish seems to consider the female self an equal partner to the male. Moreover, she argues that their union, encapsulated in their collaboration, may not be dissolved by death, since despite the death of their bodies, Wit may live on. These arguments for publication of her works that present her collaboration with William Cavendish as a happy and organic union of wits have much in common with her perception of the natural world that resolves the diversity of all matter in unity.[26]

Another argument that is particularly pertinent when considering her authorial stance is her disavowal of any hope to have the plays acted. Conceding to her husband's powers as a playwright, she addresses him in this way:

> And as for this Books of Playes, I believe I should never have writ them, nor have had the Capacity nor Ingenuity to have writ Playes, had not you read to me some Playes which your Lordship had writ, and lye by for a good time to be Acted, wherein your Wit did Create a desire in my Mind to write Playes also, although my Playes are very unlike those you have writ, for your Lordships Playes have as it were a natural life, and a quick spirit in them, whereas mine are like dull dead statues, which is the reason I send them forth to be printed, rather than keep them concealed in hopes to have them first Acted; and this advantage I have, that is, I am out of the fear of having them hissed off from the Stage, for they are not like to come thereon;[27]

She tacitly acknowledges her debt of gratitude to her husband, since a reading of his plays had inspired her to write her own, then differentiates between his plays and her own by attributing to his "natural life" and "quick spirit," qualities that make them suitable for acting on stage, thereby justifying her wish to see her plays ("dull dead statues") in print. Given the fact that William Cavendish's daughters also wrote poems and plays that were never put on the public stage,[28] together with the fact that the closing of the theatres during the Interregnum forced all plays off the stage, on a first reading her arguments here may seem to be superfluous, closet drama—and increasingly an imaginary theatre—being the staple during the Civil War and the Interregnum. On the contrary it is a strategy that encodes her basic premise to write for 'the theatre of the Brain.' Cavendish says "For all the time my Playes a making were,/ My brain the Stage, my thoughts were acting there."[29] The plays are manifestations of her "contemplations." As an amateur female playwright who exploits to the full the security offered by class and economic resources and who writes in the seclusion of her closet to please no others but herself and a small band of ideologically sympathetic readers at the most, Cavendish wrote a speculative drama in which she creates an authorial self and a fantasy female self that hold sway over a fantasy world, in frank disregard of the conventions of the theatre and staging.[30]

In a further spurt of self-effacement, she professes that she knows little of the theatre. Like her other strategies, however, this self-avowed ignorance is highly suspect—raising the question of whether she is really as "native and naturall" as she insists. In fact she shows an awareness of theatrical practices and dramaturgy that is far from uninformed. In the General Prologue to her plays she reveals that she is familiar with the plays of Shakespeare and Ben Jonson,[31] showing a perceptive understanding of their respective characteristics, attributing to Jonson his powers of judgement and plain style and attributing to "Gentle Shakespear" his fluency and truth to "Nature":

> As for Ben. Johnsons brain, it was so strong,
> He could conceive, or judge, what's right, what's wrong:
> His Language plain, significant and free,
> And in the English Tongue, the Masterie:
> Yet Gentle Shakespear had a fluent Wit,
> Although less Learning, yet full well he writ;
> For all his Playes were writ by Natures light,
> Which gives his Readers, and Spectators sight.[32]

Though Cavendish's sympathies seem to be with the 'natural' fluency of Shakespeare, in a further twist she proceeds to declare that her plays are different from all others:[33]

> But Noble Readers, do not think my Playes,
> Are such as have been writ in former daies;
> As Johnson, Shakespear, Beamont, Fletcher writ;
> The Latin phrases I could never tell,
> But Johnson could, which made him write so well.
> Greek, Latin Poets, I could never read,
> Nor their Historians, but our English Speed;[34]

Instead of retiring into modesty by confessing ignorance of the classics, however, she subverts the expectations of her readers and goes on to proclaim that "I could not steal their Wit, nor Plots out take; / All my Playes Plots, my own poor brain did make," thereby implying the positive value of the concoctions of her "own poor brain." In stressing her originality, she further displays in passing her understanding of the works from which the playwrights of "former days" derived their plots:

> From Plutarchs story I ne'r took a Plot,
> Nor from Romances, nor from Don Quixot,
> As others have, for to assist their Wit, . . .[35]

Airily passing over the importance that patriarchal writers such as Jonson attributed to *imitatio* and measuring her own practice against his,[36] far from finding herself lacking, Cavendish asserts unapologetically that she is proud of her own work since "I upon my own Foundation writ," and "All the materials in my head did grow, / All is my own, and nothing do I owe." She closes her Prologue with a rousing statement that her Works may live on to be her monument when she dies, declaring that "I care not where my dust, or bones remain, / So my Works live, the labour of my brain." Thus, she emphasizes the quality of her "native and naturall" wit, the means by which she desires to carve a monument for her authorial self through writing.

3

Cavendish's plays have been dismissed as second-rate or at best emitting an erratic brilliance—rambling, extravagant, lacking in structure and coherence. She herself acknowledged the shortcomings of her plays, accusing critical readers of preferring "Plot before Wit." The episodic structure is not as eccentric as it may seem when regarded in the context of other plays of the period. As Susan Wiseman remarks, "ten act plays were not unheard of in the explosion of dramatic genres in the 1640s and 1650s; Killigrew wrote them, and the pamphlet plays were also published in two parts."[37] It is imperative to consider her plays as speculative drama, as a vehicle for her "contemplations." As mentioned before, she explicitly states that she had no thought for their performance on the public stage.[38]

To Cavendish, writing plays, more than in any other genre, provided her with a twofold opportunity—to openly explore and establish both her authorial voice and a diversity of female selves. Many of the female protagonists of Cavendish's plays are extensions of Cavendish's selves, her thoughts turned actors. For inasmuch as the self could be conceived as amounting to acting a part or parts in the theatre of the world, the real-life Cavendish did act out her selves—her self as female scientist, as shy unworldly recluse, as manager of a noble household, as helpmate of a worthy husband, as true lover, as ambitious intellectual, or as cross-dressed *ingénue*, sometimes separately, sometimes, to the bewilderment or antipathy of her contemporaries, all at once.[39] Cavendish advocated everything that was intellectually subversive within traditional society by recourse to fantasy. Though her protagonists include a female general and a cross-dressed female warrior, the female scientist/philosopher who addresses her public audience with an authoritative voice and the female recluse who withdraws into a secluded enclosure from which she speaks to the selected few provide the most intriguing models of selfhood created by Cavendish in the theatre of the imagination, reflecting as they do two seemingly opposed ways of establishing the self that pose most poignantly the problem of subjectivity and its expression.

That Cavendish was a female philosopher and scientist of considerable interest has been reassessed on reconsideration of her philosophical works. She has been spotlighted as one of the first of the modern women philosophers who appeared during the 300 years from 1600 to 1900.[40] Influences and differences have been traced between Thomas Hobbes, Descartes, Pierre Gassendi, Johannes Van Helmont, Walter Charleton and Joseph Glanville. Her atomism and materialism have been seen as infused with the spirit of the age. She contested the dualism of Descartes, questioned the experimental philosophy of her times, followed (though disapprovingly) the scientific development of microscopes and telescopes. Here again, familial influences have been studied, and it is undeniable that she was in an exceptionally privileged position to have information as regards the intellectual state-of-the-art developments of the age via her husband and brother-in-law.[41] In this field, as in others, in creating her self as a female scientist she exhibited a daring and subversive intellectual independence,[42] while incidentally providing an example of the "scientific lady" in England.[43]

Hypotheses on the nature of the world were central to Cavendish's speculative philosophy. In this she is similar to Descartes, who held (practically, given the notorious unreliability of 17th century experimental equipment) that, in the absence of adequate methods to ascertain the complexities of the natural world, false hypotheses were better than none at all, and in contrast with Newton who declared "I do not construct hypotheses."[44] She also departed from the prevailing Baconian paradigm that held knowledge to be experimental and communal, the keynote of the Royal Society which was founded in 1662. Cavendish's skepticism about the possibility of absolute knowledge of nature led her to justify the fruits of her speculations as possible hypotheses. She suggests there are infinite worlds, both outside and inside this world—even a world in a lady's earring: "And if thus small, then ladies well might weare/ A world of worlds, as pendents in each ear."[45] Since the new science was a male prerogative,[46] with no means of developing a method of conventional knowledge, Cavendish had no choice but to advocate skepticism.[47] She attempted to establish an alternative perspective of the world relying on her speculative philosophy alone as means of discovering scientific truths, being isolated by sex and temperament from the inductive method and communal accumulation of knowledge practised by the Royal Society.[48]

In her plays, her female scientists voice their hypotheses with assurance and poise, and are greeted by admiration and applause, both male and female. According to their alternative views of the world, Nature is self-moving and perceptive. In *Youths Glory and Deaths Banquet*, the female Orator Lady Sanspareille expounds on Nature in her first oration:

> ... I shall first treat of Nature, although Nature is an endless Theam to treat of; for though that the principles of Nature, or Natures principles may be easily numbred, yet the varietyes which change doth make on those principles are infinite. . . .

Creating the Female Self

> Thus Nature the tutress to man, and onely man, have taught him to imitate her; for though she is the Mother to all other Creatures, yet man is her beloved Child . . . [49]

Thus focusing on Nature as maternal, fecund and nurturing, Sanspareille proceeds in depicting a world picture that is based on the idea of the chain of being yet surprising physical and biological. Cavendish's philosophy of nature is "empathetic" and "subjective,"[50] the same applying to the philosophy of her fictional self, Sanspareille. Nature is a "fond parent" who directs humankind to discoveries; she leads them by the three "strings" of "observation" "conception" and "experience." In a hypothetical cosmology she claims the existence of "Six Worlds" which are like "Udders" from which the "Seventh World," the Sun, sucks an oily substance. Nature's fecundity is thus an expression of an organic and ordered natural philosophy. Sanspareille sees a female transcendent Nature as the ordering principle of the world. In fact, around 1661 Margaret Cavendish changes her views from an extreme atomism to a vitalistic materialism, considering, like Sanspareille, that a hierarchy of matter composes the entire material world. All matter is animate, while the diversity of matter is resolved in unity.

In *Natures three Daughters Beauty, Love and Wit*, the female orator Mademoiselle Grand Esprit raises the question whether it is possible to obtain rational knowledge of the Gods. She asks "what Man is, or ever was created, that knows what the Gods are, or how many they are? Or what powers they have, or where they reside?" "What Man ever knew whether the Gods were Eternal . . .?"[51] Her interrogation arrives at a kind of fideism, in which she leaves the problem of God to the realm of faith, not reason. She asserts:

> this absolute, wise and Eternal power Man calls God; but this absolute power, being infinite, he must of necessity be incomprehensible, and being incomprehensible, must of necessity be unknown . . . Man is forced to set up Candels of Faith, to light them, or direct them to that they cannot perfectly know, and for want of the clear light of knowledge, Man calls all Creations of this mighty power Nature.[52]

Defending herself against accusations of atheism, Grand Esprit firmly posits a fideism or negative theology by asserting the autonomy of faith and reason. Her stance parallels that of her creator, Cavendish herself, who retracted her extreme atomism that laid her open to charges of atheism.[53] The fecundity of Nature is conceived of as the expression of God's plenitude.

Holding the organic and the autonomous as superior over all ("All the materials in my head did grow, / All is my own and nothing do I owe."), be it artistic achievement or Natural order, throughout her plays Cavendish does not refer to the Divine save in vague references to the Heavens or the Gods (almost invariably in the plural). Even when Sanspareille is dying she avows "For whilst I liv'd I worship'd Nature great, / And Poets are by Nature favoured."[54] In the Second Part of the play, Sanspareille is cut off at the peak of her success as an Orator, shortly after the Queen of Attention comes to hear her speak.[55] She becomes the cynosure of her suitors' eyes in her last oration, but disavows marriage as "a great hinderance for a speculative life."[56] The cause of her death is 'natural,' she herself merely mentions "a fainting of spirits," and her death is not seen in any way as divine retribution for any anomaly or sin, or for preservation from worldly stain. She dies *in medias res* in Part 2 Act 4, comforting her father that "life is perpetual, and death is but a change of shape."[57] Invoking a specifically female Nature to whom his daughter owes her exceptional gifts, Sanspareille's father speaks his daughter's funeral sermon before dying of a broken heart in Part 2 Act 5.

Cavendish's natural philosophy and emphasis on self-moving and feminine Nature, potentially subversive for its lack of theological qualifiers, as voiced by her female scientists, may have led her to reject ideas of God as *deus ex machina* in her speculative drama. If God was best left to faith, was it reasonable for Cavendish to employ in her "theatre of the Brain" easy resolutions relying on divine intervention, staple of court and country house masques? Thus an authorial self-consciousness reflecting Cavendish's own natural philosophy must surely account for the episodic structure of her plays, that resist any easy closure, and for the abrupt halting of the headlong career of the female self, as epitomized in Sanspareille. In other words, in her creation of Sanspareille, the female scientist, philosopher and orator *par excellence*, Cavendish gave full scope to the autonomous self, to the extent of minimizing the presence of what is determined.

If by adopting the role of orator the female philosopher Sanspareille gained the freedom to voice her hypotheses on natural science, to some of Cavendish's female protagonists a convent or monastery serves as a place of study, in which the voice of the female self could be heard in congenial surroundings. In *The Religious*, Lady Perfection decides "to enter into a Religious Order." Moreover, instead of entering an "ordinary Nunnery," where "there is too much Company,"[58] she avows to live "a kind of a Hermits life" and "incloisters" herself for nine years. This is partly to escape the attentions of the Arch-Prince who is pursuing her, partly to preserve her love for Lord Melancholy, to whom she had been betrothed since infancy but has been forced apart by parental interference. At last she talks to her betrothed through a Grate that divides them, the two contemplate double suicide, but instead resolve on marriage, after which he also enters the Religious Order, proposing a new order of Chastity in Marriage.

Thus, this cloister, admitting of marriage and a studious life rather than a holy, proposes an innovation: a secular, yet reclusive monastic life.[59] In *The Female Academy*, the women cooperate in setting up an academy for their sex in which women are voluntarily "incloistered" to spend a life of meditation and study. They discuss a wide range of subjects, ranging from discourse, truth, good behaviour, friendship, to the theatre. The men, deprived of their women, set up an academy next door to the women's, their motive being merely to gain access to the female academy. The women ignore the men, so that the men resort to making a large noise with trumpets to interrupt the women's discourse. At this threat to drown the voice of the female self, a Matron appears and satisfies the men that "an Academy is not a Cloyster but a School, wherein are taught how to be good Wives when married."[60]

In this gesture of compromise, Cavendish utilizes the typical excuse set out for female education in this period.[61] The radical implications of a woman's right to obtain a good education were deflected by the traditional motive—to become good wives and mothers. Cavendish's convents do not exclude matrimony, and in her mind, far from being an anomaly, this was eminently reconcilable with a cloistered life. As we have seen, her works are totally devoid of any religious commitment. Though she used the trappings of religion to conceive of a place of secluded study, her values were rational and secular. Her idea of a place for reclusive meditation may be visualized in the frontispiece of *The World's Olio*,[62] in which Cavendish sits alone in her study, a room that is remarkable for its complete absence of books, as if to claim a place for "native and naturall" wit in defiance to orthodox learning. Retiring for days into her study, Cavendish herself gained the freedom of the imagination into which she regressed, and by doing so, carved for herself the monument she so desired to leave to posterity. The female author's voice rings clearly in the silence of the closet—an inviolable space far removed from, yet a product of, the world-turned-upside-down.[63]

Both female orator and cloistered recluse were fictional selves that optimally endorsed intellectual activity. Since Cavendish was debarred by education and sex from full inclusion into the predominantly male academy of her day, in her fantasy she proposes her answer to her ambivalent position as a *philosophe manqué*, a woman with literary and philosophical ambitions unsupported by learning or languages, though morally and financially encouraged by her patrician husband. Furthermore, though on her own repeated admission she was painfully shy, this retiring, reclusive disposition coexisted with the need to establish herself in the eyes of society, to publicize herself and to publish her works. To her, cloistered life was a means of plausibly distancing herself from the world, yet at the same time, compatible with certain worldly criteria such as matrimony and the occasion to show oneself in public to discourse on certain subjects, whereas oration was a means of legitimately publicizing one's philosophy.

In the elaborate barrage of authorial statements prefixed to her plays, Cavendish sought to establish her own authorial voice, while in the speculative plays she placed her fictional selves in "My brain the Stage." By giving full rein to what is autonomous in the self and scorning what is determined, Margaret Cavendish sought to open up an arena within which the female self, repressed by centuries of religious and secular ideologies, is given full scope to engage with the world. At the same time, the female self, essentially elusive, retires into an enclosure, in which it revels in worlds within the world, the infinite worlds of imagination.

Notes

I am very grateful to Richard Proudfoot and Gordon McMullan for reading and commenting on a draft of this paper at ridiculously short notice. Their insights and suggestions were invaluable. I also wish to thank Hilda L. Smith and Sarah Hutton for stimulating my interest in Cavendish's philosophy. For an account of Margaret Cavendish's urge to establish the self, that involves opposing tendencies towards regression and self-aggrandizement as evinced in her life and plays, see my essay in Japanese, "'Zuno no Gekijo': Margaret Cavendish ni Miru Jikoseikei no Kokoromi" ["'My Brain the Stage': Margaret Cavendish's Self-fashioning"], *Eigoseinen* [*The Rising Generation*], 142 (1996): 243-47.

1. "Epistle to the Reader," *Nature's Pictures by Fancies Pencil to the Life* (London: 1656).
2. Margaret Cavendish was, of course, not the first woman to write. What caused consternation was her determination to publish, an attitude that even the more enterprising among her female contemporaries dared not exhibit.
3. For helpful hints in thinking about the self and setting up my paradigm for the female self in this paper, I am indebted to *Rewriting the Self: Histories from the Renaissance to the Present*, ed. Roy Porter (London: Routledge, 1996), esp. Terry Eagleton's perceptive essay, "Self-undoing Subjects," pp. 262-69.
4. The present state in studies on Margaret Cavendish was well represented in the International Conference on Margaret Cavendish held at the University of East Anglia, Norwich, in March 1996. The topics discussed ranged from the dramatic writings, the Cavendish familial writings, science and philosophy, systems of thought, to self and sexuality. The most recent International Conference on Margaret Cavendish, held at the University of Oxford in June 1997, comprised an even more diverse array of topics, including, interestingly, interpretations of physical and metaphysical space in Cavendish's writings and biographical reconstructions of Cavendish's life on the Continent. The publication of *The Description of a New World Called the Blazing World and Other Writings*, ed. Kate Lilley (London: Penguin, 1992), has made Cavendish's writing accessible to a wider public than ever before. Recent anthologies have included various aspects of Cavendish's writings. See, e.g., *Women Critics 1660-1820: An Anthology*, ed. The Folger Collective on Early Women Critics (Bloomington and Indianapolis: Indiana Univ. Press, 1995), pp. 9-16. *Women and History: Voices of Early Modern England*, ed. Valerie Frith (Toronto: Coach House Press, 1995), pp. 119-44.
5. See, e.g., Natalie Zemon Davis, "Women as Historical Writers," in *Beyond Their Sex: Learned Women of the European Past*, ed. Patricia H. Labalme (New York: New York Univ. Press, 1980). Jerome Nadelhaft, "The Englishwoman's Sexual Civil War: Feminist Attitudes Towards Men, Women, and Marriage 1650-1740," *Journal of the History of Ideas*, 43 (1982) 555-79. Hilda L. Smith, *Reason's Disciples: Seventeenth-Century English Feminists* (Illinois: Illinois Univ. Press, 1982).
6. "The Duchess of Newcastle," *The Common Reader* (1925; New York: Harcourt, Brace and World, 1953), pp. 70-79.
7. The extraordinary passage in which Cavendish declares "we are no Subjects" because of women's exclusion from the polity is from *CCXI Sociable Letters* (London: 1664), Letter XVI.
8. For example, in *The Female Academy* in *Playes* (London: 1662), citizen's wives are forbidden to enter the female academy.
9. See Jean Gagen, "Honour and Fame in the Writings of the Duchess of

Newcastle," *Studies in Philology*, 56 (1959): 519-38.

10. Apart from Cavendish's autobiography prefixed to her husband's biography (see note 12 below), the most accessible and informative biography is still Douglas Grant's *Margaret the First: A Biography of Margaret Cavendish, Duchess of Newcastle 1623-1673* (London: Rupert Hart-Davis, 1957). Others are Kathleen Jones' *A Glorious Fame: The Life of Margaret Cavendish, Duchess of Newcastle, 1623-1673* (London: Bloomsbury, 1988), Henry Ten Eyck Perry's *The First Duchess of Newcastle and her Husband as Literary Figures* (Boston: Ginn, 1918). For an interpretation of Cavendish's mentalité, see Sara Heller Mendelson's concise biography in *The Mental World of Stuart Women: Three Studies* (Brighton: Harvester Press, 1987), pp. 12-61.

11. Elizabeth Lucas was an able and calculating manager of her estate. Henrietta Maria, to whom Cavendish served as lady-in-waiting, was known for her bent for self-dramatizing her plight as courageous royal spouse in adversity.

12. For Margaret Cavendish's biography of her husband, see *The Life of William Cavendish, Duke of Newcastle*, ed. C. H. Firth (London: 1886). See also Geoffrey Trease, *Portrait of a Cavalier: William Cavendish, First Duke of Newcastle* (London: Macmillan, 1979).

13. William Cavendish's support of his wife did not go unchallenged. Samuel Pepys observes in his diary (18 March 1668) that Margaret Cavendish's biography of her husband (first published 1667, see note 12 above) "shows her to be a mad, conceited, ridiculous woman, and he [William Cavendish] an ass to suffer her to write, what she writes to him, and of him." *The Diary of Samuel Pepys*, vol. 9, ed. R. C. Latham and W. Matthews (1971; London: Harper Collins, 1995), p. 123. Cynthia M. Tuerk has suggested that this implied challenge of Pepys, that William Cavendish was an imbecile or a brow-beaten husband to allow his wife to make a fool of him in public, is taken up by John Lacy in his 1667 play *Sauny the Scot*, an adaptation of Shakespeare's *The Taming of the Shrew*, in which the Shrew is, interestingly enough, renamed Margaret. Tuerk considers it probable that Lacy renamed the Shrew after Margaret Cavendish, "a woman who asserted her right to speak and publish in a male world" who "would be, for Lacy, the perfect model of a scolding, out-spoken shrew." *Notes & Queries*, 240 (1995): 450-51.

14. To the Royalists of both sexes during the Interregnum, all power was necessarily imaginary, as Catherine Gallagher points out in "Embracing the Absolute: The Politics of the Female Subject in Seventeenth Century England," *Genders*, 1 (1988): 24-39.

15. Though she had been one herself, Cavendish detested the petitioners, and insisted that she had not hung about and exposed herself at the Courts.

16. *Poems and Fancies* (London: 1653), p. 162.

17. For a study of Christina of Sweden, see Susanna Akerman, *Queen Christina of Sweden and her Circle: the Transformation of a Seventeenth-century Philosophical Libertine* (Leiden: Brill, 1991). For the correspondence between Elizabeth of Bohemia and Descartes, see L. Dugas, *Une Amitié intellectuelle: Descartes et la Princesse Elisabeth* (Rennes: 1891). See also Louis Foucher de Cariel, *Descartes,*

La Princesse Elisabeth et la Reine Christine d'après des lettres inedites (Paris: Felix Alcan, 1909).

18. Unlike her French contemporary Marie de Rabutin-Chantal, Marquise de Sévigné (1626-96), just three years her junior, Cavendish did not establish a salon. For a readable and concise biography of the Marquise, see Jacques Hislaire, *La Marquise de Sévigné: Esquisse d'une vie au XVIIe siècle* (Brussels: Le Cri, 1996).

19. Margaret Cavendish was virtually isolated from all other female writers except her step-daughters. Though she may have become a member of the poet Katherine Philip's circle, there is no evidence of her attending its meetings. However, during the years on the Continent, Cavendish may have had links with Bathsua Makin (c. 1610-c. 1682), tutor to Henrietta Maria's daughter and sister to the mathematician John Pell, Charles Cavendish's correspondent, and perhaps the Utrecht scholar Anna Maria van Schurman (1607-1678) who corresponded with Makin. Makin certainly knew and admired Cavendish.

20. Julie Sanders suggests that patriarchal authors such as Ben Jonson presented Cavendish with a paradigm and model of authorship in her paper "'A Woman Write a Play!': Jonsonian Strategies and the Dramatic Writings of Margaret Cavendish; or, did the Duchess Feel the Anxiety of Influence?" read at the Margaret Cavendish Conference, 1996.

21. "Preface,"*Observations upon Experimental Philosophy* (London: 1666). In this it may be said that she posed as a typical Cavalier writer, such as her husband was, writing to please himself, and careless of reader response.

22. "Dedication," *Orations of Divers Sorts* (London: 1662).

23. "Epistle to the Readers," *Playes* (London: 1662).

24. For this and other insights concerning the current ramifications of collaboration for editing, I am indebted to Gordon McMullan, "'Our whole life is like a play': collaboration and the problems of editing," *Textus*, 9 (1996): 371-94. Jeffrey Masten emphasizes the idea that collaborative writing "was predicated on *erasing* the perception of any differences that might have existed . . . between collaborative parts" in "Beaumont and/or Fletcher: Collaboration and the Interpretation of Renaissance Drama," *ELH*, 59 (1992): 342.

25. In a conversation, McMullan drew my attention to the metaphor of marriage applied to collaboration that sits uneasily when applied to collaboration between two male writers, as in the case of Beaumont and Fletcher.

26. For an interesting discussion of Cavendish's philosophy, see Lisa T. Sarasohn, "A Science Turned Upside Down: Feminism and the Natural Philosophy of Margaret Cavendish," *Huntington Library Quarterly*, 47 (1984): 289-307.

27. "Epistle Dedicatory," *Playes* (London: 1662).

28. For the work of Cavendish's daughters see Bodleian MS Rawlinson Poet. 16 'Poems Song a Pastorall and a Play by . . . Lady Iane Cavendish and Lady Elizabeth Brackley.'

29. "Dedication," *Playes* (London: 1662).

30. In this context it is illuminating to compare the amateur playwright Cavendish with the professional playwright Aphra Behn (1640?-1689). There is no

evidence of Cavendish having known Behn, the social gap between them excluding familiarity. For a definitive biography of Aphra Behn, see Janet Todd, *The Secret Life of Aphra Behn* (London: Andre Deutsch, 1996).

31. Ben Jonson, whom William Cavendish respected and supported, was an important literary figure to Margaret Cavendish, a paradigm of the patriarchal playwright, and, despite her insistence to the contrary, may have provided a model for her episodic structure and characterization of stock types who do not change in the course of the action. Cavendish was one of the first critics to discern Shakespeare's self-effacement in authorship and character development, anticipating Dryden and the Romantics, particularly Coleridge. See Letter CXXIII from *CCXI Sociable Letters* (London: 1664).

32. "General Prologue," *Playes* (London: 1662).

33. It is significant that, in the absence of female playwrights to allude to as role-models or otherwise, Cavendish cites male playwrights who wrote predominantly for the stage.

34. "General Prologue," *Playes* (London: 1662).

35. "General Prologue," *Playes*. As Janet Todd suggests, interestingly, the works Cavendish insists here that she avoided are exactly the sources of Aphra Behn's early plays (p. 463, n. 9).

36. Cavendish's dichotomy between natural wit and learned judgement is a departure from the neoclassical dictum proposed by Ben Jonson. See Sylvia Bowerbank,"The Spider's Delight: Margaret Cavendish and the 'Female' Imagination, "*English Literary Renaissance*, 14 (1984): 393. For Jonson's stance towards imitation of the classics, see "Timber or Discoveries," in *The Complete Works of Ben Jonson*, vol. 8, ed. C. H. Herford et al.(Oxford: Clarendon Press, 1947), esp. 2466-2480. The idea was to study and imitate the classics in order to purify and better wit.

37. "Gender and status in dramatic discourse: Margaret Cavendish, Duchess of Newcastle," *Women, Writing, History: 1640-1740*, ed. Isobel Grundy and Susan Wiseman (London: Batsford, 1992), p. 161.

38. However, the fact that Pepys mistook William Cavendish's play *The Humorous Lovers* when he went to see it staged on 30 March 1667 for his wife's ("the silly play of my Lady Newcastle's called *The Humorous Lovers*, the most silly thing that ever came on stage") suggests that there might have been some possibility of Margaret Cavendish's plays being staged after the Restoration. See Pepys, vol. 8, p. 137.

39. The remarks of her contemporaries, Samuel Pepys and John Evelyn, attest to the bewilderment and distaste with which she was regarded in real life. Female contemporaries such as Dorothy Osborne dismissed her as completely insane.

40. See *A History of Women Philosophers*, vol.4, ed. Mary Ellen Waithe (Dordrecht: Kluwer Academic Publishers, 1991).

41. For studies of the part played by the Cavendish Circle in the development of philosophical and scientific ideas, see Robert Kargon, *Atomism in England from Hariot to Newton* (Oxford: Clarendon Press, 1966), pp. 54-76. Stephen Clucas reconsiders Kargon's overview in "The Atomism of the Cavendish

Circle: A Reappraisal," *The Seventeenth Century*, 9 (1994): 247-73. Clucas' section on the atomism of Margaret Cavendish is particularly valuable (259-64). See also Jean Jacquot, "Sir Charles Cavendish and his Learned Friends," *Annals of Science*, 8 (1952): 13-27 and 175-194. Helen Hervey, "Hobbes and Descartes in the Light of some Unpublished Letters of the Correspondence between Sir Charles Cavendish and Dr. John Pell," *Osiris*, 10 (1952): 67-91.

42. Kargon, pp. 73-76, 80, 83-84.

43. Gerald D. Meyer, *The Scientific Lady in England 1650-1750: An Account of Her Rise, with Emphasis on the Major Roles of the Telescope and Microscope* (Berkeley: California Univ. Press, 1955), pp. 1-15. Meyer sees Cavendish as a real-life precursor of the fictional Madam the Marchioness in Bernard Fontenelle's immensely popular *Entretiens sur la pluralité des mondes* (1686). However, in this work "Fontenelle" is the authority who leads the eager and pliable student, Madam, into a new Copernican universe, the two conversationalists entering a new scientific era with their sexual roles intact (Bowerbank, 404-5). This is in contrast to Cavendish's revolutionary fantasy of a woman scientist (the Empress) as leader of a scientific community in *The Blazing World*. As Bowerbank remarks, Cavendish's contemporary, Catherine, Lady Ranelagh, is the only other Englishwoman who could be considered a 'scientific lady,' but unlike Cavendish, Ranelagh always worked through her brother Robert Boyle (402).

44. Desmond M. Clarke, "Descartes' philosophy of science and the scientific revolution," in *The Cambridge Companion to Descartes*, ed. John Cottingham (Cambridge: Cambridge Univ. Press, 1995), pp. 260-271.

45. "Of many Worlds in this World," *Poems and Fancies* (London: 1653). For a discussion on the topic of the plurality of worlds, see for example, Blaise Pascal, *Pensées*, ed. Léon Brunschvicg (Paris: Librairie Générale Française, 1972) fragment 72. Similarities to the thought of Pascal, an exact contemporary of Cavendish, attest to Cavendish's responsiveness to the intellectual climate of her times.

46. Cavendish attended a series of scientific experiments by Robert Boyle and Robert Hook at the all male Royal Society in 1667, but it was not until 1945 that women were admitted as members. For Cavendish's visit see S. I. Mintz, "The Duchess of Newcastle's Visit to the Royal Society," *Journal of English and Germanic Philology*, (1952): 168-76.

47. Sarasohn, 291-94. See also Richard H. Popkin, *The History of Scepticism from Erasmus to Spinoza* (Berkeley: California Univ. Press, 1979).

48. Bowerbank, p. 402.

49. *Youths Glory and Deaths Banquet* (London: 1662), Pt. 1, 3. 9. p. 138, sig. Mm1^v.

50. Bowerbank, 400.

51. *Natures three Daughters Beauty, Love and Wit* (London: 1662), Pt. 1, 2. 7. p. 495, sig. Iiiiii2^r.

52. *Natures three Daughters*, Pt. 1, 2. 7. p. 497, sig. Kkkkkk^r.

53. Kargon, p. 75. Cavendish's fideism may be interpreted as a screen for her atheistic materialism. See Sarasohn, n. 36.

54. *Youths Glory and Deaths Banquet* (London: 1662), Pt. 2, 4. 14. p. 169, sig.

Vu^r.

55. Same-sex friendships repeatedly figure in Cavendish's works. For instance, in *The Blazing World*, the Duchess of Newcastle herself appears as female scientist and eminently suitable companion to the Empress. The letters in *CCXI Sociable Letters* are addressed to a female friend who is on an equal standing with the author. In the plays, cross-dressing blurs the thin line between platonic friendship and sexual love, as for instance in *The Convent of Pleasure* in *Plays Never Before Printed* (London: 1668), in which Lady Happy cultivates a friendship with a woman who is in fact a man dressed as a woman, and finds herself falling in love with the supposed woman.

56. *Youths Glory and Deaths Banquet* (London: 1662), Pt. 2, 2. 5. p. 159, sig. Rr2^r.

57. *Youths Glory*, Pt. 2, 4. 14. p. 169, sig. Vu^r.

58. Cavendish criticized monasticism, holding that monastics were "an idle, lazy and unprofitable people" in *The Worlds Olio* (London: 1655).

59. For women's intellectual activity in convents see Isobel Grundy, "Women's history? Writings by English nuns" in *Women, Writing, History 1640-1740*, ed. Isobel Grundy and Susan Wiseman (London: Batsford, 1992), pp. 126-38. On non-Catholic women's wish for a Protestant convent, see Bridget Hill, "A Refuge from Men: The Idea of a Protestant Nunnery," in *Past and Present: A Journal of Historical Studies*, 117 (1987): 107-30.

60. *The Female Academy* (London: 1662), 5. 29. p. 679, sig. Iiiiiiii2^r.

61. For most female advocates of women's advanced education, from Bathsua Makin (see note 20 above) to Mary Astell (1666-1731), this was the staple in strategies of negotiation. More than twenty years after Cavendish's death, Mary Astell's *A Serious Proposal to the Ladies* (1694) proposed a life of temporary studious retirement, which would equip women the better for their reentry into the world. *A Serious Proposal* ran into four editions in seven years. Even before the outbreak of the Civil War, Lady Lettice, Viscountess Falkland, expressed the need for a "Protestant nunnery" for the education of young gentlewomen and the retirement of widows. See Bridget Hill, 107-108, 111-112.

62. Frontispiece of *The World's Olio*, 1671 edition, engraved after a drawing by Abraham van Diepenbecke.

63. For the world-turned-upside-down topos see Natalie Zemon Davis, "Women on Top," *Society and Culture in Early Modern France* (Stanford: Stanford Univ. Press, 1965), pp. 130-31.

Dialogue in *Romeo and Juliet*

Tetsuo Kishi

HOW MANY TIMES do Romeo and Juliet speak to each other? No doubt the question will sound simple enough, but in reality it is concerned with a fairly complicated case of dramatic dialogue. The first and short exchange between the star-crossed lovers takes place in Act 1 Scene 5 where they meet each other for the first time and dance with each other. Next there is a long conversation in the so-called balcony scene (2. 2). Then they meet each other again in Act 2 Scene 6 before they are secretly married, and finally there is an exchange in Act 3 Scene 5 after which Romeo reluctantly leaves Verona. After this they are never given a chance to speak to each other again. In other words Romeo and Juliet speak to each other only four times throughout the play, and their exchange occupies a relatively small part in the text. Even if we add the speeches they address each other in Act 5 Scene 3, the final scene set in the tomb, the situation hardly changes. Andrew K. Kennedy takes a more strict position in *Dramatic Dialogue: The Duologue of Personal Encounter*, and says, "So intense are the main duologues of *Romeo and Juliet* in their lyricism that they seem to 'carry' the action of the play. Yet there are only three key duologues: the first encounter (1. 5), the balcony scene (2. 2) and the antiphonal verse of the wedding-night (3. 5)."[1]

The truth however is even more complicated than Kennedy might imply, for some of the exchanges between Romeo and Juliet are conducted in a situation which lacks desirable conditions for normal conversation to be carried out. Generally speaking it would be preferable that each participant of a duologue knows who the other participant is or at any rate has an adequate amount of information about the other party for verbal communication to be carried out successfully. But Romeo and Juliet know virtually nothing about each other when they first meet. As a result they do not really speak *as themselves*. Instead they create a particular situation and speak according to that situation, or more specifically, they play, respectively, roles of a man who courts a woman whom he meets for the first time at a ball and a woman who is courted by a man whom she has never met before, thus playing a kind of game. It is true of course that any speech act is more or less dramatic since it is carried out vis-à-vis a particular situation, and in this sense people never really speak "as themselves." Still, this exchange between the two is exceptionally dramatic as they know nothing about each other and consciously put themselves in a situation they create. Interestingly enough, when Romeo compares himself to a pilgrim visiting a holy shrine, Juliet immediately accepts the metaphor and makes the conversation still more dramatic. It is extremely artificial in form as well. The eighteen line exchange consists of the fourteen lines which read like a sonnet and the four lines which also rhyme. It is not at all the kind of conversation which we call "natural." While there is an undeniable harmony in the exchange, it is only so long as they happily play their roles, and we must never forget that the situation itself is far from desirable for carrying out a conversation.

The so-called balcony scene is not free from a strange restraint either. The exchange between the lovers in this scene is by far the longest of the four. The contents of the exchange are extremely important as their discourse quickly reaches a decisive conclusion, that is, they promise to marry each other. In spite of all this, they cannot see each other's face. Of course they may not be totally invisible. Romeo mentions the light from the window of Juliet's room, and so perhaps he can see Juliet at least vaguely. The scene contains a number of references to the moon, and so perhaps we may suppose that Juliet also can see Romeo at least vaguely. At the same time there are repetitive references to the darkness of the night. For instance, when Juliet warns Romeo of an imminent death when her kinsmen learn of his intrusion to the garden, the latter answers, "I have night's cloak to hide me from their eyes" (2. 2. 75).[2] There is also this speech of Juliet:

> Thou knowest the mask of night is on my face,
> Else would a maiden blush bepaint my cheek
> For that which thou hast heard me speak tonight.   (2. 2. 85-87)

The darkness which dominates the place does seem to be emphasized far more than any dim light.

In verbal communication, not only the meaning of words but various kinds of aural information such as the inflection and speed of the voice play an important part. At the same time the communication usually depends also on visual information such as facial expressions and bodily gestures and sometimes on bodily contact as well. But the dialogue between Romeo and Juliet in the balcony scene depends almost exclusively on aural information. I happened to see the now legendary Franco Zeffirelli production of *Romeo and Juliet* at the Old Vic in 1961, and I remember that in this scene Romeo climbed up the pillar supporting the balcony and tried to kiss Juliet over and over again. While I estimate very highly the liveliness and freshness of the production, I feel Zeffirelli's direction did not realize Shakespeare's intention so far as this scene was concerned. For the dense eroticism which is prevalent in the scene derives from the fact that Romeo and Juliet affirm their mutual love only with their voices and commit themselves to a decisive act of marriage.

It is intriguing to think that when the play was performed during Shakespeare's own times both the facial expressions and bodily movements of the actors were clearly visible to the audience. In other words, while the scene is supposed to be set at night, sunshine in case of an outdoor performance and probably candlelight in case of an indoor performance must have filled the theatre. To some extent the references to the darkness of the night and the moon aroused the imagination of the audience. The audience felt that they were watching what is supposed to be invisible, and we can safely assume that they tasted an almost voyeuristic pleasure. It would have been even more exciting if the actors made full use of such visible elements as facial expressions and bodily gestures. I think a modern production in which moonlight is expressed by electric lighting and the characters are only vaguely visible cannot properly achieve the effect of the scene. Since Shakespeare is making fun, so to speak, of the physical conditions of the performance, the scene should be played either without any attempt at visually showing the night, as in the Japanese Noh theatre, or with a minimal lighting under which Romeo and Juliet are virtually invisible.

In Act 2 Scene 6 the lovers meet each other for the third time. The scene is set in Friar Lawrence's cell, and it is the only occasion when their exchange is carried out in the presence of a third person. Of course many characters are on the stage in the scene of the ball, but Romeo and Juliet are separated from them—psychologically rather than spatially—and the other characters neither listen to nor interfere with the conversation between the two. It is true that the Nurse speaks to Juliet several times in the balcony scene, but she never actually appears on the stage and she does not have an inkling that Romeo is in the garden. In Act 3 Scene 5 where the lovers are about to be separated forever, the Nurse knows that Romeo is in Juliet's room and appears in the scene, but her appearance is an extremely brief one. Thus the conversation between Romeo and Juliet is essentially carried out by excluding other characters. They are very much confined in the world of their own.

But in Act 2 Scene 6 there are no conditions which could hinder the conversation such as the ignorance about each other or the invisibility of each other's face. It would be only natural to expect a smooth exchange, but the truth is quite the opposite. The lovers become relatively reticent and their exchange is short and formal. The reason why this is so is of course the presence of Friar Lawrence. In a way the Friar represents the outside world which invades the world of the lovers. He drags the lovers to a more public situation, where carrying out of conversation becomes even more difficult. The text of the play which is widely available is based on the second quarto of 1599 or the first folio of 1623, but in the so-called bad quarto of 1597 the exchange between the lovers is somewhat longer. Still they are far from eloquent. We can easily understand why Andrew K. Kennedy does not count the exchange in this scene as one of the key duologues. It is the least interesting and the least dramatic (because it does not lead to any new event) of the exchanges between the lovers.

Romeo and Juliet speak to each other for the fourth and last time in Act 3 Scene 5. Here there is absolutely no condition which might cause difficulty. The physical distance between them is minimal. They know each other most intimately. No one else is there to interfere with them. The flow of the dialogue is most smooth. It is true that they argue about whether it is still night or it is already dawn and whether they are listening to a nightingale or a lark, but this discrepancy has to do with the contents of the dialogue and there is no denying that the conversation itself is carried out most naturally.

After approximately forty lines Romeo descends from Juliet's room to the ground, or rather from the upper stage to the main stage. Strictly speaking the stage direction "He goeth down" is found only in the first quarto. Neither the second quarto nor the first folio contains such direction. But since Romeo says, "one kiss, and I'll descend," it is clear that Romeo moves over a certain distance. The result is that there is now the same distance between the lovers as the one in the balcony scene. It is no more night, but it is not yet light enough for them to see each other's face clearly. Under such circumstances another twenty lines or so are spoken by the lovers. Of course it is psychologically natural that Romeo cannot leave the place immediately, but what I think is more than accidental is that the last dialogue between them who are now intimate enough is carried out at the virtual exclusion of non-aural elements in exactly the same place as the one where their first exchange took place after they learned each other's identity.

In Shakespeare's *Romeo and Juliet* the hero and the heroine never speak to each other again, although in the final scene of the play, Act 5 Scene 3, they do address each other. Romeo speaks lengthily to Juliet who he thinks is dead and then kills himself. Juliet speaks briefly to Romeo who is really dead and then kills herself. In each case both the speaker and the audience are fully aware that dialogue in the normal sense of the word is impossible. When the central characters are about to die, Shakespeare creates a situation in which dialogue is absolutely impossible and yet makes them speak the speeches which ostensibly sound like dialogue. This ultimate paradox lies in the heart of the lovers' dialogue, and this is what makes it at once unique and dramatic.

Dialogue between lovers is among the most personal forms of dramatic dialogue and so it is not at all surprising that it tends to take place where other characters are not present. But the dialogue between Benedick and Beatrice or between Claudio and Hero in *Much Ado about Nothing*, a Shakespearean play which also deals with love, is carried out in a more public situation, in some of the scenes at any rate. These lovers do not hesitate to speak about their affection when other people are present. It is rather significant, I think, that their dialogue is free from certain restrictive conditions which accompany the dialogue between Romeo and Juliet. Like most Shakespearean plays *Romeo and Juliet* was later revised. I dare say that revisions of this play were prepared, so far as the nature of dramatic language is concerned, to get rid of such restrictive conditions, and the result was that Shakespeare's elaborate rhetoric became more logical and simpler and Shakespeare's manipulation of audience response radically changed its direction.

For instance there is a peculiar play by Thomas Otway first produced in 1679 called *The History and Fall of Caius Marius*. The scene has been shifted to Rome and the story of Romeo and Juliet is now retold as that of a heroic tragedy. Marius junior, the son of an influential politician Caius Marius, is in love with Lavinia, the daughter of another influential politician Metellus. Unlike Romeo, however, Marius junior is in love with Lavinia even before the play begins, and the fact is known to his father. Lavinia too is in love with Marius junior before the play begins. The psychological distance between the lovers is much shorter than that between the lovers in Shakespeare's original. Naturally enough there is no scene where they meet each other for the first time and fall in love.

There *is* an equivalent of the balcony scene and the situation is more or less similar to that in the original, but the dialogue in the revised version lacks the kind of quality in the original version which Andrew K. Kennedy might call "intense lyricism." If by any chance there are readers who feel that the use of metaphors and the decorative rhetoric of the dialogue in the balcony scene are excessive, then I cannot agree with them. For the first time the lovers are trying to speak to each other *as themselves*, that is, without setting up a certain dramatic situation where they can play a role. They are not so certain if they can communicate with each other without difficulty and proceed with some hesitation. The apparently excessive rhetoric corresponds to their nervousness and tension. On the other hand, in Otway's adaptation, Marius junior and Lavinia respond to each other quickly and tersely, as we can judge from the following exchange:

> *Lavinia* O *Marius*, *Marius*! wherefore art thou *Marius*?
> Deny thy Family, renounce thy Name:
> Or if thou wilt not, be but sworn my Love,
> And I'll no longer call Metellus Parent.
> *Marius junior* Shall I hear this, and yet keep silence?
> *Lavinia*   No.
> 'Tis but thy Name that is my Enemy.
> Thou would'st be still thy self, though not a *Marius*,
> Belov'd of me, and charming as thou art.
> What's in a Name? that which we call a Rose,
> By any other name wou'd smell as sweet.
> So *Marius*, were he not *Marius* call'd,
> Be still as dear to my desiring Eyes,
> Without that Title. *Marius*, lose thy Name,
> And for that Name, which is no part of Thee,
> Take all *Lavinia*.
> *Marius junior* At thy word I take thee.
> Call me but Thine, and Joys will so transport me,

I shall forget my self, and quite be chang'd.
   Lavinia Who art Thou, that thus hid and veil'd in Night
Hast overheard my Follies?
   Marius junior   By a Name
I know not how to tell thee who I am.
My Name, dear Creature, 's hatefull to my self,
Because it is an Enemy to Thee.
   Lavinia Marius? how cam'st thou hither? tell, and why?
The Orchard-walls are high, and hard to climb,
And the place Death, consid'ring who thou art,
If any of our Family find thee.
By whose Directions didst thou find this place?
   Marius junior By Love, that first did prompt me to enquire.
   . . . .
   Lavinia Thou know'st the mask of Night is on my Face,
Else should I blush for what th' hast heard me speak.
Fain would I dwell on Form; fain, fain deny
The things I've said: but farewell all such Follies.
Dost thou then love? I know thou'lt say thou dost;
And I must take thy word, though thou prove false.
   Marius junior By yon bright *Cynthia*'s beams that shines above.
   Lavinia Oh! swear not by the Moon, th'inconstant Moon,
That changes Monthly, and shines but by seasons,
Lest that thy Love prove variable too.
   Marius junior What shall I swear by?
   Lavinia   Do not swear at all.
Or, if thou wilt, swear by thy gracious Self,
Who art the God of my Idolatry,
And I'll believe thee.
   Marius junior   Witness, all ye Powr's.
   Lavinia Nay, do not swear: although my Joy be great,
I'm hardly satisfy'd with this night's Contract:
It seems too rash, too unadvis'd and sudden,
Too like the Lightning, which does cease to be
E're one can say it is. Therefore this time
Good night, my *Marius*: may a happier hour
Bring us to crown our Wishes.
   Marius junior Why wilt thou leave me so unsatisfy'd?
   Lavinia What wouldst thou have?
   Marius junior   Th' Exchange of Love for mine.
   Lavinia I gave thee mine before thou didst request it;
And yet I wish I could retrieve it back.
   Marius junior Why?
   Lavinia   But to be frank, and give it thee agen.
My Bounty is as boundless as the Sea,
My Love as deep: the more I give to Thee,

> The more I have: for both are Infinite.
> I hear a Noise within. Farewell, my *Marius*;
> Or stay a little, and I'll come agen.
>   *Marius junior* Stay? sure for ever.
>   *Lavinia* Three words, and, *Marius*, then good night indeed.
>   (2. 1. 267-294, 314-346)[3]

The overall impression is that communication is easy between these two lovers, and this impression will be justified if we compare the passage with the equivalent passage in *Romeo and Juliet*. When Lavinia learns the identity of the invisible speaker, she at once utters "*Marius*?" (289) and without waiting for Marius junior's answer goes on to ask another question, "how cam'st thou hither?" Again she does not wait for the answer but proceeds to yet another question, "By whose Directions didst thou find this place?" (293). Marius junior's line "By yon bright *Cynthia*'s beams that shines (*sic*) above" (320) is a somewhat verbose variation on "Lady, by yonder blessèd moon I vow" (2. 2. 107) of the original, but whereas the latter is followed by an exquisite description of the moonlight "That tips with silver all these fruit-tree tops," Otway's version is more concise. Lavinia simply would not allow her lover time for such poetic indulgence. Obviously she is a clever and quick-witted woman, but it is true that her response has a somewhat sobering effect as well.

What is striking about the dialogue between Lavinia and Marius junior is the alert intellect, cool objectiveness, and preoccupation with logical thinking of the two participants. One can take a simple example and compare Marius junior's line "Shall I hear this, and yet keep silence?" (271) with Romeo's line "Shall I hear more, or shall I speak at this?" (2. 2. 37). The short phrase "and yet" in the former makes the speaker far more detached. While Romeo is immersed in his own excitement and joy, there is a distance between Marius junior's emotion and his judgement. This is on the whole true about Otway's text. Such words as "still" (273), "still" (278), "Therefore" (332), and "then" (346) function similarly. Marius junior uses the word "why" in line 335 and again in line 339, but there is no equivalent of the first "why" in Shakespeare's version. The second "why" supersedes Shakespeare's "for what purpose, love?" (2. 2. 130), and the tender tone of the latter has totally disappeared from the former. The exchange between Otway's lovers is carried out smoothly and promptly, making them sound almost like Mirabell and Millamant.

Dialogue in Romeo and Juliet

Otway's play, like the original version, contains a scene in which the lovers talk to each other after spending a night together, but it is set in the garden rather than the woman's bedchamber, and so there is never a distance between the two characters as there is in the original. Throughout the scene they stay on the same level, so that the exchange is carried out without any difficulty. Finally in the closing scene of Otway's version, Lavinia is awakened while Marius junior who took poison is still alive. Naturally they can speak to each other once again. What is pathetic about Shakespeare's lovers is that they are never given a chance to speak to each other again after spending a night together for the first and last time. If they are given a chance to do so even on the brink of an imminent death, their solitude is somewhat modified, and that is exactly what happens in Garrick's adaptation as well.

David Garrick's version of *Romeo and Juliet*, which was first produced in 1748, is far more faithful to the original than Otway's version, but it is not free from a number of significant alterations either. For instance Romeo is not in love with Rosaline. Romeo loves Juliet from the very beginning and attends Capulet's ball so that he can meet her. Since Romeo has a sufficient amount of information about Juliet, the nature of the scene and the relationship between the two characters are quite different. But the most decisive difference has to with Juliet regaining consciousness while Romeo is alive. This setting, by the way, appears in Bandello's story but not in Arthur Brooke's poem on which Shakespeare probably based his own work.

I will first quote some of the last speeches of Romeo's:

> Eyes, look your last!
> Arms, take your last embrace! and, lips, O you
> The doors of breath, seal with a righteous kiss
> A dateless bargain to engrossing Death! (5. 3. 112-115)

What follows is Garrick's version of the equivalent scene, with ample additions by him:

> *Romeo* No more—here's to my love!—eyes look your last;
> [*Drinking the poison.*
> Arms take your last embrace; and lips do you
> The doors of breath seal with a righteous kiss;—
> Soft—she breathes, and stirs! [*Juliet wakes.*
> *Juliet* Where am I? defend me!
> *Romeo* She speaks, she lives! and we shall still be bless'd!

My kind propitious stars o'erpay me now
For all my sorrows past—rise, rise, my Juliet,
And from this cave of death, this house of horror,
Quick let me snatch thee to thy Romeo's arms,
There breathe a vital spirit in thy lips,
And call thee back to life and love.　　　[*Takes her hand.*
　Juliet Bless me! how cold it is! who's there?
　Romeo Thy husband,
'Tis thy Romeo, Juliet; rais'd from despair
To joys unutt'rable! quit, quit this place,
And let us fly together—　　　[*Brings her from the tomb.*
　Juliet Why do you force me so? I'll ne'er consent—
My strength may fail me, but my will's unmov'd—
I'll not wed Paris—Romeo is my husband—
　Romeo Her senses are unsettled—Heav'n restore 'em!
Romeo is thy husband; I am that Romeo,
Nor all the opposing pow'rs of earth or man,
Shall break our bonds or tear thee from my heart.
　Juliet I know! that voice—Its magic sweetness wakes
My tranced soul—I now remember well
Each circumstance—Oh my lord, my husband—
　　　　　　　　　　[*Going to embrace him.*
Dost thou avoid me, Romeo? let me touch
Thy hand, and taste the cordial of thy lips—
You fright me—speak—O let me hear some voice
Besides my own in this drear vault of death,
Or I shall faint—support me—
　Romeo Oh I cannot,
I have no strength but want thy feeble aid;
Cruel poison!
　Juliet Poison! what means my lord? thy trembling Voice!
Pale lips! and swimming eyes! death's in thy face!
　Romeo It is indeed—I struggle with him now—
The transports that I felt to hear thee speak,
And see thy op'ning eyes, stopt for a moment
His impetuous course, and all my mind
Was happiness and thee; but now the poison
Rushes thro' my veins—I've not time to tell—
Fate brought me to this place—to take a last,
Last farewell of my love, and with thee die.
　Juliet Die! was the Friar false?
　Romeo I know not that—
I thought thee dead; distracted at the sight,
(Fatal speed) drank poison, kiss'd thy cold lips,
And found within thy arms a precious grave—
But in that moment—oh—

> *Juliet* And did I wake for this!
> *Romeo* My powers are blasted,
> 'Twixt death and life I'm torn—I'm distracted!
> But death's strongest—and must I leave thee Juliet!
> Oh cruel cursed fate! in sight of heav'n—
> *Juliet* Thou rav'st—lean on my breast—
> *Romeo* Fathers have flinty hearts, no tears can melt 'em,
> Nature pleads in vain—Children must be wretched—
> *Juliet* Oh my breaking heart—
> *Romeo* She is my wife—our hearts are twin'd together—
> Capulet forbear—Paris loose your hold—
> Pull not our heart-strings thus—they crack—they break—
> Oh Juliet! Juliet!   [*Dies.*   (5. 5. 61-124)[4]

Unfortunately it is necessary to quote the passage at length to understand and appreciate the melodramatic effect and the way Garrick uses dramatic language. At the same time his professional skills are never to be ignored. First Romeo uses a third person pronoun about Juliet, so that his speeches read more like soliloquies. Then he switches to a second person pronoun and starts speaking directly to his wife. In the beginning Juliet cannot understand the situation, but eventually realizes Romeo's voice and then his face. Throughout all this they attempt various kinds of bodily contact. As Juliet regains more and more of her consciousness, Romeo becomes fainter and fainter, although quite mysteriously he can still manage to describe his physical condition in detail. Would it be impertinent to be reminded of the deaths of Pyramus and Thisbe in *A Midsummer Night's Dream*? It is true that Garrick's version conveys the characters' emotional and physical conditions very explicitly and so gives a certain kind of satisfaction to the audience, but we will no doubt get an impression that here the dialogue is all too easy.

The dialogue between Romeo and Juliet in Shakespeare's original is *just* possible in spite of a number of difficulties and restrictions. This makes their situation more intense and their plight more tragic. The star-crossed lovers have to cope with not simply the animosity between the two households. Their problem, in other words, is not only social but also linguistic. As tragic chacracters, Romeo and Juliet find themselves in a linguistically impossible situation. Shakespeare's tour-de-force materialized convincing enough dialogue when it seemed hopelessly difficult. This is no doubt one of the reasons why Shakespeare is a far more competent and formidable playwright than the likes of Otway and Garrick.

Notes

This paper was originally presented in Japanese at the 34th annual meeting of the Shakespeare Society of Japan held at Hiroshima Jogakuin University on 21 October 1995.

1. Andrew K. Kennedy, *Dramatic Dialogue: The Duologue of Personal Encounter* (Cambridge: Cambridge Univ. Press, 1983), p. 75.
2. All quotations from the play are taken from the New Cambridge Shakespeare edition of *Romeo and Juliet*, ed. G. Blakemore Evans (Cambridge: Cambridge Univ. Press, 1984).
3. *The Works of Thomas Otway*, ed. J. C. Ghosh (Oxford: Clarendon Press, 1932), Vol. 1, pp. 461-463.
4. *The Dramatic Works of David Garrick* (London: R. Bald, T. Blaw, and J. Kert, 1774), Vol. 1, pp. 264-266.

"Those Are Pearls that Were His Eyes": Shakespeare's Holographic Imagination

Mitsuru Kamachi

> What is your substance, whereof are you made,
> That millions of strange shadows on you tend?[1]

ASKS SHAKESPEARE, ADDRESSING the young man in one of his sonnets. We can perhaps pose this question back to Shakespeare himself, whose plays present those millions of strange shadows which have intrigued his audience and critics over the last four centuries. Shadows, rather than substance, seem to haunt his imagination throughout his work; and it is those strange shadows like holograms, computer graphics and what we call "virtual reality" that preoccupy our imagination now.

What I would like to suggest in this paper is a method of criticism which uses the analogy of holograms or holographic pictures in interpreting Shakespearean drama.[2] I hope it can reveal some of the striking affinities between the Elizabethan way of looking at the world and a new perspective we need towards the end of the twentieth century.

Holograms were invented in the nineteen forties, and became practicable with the advent of laser light in the sixties. They are now widely used as security figures on credit cards and in various forms of artistic representations. At first sight, a hologram looks like a blank film or screen; it is only when we catch a particular angle from which to look at it that we suddenly see an image with forms and colors within it. And the image we see there is three-dimensional. Although it is presented on a two-dimensional surface, it gives us an illusion of depth.

But the most interesting feature of a hologram is that it can contain within the same framework several different images which present themselves one by one when viewed from different angles. A holographic portrait of Shakespeare I possess, for example, can show three different faces in one picture. He looks very serious and sullen when viewed from one angle, but his expression mellows as the picture is tilted slightly; and he looks serenely happy from another angle. The color of the picture also changes constantly according to our point of view.[3]

The last feature of a hologram is the fact that its parts can contain the whole. This means that we can crack a holographic picture and look at one of the fractions; and, surprisingly enough, we can see in this tiny part not just a fraction of the original picture but its whole image.[4] We must bear in mind that the term "hologram" derives from this particular feature of "a part containing the whole." "Holo" means "the whole," and "gram" is "what is written," so the term originally means "what is written in entirety."

Now we can make some analogies between holograms and Shakespearean drama, starting from the last of these features. One of the characteristics of a Shakespearean play is that its parts can contain a picture of the whole. We see within one small passage, even just one line or one word, the whole framework of the play. It often looks puzzling or blurred, like the seemingly blank surface of a hologram. In order to get the right pictures, we have to view it from the right angles; and sometimes we have to employ a special kind of light in order to illuminate it. This light has been called by various names; historicism, new criticism, Marxism, feminism, new historicism, textual revisionism, eco-criticism, and so on.

According to the light we employ, and also according to the angle from which we view the piece, we always see within the same framework a multiple layer of pictures or shadows which keep changing their shapes like Proteus. There is no fixed image which we can call the only true Shadow which represents the Substance. Instead, what we have is those millions of strange shadows superimposed upon each other, transforming themselves every time we look at them. This is the second analogy between Shakespeare's plays and holograms.

The third analogy, of course, is their three-dimensionality. The distinguishing mark of Shakespeare's characters and situations is the roundness with which they are presented. Some of the characters in Ben Jonson or Cyril Tourneur, for example, are often deliberately two-dimensional, like the figures in a pack of playing cards. Shakespeare's main characters, on the other hand, are always depicted as three-dimensional figures and also thrive in three-dimensional situations.

"Those Are Pearls that Were His Eyes"

*

Now I should like to consider a line from *The Tempest*—"Those are pearls that were his eyes"—and see how the holographic imagination functions in this tiny fraction of his work. It has also become familiar to us because of a twentieth-century lens through which we see it: its repetition in *The Waste Land* has made it one of the most haunting lines in modern poetry as well.

But what exactly are we to depict on the canvas of our imagination when we hear the line? Each word in it is as simple as it can be. And yet one wonders how a painter would manage to illustrate this scene with a single picture, because there is a great discrepancy between the horrid image of "death by water" suggested by the line and the idyllic atmosphere created by Ariel's song. This line is much more complex than it seems, with a multiple layer of three-dimensional images hidden beneath its seemingly opaque surface. Let us now examine the line in its context, the song of Ariel heard by Ferdinand.

> Full fathom five thy father lies,
> Of his bones are coral made:
> Those are pearls that were his eyes.
> Nothing of him that doth fade,
> But doth suffer a sea-change
> Into something rich and strange . . .   (1. 2. 400-5)

What interests us is the rhyming scheme here. The first line ends with the word "lies," rhyming with "eyes" in the third line. And "made" in the second line rhymes with "fade" in the fourth line. The last two lines form a couplet, ending with "change" and "strange."

Although the word "lies" means to "lie down," to "stretch out," a faint echo of another meaning is heard when we listen to it carefully. The King of Naples is not really drowned; Ariel is "lying" to Ferdinand as he sings this song. The deceptive or illusory nature of this song is hinted at right from the beginning. The rhyme of "lies" and "eyes" reminds us that the scene presented here depends on the deception of the eyes, just as a hologram depends on the illusion of reality created by laser light.

The second rhyme of "made" and "fade" seems to suggest that every image that is "made" or "created" is destined to "fade," as all holographic images do before they are transformed into other shapes. The last couplet of "change" and "strange" refers to the effect which is brought by the transformation. "Strange" here means "marvelous" and "rare." This song, therefore, is about a marvelous transformation of the "eyes," or a surprising change in the ways of looking at the world (which, of course, is what holograms are all about.) No wonder it cannot be represented by one fixed image. It is holographic imagination that is needed here. And what we see in this hologram are some strange shadows from his earlier works, including *Richard III*, *Troilus and Cressida*, and *Pericles*.

*

The first image behind the line is the scene of the shipwreck described in the dream of Clarence in *Richard III*.

> O Lord, methought what pain it was to drown!
> What dreadful noise of waters in mine ears!
> What sights of ugly death within mine eyes!
> Methoughts I saw a thousand fearful wracks;
> A thousand men that fishes gnawed upon;
> Wedges of gold, great anchors, heaps of pearl,
> Inestimable stones, unvalued jewels,
> All scatt'red in the bottom of the sea.
> Some lay in dead men's skulls; and in the holes
> Where eyes did once inhabit there were crept,
> As 'twere in scorn of eyes, reflecting gems,
> That wooed the slimy bottom of the deep,
> And mocked the dead bones that lay scatt'red by.   (1. 4. 21-33)

This vivid description of a grotesque scene in which jewels glitter in skulls reminds the modern reader of surrealistic paintings. For the Elizabethans, however, the combination of the jewel and the skull was more "real" than "surreal." Their rings, brooches and golden ornaments were often engraved with the figure of a skull. Their precious stones were placed right next to the real skulls which decorated their studies as a symbol of memento mori. Their insatiable greed for wealth and fame prompted them to go out to the sea, where so many of them actually suffered shipwreck. This passage, therefore, must have presented a three-dimensional, life-size vision of horror to the Elizabethans, whose desire was always placed side by side with their realization of the vanity of such an endeavor.

If a skull is a symbol of mortality, a jewel is that of immortality. Here in the dream of Clarence, immortal objects are personified by malicious beings who mock and scorn the misery of the mortal. But the irony goes further. By replacing the human eyes and glittering in the eye-sockets of the skulls in scorn of mortality, those immortal jewels have also become completely worthless themselves. Because it was the human eyes which gave them value, those gems are simply useless stones scattered at the bottom of the sea when there are no human eyes to look at them.

Shakespeare was probably thinking of one of his favorite puns here: that of the "eye," the visual organ, and of the "I," the "Self" or "Ego." (A pun, of course, is a kind of hologram, with a multiple layer of meanings hidden in a single word.) In their pursuit of pretty objects to please their eyes and inflate their Ego, those men have wrecked themselves and have lost their eyes; that is, their true Self, their real identity. Because their eyes are replaced by the jewels they were so eagerly seeking, they can no longer "see" the intrinsic value of things.

Here is another pun which is just as important. That of the "sea," the ocean, and of the verb "see," "to view" and "to comprehend." The sea for the Elizabethans had become a place for achieving their ambitions. Their vision had seemingly extended beyond the small compass of a country or a continent. Their loss, however, was equally great. In their egotistic pursuit of wealth and fame, they do not seem to appreciate that the sea is a mythical area which is their womb as well as their tomb. Because they are interested only in the inorganic glare of the gems, they can no longer see the beauty of the sea any more; and they lose their sight completely at the bottom of the sea, which hides the secrets of great creating Nature. All they are concerned with is the tiny gems of their Ego, which rot away immediately when they are overwhelmed by the waves. They must remain eyeless in the depth of the sea.

*

The same theme continues in *Troilus and Cressida*, in which Troilus compares Cressida to a pearl in India. When expecting to visit her for the first time with the help of Pandarus, he says:

> Her bed is India; there she lies, a pearl;
> Between our Ilium and where she resides
> Let it be called the wild and wandering flood;
> Ourself the merchant, and this sailing Pandar,
> Our doubtful hope, our convoy and our bark. (1. 1. 102-6)

Just like those merchants who went out to the Indian Sea for the "orient pearls," Troilus goes out to get his beloved lady Cressida. Just like those men who are shipwrecked after obtaining those "heaps of pearl" in Clarence's dream, Troilus suffers a spiritual shipwreck immediately after acquiring his precious pearl.

The morning after he spends his first night with her, he gives us one of the strangest aubades to be found. He is apparently trying to persuade Cressida to go back to her bed again rather than to see him off at the gate:

> *Troilus* To bed, to bed! Sleep kill those pretty eyes,
> And give as soft attachment to thy senses
> As infants empty of all thought!
>   *Cressida*   Good morrow, then.
>   *Troilus* I prithee now, to bed!
>   *Cressida*   Are you aweary of me?
>   *Troilus* O Cressida! But that the busy day,
> Waked by the lark, hath roused the ribald crows,
> And dreaming night will hide our joys no longer,
> I would not from thee.
>   *Cressida*   Night hath been too brief.
>   *Troilus* Beshrew the witch! With venomous wights she stays
> As tediously as hell, but flies the grasps of love
> With wings more momentary-swift than thought.
> You will catch cold, and curse me. (4. 2. 4-15)

What puzzles us here especially is the sentence: "Sleep kill those pretty eyes." It does not give us a clear image, as if there is a blot or smudge in the middle of the picture. Or it is like a blank film of a hologram when we do not know the right angle to look at it. It is a very complex line, because it is actually a double hologram within a hologram, offering us two sets of images which transform themselves in dramatic ways in a wider context of the holographic line in *The Tempest*. The first set of images turn around the "pretty eyes" of Cressida, who is compared to a pearl. The second set is related to the image of the infants suggested in the third line. And the key to finding the right angles for seeing these holographic transformations is the word "kill."

Scholars have always found this word rather annoying, because it looks totally inappropriate in the context of an aubade. John Dryden, for example, changed this word to "seal," in his usual effort to "improve" Shakespeare. In his version, therefore, Troilus says: "Sleep seal those pretty eyes."[5] He has certainly normalized the picture, but in doing so, he has turned this Shakespearean hologram into a flat painting. Here Troilus is simply saying to his love: "go back to your bed, close your eyes, and sleep like an innocent baby."

It has always been safer, though, to pause before "improving" Shakespeare; both the Quarto and Folio editions clearly give us "kill." And the original picture with this ominous word in it presents before us, with a slight turn of the angle, an image which is as gruesome and scary as the one in *Richard III*. We can find the right angle for it by recalling that the play of *Troilus and Cressida* abounds with the images of blindness. Ajax, for example, is called "a purblind Argus, all eyes and no sight" (1. 2. 29-30); and the lovers have a curious conversation when they meet each other for the first time.

> *Troilus* What too curious dreg espies my sweet lady in the fountain of our love?
> *Cressida* More dregs than water, if my fears have eyes.
> *Troilus* Fears make devils of cherubins; they never see truly.
> *Cressida* Blind fear, that seeing reason leads, finds safer footing than blind reason stumbling without fear: (3. 2. 65-71)

The fountain of their love, which is also a symbol of the lovers' eyes, is so full of dregs that they cannot see the bottom of it. The malady of the "eye" is that of the "Ego." Cressida is imprisoned in the tiny cell of her ego, with her "fears" serving as the windows to the outside world. Those "fears" also function as her eyes, but "they never see truly"—in fact they are all blind. It is as if Cressida were turned into "a purblind Argus, all eyes and no sight." The image of blindness here is not that of Cupid, as one would expect, but of a cataract.

When we remember that a cataract was called "a pearl of the eye" in Elizabethan times, and that the original meaning of the word "pretty" was "cunning" or "shifty," a new picture reveals itself in the hologram. "Sleep kill those pretty eyes" can be interpreted as "May sleep give those cunning eyes cataracts." We see Cressida's eyes turning pale and opaque, until they are changed into a pair of pearls in her head.

Then a further image emerges as we keep tilting the hologram. Troilus called her a pearl in the Indian Sea; with his word "kill," however, this magnificent pearl turns itself into an object with the same spherical shape and the same off-white color—a skull lying at the bottom of the sea. While the skulls in Clarence's dream had "reflecting gems" in their eye-sockets, this skull of Cressida has pearls as her eyes, symbolizing the irredeemable blindness of her soul.

Now I should like to turn to another hologram within a hologram we can see in this scene, by referring to the other emendation of the word "kill." This was proposed by Lettsom and has been supported by scholars like John Dover Wilson and Gary Taylor.[6] They have changed the word to "lull," so the whole sentence becomes "Sleep lull those pretty eyes, / And give as soft attachment to thy senses / As infants empty of all thought." This seems to be an ingenious emendation which depicts a sweet picture of Cressida as an innocent baby sleeping in heavenly peace.

The only problem with this portrait is the imagery of darkness which predominates in Troilus's aubade in the same scene. We hear words like "crows," "night," "hide," "witch," "venomous," "hell," "cold" and "curse" coming out of his mouth in succession. "Kill" would be far more appropriate than "lull" in this context. If we only reverse the order of the words "Sleep kill," we have "kill Sleep," reminding us of the cry of Macbeth: "Glamis hath murdered sleep, and therefore Cawdor / Shall sleep no more: Macbeth shall sleep no more!" (*Macbeth*, 2. 2. 42-43). Troilus's obsessive repetition of "to bed" (4. 2. 4 & 7) seems to presage Lady Macbeth's same phrase in her sleep-walking scene (5. 1. 65 & 67). Even the "infants empty of all thought" (4. 2. 6) in Troilus's speech seem to be superimposed on the imagined scene of Lady Macbeth dashing "the brains out" of the "babe that milks" her (1. 7. 54-58). What looms up behind this aubade is the allegorical figure of Night, who is invoked by Lady Macbeth and cursed by Troilus. She is the key figure in presenting the second hologram within a hologram we see in the line in question.

"Night" in the sixteenth century was often represented as a woman with wings who carried her twin babes in her arms. The one in her left arm, a fair baby sleeping innocently, was called "Sleep." The one in her right arm, a dark baby who was wide awake, was called "Death." Now we can see the dramatic reversal of images in the hologram. The emended version of "lull" presents Cressida as a fair baby of Sleep, but the original word "kill" inevitably tilts the picture back to reveal her as the dark baby of Death. And this new portrait of Cressida as Death in the arm of its mother Night is superimposed on the first image we saw, a skull lying on the bed of the murky sea.

We have to think, however, why the emendation of the word "kill" into "lull" has been so popular as to continue into the present day. It may reflect our heartfelt desire to restore the picture of the fair baby of Sleep. Like Macbeth who murdered Sleep, modern men and women suffer from sleeplessness night after night. We need to "lull" our cunning egos in order to get some sleep, but our problems and worries do not allow us to do so.

"Sleep," after all, has not been able to "lull" our "pretty eyes"; then it will have to resort to a more drastic measure. The original word "kill" has a new significance in this context. "Sleep kill those pretty eyes" could be a desperate cry of someone who wants the power of Sleep, or great Nature, to "kill" our "cunning egos" so that we could regain our true selves, which are just a part of Nature. This line is perhaps looking ahead towards the world of the Romances, where the hologram is tilted in the opposite direction: from the dark baby of Death to the fair baby of Sleep.

*

The following passage in *Pericles*, the first of the Romances, gives us the final image which we can see behind the holographic line in *The Tempest*. After apparently losing his wife Thaisa in childbirth, Pericles is compelled to cast her body into the sea. Although his words are filled with dark images of death, there is a sudden change of keynote in the last couple of lines:

> A terrible childbed hast thou had, my dear;
> No light, no fire: th'unfriendly elements
> Forgot thee utterly; nor have I time
> To give thee hallowed to thy grave, but straight
> Must cast thee, scarcely coffined, in the ooze;
> Where, for a monument upon thy bones,
> And e'er-remaining lamps, the belching whale
> And humming water must o'erwhelm thy corpse,
> Lying with simple shells.   (3. 1. 56-64)

Instead of an imperishable grave with its "monument" and "e'er-remaining lamps," Thaisa has a vast watery grave where the natural cycle of birth and death continues to whirl round. There is something warm and friendly, even humorous, about the unaffected simplicity of the "belching whale." "The dreadful noise of waters" in *Richard III* is now changed into the "humming water," suggesting the peaceful harmony of a dreamy lullaby. Instead of the "reflecting gems" which "mocked the dead bones," the body of Thaisa has "simple shells" as her company. Human bones are no longer scorned by the immortal, but are at peace with all the other mortal images of Nature. It is as though time had ceased to hurry along its linear course and had joined the eternal tide of the sea. This impression is enforced by the repetition of the "-ing" form in the last three lines of the passage: "e'er-remaining," "belching," "humming" and "lying."

This last word "lying" again reminds us of the fact that the scene is not a presentation of reality but is a spiritual landscape imagined by Pericles, just like Clarence's dream or Ariel's song. But the original meaning of lying gently at the bottom of the sea is also significant. It is a symbolic death, a necessary process for the rebirth of the soul in the womb of the sea.

The image of the jewels, which was so dominant in the dream of Clarence, also undergoes a great change. After retrieving the coffin of Thaisa from the sea, Cerimon succeeds in making her "blow / Into life's flower again" (3. 2. 100-1).

> She is alive; behold,
> Her eyelids, cases to those heavenly jewels
> Which Pericles hath lost, begin to part
> Their fringes of bright gold; the diamonds
> Of a most praised water doth appear
> To make the world twice rich.   (3. 2. 103-8)

The word "water" in the fifth line means the "luster of a diamond" in this context; but it gives us the inevitable association of her tears, and of the depth of the sea from which she has returned. The salt water is crystallized into her tears, then to her eyes, and finally into most precious diamonds. The mortal and the immortal are fused into one at this supreme moment of "resurrection." Thaisa's eyes are not lost in the sea but have been transformed into something of great value which the hands of time cannot touch. We have come a long way from the jewel imagery in *Richard III*; and only a slight turn of the angle brings us back to the picture where we started from, the song of Ariel in *The Tempest*.

While Thaisa's eyes were transformed into diamonds, that is, inorganic stones, Alonzo's eyes have been turned into pearls, the organic jewel produced by "simple shells." His bones are also changed into corals, another natural product of the sea. The fusion of the human body into the elements of the sea is now complete. Alonzo is at one with great creating Nature, and his mortality ceases to be a problem when his "eye" or "ego" is dissolved into some wider being, only to be crystallized again into a pearl: a symbol of the intrinsic beauty of the soul.

It is also important to note that a real pearl is created around a foreign body in an oyster; either a grain of sand or a small pebble which enters the shell by chance. It is more than a mote in the eye for the poor oyster; sometimes it dies of it. For those oysters which survive, the larger their predicament, the more magnificent the pearls they produce.

The word "suffer" in Ariel's song reverberates this element of pain involved in the transformation. Although it simply means to "experience" or "undergo," a distant echo of the shipwreck is undeniably there, like a ghastly image hidden underneath a happy picture in a hologram. The following words of Alonzo should not be overlooked in this context. Repenting his trespass on Prospero's rights, he says:

> Therefore my son i'th'ooze is bedded; and
> I'll seek him deeper than e'er plummet sounded,
> And with him there lie mudded.   (3. 3. 100-2)

These lines serve as a parallel to Ariel's song, throwing light on the deeper significance of the "sea-change." They reveal the concept of penitence and sorrow involved in the process of purgation. The "sea-change" is a "*see*-change": a change in one's view of the world, which is always accompanied by pain. It is only after going through this pain that one can obtain a vision of the miraculous transformation of a pearl: from a symbol of the Ego to that of the Self, from a symbol of irredeemable blindness to that of eternal eyesight.

*

The beauty of the undersea imagery in the hologram we have seen may be compared to a thin veil of silk laid over the dark abyss of reality. It is not the absolute and imperishable beauty set apart from the pains and sufferings of everyday life. It is a vision which, at the slightest change of the angle, fades away to reveal most frightful images behind it. And yet—or rather because of it—we are led to believe in its immanent value. It is almost a silent prayer for those who rest in the "ooze" of this vast sea of life.

The hologram also reminds us of one of the essential teachings of Buddhism: the realization that everything in this world fades away and changes into some other form of existence. The main cause of human suffering, it says, is the obsession with a single form in this perpetual process of change, mistaking it for the only fixed possibility. A human being, like everything else, is a crystallization of all kinds of different elements in the universe. When it dissolves, it simply goes back to the elements again, in order to take other forms and shapes in the whirlpool of creation. Shakespeare's holographic picture shows us the very process of change in this mysterious universe, where every single thing is connected with everything else in the Great Chain of Being.

It is exactly this flexibility and wholeness we need towards the end of the twentieth century: a century of division, specialization, particularization and fragmentation. This is a period in which we have dissected the great creating Nature into bits and pieces in our egotistic pursuit to make her serve our purposes. As a result, we have lost our eyes, or our true selves, and cannot see Nature's whole figure any more. It is perhaps high time we acquired, once again, the Shakespearean way of looking at the universe, which I have termed, with all its anachronism, "the holographic imagination."

Notes

This paper was presented at the sixth World Shakespeare Congress held in Los Angeles in April 1996. A part of the section on *Troilus and Cressida* was published in Japanese in *The Review of English Literature*, 68 (1995): 1-16.

1. Sonnet 53, 1-2. Quotations from Shakespeare are based on the editions by John Dover Wilson (Cambridge: Cambridge Univ. Press), with the exception of *Richard III*, 1. 4. 26 and *Troilus and Cressida*, 4. 2. 4.

2. A hologram is a three-dimensional image recorded on a photographic plate in the form of an interference pattern between two portions of a laser beam. By illuminating it either with a laser beam or with ordinary white light, one can

see a reconstructed image of the original object.

3. This type of hologram can be seen with natural white light and is called a "rainbow hologram" because of the colors it presents. Most holograms in everyday use belong to this type.

4. This particular feature applies not to the "rainbow" holograms mentioned above, but to the kind of holograms whose images can be reconstructed only with laser beams.

5. John Dryden, *Troilus and Cressida, or, Truth Found too Late* (London, 1679; facsimile edition, London: Cornmarket Press, 1969), p. 33.

6. See John Dover Wilson, ed., *Troilus and Cressida* (Cambridge: Cambridge Univ. Press, 1957), p. 75 & 196; Stanley Wells and Gary Taylor, ed. *William Shakespeare: The Complete Works* (Oxford: Clarendon Press, 1986), p. 830.

Coriolanus and the Body of Satan

KOICHI MURANUSHI

WHILE IT IS possible to pursue in Shakespeare's *Coriolanus* the fantasy elements which play an important part in the imagination of Coriolanus and his mother, I would like to show in this essay the conception of the body of Satan which is embedded in the realistic elements of the play. The hunger of the plebeians is realistically presented at the beginning of the play and is closely connected with the linguistic anxiety prevalent throughout the play. To put it in another way, while Coriolanus-related fantasy spun out of such raw materials as corn, milk and blood is the result of regarding those materials as equivalent, there is another way of reading the play, which does not figuratively identify them but literally looks upon them as different materials.[1] While the former poetic reading of the play contributes greatly to the formation of Volumnia's vision of superhuman masculinity, the latter realistic reading will produce a serious criticism of the political and ideological system of Rome in general, and Coriolanus as the embodiment of his mother's vision in particular. The latter reading is a spell, as it were, which conjures up the body of Satan.

Coriolanus is a story of the body. While the Roman citizenry cries "The people are the city" (3. 1. 198),[2] Coriolanus, sentenced to banishment, contemptuously says to them, "I banish you" (3. 3. 123) as if he were Rome itself. Volumnia compares her son's aggression on his native country to an act of treading on "thy mother's womb" (5. 3. 124). The Roman citizenry, Coriolanus, and Volumnia try to represent Rome by identifying their bodies with the body politic of the city. In the history of *Coriolanus* criticism it has been a truism to call this play a story of plural bodies. I would like to argue, however, that Rome has a fourth corporeality, the body of Satan. The purpose of this essay is to reveal the biblical subtext working under the surface of the play. First, I would like to discuss the motif of the tower of Babel which underlies the text of the play, because this motif is, as I will show a little later, a variation of the body of Satan.

The Tower of Babel

In Act 1 Coriolanus would deny the Roman plebeians not only corn but also "good words" (1. 1. 166). In the scenes of the election campaign in Acts 2 and 3, he is compelled to feign generosity with kind words and, in many patricians' view, it is not a difficult procedure if a candidate can deceive the plebeians with polite manners. That's why both tribunes and citizens pay attention to Coriolanus's behavior, which is the main dramatic interest in the election campaign scenes. But citizens' recent hunger and Coriolanus's central role among the privileged in denying them corn are still fresh in their memory and they cannot restrain themselves from referring to it when they see again Coriolanus's haughty behavior. Thus the topic of corn reappears in these scenes. The hungry citizens demand food, not "good words." But it is only through words that the patricians can make a promise to give them corn. As Sicinius says, "you might / As cause had call'd you up . . . have held" (2. 3. 191-92) Coriolanus to his gracious promise, the plebeians seem to take it for granted that, once a verbal promise is made by the patricians, there is no doubt about its fulfillment. Especially for the citizens, spoken words are essential. English Renaissance playwrights frequently dramatized sycophants' flattery and tried to reveal its evil influence on rulers. In spite of the inherent danger of flattery, however, it will be relatively easy for a superior to take flattering words from an inferior without concerning himself with the genuineness of those words, for the substance of those words rarely affect their biological existence itself. In this play, however, a superior gives flattering words to an inferior. Because of the plebeians' powerless position in Roman society, they cannot help believing words. To the citizenry, words are a matter of life or death.

In Act 3 the crisis threatening the Roman society has an aspect of linguistic crisis. There the collapse of a society and the collapse of language are conterminous as in the myth of the Tower of Babel, where the disorder of language involves a city's destruction.

The Roman plebeians regard Coriolanus, with his proud behaviour and haughty language, as the cause of the linguistic disorder. This reminds us of the myth of the Tower of Babel which is, as Guiseppe Mazotta in his study of the *Divine Comedy* says, the opposite of the Incarnation of Christ.

> In general, the symbolic interaction of city and language is a persistent motif in Dante's imagination, so much so that they are often interchangeable terms: Babel, the literal city of language and the radical emblem of chaos is, in Dante's typology, the antitype of the Incarnation. If the Incarnation is the account of the descent into humility of the Word as it bridges the gap between Heaven and Earth, Babel is the allegory of the confusion of tongues, the narrative of the failure of language to bridge that gap.³

Helplessly involved in the uproar in 3. 1, Menenius is so upset that he does not know what he is saying. He uses the word "confusion" to describe the disorder of the city:

> What is about to be? I am out of breath;
> Confusion's near, I cannot speak. You, tribunes
> To th'people! Coriolanus, patience!
> Speak, good Sicinius! (187-90)

And this linguistic disorder will become greater with the additional noise of instruments in 3. 3.

> And when such time they have begun to cry,
> Let them not cease, but *with a din confus'd*
> Enforce the present execution
> Of what we chance to sentence. (19-22, italics mine)

As the Tower of Babel is called by Mazotta "the radical emblem of chaos," so Shakespeare uses the word "confusion," by which he means "cataclysm and chaos."⁴

The disorder of the Roman citizens grows into a violent class struggle, which was so far avoided by the patricians' conciliatory measure. In the patricians' eye this uproar is the destruction of the Roman society, which is figured as the collapse of a building. Their society is in danger of losing its vertical order to be reduced to a horizontal chaos.

> That is the way to lay the city flat,
> To bring the roof to the foundation,
> And bury all which yet distinctly ranges

>   In heaps and piles of ruin. (3. 1. 202-05)

The breakdown of verbal communication in the image of an architectural collapse again reminds us of the Tower of Babel.

Genesis tells a story of people trying to build "a citie and a tower, whose toppe may reach unto the heaven" (11:4)[5] when "the whole earth was of one language and one speech" (11:1). Then the Lord "confounde[d]" their language and "scater[ed] them upon all the earth" (11:9). The Bible says that Babel means confusion, and the Geneva version actually uses the word "confusion" in the gloss when it interprets the Lord's message in the story:

> By this great plague of the confusion of tongues, appeareth Gods horrible judgement against mans pride and vaine glorie. (11:9, gloss)

The disorder of Rome in *Coriolanus* gradually resembles the myth of the Tower of Babel. The disintegration is triggered by Coriolanus, "proud . . . even to the altitude of his virtue" (1. 1. 38-39); the word "confusion" is used as a condensed expression of the social disorder; and the disorder of language is depicted in the image of a building collapsing.

The biblical account of the Tower of Babel was, as Sir James G. Frazer's *Folk-lore in the Old Testament* abundantly demonstrates,[6] variously embellished by later ages. According to John Lydgate's compendious version of the story in his *Fall of Princes*, Nimrod's purpose in building the tower was to secure himself against "watris vilence" (I, 1085) after the Deluge.[7] In the confusion of Rome in our play, the agitated crowd is imaged as "interrupted water" (3. 1. 247) whose rage the bank cannot constrain. Lydgate's words about the divided people, "So as the chaung was maad off ther languages, / So off ther hertis was maad dyuysioun, / Bothe off ther will, and off ther corages" (I, 1220-1222), correspond with the sharply divided opinions and interests of the Romans in *Coriolanus*. In Lydgate, when the tower was eventually abandoned and Babel deserted, the ruin could still be seen, but only from a safe distance.

>   Off which[e] werk thus it is befall,
>   Off serpentis and many a gret dragoun
>   It is now called cheeff habitacioun . . . . (I, 1139-41)

The deserted Babel inhabited by dragons appears also in Jeremiah (51: 37-43).

> And Babel shalbe as heaps, a dwelling place for dragons, an astonishment, and an hissing, without an inhabitant.... Her cities are desolate: the land is drie and a wildernes.

In the play, the plebeians refer to Coriolanus as a "viper" (3. 1. 261) and, after the scenes of the confused Rome, Coriolanus figures himself as "a lonely dragon that his fen / Makes fear'd and talk'd of more than seen" (4. 1. 30-31). Moreover Nimrod was regarded as the founder of idolatry[8] and also the founder of monarchy[9] in Renaissance England. These again correspond to the Romans' figuring Coriolanus as the reincarnation of a godly king (e.g., 4. 6 .91-93; 5. 4. 24-25) in Republican Rome.

The ultimate vision of the disorder of Rome is presented by the First Senator as a gigantic pool of blood, beneath which Coriolanus will submerge both patricians and plebeians (cf. 3. 1. 324-26). This outrage against "my sworn brother the people" (2. 3. 95) has an implication of fratricide. The biblical archetype of fratricide is Cain's killing of Abel. As Cain was punished by the Lord to be "a vagabonde and a rennegate . . . in the earth" (Genesis 4:14), so Coriolanus, as he and Cominius imagine, will "O'er the vast world . . . go rove" (4. 1. 42-46). When Coriolanus visits Aufidius's house, he says to the Third Servingman that he is living "I'th'city of kites and crows" (4. 5. 43), which suggests that he is now an exile banished from Rome. "Cain's punishment, which makes him a wanderer across the earth," according to David Quint, "is the same as his fratricidal crime: a violation of human community. Saint Augustine describes Cain as the typological founder of Babel-Babylon."[10] While Abel's blood is a type of Christ's blood reconciling God and mankind (Hebrew 12:24), the blood which flows within Rome will not serve as the mediator of Roman society.

Babylon as the Double of Babel

According to S. F. Johnson, the two geographical names "Babel" and "Babylon" were frequently confused in Shakespeare's time. The Geneva Bible uses "Babel" both for the site of the Tower and for the later city or empire throughout the Old Testament.[11] The traditional image of Babel and Babylon was as the enemies of the chosen people, the Israelites, the early Christians, and the Protestant nations, particularly the English in Shakespeare's time.

Maerten de Vos (?), Allegory of the Power of Woman, late sixteenth-century drawing, formerly in the collection of C. Fairfax. Present location unknown. Reproduced from Norma Broude and Mary D. Garrard, ed. *Feminism and Art History* (New York: Harper & Row, 1982), p.137

    This confusion enables us to shift our attention a little from Babel to Babylon, its biblical double, because we are still dealing with the notion of the body of Satan. To Protestant interpreters, Babylon in Revelation was a symbol of Catholic Rome. Originally in its background, Revelation had the Roman empire which persecuted the early Christians. The destruction of the historical and Apocalyptic Babylons is prophesied in Isaiah 13, Jeremiah 50-51 and Revelation 18. Act 5 of *Coriolanus*, where Volumnia tries for the second time to rule over her son, has a strong association with the biblical description of Babylon: as the city of Babylon is usually imaged as a woman, so the city of Rome is here represented by Volumnia. And the prophesied conflagration of Babylon[12] corresponds to *Coriolanus*'s Rome trembling at the thought of consuming fire.

A late sixteenth-century drawing entitled "Allegory of the Power of Woman" (see the figure) reminds us of a close resemblance between Volumnia and Babylon. It represents a woman who stands nursing an infant in one arm, holding a royal scepter and golden chain in the other, treading on the broken shield and sword, symbols of defeated male power, and in the upper right are the women who tempted Solomon to idolatry (and hence, ultimately, into Babylon).[13] In the play, Volumnia insists on her experience of nursing her son as the source of power over him and she keeps him from using a sword in the two critical moments in Act 3 and 5; in the last third of the play Coriolanus is given an appearance of divinity in the imagination of the Romans; the three women's success in their diplomatic action and their resultant triumph deprive Coriolanus of his own glory.

The Body of Satan

The action of *Coriolanus* shows resemblances to the Tower of Babel mainly in Act 3, and resemblances to Apocalyptic Babylon mainly occur in Act 5. This leads us to reconsider the problem of Rome's corporeality. According to Robert M. Durling, the structure of Hell in Dante's *Divine Comedy* parallels the form of human body. The portion of the *Inferno* allotted for the sinners of fraud corresponds to the human belly. Both in the punishments for the fraudulent and in his conception of the sin itself, Dante draws upon the idea of the preparation and digestion of foods.

> This giant projection of the human body draws upon the traditional notion of the Body of Satan as the infernal counterpart of the Body of Christ, the Church. It is Babylon, Babel, or confusion; among the persistent motifs of the *Inferno* is the association of sin with perverted or distorted bodily functions.[14]

The body of Satan with these features resembles Rome in *Coriolanus*, which is a story of bellies and foods.

Our awareness of the human body as the figure of a city is first awakened by the fable of the belly told by Menenius at the beginning of the play. There the hungry plebeians gather to start a food riot. In order to appease them, he tells a story likening a city-state to the human body. Indeed in order to negate any rioters' cause the image of a state as an organism could be applied by its rulers, but the most serious social problem now is the hunger of the citizenry and their complaint that the patricians have more than sufficient corn: "For corn at their own rates, whereof they say / The city is well stor'd" (1. 1. 188-89). Accordingly the purpose of Menenius's fable here is to argue against the plebeians' insistence that the privileged are monopolizing corn.

Taking this fable literally and looking at the citizens' situation through the fable, it is reasonably said that the digestive function of Rome as the body politic is now in bad condition. To the plebeians, the belly of Rome is suffering from constipation. While Menenius, saying "all / From me do back receive the flour of all, / And leave me but the bran" (1. 1. 143-45), stresses that the belly is almost empty, the hungry citizens' imagination pictures the belly full of rotten food, as their characterization of the belly as "the sink o'th'body" (1. 1. 121) implies. If the food is bad, it will not save the hungry people:

> If they would yield us but the superfluity while it were wholesome, we might guess they relieved us humanely .... (16-18)

Interestingly, food is not the only thing that will go bad in 1. 1. This is not the first time that the fable of the belly has struck the plebeians' ear.

> I shall tell you
> A pretty tale; it may be you have heard it,
> But since it serves my purpose, I will venture
> *To stale't a little more.* (88-91, italics mine)

The fable is significantly located in the dialogue between Menenius and the citizens. Menenius's narration of the fable is interrupted by the First Citizen, and the interruption surprises the narrator because the citizen has known the fable so well that he can add his own version of the subsequent part of the fable. To repeat a familiar story will be to "stale" it. It can be said that words as well as food go bad. And we have another detail which implies the rottenness of words. Menenius makes the belly speak the moral of the fable.

> With a kind of smile,
> Which ne'er came from the lungs, but even thus—
> For look you, I may make the belly smile,
> As well as speak—it tauntingly replied
> To th'discontented members .... (106-10)

Voice or sound that "ne'er came from the lungs" is either belch or fart,[15] which implies that Menenius's speech itself is accompanied by a digestive disorder.

The plebeians have protested against the patricians' hoarding and concealing food, and in Menenius's fable it has been implied that words go bad, too. Therefore the citizenry's food riot is an appropriate event for symbolizing Rome's disorientation in verbal communication. Behind the image of words' rottenness is working an association of food and words. Words, knowledge and truth nourish the soul just as food nourishes the body. To the hungry plebeians Menenius gives not corn but a fable, or words. Being unaware that his words have been rotten, he tells them to "*digest . . . rightly*" (1. 1. 149, italics mine) his words or his truth. This association of food and knowledge is ancient and, I suppose, ubiquitous; it all began when Adam and Eve ate the apple. For Christians, the Truth—Christ—was the Bread of Life, both as Eucharist and as the Logos. St. Paul develops the analogy between food and truth at some length in 1 Corinthians 3.

In this play there is an implication that Coriolanus is a small eater. Its first indication is in Volumnia's "I had rather had eleven die nobly for their country, / than one voluptuously surfeit out of action" (1. 3. 24-25).[16] But in 1. 1, it seems that the rioters do not associate their supposed deadly enemy with a small appetite.

> *First Citizen* Let us revenge this with our pikes, ere we become rakes. For the gods know, I speak this in hunger for bread, not in thirst for revenge.
> *Second Citizen* Would you proceed especially against Caius Martius?
> *All* Against him first. He's a very dog to the commonality.
> (21-28)

Though it is not certain that Rome's granary is so filled as the citizens imagine, yet they are convinced of the privileged class hoarding corn after the traditional association of the privileged and heavy eating.[17] In the above quotation Martius is the representative of the patricians. By the plebeians he is looked upon as one of his fellow gormandizers. And the patricians' secret big appetite is suggested by Menenius's fable, too. The belly in his fable stands for the privileged.

In 1. 1, another element shows Martius's big appetite. In the first dialogue between Martius and the citizens he shows a peculiar manner of speech and behavior:

> *Martius* What's the matter, you dissentious rogues
> That, rubbing the poor itch of your opinion,
> Make yourselves scabs?
>   *First Citizen*   We have ever your good word.
>   *Martius* He that will give good words to thee, will flatter
> Beneath abhorring.   (163-67)

According to R. F. Yeager, "a tradition existed in the later Middle Ages in England which included, under gluttony, not only excessive eating and drinking, but also great swearing and blasphemy . . . ."[18] And this idea of gluttony is, as Yeager explains, consistent with "Christian logocentrism, and the value placed by Christian teachings on the Divine Word."[19] Martius is using here such abusive words as "Hang 'em!," "'Sdeath," and so on and they might, in this later medieval tradition of gluttony, contribute to the formation of the citizens' bitter mental landscape of extremely unequal distribution of food because Martius's peculiar language itself implies his full stomach.

Again in Act 3, the topic of denied food triggers off Coriolanus's contemptuous language towards the plebeians. Giving a promise, or words, always comes before giving food in Rome. This situation seems to give the patricians' language promised materiality which is not necessarily reliable and involves the common people in the duality of container and things contained. In Menenius's fable the belly is presented as an important container. Once the plebeians believe and "digest" this story of the belly, they are deceived by the city-state because they cannot be sure whether they can "gnaw their [the Volscians'] garners" or "the present war devour[s]" (1. 1. 248; 257) them. The theme of reversal of container and things contained, reversal of eater and what is eaten, is found in the plebeians' anxiety about the deceptiveness of both the city-state and Coriolanus. And later such anxiety infects the Volscians too. Coriolanus in Antium is imaged as an invited cannibal and, according to the Second Servingman, "And he had been cannibally given, he might have broiled and eaten him [Aufidius] too" (4. 5. 193-94). In such a linguistic situation an extreme care in communication would be required to create understanding between different social classes. But Rome's solution to this problem is impossible from the start because Coriolanus's spoken language in public places is usually heard not as voice but as sound, for instance, as "The thunder like percussion of thy sounds" (1. 4. 59),[20] which does not change even in peacetime.

Durling summarizes the theory of digestion, explaining the four stages of digestion as follows:

> After food has been softened and partly liquefied in the mouth (no digestion, properly speaking, taking place there), the stomach performs the so-called first digestion, reducing the food to chyle, a fluid from which the usable portion is extracted by the intestines. The intestines then send the chyle via the mesenteric veins to the liver, where the so-called second digestion takes place, the conversion of the chyle to blood. There were also thought to be a third digestion, in which the heart further refined a portion of the blood and combined it with spirit, carried in the arteries; and a fourth digestion, whereby a small portion of heart's blood was further refined into semen.[21]

Viewed in terms of the fable of the belly, the plebeians' hunger in 1. 1. comes from the disordered digestion in the body of Rome, and specifically the disorder of the "second digestion"; the aristocratic belly is not properly converting the chyle into blood; the belly becomes, instead, "the sink" that cannot be assimilated by the body.

Rome, where the plebeians transform Menenius's fable of the belly into another figure which has a counter-message that food hoarded by and in the belly perhaps goes rotten, is far from the body of Christ, the Church which nourishes people by the Divine Word as food. Rome is now comparable to the body of Satan, which has its facets of Babel, Babylon and confusion as Durling says, and we can say that *Coriolanus* has the body of Satan as its biblical subtext.[22] There is a single reference to the protagonist as "the devil" (1. 10. 16) in the play, and the appellation does not appeal to Aufidius who regards it as inappropriate for Martius. In spite of that, the sick body of Rome more resembles the body of Satan than the body of Christ.

In this new context of the body of Satan, it is possible, I suppose, to find a new meaning in Volumnia's often quoted speech:

> The breasts of Hecuba
> When she did suckle Hector, look'd not lovelier
> Than Hector's forehead when it spit forth blood
> At Grecian sword contemning.   (1. 3. 40-43)

Critics, especially Janet Adelman and Stanley Cavell, have produced subtle interpretations of this speech; they have regarded its poetry as closely connected with the core fantasy of the play.[23] In Cavell's poetic reading, Volumnia's nursing and Martius's spilling of blood are identified. Coriolanus's experience of sucking his mother's breast gives him an idea that he too has to nurse Rome by his blood. But here I wonder what it is that feeds Rome, not at the breast but at some other part of the body. This is a question nobody has asked before as far as I know. Two answers will be possible, a sacred answer and a diabolic.[24] The sacred answer includes the image of a pelican that wounds her breast to feed her young and the image of Christ, depicted in parallel to the lactating Virgin, who feeds by his bleeding on the cross. We should remember here that, to contemporary natural philosophers, breast milk was transmuted blood. On the other hand, the diabolic answer involves the witch's teat.[25] Witches were supposed to have queer marks on their bodies (a third nipple) at which they nursed their demonic familiars. The witch's teat was sometimes confused with the Devil's mark, which was a cavity or protuberance discovered on the surface of the body and was considered as an explicit proof of her pact with the Devil. When the confusion took place, the Devil's mark was considered to have the same function as the witch's teat. Volumnia's speech quoted above implies the two antithetical answers to the question of what kind of nurse Coriolanus is. Our reading of Rome as the body of Satan makes us choose the answer that Coriolanus's bleeding and feeding is witch's (cf. "witchcraft" 4. 7. 2) suckling. The body of Rome is nursed by Coriolanus, a male witch. In *Coriolanus*, while the image of diabolical lactation develops to cover the whole society of Rome, the image of sacred lactation grows around the protagonist imagined to be endlessly bleeding in dedication to Rome (see 3. 1. 296-98).

Volumnia's speech beginning with "The breasts of Hecuba" is the poetic matrix in which the two contradictory images of sacred and diabolical lactations emerge, and out of which the two images develop almost in parallel. What is characteristic of this play is the facility with which one theological extreme turns into the other extreme. This may have been reinforced by a religio-political tendency in the age of Reformation. Stephen Greenblatt in his *Renaissance Self-Fashioning* says that both Catholic Sir Thomas More and Protestant James Bainham had the conception of "a demonic church." Neither Catholics nor Protestants "could resist invoking it, for it had both powerful doctrinal precedent and psychic force, but it was dangerously reversible."[26] This "sinister

Doppelgänger"[27] is also pointed out by Carlo Ginzburg in his essay entitled "Witchcraft and Popular Piety: Notes on a Modenese Trial of 1519." In the process of inquisitorial trials of a Modenese peasant woman accused of witchcraft, the judge superimposed his predetermined ideas on her confession. There was a transparent attempt on the part of the judge to make her confession coincide with his perception of the truth. Hence Ginzburg concludes:

> And it does not matter whether it is a heavenly or diabolical being. The convergence of orthodox and diabolical religion in common piety clearly shows how thin the line separating the two could be in the mind of the believer, especially in rural areas where the faith was often mixed with superstitious elements or even pre-Christian residues.[28]

In the context of the instant reversibility of the opposing theological images in the play, it is understandable that both of the contrasting images are inscribed in the protagonist's name. The first three letters of "Coriolanus," "cor," suggest the heart.[29] It functions, in the four stages of digestion that we have seen, as one of the important digestive organs which conveys received food to every part of the whole body. "Cor" in that sense can be the core of the sacred fantasy of the play. On the other hand, the last four letters of the hero's name, "anus," mean an organ through which waste matter leaves the body. This can be said to be an imaginative focus of the body of Satan with its related images of the rottenness of food and words.

Dealing with Menenius's fable, I have suggested a possibility that rotten words come out of the anus, and this leads us to consider the fecal nature of Coriolanus's words. As Cavell has noted, while the explicit theme of orality in this play has received much analysis from critics, the implicit theme of anality has not received much critical attention. Only Kenneth Burke shows an insight, saying that "in the light of Freudian theories concerning the fecal nature of invective, the last two syllables of the hero's name are so 'right'."[30] The body which discharges rotten words from the anus and discharges "muck" (2. 2. 126) or waste matter from the mouth—this is a body upside-down, which is, as Durling says, the body of Satan:

> The body of Satan is upsidedown[sic]: functions are misdistributed and perverted: in the intestine-like Malebolge we

find those who corrupt and sever the bond of love that should unit [sic] the body politic—instead of the healthy currency of faith and mutual trust, their perversion of *digestion* produces alloys, hydroptic humors, pitch.... After Virgil carries Dante down Satan's side, turns laboriously around, and climbs up out of Hell (at a point corresponding to the anus, as Norman O. Brown pointed out years ago), they are in a position to see Satan from a truer perspective—as upside down.[31]

Notes

An earlier version of this essay was read at the annual meeting of the Shakespeare Society in Japan held at Hiroshima Jogakuin University, 1995 and the longer version was originally published as "*Coriolanus* and the Body (2)," *Studies of Language and Culture* [Nagoya Univ.], 17 (1996) 37-53 (in Japanese). This essay is part of a larger research project funded by the Fukuhara Foundation, whose support is gratefully acknowledged.

1. For instance, the play as one of its important themes deals with the growing up not only of Coriolanus but also of the Roman citizens in terms of the kind of food which they literally or figuratively require. Some critics tend to easily identify Coriolanus with the Roman citizens, observing that both of them stay in the oral stage of development. In the literal reading, however, the kind of food which the citizens want to have is different from that related to Coriolanus. The citizens want to have corn which is the hard kind of food. And it is thematically contrasted with milk, the soft kind of food, which Volumnia says her son still needs. As regards this contrast of hard and soft kinds of foods, we should consider 1 Corinthians 3:2 which says: "I fed you with milk, not solid food, for you were not ready for solid food" and also the possibility of growing teeth on the part of the citizens (cf. "You being their mouths, why rule you not their teeth?" 3. 1. 35). Incidentally, we should consider also the problem of Volumnia's growing and weaning. On these points, see my "Children Who Never Grow: *Coriolanus* Act 3 Scene 3," *Studies of Language and Culture* [Nagoya Univ.], 16 (1995) 147-55 (in Japanese).

2. Quotations from *Coriolanus* refer to the Arden edition, ed. Philip Brockbank (London: Routledge, 1976).

3. Giuseppe Mazzotta, *Dante, Poet of the Desert: History & Allegory in the Divine Comedy* (Princeton, N. J.: Princeton Univ. Press, 1979), p. 73.

4. Brockbank, note to 3. 1. 109.

5. Quotations of the Bible are from *The Geneva Bible: A Facsimile of the 1560 Edition* (Madison, Wisc.: The Univ. of Wisconsin Press, 1969).

6. Sir James G. Frazer, *Folk-lore in the Old Testament: Studies in Comparative Religion, Legend, and Law* (London: Macmillan, 1967), I, 362-90.

7. John Lydgate, *Lydgate's Fall of Princes,* Early English Text Society, Extra

Series, No. 121 (1924; London: Oxford Univ. Press, 1967). Quotations from *Fall of Princes* are from this edition.

8. Lydgate, I, 1254-1260.

9. Sir Robert Filmer, *Patriarcha and Other Writings*, ed. Johann P. Sommerville (Cambridge: Cambridge Univ. Press, 1991), p. 8.

10. David Quint, "Rabelais: From Babel to Apocalypse," in his *Origin and Originality in Renaissance Literature: Versions of the Source* (New Haven: Yale Univ. Press, 1983), p. 178.

11. S. F. Johnson, "*The Spanish Tragedy*, or Babylon Revisited," in *Essays on Shakespeare and Elizabethan Drama in Honour of Hardin Craig*, ed. Richard Hosley (London: Routledge & Kegan Paul, 1963), pp. 24-25. See also St. Augustine, *Concerning the City of God against the Pagans*, trans. Henry Bettenson (1972; Harmondsworth: Penguin Books, 1984), pp. 657, 677, which looks upon Babel as "none other than Babylon" and Rome as "the second Babylonia, as it were, the Babylonia of the west."

12. For instance, Revelation 18:8-9.

13. On the description of this picture, see Madlyn Millner Kahr, "Delilah," in *Feminism and Art History: Questioning the Litany*, ed. Norma Broude and Mary D. Garrard (New York: Harper & Row, 1982), p. 138 and Patricia Parker, *Literary Fat Ladies: Rhetoric, Gender, Property* (London: Methuen, 1987), p. 57.

14. Robert M. Durling, "Deceit and Digestion in the Belly of Hell," in *Allegory and Representation*, ed. Stephen Greenblatt (Baltimore: The Johns Hopkins University Press, 1981), p. 61. On hell as digestion, see also Caroline Walker Bynum, *The Resurrection of the Body in Western Christianity, 200-1336* (New York: Columbia Univ. Press, 1995), plates 3, 6, 12-16 and 28-32.

15. Cf. Roy W. Battenhouse, *Shakespearean Tragedy: Its Art and its Christian Premises* (Bloomington: Indiana Univ. Press, 1969), p. 342; Stanley Cavell, *Disowning Knowledge in Six Plays of Shakespeare* (Cambridge: Cambridge Univ. Press, 1987), p. 169; Brockbank's note to 1. 1. 208.

16. Another indication is in Coriolanus's "Better it is to die, better to starve" (2. 3. 112)

17. Stephen Mennell, "On the Civilizing of Appetite," *Theory, Culture & Society*, 4 (1987): 373-403. On the other hand, concerning Volumnia's vision of her son with a small appetite, we can point out another tradition which associates the political leader and a small appetite. See Marcus Aurelius's *Meditations*, Niccolò Machiavelli's *The Discourses*, King James I's *Basilicon Doron* and so on.

18. R. F. Yeager, "Aspects of Gluttony in Chaucer and Gower," *Studies in Philology*, 81 (1984): 45.

19. Yeager, pp. 50-51.

20. According to *OED*, this is the first instance of "percussion" which has a meaning of sound. This again would distance the hero's voice as a means of communication in society.

21. Durling, p. 68.

22. Cf. Barbara L. Parker, "The Whore of Babylon and Shakespeare's *Julius Caesar*," *SEL*, 35 (1995): 251-69, which, pointing out Rome's association with homosexuality from the viewpoint of Protestant England, regards the play's

Rome as diabolical.

23. Janet Adelman, "'Anger's My Meat': Feeding, Dependency, and Aggression in *Coriolanus*," *Representing Shakespeare: New Psychoanalytic Essays*, ed. Murray M. Schwartz and Coppélia Kahn (Baltimore: The Johns Hopkins Univ. Press, 1980), pp. 129-49 and Cavell, pp.143-78.

24. Cf. Caroline Walker Bynum, *Holy Feast and Holy Fast: The Religious Significance of Food to Medieval Women* (Berkeley and Los Angeles: Univ. of California Press, 1987), p. 270.

25. On the witch's teat and the Devil's mark, see G. R. Quaife, *Godly Zeal and Furious Rage: The Witch in Early Modern Europe* (New York: St. Martin's Press, 1987), p. 55; Keith Thomas, *Religion and the Decline of Magic: Studies in Popular Beliefs in Sixteenth and Seventeenth Century England* (London: Weidenfeld and Nicolson, 1971), p. 446; Laura Levine, *Men in Women's Clothing: Anti-theatricality and Effeminization 1579-1642* (Cambridge: Cambridge Univ. Press, 1994), p. 120.

26. Stephen Greenblatt, *Renaissance Self-Fashioning: From More to Shakespeare* (Chicago: The Univ. of Chicago Press, 1980), p. 82.

27. Cited by Greenblatt, p. 269, n. 19. The phrase was originally used by Peter Brown in his *Augustine of Hippo* (Berkeley: Univ. of California Press, 1969), p. 213.

28. Carlo Ginzburg, "Witchcraft and Popular Piety: Notes on a Modenese Trial of 1519," in his *Clues, Myths and the Historical Method*, trans. John and Anne C. Tedeschi (Baltimore: The Johns Hopkins Univ. Press, 1989), p. 13.

29. Harold C. Goddard, *The Meaning of Shakespeare* (Chicago: Univ. of Chicago Press, 1951), I, p. 210.

30. Kenneth Burke, "*Coriolanus*—and the Delights of Faction," in his *Language as Symbolic Action: Essays on Life, Literature and Method* (Berkeley: Univ. of California Press, 1966), p. 96. I first met this citation from Burke in Cavell, p. 174. I guess that the critical neglect of anality has been partly caused by the difficulty of linking the theme with the problem of Coriolanus's psychological growing. Volumnia's control of her son is strongly indicated in the play and she always appeals to her exprience of nursing him as the source of power over him. It is easy to talk about Coriolanus's staying at the oral stage of development, while it would be hard to argue that he stays at the anal stage. Though Kenneth Burke's remark about the anality of Coriolanus's characteristic language is Freudian, I feel that we cannot pursue the theme of anality psychoanalytically and we need a different referential framework. In this essay I have suggested a biblical answer to the problem.

31. Robert M. Durling, "'*Io son venuto*': Seneca, Plato, and the Microcosm," *Dante Studies*, 93 (1975): 119.

The Bee Emblem in *The Rape of Lucrece*

Misako Matsuda

THE STORY OF the rape and suicide of Lucrece in Livy's *The History of Rome* (II, 57-60) provided an important source for Renaissance art and literature. The episode seems to have been popular not only because of its erotic and sensational implications but also because the incident was commonly interpreted as serving the goal of establishing a republic in Rome by banishing Tarquin. The protagonists of the story can therefore be either Lucrece or Brutus, depending on how writers and artists interpreted its moral. In art, Lucrece is primarily represented alone as a naked and helpless woman, at the moment of her suicide to intensify her tragic isolation and purity, as we can see in Cranach's *Lucretia* (1533; Staatliche Museen Preussischer Kulturbesitz, Berlin) and Veronese's (1580-85; Kunsthistorisches Museum, Vienna). But *The Tragedy of Lucretia* by Botticelli (c.1499; Isabella Stewart Gardner Museum, Boston) depicts the entire story on a single panel, in which three representative episodes show how her tragic death brought about the end of tyranny. On the left, Tarquin threatens Lucrece with a knife (beneath a relief of Judith and Holofernes); on the right, the dead Lucrece is held by her husband and father (beneath a frieze of a defender of the Republic, Horatius), while in the centre, Brutus urges the Romans to avenge her death in the Forum (beneath the figures of famous heroes such as David). In Botticelli's painting, a statue of David holding the head of Goliath stands high above the dead Lucrece in the Forum; near David is Judith with the head of Holofernes. Lucrece is not only a defiled woman, but a woman with power and authority like Judith, overcoming her suffering despite her passivity, frailty, and self-destruction. As in Cranach's now lost panels of *Lucretia and Judith* (after 1537; formerly in the Gemäldegalerie, Dresden),[1] Lucretia is paired with Judith to emphasize her power in bringing down her enemies. Botticelli relates her death to the political victory of Brutus, and there is an echo of Ovid's rhetorical question to Tarquin after the rape: "Quid victor gaudes? haec te victoria perdet" (*Fasti*, 811). The line, according to Bate, is translated by Shakespeare as "A captive victor that hath lost in gain" (730); although Bate sees little political implication here,[2] the interplay of loss and gain here alerts the contemporary reader well-versed in the Roman history who became the ultimate victor.

Shakespeare makes no attempt to change the traditional historical framework of this story, nor the established interpretation of the episode within Roman history, although he closes the narrative hastily after her suicide. As Livy, Ovid, and William Painter's *The Palace of Pleasure* (1566) indicate, the story is basically regarded as a justified revolt against tyrannical monarchy.[3] After the Dedication to the Earl of Southampton, Shakespeare pays due respect to the two classical authors in the Argument, which is a prose summary of the narrative based on Ovid and Livy. Compared with the frustrated discourse on moral problems like virginity and violation, the political lesson of the narrative is rather straightforward. As Camino argues, like Lydgate's *Serpent of Division*, written in the early fifteenth century and reprinted in 1590, Sir Thomas Elyot's *The Boke Named the Governour*, and Holinshed's *Chronicles*, Shakespeare uses Tarquin's rape as an admonition against the dangers inherent in tyrannical systems of government.[4]

While the admonition against the danger of tyranny is a primary political lesson of the poem, Shakespeare puts another important political sub-theme especially in the long lament where Lucrece blames her disaster on "Night, Opportunity, and Time." Even though nearly half of the speeches in the entire narrative are direct speeches, they are monologues most of the time and become even more so in Lucrece's long lament over the loss of her marital chastity. Because the poem lacks a dramatic interplay between Lucrece and Tarquin, it was undervalued by some critics; Douglas Bush called it "a would-be dramatic but quite bookish poem."[5] The political imagery warning against unexpected invasion, however, is developed persistently throughout the long lament. Approaching the chamber of Lucrece, Tarquin is described as a ferocious beast, in terms of such expressions as a "grim lion" (421), "falcon" (506), "cockatrice" (540),"vulture" (556), and "wolf" (677). On the other hand, Lucrece is associated with a powerless "dove" (360), "white hind" (543), and "poor lamb" (677). The powerless, pitiful portrait of

Lucrece is clearly contrasted with the violent, relentless imagery of Tarquin. Shakespeare tries to save Lucrece from moral censure partly by intensifying our sense of her vulnerability being overpowered by Tarquin's physical force, whereas Chaucer, for example, does so more mechanically by having Tarquin violate her while she lies in a swoon.[6] Because Shakespeare's Lucrece is fully awake, her desperate plea illuminates the social as well as moral consequences of Tarquin's act whose violence also receives a more explicit emphasis. Before the rape, Lucrece entreats Tarquin to suppress his lust to keep a royal duty. Although he never lends his ear to her plea, her speech is based on the theme of government, "For kings like gods should govern every thing" (602). At this point, Tarquin, who cannot control his own desire, clearly deviates from the tradition of the mirror of magistrates.

Throughout the first part of the narrative, we find the metaphorical expressions of a revolt against a ruler and a deviation from the respectable ruler again and again, suggesting both sexual and mental disorder. With Tarquin "treason works ere traitors be espied" (361) and "like a foul usurper" (412), he approaches Lucrece, a faithful wife to Collatine. His dark desire is described as a rebel against "a pure heart" (625) and Tarquin's soul, described as a "spotted princess" (721), has been assaulted and its immortality is in captivity:

> She says her subjects with foul insurrection
> Have battered down her consecrated wall,
> And by their mortal fault brought in subjection
> Her immortality, and made her thrall
> To living death and pain perpetual;   (722-26)

The rape indicates not only a physical and forced attack on Lucrece's body but the self-destruction of Tarquin's spiritual kingdom. The purity of the immortal soul stands in contrast to the danger and miserable consequence of invasion.

On the other hand, the hapless Lucrece regards her misfortune as a tragic loss, and blames Opportunity by citing many examples of unexpected misfortunes falling upon innocent and unwary victims, such as the worm intruding into a maiden bud and hateful cuckoos hatching in sparrows' nests. A series of such metaphors indicate that, once the enemy's invasion is accomplished, the apparent safety of these closely guarded spaces soon turns out to be deceptive and illusory. One of the first metaphors used in Lucrece's complaint against Opportunity is that of a bee-hive, and this is significant in terms of the underlying political theme. The violence and ruthlessness of Tarquin's attack on Lucrece is effectively foreshadowed by a series of military images and metaphors of a siege and an attack on a walled city. The resolute Tarquin, with affection as his "captain" (271), "marcheth to Lucrece's bed"(301) to "scale/ Thy [Lucrece's] never-conquered fort" (481-82). Tarquin's hand is likened to "Rude ram to batter such an ivory wall" (i.e. Lucrece's breast) (463), and his desire is to "make the breach and enter this sweet city" (469). Such passages are more than illustrative metaphors; the personal and private struggle between Lucrece and Tarquin is simultaneously turned into an extended metaphorical narrative of a military campaign which adds another, public dimension to this personal tragedy. Lucrece's personal loss of marital chastity caused by an sudden invasion of a single enemy may well be transformed into the warning to a peaceful city, which should protect itself against unseen enemies. The image of a bee-hive, which begins Lucrece's lament over the sudden tragedy, introduces the theme of destruction caused by sudden intrusion:

> If, Collatine, thine honour lay in me,
> From me by strong assault it is bereft;
> My honey lost, and I, a drone-like bee,
> Have no perfection of my summer left,
> But robbed and ransacked by injurious theft.
> In thy weak hive a wand'ring wasp hath crept,
> And sucked the honey which thy chaste bee kept.   (834-40)

Lucrece, who led a happily married life as a diligent bee, is now a useless drone, for a wasp, Tarquin, suddenly invaded the hive to violate her chastity. Collatine's hive which has previously seemed a happy and safely guarded place, turns out to be a "weak hive" hardly aware of imminent danger. The image of a bee hive attacked by wasps is also used in *The Two Gentlemen of Verona*. Julia reproaches herself for tearing Proteus' letter as follows: "O hateful hands, to tear such loving words! / Injurious wasps, to feed on such sweet honey, / And kill the bees that yield it with your stings!" (1. 2. 102-104) The contrast of wasps and bees highlights Julia's perspective to regard her hands which committed the ungrateful act as independent of her will. The comic effect of these lines owes itself to the contrast inherent in the two types of bees, bringers of wealth and pillaging intruders, just as the same contrast reinforces the sudden and unexpected nature of the personal tragedy that fell upon Lucrece's married life.

We can notice how the bee hive imagery has a further, more political dimension, if we pay attention to the distinctive roles that the bee, wasp and drone play. The imagery of bees was indeed a popular motif in contemporary emblem books. The emblem books had been a favourite hunting ground for sources of Shakespeare and other Elizabethan dramatists, especially toward the end of the nineteenth century. Although the difficulties involved in citing them as a direct source of Renaissance literature has since been recognized, recent systematic researches toward comprehensive iconographical catalogues of emblems led by P. M. Daly as well as the renewed emphasis on the "iconic" or emblematic nature of Shakespeare's works are making it possible to approach the problem of the influence and reception of contemporary emblems in more concrete terms.[7] A knowledge of the emblem literature clarifies a political theme in this poem and allows us to surmise how it is related to the more personal aspect of Lucrece's tragedy.

The commonest association bees conveyed to the sixteenth-century mind was perhaps that of a Petrarchan contrast between sweet love and bitter love, which is derived from the well-known fact that bees have both honey and a poisonous sting. In Andrea Alciati's *Emblematum Liber* (Padua, 1621), there is a classical motif which can be traced back to Theocritus (Plate 1).[8] Cupid, who was stung by a bee, shows his hurt to his mother, Venus; the woodcut shows the two aspects of a bee that has a sting as well as honey in the plainest terms. Shakespeare uses "sting" several times in the poem (40, 364, 493) to describe jealousy and the illicit desire Tarquin feels towards Lucrece when listening to Collatine's boastful praise of his wife. Added to these, Tarquin's own words, "I think the honey guarded with a sting" (493) suggests the ironic duality of love. Similarly, Jacob Cats depicts a bee that stings a girl gathering roses in his *Emblemata Moralia et Aeconomica* (Rotterdam, 1627), where he develops the two aspects of the bee, the sting and honey.[9] The association of outward sweetness, which often conceals poisonous venom, leads with little difficulty to Tarquin whose outward appearance belies his inner thought.

Perhaps more so than a bee sting, there was also a frequent association of the bee hive—in which a king bee presides over his ordered servants—with a nation or human society in general. Medieval bestiaries often describe bees as forming a militant society lead by a king (rather than a queen) bee.[10] The popular belief that the ruler of the hive is a male is shared by bee masters of the sixteenth and seventeenth centuries. Thomas Hyll whose *Proffitable Instructions of the Perfite Ordering of Bees* (published with his *Profittable Arte of Gardening* in 1572) is the earliest bee-book in the English language, also thought in terms of a king bee; Hyll, however, was, well aware of the distinction that existed between the bees gathering honey and the drones which stay in the hive. Hyll's treatise emphasizes that there exists such an intimacy and loyalty between the king bee and his servants that when the king dies, bees stop gathering honey out of grief and the whole hive may die out unless a new king appears from among them. A king bee was also sometimes erroneously believed to be without a sting, creating an association with a generous ideal ruler.[11] In Horapollo's *Hieroglyphica*, which was as popular as Alciati's *Emblematum Liber*, depicts a bee house to indicate that only bees among all animals have a ruler and the other bees serve him sometimes with honey and sometimes with a sting (Plate 2).[12] A bee is indeed a mirror for a ruler as Joachim Camerarius's emblem indicates. Using a bee hive as a political model, he tells us that we should learn the ideal form of government from the ordered relationship between a king bee and his servants in the hive.[13] Wasps on the other hand stand for revolt and mutiny, as in Jacobus à Bruck, *Emblemata Moralia et Bellica* (Strasbourg, 1615). The woodcut shows wasps attacking a hand with a stick trying to break the hive, and the accompanying verse relates the emblem to the popular mutiny. Bellicose and wrathful wasps often stand in contrast to orderly society of bees.[14]

The association of a bee-hive with a nation is seen for example in Geffrey Whitney, *A Choice of Emblems and Other Devices* (Leiden, 1586) which describes loyal servants in terms of bees returning to their hive without fail. Loyalty and trust should also be at the basis of a commonwealth (Plate 3):

> The bees at lengthe retourne into their hiue,
> When they haue suck'd the sweete of FLORAS bloomes;
> And with one minde their worke they doe contriue,
> And laden come with honie to their roomes:
> . . . .
> The maister bee, within the midst dothe liue,
> In fairest roome, and most of stature is;
> And euerie one to him dothe reuerence giue,
> And in the hiue with him doe liue in blisse:

> Hee hath no stinge, yet none can doe him harme,
> For with their strengthe, the rest about him swarme.
> ....
> A Comon-wealthe, by this, is right expreste:
> Bothe him, that rules, and those, that doe obaye:
> Or suche, as are the heads aboue the rest,
> Whome here, the Lorde in highe estate dothe staye:
> By whose supporte, the meaner sorte doe liue,
> And vnto them all reuerence dulie giue.[15]

The hive is a model of a nation while its "tennaunts" are the bees who have their places in it each in accordance with their degrees. Shakespeare also refers to similar images of bees and a bee-hive when his characters speak of the necessity of civic or military order. Ulysses' famous speech on degree in *Troilus and Cressida* begins with bee hive imagery, in which he likens a general to a bee hive that "the foragers shall all repair" (1. 3. 81). Furthermore, Canterbury's speech in *Henry V* fully develops the bee and bee-hive imagery as a form of an ideal nation, in order to persuade the King to wage a just war on France:

>   for so work the honey-bees,
> Creatures that by a rule in nature teach
> The act of order to a peopled kingdom.
> They have a king, and officers of sorts,
> Where some, like magistrates, correct at home;
> Others, like merchants, venter trade abroad;
> Others, like soldiers, armed in their stings,
> Make boot upon the summer's velvet buds,
> Which pillage they with merry march bring home
> To the tent-royal of their emperor;
> Who busied in his [majesty] surveys
> The singing masons building roofs of gold,
> The civil citizens kneading up the honey,
> The poor mechanic porters crowding in
> Their heavy burtherns at his narrow gate,
> The sad-ey'd justice, with his surly hum,
> Delivering o'er to executors pale
> The lazy yawning drone.   (1. 2. 187-204)

While the ordered harmony of the society of bees is frequently used as a model for good government, the hive itself could also be put to a more cautionary use by contemporary emblematists. A variation on the above emblems of bees and the hive is that of a war helmet used as a bee hive, signifying the end of war and the coming of peace. An occasional verse by George Peele (1530-1610) for the retirement of Sir Henry Lee uses this image: "His helmet now shall make a hive for bees, / And, lovers' sonnets turn'd to holy psalms."[16] Its significance could be carried further; it could be a warning against sloth and over-confidence. Robert Greene uses it to represent sloth as one of seven deadly sins.[17] A swarm of wasps, referring to "vespa" in Italian implying the name of the lady who is depicted as Venus, also appears around Mars's helmet in Botticelli's *Venus and Mars* (National Gallery, London). It was painted initially for the bedchamber of the newly wed. The defenceless figure of the Mars in deep slumber, combined with a group of erotic satyrs who replace more usual Cupids, implies that the emblematic association of bees around the helmet contains satire or even a degree of moral censure, pointing to sloth and erotic fatigue rather than to peace and rest.

The same image appears as one of emblems in a more political context in George Wither's *Collection of Emblemes, Ancient and Moderne* (London, 1635; Plate 4):

> When you have heeded, by your Eyes of sense,
> This Helmet, hiving of a Swarme of Bees,
> Consider, what may gather'd be from thence,
> And, what your Eye of Understanding sees.
> That Helmet, and, those other Weapons, there,
> Betoken Warre; the Honey-making, Flyes,
> An Emblem of a happy Kingdome, are,
> Injoying Peace, by painfull Industries:
> ....
> So when a People, meerely, doe affect
> To gather Wealth; and (foolishly secure)
> Defences necessary, quite neglect;
> Their Foes, to spoyle their Land, it will allure.
> Long Peace, brings Warre; and, Warre, brings Peace, againe:
> For, when the smart of Warfare seizeth on them,
> They crye, Alarme; and, then, to fight, are faine,
> Vntill, their Warre, another Peace, hath wonne them;
> And, out of their old rusty Helmets, then,
> New Bees doe sworme, and, fall to worke agen.[18]

The moral of this emblem is a political one warning a peaceful kingdom to be constantly vigilant in defending itself from external enemies. In Henry Peacham's *Basilikon Doron*, the same association applies more straightforwardly to James I and Prince Henry, to whom the book is dedicated.[19] As a mirror for princes, the book includes various political emblems including that of a bee flying over the tomb of the Emperor Domitianus, a Roman tyrant murdered by his servant. The same emblem appears in Peacham's *Minerva Britanna* (London, 1612; Plate 5):

> Once NERO's name, the world did quake to heare,
> And ROME did tremble, at DOMITIAN's sight:
> But now the Tyrant, cause of all this feare,
> Is laid full low, vpon whose toombe do light,
>   To take revenge, the Bee, and summer Flie,
>   Who not escap't sometime his crueltie.[20]

A swarm of bees represents the oppressed people who now take revenge upon the dead tyrant, implying revolt and protest instead of order and obedience. The verse may be aimed specifically at a monarch or a ruler as it conveys a warning against tyranny and oppression.

Bees can therefore appear in the context of treachery and revenge, while they are also symbols of peace and order. The contrastive and dual aspects of the emblems related to bees lie behind Lucrece's lament that a single wasp could disrupt the peace of a nation. She inveighs against Opportunity that the change brought by an opportunity is nothing but a loss and honey turned to gall (889). The same association is also conveyed by a tapestry of the Trojan War described in detail by Lucrece herself. After making up her mind to compensate her lost honour by a dagger, she tries to understand her destiny by comparing her own tragedy with the fall of Troy. Lucrece's eyes follow the tragic scenes of the fall in order, but Shakespeare deliberately changes the sequence and places the passage on Sinon at the end. Thus the whole passage, original to Shakespeare, focuses on Sinon whose intrigue made the Trojans open the gate and bring the horse in. Just as the fall of Troy was brought about by the deceit of a single man, so was, Lucrece thinks, her tragedy caused by the invasion of a single man. The analogues go further. Lucrece understands that she entertained Tarquin, just as Priamus did Sinon:

> "For even as subtle Sinon here is painted,
> So sober-sad, so weary, and so mild
> (As if with grief or travail he had fainted),
> To me came Tarquin armed, too beguild

> With outward honesty, but yet defiled
> With inward vice. As Priam him did cherish,
> So did I Tarquin; so my Troy did perish." (1541-47)

The association of deceit by a friendly face is enhanced by Tarquin's ambush of Gabi, described in the Ovidian version of the Lucrece story in *Fasti* (783). Lucrece brings out a social implication of her personal loss by calling her body "my Troy" (1547); to violate it is to disrupt the social tie that binds together her family and relatives.

The emblematic image of bees effectively links a personal tragedy to disorder at a national level. Tarquin is a wasp invading Lucrece's bedroom, but he is also a king bee murdered by his people because he did not act properly in his own hive. Tarquin revolted against the ideal image of a ruler as well as against his own reason, and, in turn, prompted a just revolt against him by his people. At the same time, Lucrece's lament shows that even a great city like Troy can be ruined by one enemy who needs only a single opportunity to enter secretly. This aspect is also linked, by means of the emblematic association of a bee-hive as well as by the story of the fall of Troy, to a general political admonition to be vigilant against unexpected enemies.

The political consequence of the rape of Lucrece remained a major concern of classical authors. In Livy, the personal tragedy of Lucrece swiftly becomes an occasion for political change. The sword with which Lucrece kills herself literally becomes the emblem of political reform for Brutus who interprets the rape of Lucrece as the sack of all Rome.[21] Lucrece's suicide becomes a golden opportunity for Brutus, who taking it by the forelock, turns it into the occasion of his own revenge against Tarquin. The opportunity which only brought loss to Lucrece, becomes a generous bringer of profit to Brutus. Brutus is later revered as the liberator of Rome for his moral rectitude, but this fact does not appear in *The Rape of Lucrece* nor is the role of Brutus given much prominence, although Shakespeare otherwise follows the accounts of Livy and Ovid. The poem ends with the banishment of Tarquin without any specific mention of the future republic. Still, the emblematic image of bees which appears in the poem cannot fail to convey the political theme within Lucrece's personal lament. An episode of Roman history was indeed a proper place to develop such an argument as we can see from Machiavelli. Although Shakespeare is never explicit about any possible political message the poem might convey, the analysis of the poem's dominant emblematic image indeed allows us to read into it a political theme such as peacetime defence against unseen enemies. The fact that the poem went into nine editions between 1594 and 1655 and was not published after that until the second half of the eighteenth century may be taken to indicate that the seventeenth-century reading of the poem was also to read it in connection with contemporary political situations in England and to reassure a traditional morality that the Lucrece episode had conveyed in Livy and Ovid.[22] The popularity of a variety of bee-related emblems seems to indicate that such an interpretation was possible at least for those well-versed in contemporary emblem books.

Notes

An earlier version of this paper was read at the 65th General Meeting of the English Literary Society of Japan, held at the University of Tokyo in May 1993. I am grateful to Glasgow University Library, Department of Special Collections for permission to publish illustrations from the emblem books in their collection (plates 1, 3, 4, 5).

    1. See Ian Donaldson, *The Rapes of Lucretia: A Myth and its Transformation* (Oxford: Clarendon, 1982), plate 8.
    2. Jonathan Bate, *Shakespeare and Ovid* (Oxford: Clarendon, 1993), p. 74. All quotations from *The Rape of Lucrece* are taken from *The Poems*, ed. John Roe, The New Cambridge Shakespeare (Cambridge: Cambridge Univ. Press, 1992). Quotations from all other plays and poems are from *The Riverside Shakespeare* (Boston: Houghton Mifflin, 1974).
    3. D. C. Allen, *Image and Meaning: Metaphoric Traditions in Renaissance Poetry*, rev. ed. (Baltimore: The Johns Hopkins Univ. Press, 1968), p. 58.
    4. Mercedes M. Camino, *"The Stage Am I": Raping Lucrece in Early Modern England* (Lewston, NJ: The Edwen Mellen Press, 1995), p. 15.
    5. *Mythology and the Renaissance Tradition in English Poetry*, rev. ed. (New York: Norton, 1963), p. 154.
    6. Clark Hulse, *Metamorphic Verse: The Elizabethan Minor Epic* (Princeton, NJ: Princeton Univ. Press, 1981), p. 179.
    7. See the preliminary survey edited by P. M. Daly, *The European Emblem: Towards an Index Emblematicus* (Waterloo, Ont: Wilfred Laurier Univ. Press, 1980) as well as the actual indices so far published: *Andreas Alciatus*, 2 vols. ed. P. M. Daly, V. W. Callahan and S. Cuttler (Toronto: Toronto Univ. Press, 1985); *The English Emblem Tradition*, 2 vols, ed. P. M. Daly, L. T. Duer and A. Raspa (Toronto: Toronto Univ. Press, 1988, 1993). See also Huston Diehl, *An Index of Icons in English Emblem Books 1500-1700* (Norman, OK: Univ. of Oklahoma Press, 1986). John Doebler, *Shakespeare's Speaking Pictures: Studies in Iconic Imagery* (Albu-

querque, NM: Univ. of New Mexico Press, 1974), is one of the first studies to apply the emblematic approach to Shakespeare. For recent developments, see John Doebler, "Bibliography for the Study of Iconography in Renaissance English Literature," *Research Opportunities in Renaissance Drama*, 22 (1979): 45-55; Peggy M. Simonds, *Iconographic Research in English Renaissance Literature: A Critical Guide* (New York: Garland, 1995).

8. Andreas Alciatus, *Emblematum Liber* (Padua, 1621), no. 112 (with the motto "Dulcia quandoque amara fieri"), reprinted in Daly, *Andreas Alciatus*, vol. 1. A full discussion of this motif can be found in Michael Bath, "Honey and Gall or: Cupid and the Bees. A Case of Iconographic Slippage," in *Andrea Alciato and the Emblem Tradition: Essays in Honor of Virginia Woods Callahan*, ed. Peter M. Daly (New York: AMS Press, 1989), pp. 59-94.

9. No. 32, reproduced in *Emblemata: Handbuch zur Sinnbildkunst des XVI. und XVII. Jahrhunderts*, ed. Arthur Henkel and Albrecht Schöne (Stuttgart: J. B. Metzlersche Verlagsbuchhandlung, rev. ed. 1976), p. 922.

10. *The Book of Beasts*, trans. and ed. T.H. White (Gloucester: Alan Sutton, 1984), pp. 153-56.

11. Eleanour S. Rohde, *Shakespeare's Wild Flowers: Fairy Lore, Gardens, Herbs, Gatherers of Samples and Bee Lore* (London: The Medici Society, 1935), p. 202.

12. *Ori Apollinis Niliaci, de sacris notis et sculpturis libri duo* . . . (Paris: Jacobus Kerver, 1551), p. 87. See also *The Hieroglyphics of Horapollo*, trans. George Boas, new ed. (Princeton, NJ: Princeton Univ. Press, 1978), p. 70. Plate 2 is reproduced from a copy in private hands.

13. Joachim Camerarius, *Symbolorum et Emblematum* . . . (Nuremberg, 1596), no. 90, reproduced in Henkel and Schöne, p. 926.

14. No. 3; Henkel and Schöne, p. 929.

15. Geffrey Whitney, *A Choice of Emblemes*, introd. John Manning (London: Scolar, 1989). pp. 200-1. The emblem is dedicated to Richarde Cotton with the motto "Patria cuique chara."

16. *The Works of George Peele*, ed. A. H. Bullen (1888; Port Washington, NY: Kennikat Press, 1966), II, 302.

17. William M. Carroll, *Animal Conventions in English Renaissance Non-Religious Prose (1550-1600)* (New York: Bookman Associates, 1954), p. 77.

18. George Wither, *A Collection of Emblemes, Ancient and Moderne* (1635), introd. Rosemary Freeman (Columbia, SC: Univ. of South Carolina Press, 1975), p. 90. The motto is "The Bees, will in an Helmet breed; / And, Peace, doth after Warre, succeed."

19. Robert J. Clements, *Picta Poesis: Literary and Humanistic Theory in Renaissance Emblem Books* (Rome: Edizioni di Storia e Letteratura, 1960), p. 73.

20. Henry Peacham, *Minerva Britanna* (London 1612), The English Experience, 407 (Amsterdam: Theatrum Orbis Terrarum, 1971), p. 144. The motto is "Et minimi vindictam."

21. Donaldson, p. 8.

22. Thomas Simone, *Shakespeare and Lucrece: A Study of the Poem and Its Relation to the Plays* (Salzburg: Institut für englische Sprache und Literatur, Universität Salzburg, 1974), p. 91.

The Bee Emblem in The Rape of Lucrece

Plate 1. Andreas Alciatus, *Emblemata* (Padova, 1621), no.112, reprod. from *Andreas Alciatus 1: the Latin Emblems, Indexes and Lists*, ed. P. M. Daly, et al. (Toronto, 1985).

Plate 2. (Horapollo), *Ori Appolinis Niliaci, de sacris notis et sculpturis libri duo* . . . (Paris, 1551), p.87.

Plate 3. Geffrey Whitney, *A Choice of Emblemes* (Leiden, 1586), pp.200-1, reprod. from Geffrey Whitney, *A Choice of Emblemes*, intro. J. Manning (London, 1989).

Plate 4. George Wither, *A Collection of Emblemes, Ancient and Moderne* (London, 1635), p.90, reprod. from George Wither, *A Collection of Emblemes, Ancient and Moderne (1635)*, intro. R. Freeman (Columbia, SC, 1975).

Plate 5. Henry Peacham, *Minerva Britanna* (London, 1612), p.144, reprod. from The English Experience 407 (Amsterdam, 1971).

Overlapping Exits and Entrances in Shakespeare's Plays

Mariko Ichikawa

1

IN SHAKESPEARE'S PLAYS, there are a significant number of instances in which about four lines are delivered between the point at which a major character enters and the point at which he either speaks or is addressed by another character already on stage, as the following illustrates:

>   *Enter* Romeo.
> *Tyb.* Well peace be with you sir, here comes my man.
> *Mer.* But ile be hangd sir if he weare your liuerie:
> Marrie go before to field, heele be your follower,
> Your worship in that sense may call him man.
> *Tyb. Romeo*, the loue I beare thee, can affoord
> No better terme then this: thou art a villaine.
>   (*Romeo and Juliet* Q2, sig. F3^R; 3. 1. 55-60) [1]

It is also noteworthy that, in most cases, at least four lines are delivered between the point at which a major character begins to exit and the point at which either he re-enters or the character summoned by him enters. This pattern can be seen in the following example:

> *Othe.* Bid her come hither: go.   *Exit AEmilia.*
> She saies enough: yet she's a simple Baud
> That cannot say as much. This is a subtile Whore:
> A Closset Locke and Key of Villanous Secrets,
> And yet she'le kneele, and pray: I haue seene her do't.
>   *Enter Desdemona, and AEmilia.*
> *Des.* My Lord, what is your will?
>   (*Othello* F1, TLN 2708-14; 4. 2. 20-25)

From these observations it can be concluded that in Shakespeare's plays major characters are usually allowed about four lines to make entrances and exits, that is, to walk the distance between one of the two (or three) doors in the tiring-house facade and the main acting area, i.e., front-stage.[2]

With this in mind, let us consider the following passage:

> *Bast.* . . .
> Yeeld, come before my Father, light hoa, here,
> Fly Brother, Torches, Torches, so farewell.
> *Exit Edgar.*
> Some blood drawne on me, would beget opinion
> Of my more fierce endeauour. I haue seene drunkards
> Do more then this in sport; Father, Father,
> Stop, stop, no helpe?
> *Enter Gloster, and Seruants with Torches.*
> *Glo.* Now Edmund, where's the villaine?
> (*King Lear* F1, TLN 963-71; 2. 1. 31-36)

Gloucester and his servants do not enter just after the Bastard's first call, but do so three and a half lines after Edgar begins to exit. The exit and the entrance are presumably made through different doors. This three-and-a-half-line gap ensures that the entrance of Gloucester and his servants does not overlap with Edgar's exit, though Edgar probably does not need all three and a half lines, since he exits running. No stage lighting was used in Elizabethan public playhouses and players acted in broad daylight.[3] Neither Edgar's exit nor Gloucester's entrance could be cloaked in darkness. Under such stage conditions, the overlapping of the exit and entrance would have seemed inconsistent with the succeeding dialogue. It seems likely, therefore, that the three-and-a-half-line gap reflects Shakespeare's wish to prevent Gloucester's entrance overlapping with Edgar's exit.

In Shakespeare's plays, there are a great number of instances where no sooner has a character begun to exit than another character enters. It can be assumed that in such instances overlapping of exits and entrances is intended or at least permitted. In most cases, though, whether the exits and entrances overlap or not may be of no consequence. Exiting characters rarely attract the audience's attention, unless they speak or are spoken to or referred to. However, there are some cases in which the overlapping of exits and entrances can be meaningful. The purpose of this paper is to examine several of these cases and consider what kinds of effect Shakespeare sometimes achieves by overlapping exits and entrances.

2

In *The Merry Wives of Windsor*, 3.3, the moment the servants begin to exit, Ford enters with others, probably through the door opposite the one towards which the servants are making their exit.[4]

> M. Ford. ... Carry them to the Landresse in Dat-
> chet mead: quickly, come.   [*Servants begin to exit.*] [5]
>   [*Enter Ford, Page, Caius, and Evans.*]
> Ford. 'Pray you come nere: if I suspect without cause,
> Why then make sport at me, then let me be your iest,
> I deserue it: How now? Whether beare you this?
> Ser. To the Landresse forsooth?
> M. Ford. Why, what haue you to doe whether they
> beare it? You were best meddle with buck-washing.
>   (*The Merry Wives of Windsor* F1, TLN 1480-87; 3. 3. 141-49)

Clearly, the servants cannot walk quickly, because they are carrying the basket in which the fat knight, Falstaff, is hiding. After speaking two or so lines, while walking towards front-stage, Ford interrupts the servants' move and questions them about the move itself. Watching the basket and Ford, the audience could well imagine the poor knight holding his breath and shrinking under the dirty linen, wishing that the servants would move more quickly and praying that Ford would not search the basket. The humour of the situation, which the audience shares with Mistress Ford and Mistress Page, is clearly based on this image of Falstaff created in the audience's mind.

In *Antony and Cleopatra*, 1.2, although Cleopatra has been seeking Antony, she impulsively begins to exit the moment she recognizes his entrance.

> Cleo. Seeke him, and bring him hither: [*Enobarbus begins to exit.*]
>   wher's *Alexias*?
> Alex. Heere at your seruice.
> My Lord approaches.
>   *Enter Anthony, with a Messenger.*
> Cleo. We will not looke vpon him:
> Go with vs.   *Exeunt* [*Cleopatra, Enobarbus, and Train*].
> Messen. Fuluia thy Wife,

> First came into the Field.
> *Ant.* Against my Brother *Lucius*?
>
> (*Antony and Cleopatra* F1, TLN 167-75; 1. 2. 79-83)

On the other hand, Antony, who in only the previous scene made the forthright pronouncement, "Let Rome in Tyber melt" (TLN 44; 1.1.35), walks towards front-stage, listening attentively to a messenger from Rome, and does not even perceive her leaving. Their manner of exiting and entering signifies that Rome is everything to Antony now and that Cleopatra instinctively feels that it would be vain to compete with Rome.

The Q2 version of *Hamlet* provides another example.

> *Fortin.* Goe Captaine . . .
> *Cap.* I will doo't my Lord.   [*Begins to exit.*]
> *For.* Goe softly on.   [*Exit with his army.*]
>   *Enter Hamlet, Rosencraus, &c.*
> *Ham.* Good sir whose powers are these?
> *Cap.* They are of *Norway* sir.
> *Ham.* How purposd sir I pray you?
> *Cap.* Against some part of *Poland*.
> *Ham.* Who commaunds them sir?
> *Cap.* The Nephew to old *Norway, Fortenbrasse.*
> . . .
> *Cap.* God buy you sir.   [*Exit.*]
>
> (*Hamlet* Q2, sig. K3^R; 4. 4. 1, 9-)

Just after the Captain begins to exit towards one door, Fortinbras also begins to exit with his army towards the other door. Then Hamlet enters through the door towards which the Captain is going. He interrupts the Captain's exit and questions him about the exit which Fortinbras and his army are now making. In this way Shakespeare makes Hamlet see Fortinbras only from a distance. This encounter is highly significant, because in the final moments of the tragedy Hamlet gives his dying voice to Fortinbras and entrusts the future of Denmark to him. However, this encounter is missing in the F1 text, which was printed from a transcript of the prompt-book reflecting Shakespeare's revision.[6] It seems that Shakespeare eventually chose to allow only the audience, and not Hamlet, to meet Fortinbras at this stage.[7] Still, it is interesting that Shakespeare originally intended Hamlet to see Fortinbras by overlapping Hamlet's entrance with Fortinbras's exit, for, in both versions, they are destined not to meet each other. At the end of the play, a "warlike noise/noyse" (Q2, sig. O1^V/ F1, TLN 3837; 5. 2.

301) from Fortinbras's army and Hamlet's "dying voyce" (Q2, sig. O1^V/ F1, TLN 3845; 5. 2. 308) merely overlap, and Fortinbras's entrance is too late to be received by Hamlet.

The following example is somewhat ambiguous:

> *Pol.* I heare him comming, let's withdraw my Lord.
> *Exeunt* [*King and Polonius*].
> *Enter Hamlet.*
> *Ham.* To be, or not to be, that is the Question:
> Whether 'tis Nobler in the minde to suffer
> The Slings and Arrowes of outragious Fortune,
> Or to take Armes against a Sea of troubles,
> And by opposing end them . . .
>
> (*Hamlet* F1, TLN 1707-14; 3. 1. 57-62)

It is not absolutely certain that the exit and the entrance are intended to overlap, for Polonius seems to have perceived Hamlet's approach only aurally, and Hamlet neither speaks to the exiting characters nor refers to their exit. Hamlet may possibly enter after the King and Polonius complete their exit.[8] But in this instance, Ophelia, who is on stage, speaks no lines to fill the gap, as we saw the Bastard do in *King Lear*, 2.1. Let us suppose that while the King and Polonius are exiting towards one door, Hamlet enters through the other door. The overlapping of the exit of the King and Polonius and the entrance of Hamlet adds to the suspense. Even though the entering character seems not to notice the exiting characters, the audience cannot but suspect that Hamlet may possibly be aware of the King and Polonius, for Hamlet and the King have been trying to conceal their own real intentions and probe each other's heart. After a short while, when Hamlet abruptly asks Ophelia, "Where's your Father?" (TLN 1785; 3.1.132), and aggressively says, "Those that are married already, all but one shall liue" (TLN 1803-4; 3.1.150-51), the audience would feel as if Hamlet intended these speeches to be heard by Polonius and the King, who are listening behind the door through which they have exited.[9]

As I have already mentioned, I do not think that the overlapping of exits and entrances is always so effective or meaningful. There are relatively few instances in which some effect or meaning can be confidently attributed to it. I admit that the effect resulting from it is often very subtle. But, however vague what results from the overlapping of an exit and an entrance may be, if it was an element in the experience of

Shakespeare's original audience, we should not ignore it.

3

A Shakespearean scene generally concludes with the exit of all characters and opens with the entrance of other characters. It is reasonable to assume that the closing exit and the opening entrance are made through different doors. We should consider the possibility that the exit made at the end of one scene and the entrance made at the beginning of the next might have overlapped in Shakespeare's playhouses.

Bernard Beckerman argues that overlapping exits and entrances were not the habit of the Globe company and that separation and pause were the more likely method. He gives five reasons. (i) Actors or stage attendants, on occasion, had to bring out props. (ii) In theatrical plots, a line was drawn across the page to separate one scene from another. It had the effect of fixing scene divisions firmly in the actor's mind. (iii) Together with the rhyming couplet which concluded so many scenes, the line may have encouraged the insertion of a slight pause between scenes. (iv) Exit lines stressed the conclusion of the scene, and they bridged moves across the large platform stage. (v) There are instances where characters enter through different doors at the beginning of a scene, and there are instances where characters depart through different doors at the end of a scene.[10]

The occurrence of split entrances and exits (v) is a sufficient reason for suggesting that the closing exit of one scene and the opening entrance of the next did not always overlap, because where both doors are simultaneously used for the exit or the entrance, the entrance cannot be made until the exit is completed. But, as for (i), it is clear that the actors or stage attendants played characters, such as servants or attendants, by bringing on [and carrying off] [11] props. Exceptions to this would be where they carried on [and off] something that is seldom carried about in ordinary life, such as a bed, tree, tomb, or the like.[12] Although (ii), (iii), and (iv) are sufficient reasons for assuming a pause between the concluding speech of one scene and the opening speech of the next, they are not adequate reasons for insisting that actors did not make the opening entrance of a new scene while other actors were still making the closing exit of the previous scene.

I agree with Beckerman when he suggests that characters took several paces towards the centre or front of the stage before speaking at the beginnings of scenes, and that this action may have provided a hia-

Overlapping Exits and Entrances in Shakespeare's Plays 151

tus sufficient to mark a new scene.[13] It is certain that there was a pause between the concluding speech of one scene and the opening speech of the next. However, scenes change very frequently in Shakespeare's plays. There are many scenes which run for only ten or so lines. Must we assume that, after it took four lines for characters to complete their exit, it took a further two to four lines for other characters to walk towards the centre or front of the stage, and that therefore there was a six-to-eight-line pause at every scene-break?

In the extant manuscript of Thomas Heywood's *Captives*, the book-keeper almost regularly places the word "clere" at the ends of scenes.[14] This is weighty evidence, even taking into account the fact that it comes from the Cockpit company, not the Globe. However, did the book-keeper insert the word to indicate that the entering characters should not appear until the exiting characters have completely disappeared from the stage? The following passage is from John Marston's *Antonio and Mellida*, a Paul's Children play:

> Feli. Peace, here comes the Prologue, cleare the Stage.
> *Exeunt.*
> *The Prologue.*
> THE wreath of pleasure, and delicious sweetes,
> ...
> (*Antonio and Mellida* Q, TLN 153-57)[15]

It is surely unlikely that the Prologue's entrance takes place only after Feliche and others have disappeared from a stage door. Feliche's last speech referring to the Prologue's entrance serves as a bridge between the Induction and the Prologue. The exit of Feliche and others and the entrance of the Prologue overlap. Since, in this instance, "cleare the Stage" means "let us all leave the stage," it may be that the Cockpit book-keeper also used "clere" only to indicate that all the on-stage characters should exit.[16]

Ghismonda (British Library, MS. Additional 34,312) contains a stage direction indicating an overlapping or simultaneous exit and entrance:

> Guisc: ....
> He's dull that stayes when such an Angell Calls
> and doth inuite him wth so faire a sumons
> lett me be cald pigritia's son & heire
> if I be slow in following this affaire
> *Exit Guiscardo interim Enter pasquino*
> *at an other dore*

> *Pasq:* Well no more to the Kinge=
>   *Enter Tancred, Glausamond, & Gabriello*
> =But new gone out ant
> please your Maiesty
> *Tanc*: I wonder at it, his care vsed to be greater   (fol. 166ᵛ) [17]

This play may have been written only for a private performance, but the author may have been influenced by the contemporary playhouse practice. Either he continues the scene by overlapping the exit of Guiscardo, who has been alone on stage, with the two successive entrances of Pasquino and Tancred, Glausamond, and Gabriello, or he bridges the gap between two scenes by overlapping the exit and the two entrances.

There are similar instances in *Measure for Measure* F1 and *Cymbeline* F1:

> *Bawd.* What's to doe heere, *Thomas* Tapster? let's withdraw?
> *Clo.* Here comes Signior *Claudio*, led by the Prouost to prison: and there's Madam *Iuliet*.   *Exeunt.*
>
>   *Scena Tertia.*
>
> *Enter Prouost, Claudio, Iuliet, Officers, Lucio, & 2. Gent.*
> *Cla.* Fellow, why do'st thou show me thus to th'world?
>   (*Measure for Measure* F1, TLN 201-7; 1. 2. 104-8)
>
> 1 We must forbeare. Heere comes the Gentleman,
> The Queene, and Princesse.   *Exeunt*
>
>   *Scena Secunda.*
>
> *Enter the Queene, Posthumus, and Imogen.*
> *Qu.* No, be assur'd you shall not finde me (Daughter)
> . . .
>   (*Cymbeline* F1, TLN 80-84; 1. 1. 69-71)

In each case, if there really is a scene change where the new scene is indicated, these passages can be treated as instances of overlapping exits and entrances at scene-breaks. However, if the scene divisions are merely scribal in origin and have nothing to do with theatrical practice,[18] for the F1 texts of *Measure for Measure* and *Cymbeline* were printed from literary transcripts by Ralph Crane, then in each case Shakespeare continues the scene by overlapping the exit and the entrance.[19]

In the following example, it is absolutely certain that the stage is not cleared at the end of the scene but that the scene flows into the next.

> Ro. ...
> But he that hath the stirrage of my course,
> Direct my sute, on lustie Gentlemen.
>   Ben. Strike drum.
>   *They march about the Stage, and Seruingmen come forth with Napkins.*
>   *Enter Romeo.*
>   Ser. Wheres Potpan that he helpes not to take away?
> He shift a trencher, he scrape a trencher?
>   (*Romeo and Juliet* Q2, sig. C2^V; 1. 4. 112-15, 1. 5. 1-2)

Since Romeo and his friends do not leave the stage altogether but only move aside at the end of 1. 4, the Q2 stage direction indicating Romeo's entrance at the beginning of 1. 5 is an error. This is an example of the overlapping of action on stage and an entrance. This overlapping is never intended to imply that the two groups of characters are in the same location. It is, as it were, a theatrical convention which shortens the running time of the play. Despite the presence of Romeo and others on stage, the entrance of the servingmen establishes the new locality, "a hall in Capulet's house" and opens the new scene. In *A Midsummer Night's Dream* the lovers do not exit but remain asleep at the end of act 3 (Q1, sig. F2^V/ F1, TLN 1507).[20] It is obvious that in Shakespeare's plays one scene is not always separated definitely from the next. It is not unreasonable therefore to assume the possibility that concluding exits and opening entrances overlap at scene-breaks.

In Shakespeare's plays, there are a great number of instances in which a character exits at or around the end of a scene and enters at or around the beginning of the succeeding scene. In these instances, if scene-breaks did not provide the time necessary for the actors to complete their exits and also move across off-stage to the opposite door, the necessary time had to be built into the dialogue. Using the Quarto and Folio texts of Shakespeare's plays, I have collected all the instances where a character appears in two consecutive scenes, and in each case counted the number of lines delivered between the point at which the character begins to exit and the point at which he re-enters.[21] (The number of lines delivered between the point at which a character begins to exit in a scene and the point at which he enters in the next scene shall be hereafter referred to as "NL.") However, I have restricted myself to those instances in which the exit and the entrance are both made on the main stage, leaving aside those in which the exit or the entrance is made on the "upper stage."[22]

The collected instances can be divided into the following six kinds, according to the conditions found between the exits and the entrances, mainly either at the ends of the preceding scenes or at the beginnings of the succeeding scenes.

1) Excursion . . . An excursion, military marching, or the like takes place.
2) Action . . . . . . Another kind of action is made.[23]
3) Last . . . . The character enters last after several other characters have entered.[24]
4) Sound . . . . . . An off-stage sound or music is heard.
5) Split . . . . The closing exit or the opening entrance is [probably / possibly] split.[25]
6) None . . . . None of the above five conditions is fulfilled.

Needless to say, it is only the distribution of instances of the last category that can reveal how many lines are allowed for characters to exit and walk to the opposite door. But it is also important to grasp the difference between the distribution of instances fulfilling any of the first five conditions and that of instances of "None." It will be sufficient for the present purposes to show the number of instances fulfilling each condition in which NL is between 0 and 10. For the instances themselves, see Appendix 1. However, for reasons of space, only the instances in which NL is between 0 and 6 are listed.

Table 1
Instances Fulfilling Each Condition

Condition	NL										
	0	1	2	3	4	5	6	7	8	9	10
Excursion	17	0	0	1	1	0	1	0	1	0	0
Action	3	0	0	0	0	0	0	2	0	0	0
Last	5	0	0	0	0	0	0	0	0	0	0
Sound	11	0	1	0	4	0	2	0	1	2	3
Split	0	1	0	0	0	1	0	1	0	1	2
None	5	0	0	1	2	3	7	6	4	12	4

Notes:
[a] In this table, extra half lines are counted as full lines.
[b] Where an instance fulfills two or more conditions, I have chosen only one condition, giving priority to one over the other(s) according to the order indicated in the table.
[c] Where characters who have simultaneously exited enter at different times,

and where characters who have exited at different times enter simultaneously, I have counted only the instance in which NL is smaller or the smallest.

While there are numerous instances fulfilling any of the first five conditions in which NL is 0, there are only a few instances of "None" in which NL is below six. Further, *The Tempest*, 4. 1. 264-5. 1. 0 and possibly *Titus Andronicus*, 3. 2. 84-4. 1. 0 need not be counted as instances of "None=0." This is because the Blackfriars, for which *The Tempest* was written, used act-intervals, and *Titus Andronicus*, 3. 2. 84-4. 1. 0, which occurs only in the F1 text, appears to reflect later staging after the practice of act-intervals was adopted by the public playhouses (c. 1607-10).[26] There are instances in which the actor must change costumes off-stage between his exit and re-entry. But, as Appendix 2 shows, where none of the five conditions is fulfilled, NL is never fewer than 16. As has been mentioned earlier, in Shakespeare's plays characters are usually allowed about four lines to walk from front-stage to a stage door. It can therefore be concluded that in almost all the cases where no action is made or no sound is heard, a sufficient number of lines are spoken to fill not only the time for the characters to complete their exits but also at least part of the necessary time for them to move across to the opposite door off-stage.[27]

I am inclined to believe that it may have been usual, at least at the Theatre and the Globe, for actors to enter and open a new scene while other actors were still making their exit at the end of the previous scene, except where both stage doors were simultaneously used for the closing exit or the opening entrance. This may not apply to the staging at the Rose and the Blackfriars, for the stages of these playhouses were considerably smaller.

4

What would happen, if exits and entrances overlapped at scene-breaks? Take for example the scene-break between 3. 3 and 3. 4 of *Antony and Cleopatra*, a Globe play:

>   *Cleopa.* I haue one thing more to aske him yet good *Charmian*:
> but 'tis no matter, thou shalt bring him to me where I will write;
> all may be well enough.
>   *Char.* I warrant you Madam.   *Exeunt.*
>   *Enter Anthony and Octauia.*
>   *Ant.* Nay, nay, Octauia, not onely that,
> That were excusable, that and thousands more
> Of semblable import, . . .
>   (*Antony and Cleopatra* F1, TLN 1680-87; 3. 3. 44-47, 3. 4. 1-3)

The exit of the Egyptian characters and the entrance of the Roman characters, even if they overlap, establish a scene-break, which the audience cannot fail to notice. But they could never miss the overlapping of the moves, since while Cleopatra is leaving, satisfied with the messenger's false report on Octavia's features and hopeful of regaining Antony's love, Antony himself enters with Octavia. Judging from Antony's speech, they clearly do not enter like a devoted couple. With Cleopatra's exit functioning, as it were, as a background, the audience would be visually aware that Antony is now in a very critical situation—his body still in Rome but his heart already in Egypt.

At the turning point of *Richard II*, written for the Theatre, the departure of Richard and his friends is followed by the arrival of Bolingbroke and his followers.

> *King* He does me double wrong,
> That wounds me with the flatteries of his tong,
> Discharge my followers, let them hence away,
> From Richards night, to Bullingbrookes faire day.   [*Exeunt.*]
>   *Enter Bull. Yorke, North.*
> *Bull.* So that by this intelligence we learne
> The Welch men are disperst, and Salisburie
> Is gone to meete the King, who lately landed
> With some few priuate friends vpon this coast.
>   (*Richard II* Q1, sig. F3^V; 3. 2. 211-14, 3. 3. 1-4)

The overlapping of the exit of a character who has sunk into the depths of despair with the entrance of the one who has driven him to that despair would stress the contrast between the falling fortunes of Richard and the rising fortunes of Bolingbroke, and show the exit of Richard and his friends as more miserable and the entrance of Bolingbroke and his followers as more powerful.

In these passages, even if the exits of Cleopatra and Richard did not overlap with the entrances, respectively, of Antony and Bolingbroke, the juxtaposition of the scenes would bring about almost the same effects. What I should like to note is the possibility that at the Theatre and the Globe the overlapping of the closing exit of one scene and the opening entrance of the next occasionally made the juxtaposition of the two scenes obvious and intensified the effect of the juxtaposition itself.

5

The exit of all characters normally indicates the end of a scene. It seems, however, that a general exit is not always a crucial factor in distinguishing one scene from another. The second platform scene of Hamlet is usually treated as two scenes.

> *Ham.* . . .
> By Heau'n, Ile make a Ghost of him that lets me:
> I say away, goe on, Ile follow thee.
> Exeunt Ghost & Hamlet.
>   *Hor.* He waxes desperate with imagination.
>   *Mar.* Let's follow; 'tis not fit thus to obey him.
>   *Hor.* Haue after, to what issue will this come?
>   *Mar.* Something is rotten in the State of Denmarke.
>   *Hor.* Heauen will direct it.
>   *Mar.* Nay, let's follow him.   *Exeunt.*
>   Enter Ghost and Hamlet.
>   *Ham.* Where wilt thou lead me? speak; Ile go no further.
>   (*Hamlet* F1, TLN 672-82; 1. 4. 62-68, 1. 5. 1)

There is no break in the action between the two scenes now numbered 1. 4 and 1. 5, though Hamlet's first speech after his re-entrance seems to suggest some change of location. Let us suppose that while Horatio and Marcellus are still moving towards the door from which the Ghost and Hamlet have made their exit, the Ghost and Hamlet enter through the other door. The audience would never be aware of any scene change. The F1 text provides scene divisions in Acts 1 and 2, though the scenes now generally known as 1. 3, 1. 4, and 1. 5 are combined and designated as "Scena Tertia" (TLN 460). However, whereas there is blank space between 1. 3 and 1. 4 (TLN 602-3), there is no space between 1. 4 and 1. 5 (TLN 680-81). Do these spacings accurately reflect the printer's copy? If so, does that signify that 1. 4 and 1. 5 may have been treated as a single scene? Unfortunately we cannot answer these questions, but it is not absolutely necessary to introduce a scene-break at 1. 4. 68, and at least from the viewpoint of the original staging of Shakespeare's plays or the original audience's experience, the division seems improper.[28]

In the Oxford *Complete Works*, the traditional 3. 2 of *A Midsummer Night's Dream* is broken into two scenes.

>   *Lys.* I will be with thee straight.

> *Rob.* Follow me then to plainer ground. [Exit Lysander.]
> *Enter* Demetrius.
> *Deme. Lysander*, speake againe.
> Thou runaway, thou coward, art thou fled?
> Speake in some bush. Where doest thou hide thy head?
> *Rob.* Thou coward art thou bragging, to the starres,
> Telling the bushes that thou look'st for warres,
> And wilt not come? Come recreant, come thou childe,
> Ile whippe thee with a rodde. He is defil'd,
> That drawes a sword on thee.
> *De.* Yea, art thou there?
> *Ro.* Follow my voice: weele try manhood here. *Exeut.*
> [*Enter* Lysander.]
> *Lys.* He goes before me, and still dares me on:
> When I come where he calles, then he is gon.
> (*A Midsummer Night's Dream* Q1, sig. F2^R; 3. 2. 404-13, 3. 3. 1-2)

Gary Taylor notes that "although the action of Robin's abuse of the men clearly continues, the cleared stage can suggest a gap in time and place, which usefully contributes to the ease with which an audience accepts the subsequent wearied surrender of Lysander and Demetrius."[29] But I do not think that there is anything wrong with the interpretation that there is no change of place nor lapse of time between the exit of Robin and Demetrius and the entrance of Lysander. It is highly amusing that, when the two lovers are running after each other, bewitched by Robin, the one enters as the other exits, neither noticing each other's arrival or departure. Their joint entry and departure takes place as often as twice in the space of only about ten lines. This would also make their wearied surrender understandable and acceptable. The Oxford editors seem to observe the general principle concerning the exit of all characters too strictly.[30] If they had taken into account the time necessary for characters to exit, and allowed the possibility of overlapping in certain exits and entrances, their attitude towards the exit of all characters would have been different.

Appendix 1
Instances Fulfilling Each Condition in which NL is between 0 and 6

Excursion=0:
1. 2H6 4.2.189-4.3.0	Cade, etc.		(Sound)
2. 2H6 4.6.15-4.7.0	Cade, etc.		(Sound)
3. 3H6 2.2.177-2.3.0	Warwick		(Sound; Split)
4. 3H6 2.3.56-2.4.0	Richard		(Split)

Overlapping Exits and Entrances in Shakespeare's Plays 159

    5. 3H6 5.1.116-5.2.0   Edward   (Sound)
    6. 3H6 5.4.82-5.5.0   Edward, etc.   (Sound)
    7. 1H6 1.2.21-1.3.0   Charles, Alençon, René   (Sound)
    8. 1H6 3.4.5-3.5.0   Joan   (Sound)
    9. 1H6 4.5.55-4.6.0   Talbot, John Talbot   (Sound)
  10. 1H6 4.6.57-4.7.0   Talbot   (Sound)
  11. 1H6 5.2.21-5.3.0   Joan   (Sound)
  12. 1H6 5.3.29-5.4.0   Joan
  13. R3 5.6.81-5.7.0   Catesby   (Sound)
  14. JN 3.2.10-3.3.0   John, Arthur, Hubert   (Sound; Split)
  15. 1H4 5.2.100-5.3.0   Douglas   (Sound)
  16. ANT 3.9.4-3.10.0   Enobarbus   (Sound)
  17. COR 1.4.29-1.5.0   Martius   (Sound)

Excursion=3:
    1. COR 1.5.33-1.6.3   Martius, Lartius   (Sound)
    i) JN 3.1.273-3.2.4[3]   John   (Sound; Split)

Excursion=4:
    1. JN 3.1.273-3.2.4[3]   John   (Sound; Split)

Excursion=6:
    1. 1H4 5.3.55-5.4.0   Prince Henry   (Sound)

Action=0:
    1. SHR 5.1.141-5.2.0[1]   Petruccio, Katherine, Grumio   ?
    2. TIM 1.1.286-1.2.0   Lords   (Sound)
    3. PER 6.62-7.0   Simonides, Thaisa   (Sound)

Last=0:
    1. 2H6 2.2.82-2.3.0   York, Salisbury, Warwick   (Sound)
    2. JC 1.1.75-1.2.0   Flavius, Murellus
    3. WT 1.1.46-1.2.0   Camillo
    4. CYM 5.1.33-5.2.0   Posthumus   (Split)
    5. CYM 5.5.94-5.5.94[2] Posthumus, Captains   ? ; sb?

Sound=0:
    1. 2H6 5.1.214-5.3.0   Warwick   (Split)
    2. 3H6 4.3.27-4.4.0   Warwick
    3. TIT 1.1.491-2.1.0   Aaron   in F1 only
    4. 1H6 1.6.89-1.7.0   Talbot
    5. 1H6 2.5.129-3.1.0   Richard Plantagenet
    6. R3 2.4.72-3.1.0   Cardinal
    7. R3 5.7.13-5.8.0   Richard   (Split)
    8. JC 5.1.126-5.2.0   Brutus
    9. JC 5.3.109-5.4.0   Brutus, etc.
  10. AWW 5.2.54-5.3.0   Lafeu

11. ANT 4.8.13-4.9.0   Antony

Sound=2:
1. COR 1.9.13-1.10.0   Martius   (Split)

Sound=4:
1. 1H4 5.4.158-5.5.0   Prince Henry, Lancaster
2. MAC 5.6.10-5.7.4   Young Siward   ?
3. ANT 4.4.34-4.5.0   Antony, Eros   (Split)
4. COR 4.4.26-4.5.4   Coriolanus

Sound=6:
1. 2H6 4.7.224-4.8.6   Buckingham, Clifford
2. R2 1.2.74-1.3.6   Gaunt   (Split)

Split=1:
1. 3H6 4.9.31-4.10.0   Henry   ? ; sb?

Split=5:
1. ROM 4.2.47-4.3.5   Lady Capulet

None=0:
1. SHR 3.2.127-3.3.0   Lucentio   ? ; sb?
2. TIT 3.2.84-4.1.0   Young Lucius, Lavinia   in F1 only
3. R3 3.3.24-3.4.0   Ratcliffe   in F1 only
4. CYM 5.5.94-5.5.94[3]   Posthumus, Jailers   ? ; sb?
5. TMP 4.1.264-5.1.0   Prospero, Ariel   act-interval

None=3:
1. TIM 3.4.96-3.5.0   Timon

None=4:
1. SHR 4.4.67[66]-4.5.0   Biondello   ? ; sb?
2. CYM 2.4.149m-2.5.0   Posthumus

None=5:
1. 1H4 2.2.89-2.3.5   Falstaff, etc.   sb?
2. HAM 1.4.63-1.5.0   Ghost, Hamlet   sb?
3. TRO 5.1.95-5.2.5[8]   Thersites
i) SHR 4.4.67[66]-4.5.0   Biondello   ? ; sb?

None=6:
1. SHR 3.1.84-3.2.0   Bianca
2. H5 1.1.99-1.2.6   Archbishop, Ely
3. HAM 5.1.291-5.2.0   Horatio
4. TRO 5.5.43-5.6.0   Ajax
5. TRO 5.5.44-5.6.1   Diomedes

6. MM 3.1.538-4.1.6   Duke
   7. ANT 4.15.138-4.16.6m   Diomedes

Notes to Appendix 1:

Instances listed under "Excursion=0," for example, are those fulfilling the condition of "Excursion" in which NL is 0.

The abbreviations of titles of plays are those used in C. T. Onions, *A Shakespeare Glossary*, enlarged and revised throughout by Robert D. Eagleson (Oxford: Oxford Univ. Press, 1986).

"m" added to a line number indicates the middle of the line.

"?" in the third column indicates that it is not certain whether the exit and entrance actually occur or not.

"sb?" in the third column indicates that it is doubtful whether there is really a scene-break between the exit and the entrance.

[1] It is clear that there is some problem with SHR 5.1.141-5.2.0. The opening stage direction of 5.2 (F1, TLN 2534-37) mentions Tranio twice, but unaccountably makes no reference to Petruccio and Katherine. Although this stage direction indicates that Tranio and other servingmen bring in a banquet after the entrance of Baptista, Vincentio, Gremio, Pedant, Lucentio, and Bianca, it seems equally likely that the banquet is carried in first. This is because the listing of the characters may be in order of seniority rather than practical appearance. (In English Renaissance plays, there are a great number of banquet scenes. In these scenes, it is usual for the banquet to be brought in just before the guests enter.) In either case, Petruccio and Katherine probably enter after the six characters mentioned above.

[2] The Second Captain's "bring him to'th'King" (*Cymbeline* F1, TLN 3028; 5.5.94) implies that the Captains and soldiers lead Posthumus off the stage. Although the F1 text inserts a scene-break at TLN 3032, it seems more likely that a new scene opens at TLN 3029 with the entrance of Cymbeline, Belarius, Guiderius, Arviragus, Pisanio, and Roman captives, and that the Captains return with Posthumus after the entrance of Cymbeline and the others. See Irwin Smith, "Their Exits and Reentrances," *Shakespeare Quarterly*, 18 (1967): 13-14.

[3] See n 2.

Appendix 2

Instances with Costume Changes in which NL is between 0 and 25

   1. CYM 5.1.33-5.2.0 (Last; Split=0)
      Posthumus dresses himself like a poor soldier.
   2. LR 3.7.92m-4.1.9m (None=13) [act-interval][1]
      Gloucester changes clothes and puts plasters on his eyes.
   3. PER 9.113-10.14 (Action; Split=14)
      Thaisa dresses herself like a woman with child.

4. 1H4 2.2.73-2.3.0 (Action=16) [scene-break?][2]
   Prince Henry and Poins disguise themselves in Buckram.
5. PER 21.248-22.16 (None=16)
   Pericles takes off the wig and false beard he has worn.
6. TIT 5.2.204-5.3.25 (Sound=25)
   Titus dresses himself like a cook and Lavinia puts on a veil over her face.

There are two other examples, in which entrances onto the "upper stage" are involved:

i) SHR 0.1.136-0.2.0 (Last=0)
   Lord dresses himself like a servant.
ii) MV 2.5.56-2.6.25 (None=25)
   Jessica dresses herself like a boy.

Notes to Appendix 2:

[1] In the Q1 version, NL of the corresponding instance, i.e., LR 14.92m[95m]-15.6, is 19.5[16.5]. Gary Taylor points out that the act-division makes the F1 omission of the dialogue of the two servants at the end of 3.7 possible. See Taylor and John Jowett, *Shakespeare Reshaped: 1603-1623* (Oxford: Clarendon Press, 1993), pp. 48-49.

[2] I do not think that there is a scene-break between 2.2.89 and "2.3.0" in *1 Henry IV*. Shakespeare clearly combines into a single scene the parts which are designated as 2.2 and 2.3 in the Oxford *Complete Works* by giving Prince Henry a speech implying that he saw the exit of Falstaff and others as he entered (2.3.1).

Notes

This paper was originally published in Japanese in *Studies in English Literature* (The English Literary Society of Japan), 71 (1994): 1-18. I should like to express my gratitude to Andrew Gurr, Alan C. Dessen, Raymond Powell, and James House for their invaluable comments on earlier English versions.

1. Quarto and Folio readings are from *Shakespeare's Plays in Quarto: A Facsimile Edition of Copies Primarily from the Henry E. Huntington Library*, ed. Michael J. B. Allen and Kenneth Muir (Berkeley and Los Angeles: Univ. of California Press, 1981) and *The First Folio of Shakespeare*: The Norton Facsimile, ed. Charlton Hinman (New York: W. W. Norton, 1968). Act-scene-line references are those of *William Shakespeare: The Complete Works*, ed. Stanley Wells and Gary Taylor (Oxford: Clarendon Press, 1986).

2. By contrast, minor characters, such as servants and attendants, are usually allowed about two lines, and occasionally only one line or less, to complete their exits. Clearly the reason why they are given much less time than major characters is that their acting area is ordinarily the rear of the stage, and

that they are usually expected to move very quickly. I have fully discussed this question in my "Time Allowed for Exits in Shakespeare's Plays" in *Japanese Studies in Shakespeare and His Contemporaries*, ed. Yoshiko Kawachi (Cranbury, N. J.: Associated Univ. Presses, forthcoming).

It used to be thought that the size of the Globe stage was forty-three feet wide by twenty-seven and a half feet deep. But this estimate, which is a deduction from the building contract for the Fortune, has been seriously questioned, particularly since the Rose excavation. John Orrell argues that both the stages and tiring-houses were commonly built in the yards of public playhouses, and insists on the likelihood that the Globe stage was wide but comparatively shallow. See "Beyond the Rose: Design Problems for the Globe Reconstruction," in *New Issues in the Reconstruction of Shakespeare's Theatre*, ed. Franklin J. Hildy (New York: Peter Lang, 1990), pp. 111-16. See also Hildy, "Reconstructing Shakespeare's Theatre," in *New Issues in the Reconstruction of Shakespeare's Theatre*, pp. 13-17. Unfortunately, the precise size and design of the Globe stage have not yet been confirmed. However, it seems very likely that the stages of the Theatre and its reincarnation, the Globe, were larger than the stages of the Rose and the Blackfriars. The Shakespearean passages I have chosen are all from the plays which were originally performed in the Theatre or the Globe. For the playhouses in which the plays of Shakespeare and his contemporaries were staged, I have relied on Alfred Harbage, *Annals of English Drama: 975-1700*, 3rd edition, ed. Sylvia S. Wagenheim (London: Routledge, 1989); Andrew Gurr, *The Shakespearean Stage: 1574-1642*, 3rd edition (Cambridge: Cambridge Univ. Press, 1992), pp. 232-43.

3. Alan C. Dessen stresses this point and discusses effects resulting from the overlapping and juxtapositions of several kinds of elements. See "'Taint Not Thy Mind . . .': Problems and Pitfalls in Staging Plays at the New Globe," in *New Issues in the Reconstruction of Shakespeare's Theatre*, pp. 135-58.

4. In this instance, the exiters and the enterers may use the same door. But it seems reasonable to assume that where the exit of a character and the entrance of another character are made almost simultaneously or successively, the exiter and the enterer are generally expected to use different doors. Bernard Beckerman's hypothesis that entrances were usually made at one door and exits were made at the other is attractive. See "Theatrical Plots and Elizabethan Stage Practice," in *Shakespeare and Dramatic Tradition*, ed. W. R. Elton and William B. Long (Newark: Univ. of Delaware Press, 1989), pp. 109-24. See also Long, "*John a Kent and John a Cumber*: An Elizabethan Playbook and Its Implications," in *Shakespeare and Dramatic Tradition*, pp. 136-37.

5. In this paper, the stage directions printed within square brackets are my additions. In those cases where the exit is interrupted, I have added the stage direction "begin[s] to exit." The fact that interrupted exits are common in Elizabethan plays may suggest that the depth of Elizabethan stages was generally quite considerable.

6. For the nature of the early texts of Shakespeare's plays, I have relied on Stanley Wells and Gary Taylor (with John Jowett and William Montgomery), *William Shakespeare: A Textual Companion* (Oxford: Clarendon Press, 1987).

7. In the F1 version, however, the Captain and the rest of the army may be

expected to use the same door for their exits. For one thing, the split exit at the end of the scene would have been undesirable for the smoothness of the scene change. For another, a short march scene ordinarily consists of a general entrance by one door and a general exit by the other door. The Captain would leave the stage first while the others are still marching.

8. The Q2 text places the stage direction for Hamlet's entrance just before Polonius's speech (sig. G2^R). It may be that, in the F1 version, either Shakespeare or the book-keeper moved down the entry stage direction to avoid Hamlet's entrance overlapping with the exit of the King and Polonius.

9. Even if the King and Polonius did not really exit but went behind the arras, the overlapping of their move and Hamlet's entrance would bring about almost the same effect. See G. R. Hibbard, ed., *Hamlet*, The Oxford Shakespeare (Oxford: Oxford Univ. Press, 1987), p. 239 n.

10. See Bernard Beckerman, *Shakespeare at the Globe: 1599-1609* (New York: Macmillan, 1962), p. 176-78.

11. However, in certain cases, the props used in a scene may have been left on stage during the next. See Dessen, "'Taint Not Thy Mind . . .'," pp. 148-53.

12. These items are included in the list of properties that Henslowe compiled in March 1598. See Gurr, *Shakespearean Stage*, pp. 187-88.

13. See *Shakespeare at the Globe*, p. 179.

14. See *The Captives* by Thomas Heywood (The Malone Society Reprints, 1953). In a copy of the fourth edition of *A Looking-Glass for London and England*, which was used as a prompt-book sometime in the first half of the seventeenth century, the book-keeper regularly adds the word "clear" at the ends of scenes. See *A Looking-Glass for London and England* by Thomas Lodge and Robert Greene (The Malone Society Reprints, 1932), pp. xxviii-xxxiii. "Exeunt cleere/clear" appears twice in the Qq2-6 and F2 versions of Beaumont and Fletcher's *A King and No King*. See Fredson Bowers, gen. ed. *The Dramatic Works in the Beaumont and Fletcher Canon*, II (Cambridge: Cambridge Univ. Press, 1970), pp. 311-12. I am indebted to Alan C. Dessen for these very important facts.

15. Antonio and Mellida & Antonio's Revenge by John Marston (The Malone Society Reprints, 1921).

16. Evidently he emphasises scene-breaks by inserting the word. However, in the two cases where he indicates that the sound of "Storme" or "Tempeste/Thunder" should bridge two consecutive scenes (TLN 651, 901-3), he does not mark "clere" at the scene-breaks. From these exceptional cases, it can be inferred that the Cockpit book-keeper may have thought of scenes in terms of fictional time and place. See David Bradley, *From Text to Performance in the Elizabethan Theatre* (Cambridge: Cambridge Univ. Press, 1992), pp. 30-31.

17. The transcription is by Mariko Ichikawa.

18. See Gary Taylor and John Jowett, *Shakespeare Reshaped: 1616-1623*, pp. 239-41.

19. Taylor and Jowett discuss the changes made in *Measure for Measure*, 1. 2 after Shakespeare's death. According to their view, in the original form of the passage quoted above, only Provost and Claudio entered as Bawd and Clown exited. See *Shakespeare Reshaped*, pp. 151-71.

20. In *King Lear*, 2. 2, while Kent is sleeping on stage, Edgar enters, solilo-

quizes, and exits. Although the F1 text provides act-scene divisions, it does not mark a new scene at Edgar's arrival (TLN 1251; 2. 2. 164). However, as Bernard Beckerman says, whether Edgar was supposed to be in the same part of the castle yard or another part does not much matter. See *Shakespeare at the Globe*, p. 159.

21. In the cases of multiple-text plays, I have basically chosen to use the text closer or closest to the prompt-book of Shakespeare's company, while also consulting the other text[s].

It is very difficult to determine when characters begin to exit and when they enter. I have tentatively placed the beginnings of exits just after those speeches which serve as exit cues, and I have placed entrances in one of two positions: either just before those speeches which are delivered to or spoken by the enterers, or just before those speeches which refer to the approach of the enterers. Where stage directions indicate different points, I have accepted them as alternative possibilities, unless it is unreasonable to assume that the characters begin to exit or enter at the points.

22. E.g., *The Taming of the Shrew*, 0. 1. 136-0. 2. 0 (Lord); *3 Henry VI*, 5. 6.94-5. 7. 0 (Richard).

23. There are several instances in which a banquet is prepared. In all the instances of "Action" counted in Table 1 the preparation of a banquet is found at the beginning of the scene.

24. For example, Julius Caesar F1 has a stage direction reading "*Enter Caesar, Antony for the Course, Calphurnia, Portia, Decius, Cicero, Brutus, Cassius, Caska, a Soothsayer: after them Murellus and Flauius*" (TLN 84-86; 1. 2. 0).

25. Since it is sometimes extremely difficult to decide whether closing exits and opening entrances are split or not, I have included probable and less probable instances.

26. See Wilfred T. Jewkes, *Act Division in Elizabethan and Jacobean Plays: 1583-1616* (1958; New York: AMS Press, 1973); Taylor and Jowett, *Shakespeare Reshaped*, pp. 3-50; Andrew Gurr, "*The Tempest*'s Tempest at Blackfriars," *Shakespeare Survey*, 41 (1989): 91-102.

27. Irwin Smith also insists that Shakespeare provides characters with sufficient time to move backstage from one door to the other, even in those instances where the so-called "Law of Re-entry" seems to be violated. See "Their Exits and Reentrances," *Shakespeare Quarterly*, 18 (1967): 7-16.

28. Mark Rose treats 1. 4 and 1. 5 as a single scene and shows the design of the whole scene. See *Shakespearean Design* (Cambridge, Mass.: Harvard Univ. Press, 1972), pp. 103-6.

29. Wells and Taylor, *Textual Companion*, p. 280.

30. For some other examples, see *1 Henry IV*, 2. 2. 89-2. 3. 0; *King Lear*, 2. 2. 164-64, 184-85. See also Appendix 2, n 2.

Theories of Nature and Political Legitimation: Two Orestes Plays in English Renaissance Drama

Aya Mimura

FEW PLAYWRIGHTS IN Renaissance England seem to have dared to challenge the Greeks by staging the gory story of Orestes—one of the most problematic of mythological revengers, the killer of his own mother for the sake of his father. Even those Kydian revenge tragedy writers known for their so-called debt to Seneca shied away from it. There were some, however, who were indeed bold enough to attempt the adaptation of this myth—those from another theatre tradition who were haunted by the classics, who took pride in the dramas they themselves had written and disdained the "popular" theatre, and who now in our present age suffer from complete neglect. These were the people of the court and the universities.

At least two Orestes plays are extant.[1] One is an interlude by a courtier named John Pickering (*A Newe Enterlude of Vice conteyninge the Historye of Horestes with the cruell revengment of his Fathers death upon his one naturall Mother*, 1567), and the other is a revenge tragedy by an Oxford student Thomas Goffe (*The Tragedy of Orestes*, c.1613-18).[2] Strikingly, although these two plays are based on the same myth, their protagonists experience extremely different fates: the interlude ends with the protagonist's coronation and marriage, while the revenging hero in the Oxford play suffers banishment and madness, subsequently committing suicide.

In other words, Pickering presents the deposing of an erring queen for the sake of peace and order as justified, whilst Goffe, writing several years after James' succession, concentrates on the disturbance caused by the change of government, rather than the restoration of order. Through comparing these two contrary interpretations of the Orestes myth, this paper attempts to reveal what roles these works had in Elizabethan and Jacobean contexts respectively.

Pickering's *The History of Horestes*

It has been suggested that the author of *The History of Horestes* was probably identical with John Puckering, later Speaker of the House of Commons and Lord Keeper in Elizabeth's government. Although there is scarcely any proof of authorship, the remarkable similarity between the plot of the play and the course of events in Scotland in the very year of its performance at court would seem reasonably to associate the work with Puckering, whose reputation as an Elizabethan public servant rests mainly on his activities as an ardent foe of Mary Queen of Scots.

It was in early 1567 that Mary Stuart was accused of being an accomplice in the murder of her consort, Henry Darnley. Only three months later, she married the suspected assassin, the Earl of Bothwell. Antipathy towards the Queen among the Scottish Protestant nobles became so strong that she was finally forced to abdicate the throne in favour of her one year-old son, James. I agree with Phillips when he says that Pickering must have been "attempting to demonstrate . . . the circumstances under which one queen might properly be deposed without violating the principle of royal sovereignty everywhere."[3]

The story of *The History of Horestes* is as follows: while the Vice is causing turmoil amongst the people, Horestes arrives and prays that the gods "declare to [him their] gracious mind", asking if he should "revenged be of good Kynge Agamemnones death", or "let the adulltres dame styll wallow in her sin" (185-7). The Vice appears to Horestes as a messenger from heaven sent to support his plans of revenge, and to encourage the wronged prince to make war against his mother. Horestes succeeds in seizing the city, leaving Clytemnestra to the Vice to be duly executed. Accused of matricide at the ensuing trial, he defends himself by saying that he acted only according to the demands of the gods. His coronation and marriage are celebrated by Duty and Truth, as well as by noblemen of the land and neighbouring rulers.

This play was written very late in the history of the interlude, and it is quite ambiguous whether the Vice is a traditional figure of evil who seduces Mankind, or indeed the representative of the gods who approve of Horestes' revenge. However, it is this very ambiguity which allows a justification of Horestes' action. The responsibility is shifted to the Vice, who absorbs all the evil elements of the deed to leave Horestes innocent. The Vice is banished in the end and forced to leave with a beggar's staff and dish, as if he were a *pharmakos* sacrificed to cleanse the land.

One wonders if this seemingly happy ending tries to extinguish, rather than solve, the old dilemma. Comparison of the play with its classical predecessors will obviously help to clarify the nature of the question.

*

The true horror of the Orestes myth is that the protagonist is compelled to destroy the maternal body, to annihilate the origin of his own being. Let us look at the famous climax of Aeschylus' *The Libation Bearers*, where the mother thrusts out one of her breasts and cries:

> *Clytaemnestra*:
> Wait, my son—no respect for this, my child?
> The breast you held, drowsing away the hours,
> soft gums tugging the milk that made you grow?[4]

The vehemence of the confrontation is modified in Euripides' *Electra*, where it is recalled after the murder, although in such a way as to lose none of its overwhelming intensity:

> *Orestes*:
> Did you see how, in her agony,
> She opened her gown, thrust forth her breast,
> And showed it to me as I struck?
> Her body that gave me birth
> Sprawled there on the ground.
> I had her by the hair . . .[5]

Such vivid expressions are, however, assiduously, and disappointingly, avoided in Pickering's play: there is only a minimal residue of the presentation of corporeality. Clytemnestra appeals to her son: "Yf aney sparke of mothers bloud remayned within thy breaste"(730); "Consider that in me thou hadest they hewmayne shape composid"(801). Here the "breast" is not the mother's but the son's—changed from "mammary" into "chest"—erasing the display of motherhood and leaving the bodily bond between the two quite abstract.

Pickering's Horestes does not hesitate. He rejects his mother's plea outright: "For to repent this facte of thyne, now that is to late, / Can not be thought a recompence for kylling of thy mate" (736-7). Even with his "bitter sigh", Horestes only means that "By all the godes, my hart dyd fayle, my mother for to se / From hye estate for to be brought to so great myserey" (750-1). This is precisely what tragedy was held to be at that time: the fall of the great from the peak of glory to irrevocable destruction. Here Horestes is lamenting over, or rather commenting on, the queen's fall in general terms—as if he were a member of the audience who had no part in the act of matricide.

This firmness in Horestes' attitude is most apparent in his argument with the goddess Nature, another mother figure who calls him "Horestes myne", "my child." Nature, admitting that the murder of Agamemnon was "a wycked facte" (414), still tries to dissuade him from avenging himself on his mother. She tries to remind him of the bonds between mother and son even more evocatively than Clytemnestra herself; indeed if any echo of the Aeschylean mother's plea is to be found in this interlude, it is in Nature's appeal.

> *Nature*:
> Canst thou (a lacke, unhappey wight!) consent revenged to be
> On her whose pappes, before this time, hath given foud to the?
> (416-7)

Considering the custom of wet-nursing and fosterage prevalent in the Elizabethan age, it must have been the nourishing of a child rather than conception and delivery that constituted the idea of maternal care. Horestes, however, has no ears at all for the appeal from maternity, and instead sees the matter in a completely different perspective:

> *Horestes*:
> Who offendith the love of God, and eke mans love with willing hart,
> Must by [that] love have punnishment as dutey due for his desart.
> For me therfor to punnish hear, as law of gods and man doth wil,
> Is not a crime, though that I do, as thou dost saie, my mother kil.
> (420-3)

His argument is concentrated on only one side of his act, that of regicide. The other side, that of matricide, is patently ignored, for it is Pickering's main concern to bring into focus the resistance of the people against an evil monarch. He employs Clytemnestra's figure only because she is a typical example of an adulterous wife and wicked queen. The question he is really interested in is whether it is right or wrong for a subject to kill his/her ruler—not whether it is right or wrong for a son to kill his mother.

Since Clytemnestra offends the love of "gods *and* men", she is rightly punished according to the law of "gods *and* men." This small conjunction in Horestes' speech deserves more than a glance. It guarantees that there is no conflict between the two, gods and men. The steadfastness of Pickering's Horestes comes from the assumption of this happy agreement. The paradigm is neat: "mother versus father" means "Nature versus State", with God firmly on the side of State, justifying the revenger in the end. Nature has her own logic, but it is "hierarchically inferior"[6] to the logic which demands that Horestes seek revenge. She is subordinate, subsidiary and complementary to the "justice" dominant on the stage.

By subordinating nature to politics, and by eliminating the vivid presentation of the maternal body, Pickering gains safe generalization, which is the only way to give an unconditional justification of Horestes' action. He avoids facing the double-sided nature of Horestes' problem, the vexing aporia of being, at one and the same time, a subject and a child to her whom he has to kill. That is how Pickering sets himself free to concentrate on the legal question of deposing a monarch.

*

Pickering's Horestes calls his mother "thadulltres [sic] dame", who is "not contented her spousaule bed to fyll / With forrayne love, but sought also my fatal thred to share / As, erst before, my fathers fyll in sonder she dyd pare" (175-8). Note his complaint about his interrupted succession to the throne; adultery is condemned since it disturbs the male line of inheritance.

Sexuality, particularly female sexuality, becomes, therefore, something which should be put under firm control within the marriage system. Female sexuality was, indeed, a constant source of male anxiety, providing a fear that it might at any moment slip beyond control, producing children to threaten men as patriarch or heir. Sex has to be safely placed "under God's commandments to be fruitful and multiply and avoid illicit fornication."[7]

In Pickering's binary opposition—"mother versus father" means "nature versus law of god and man"—the crucial point is whether motherhood can be considered as "natural" at all. Is the mother not rather a composing element of the social system of marriage? Is a "loving mother" not an invented image, a myth, in order to keep the patriarchal system stable? St. Paul tells us: ". . . Adam was not deceived, but the woman was deceived and became a transgressor. Yet woman will be saved through bearing of children, if she continues in faith and love and holiness, with modesty."[8] Woman as a daughter of Eve is a corrupt creature, even more corrupt and vulnerable to temptation than man. Yet motherhood, in particular the Virgin Mary, blesses womankind and purifies a child from being the mere fruit of the sexual intercourse of its parents.

This inevitably reminds one of Elizabeth I, who claimed herself to be a "virgin mother" of her people:

> To conclude, I am already bound unto an Husband, which is the Kingdom of England, and that may suffice you. . . . And reproch mee no more, (quoth shee) that I haue no children: for euery one of you, and as many as are English, are my Children, and Kinsfolkes.[9]

Nevertheless, there was no way for Elizabeth to evade the problem of succession, given the fact that she had no children of her own. It is impossible to de-sexualize the mother completely, for her role in the family system is inevitably connected to procreation.

Interestingly, Goldberg points out that Mary Stuart, the Renaissance Clytemnestra, repeatedly exaggerated her maternal love to her young son James.

> Although the king and his mother had been separated when he was ten months old and never saw each other again, Mary preserved the show of a sentimental attachment to her son. . . . During their twenty-year separation she continued writing to him as if the narrow thread that bound them together had not been untied. Yet he was king because she was not queen and the throne of Elizabeth would be his if it were not hers. During her last years, he was corresponding with Elizabeth and had broken off communication with his mother. . . . James had replace his mother with Elizabeth; angling for her inheritance, he sacrificed his mother for it.[10]

In a sense, James was shrewd enough to split the mother in two, namely, the "real" one who gave birth to him and the "ideal" one who assures his position in this world. He took these two aspects from two mothers,

Mary and Elizabeth respectively.[11]

The happy ending of Pickering's interlude is, in short, far-fetched. It hardly provides a convincing resolution to the ancient dilemma. Yet it is remarkable that this play did foreshadow what would happen to the throne of England a few decades later.

Goffe's *The Tragedy of Orestes*

Little is known about the author of *The Tragedy of Orestes*, either. The play is said to have been performed at Christ Church, Oxford, where Goffe was actively involved in drama as a student. Later he became a clergyman and married the widow of his predecessor, who turned out to be "a meer *Xantippe*", and "his Life being much shortned [sic] thereby, [he] died at length in a manner of heart-broken", in 1629, at the age of thirty-seven or eight.[12] The dates when *Orestes* was written and first performed are also uncertain,[13] but it seems safe to say that *Orestes* is contemporaneous with *The Duchess of Malfi* (c.1614) and *Women Beware Women* (c.1621).

Orestes begins with the triumphant return of Agamemnon from Troy. He is greeted by Orestes, already an adult, unlike his counterpart in the classical sources. When his father is found killed, Orestes flees the court with his cousin Pylades, and is told of the identity of the murderers by the witch Canidia. The two friends return to the court disguised as physicians, deceive Clytemnestra and Aegisthus by feigning to give them some medical treatment, and kill them together with their new-born son. Orestes, however, fails in his claim to the throne, is banished, and becomes deranged. Finally he and Pylades die by each other's swords.

The number of borrowings in this play, particularly from Seneca, is enormous. The structure and speech in the scene of Agamemnon's death are obviously inspired by the equivalent scene in Seneca, and there are continual echoes of Stoicism throughout the play. In addition, O'Donnell points out that although the contemporary amateur playwrights in Oxford had only "lofty contempt" for and "pedantic hostility" towards the popular theatre, Goffe did not share this attitude.[14] *The Tragedy of Orestes* also owes much to *Antonio's Revenge* (for the ghost and the infanticide scenes), to *Hamlet* and *The Revenger's Tragedy* (for the skull scene), perhaps even to *Macbeth* or other witch plays. His Orestes' boasting, "Reuenge is lost, vnlesse we doe exceed" (3. 4. 93), is typical of the spirit of Kydian heroes. Above all, the protagonist's ruin by his own hand clearly distinguishes this play both from Greek drama, in which

Orestes is ultimately forgiven and saved in one way or another, and from Seneca's tragedies, in which the murderers go triumphantly free without punishment.

One remarkable point about Goffe's tragedy is that the father, King Agamemnon, is an omnipresent and dominant figure throughout the course of events, a stark contrast to his total absence from Pickering's interlude.

*

In his speech at the beginning of the play, Agamemnon addresses his land as if it were his bride—just as another absolutist monarch, James I, did in his call for union with Scotland.

> *Agamemnon*:
> Now a faire blessing blesse my dearest earth,
> And like a Bride adorne thy royall brow,
> With fruits rich Garland; a new married Bride
> Vnto thy King and Husband, who too long
> Hath left thee widdowed . . .   (1. 1. 1-5)

Compare James's famous statement: "I am the Husband and all the whole Isle is my wife."[15] It should be noted here that his famous doctrine of the Divine Right was essentially founded on the symbolical equation of father/king/god.

> The State of MONARCHIE is the supremest vpon earth; For Kings are not only GODS Lieutenants vpon earth, and sit vpon GODS throne, but euen by GOD himself they are called GODS . . . . In the Scriptures Kings are called GODS, and so their power after a certain relation compared to the Diuine power. Kings are also compared to Fathers of families: for a King is trewly Parens Patriae . . . .[16]

This employing of family metaphors is typical of patriarchism, and sounds rather less inventive than Elizabeth's self-representation as a bride and mother of her people. James' strategy here was to claim the title of "natural" father of the people, whose patriarchal power over them was given by God and hence secured as "natural." Here one can see the opposition between nature and state, on which Pickering, and even the Greek poets, constructed their drama concerning Orestes'

Theories of Nature and Political Legitimation

matricide, dissolved into the figure of the "father-king." By emphasizing the "natural" bonds between monarch and subject, James has "nature" support his political authority rather than opposing it to the state.

Let us look further at why the power endowed by God can be regarded as "natural." There was a conflict between roughly two kinds of thinking at that time, namely, Augustinianism and Aristoteleanism. The former condemned human nature as corrupt, while the latter maintained, interpreting the pagan sage in Christian terms, that God had given reason to everyone, and called its precepts the law of nature. It was also held that "the law of nature, upon which civil government was based, was a part of God's law and as such was compatible with the teaching of Christianity and with the authority of the church."[17]

Here one can see two contrary notions of nature: corrupt and godly. This contradiction, or rather, this instability in the definition of nature, was not only the point at issue in the religio-political controversy of the time, but also threatened King James's claim as a "natural" father of the state—which was based on the notion of nature as "god-given." The Puritan emphasis on the corruption of human nature was always at odds with the elevated notion of nature, a notion on which the monarch's metaphor depended.

Given such an unstable notion of nature, the danger that one might forge a definition of nature to suit one's own convenience was always there. Thus it is significant that Goffe's Agamemnon is murdered so miserably. As a father king, he should have been protected by the doctrine of Divine Right, which condemns the resistance of subjects to their monarch, to say nothing of regicide.[18] Moreover, the "skull" scene, much abused as being derivative, comes to have another implication rather than simply being a mere imitation of the equivalent scenes in *Hamlet* (5. 1) and *The Revenger's Tragedy* (1. 1).

> *Orestes:*
> Where be these Princely eyes, commanding face,
> The braue Maiesticke looke, the Kingly grace,
> Wher's the imperious frowne, the Godlike smile,
> The gracefull tongue, that spoke a soldiers stile?
> Ha, ha, worms eate them . . .
> . . . O, I remember, here
> Ran the strong sinews, 'twixt his knitting ioynts,
> Here to this bone was ioyn'd his Princely arme,
> Here stood the hand that bare his warlike shield,

> And on this little ioint was place't the head,
> That *Atlas*-like bare vp the weight of Greece,
> Here, here betwixt these hollow yawning iaws
> Stood once a tongue, which with one little word
> Could haue commanded thousand souls to death.... (3. 4. 9-13, 50-58)

This minute, typically Senecan description of the bones[19] utterly runs against the mystification of the king's body, and dissolves all the majestic images into a mere heap of skeleton.

*

Yet Agamemnon has to be idealised as a perfect king—although less a good ruler than a triumphant conqueror—if his demand for revenge is to have absolute authority over his son. Goffe's Agamemnon is elevated as a noble figure, "a deare, deare father, / A King, a braue old King, a noble souldier" (3. 3. 16-7). Orestes is overjoyed at his father's return from Troy:[20]

> *Orestes*:
> ... those syluer hayres,
> Which Time hath crown'd my Fathers brow withall,
> Doe shine within mine eyes, and like the Sunne,
> Extract all drossy vapors from my soule   (1. 3. 4-7)

In his son's eyes, Agamemnon almost becomes free from any human weakness—quite unlike Aeschylus' King, who cannot resist the hubris of walking down the royal carpet to show off his triumphant return from Troy (Aeschylus, *Agamemnon*, 897-976); or Seneca's, who has only a small number of unimpressive lines which seem merely intended to show his blindness towards his fate (Seneca, *Agamemnon*, 782-807).

In order to "purify" his father, Goffe's prince directs all criticism at his mother.[21] He calls her "that *Hiena*," and declares: "No more my mother, I abiure the name, / She did not bring me forth, I know she did not" (3. 4. 43, 44-45). Moreover, Goffe refers to Clytemnestra's sensuality over and over again, turning her into a sexually frustrated wife who detests her aged husband. She scornfully says of him:

> *Clytemnestra*:
> Could the old dry bon'd dotard euer dreame,
> Now he had drawn forth all his strength abroad,

> He could be welcome to lye bedred here
> And supple his numbe ioynts in my fresh armes?   (1. 4. 22-25)

The contrast between Agamemnon's old age and Clytemnestra's youth is repeatedly stressed in this play, an aspect which does not appear in the classic tragedies and therefore is obviously Goffe's invention.

Ironically, however, once Orestes begins to suspect his mother's chastity, his belief in his role as revenger is shaken to its roots. The mother's sexuality "threatens," to borrow Adelman's phrase, "to annihilate the distinction between the fathers [i.e. the "true" father and the "false" one(s)] and hence problematizes the son's paternal identification."[22] The sexualized maternal body begins to disturb the son's idealization of the father. In fact, of course, the son can never "abiure [the mother's] name," while the mother is in a position of being able to deprive the son of the "true" father with one word of disproof of parentage.

It is difficult not to observe how Goffe's Orestes' desperate attempt to set up the binary opposition of "mother versus father" collapses.

> *Clytemnestra*:
> Why sonne, whose death is it thou dost reuenge?
> Thy fathers? but on whom? vpon thy mother!
> On her which brought thee forth, which took most care,
> To bring thee vp, from whom thou tookst thy selfe,
> Thou'rt sure thou art mine, but dost not know,
> Who twas begat thee.
>   *Orestes*:   Wil't Bastardize me?
> Yes, mother, yes, I know I was his sonne:
> Alas! why, what are you? a senselesse peece;
> Of rotten earth can doe as much to come,
> As you to me, beare it, and bring it forth,
> But *Agamemnon* he that seed did sow,
> And onely vnto him my selfe I owe:
> And for him thou shalt die.   (5. 7. 115-27)

This logic is obviously inspired by that of Apollo in the trial scene in Aeschylus' *Eumenides*, who, arguing for Orestes, presents the case for domination of patrilinear over matrilinear inheritance.[23] Nevertheless, a slight alteration radically subverts the whole argument: Orestes, however desperately he tries, cannot really prove that Agamemnon begot him. This is another example of the Renaissance obsession that there is actually no way to know who the father of a child is.[24] The mother is a menacing presence who, claiming that she alone is the true origin of the child, can "bastardize" him and deprive him of the ideal father, whom he depends upon as a model to construct his identity.

The Tragedy of Orestes might be "the queerest hotch-potch";[25] or "a curiosity rather than masterpiece," "an astonishing loose-leaf collection of scenes."[26] Nevertheless, its incoherence as a play is all the more important, since it discloses the very incoherence of Jacobean ideologies.

*

It is understandable that the myth of Orestes, in which the problem of regicide is inextricably linked with that of kin-murder, attracted attention during a period when the metaphor of the family was often employed in considering royal affairs. The crucial point was the notion of nature, which was molded to suit the dominant ideology. Sometimes it was subordinated to the state; at other times it was exploited in order to justify and mystify the power of the monarch.

Undergoing such frequent and arbitrary modification, however, the notion of nature remained unstable, and thus threatened to undermine those ideologies it was deployed to support. The incoherence and distortion in the two revenge plays we have looked at are not (merely) due to a lack of skill on the part of the playwrights. They are also a result of the fact that the ideological frameworks within which the plays were written were themselves incoherent and distorted. And one should also add here that it is not only a matter of absolutism in the sixteenth and seventeenth centuries. The systematic exploitation of theories of nature is indeed still at work today, legitimating authority in the name of nature.

Notes

1. There seems to have been a play titled *Agamemnon* written by Chettle and Dekker (1599), which may be identical with *Orestes Furens* (or *Orestes Furious*, or *Orestes' Furies*) by the same authors in the same year. An anonymous play *Agamemnon and Ulysses* is also on the record (1585), and a playwright named Cosmo Manuche wrote an uncompleted manuscript *Agamemnon* after the closure of the theatres (published in 1665). All of these plays are now lost, except Manuche's fragment. See E. K. Chambers, *The Elizabethan Stage* (4 vols. Ox-

ford: Clarendon Press, 1925); Gerald Eades Bentley, *The Jacobean and Caroline Stage: Plays and Playwrights*, Vol. IV (Oxford: Clarendon Press, 1956); Alfred Harbage, *Annals of English Drama 975-1700*, rev. by S. Schoenbaum, 2nd ed. (London: Methuen, 1964); A. W. Pollard and G. R. Redgrave, *A Short-title Catalogue of Books Printed in England, Scotland, and Ireland and of English Books Printed Abroad: 1475-1640*, rev. by W. A. Jackson, F. S. Ferguson and K. F Pantzer, 2nd ed. (London: The Bibliographical Society, 1976-1991).

2. The texts used here are: Marie Axton ed. *Three Tudor Classical Interludes: Thersites, Jacke Jugeler, Horestes* (Cambridge: D. S. Brewer, 1982), and Norbert F. O'Donnell, "*The Tragedy of Orestes* by Thomas Goffe: A Critical Edition," unpubl. diss. Ohio State University, 1950.

3. James E. Phillips, "A Revaluation of *Horestes* (1567)," *Huntington Library Quarterly*, 18 (1955): 230.

4. Aeschylus, *The Oresteia (Agamemnon / The Libation Bearers / The Eumenides)*, trans. by Robert Fagles (1975. New York: Penguin Books, 1979), pp. 883-5.

5. Euripides, *Medea and Other Plays*, trans. by Philip Vellacott (London: Penguin Books, 1963), 1206-9.

6. Robert S. Knapp, "*Horestes*: The Uses of Revenge," *English Literary History*, 40 (1973): 218.

7. Steven Ozment, *When Fathers Ruled: Family Life in Reformation Europe* (Cambridge, Mass.: Harvard University Press, 1983), p. 11.

8. 1 Timothy 2:14-15. Revised Standard Version, from *Eight Translation New Testament* (Wheaton, Illinois: Tyndale House Publishers Inc., 1974), p. 1511.

9. William Camden, *Annales Rerum Anglicarum: The History of the Most Renowned and Victorious Princess Elizabeth, Late Queen of England* (Selected Chapters), 4th ed. Wallace T. MacCaffrey ed. (Chicago: University of Chicago Press, 1970), p. 28.

10. Jonathan Goldberg, *James I and the Politics of Literature: Jonson, Shakespeare, Donne, and Their Contemporaries* (Stanford: Stanford University Press, 1989), pp. 14-16.

11. This division reminds us of the Elizabethan theory of the monarch's two bodies, the body natural and the body politic.

12. Bentley, p. 498.

13. Bentley rejects Schelling's dating of 1623 (*Elizabethan Drama*, ii. 45) as unsupported by evidence, and suggests instead that it must have been written between 1613, when Goffe took his bachelor's degree, and 1618, when his *The Courageous Turk* was written; for this Turk play was his third one, and since Goffe's prologue to *Orestes* implies its immaturity, it is supposed to be either his first or second work. Bentley also states that "Goffe's contemporary reputation was greater than has been commonly recognized", showing the playwight's name often compared to that of Beaumont, Fletcher, Massinger, Dekker, Jonson, Webster, even Shakespeare, or Euripides and Sophocles.

14. See O'Donnell, Introduction.

15. *The Political Works of James I*, rpt. from the edition of 1616, ed. by Charles Howard McIlwain (1918. New York: Russell and Russell, 1965), p. 272.

16. *The Political Works of James I*, p. 307.

17. J. P. Sommerville, *Politics and Ideology in England 1603-1640* (London: Longman, 1986), p. 14.

18. Here is another example: as Orestes never stops lamenting over his dead father, his uncle Strophius tries to console him.

> *Strophius*:
> Yet all thi's but a man; Therefore must die:
> . . .
> His booke of life the Fates had ouer-read,
> And turn'd the leafe where his last period stood.
> Now an immortall wreath circles his brow,
> And makes him King in heauen, who was before
> At most a God on earth; Hence difference springs,
> Kings are earths Gods, and Gods are heauenly Kings.
> (II. iii. 15, 17-22)

Agamemnon died, but as a king, he was once an earthly god, so he was indeed more than an ordinary man; yet he could not escape from the death anyway. Trying to mystify the monarch's body, Strophius unwittingly betrays the contradiction.

19. Its almost absurd grotesqueness reminds us, for example, of the last scene of Seneca's *Phaedra*, where Theseus tries to assemble the torn limbs of his dead son:

> *Theseus*:
> . . . Trembling hands, be firm
> For this sad service; cheeks, dry up your tears!
> Here is a father building, limb by limb,
> A body for his son . . . . Here is a piece,
> Misshapen, horrible, each side of it
> Injured and torn. What part of you it is
> I cannot tell, but it is part of you.
> . . . Was this
> The face that shone as brightly as a star,
> The face that turned all enemies' eyes aside?

Seneca, *Four Tragedies and Octavia*, trans. by E. F. Watling (London: Penguin Books, 1966), 1260-66, 1268-70.

20. There is of course an unmistakable similarity between this passage and Hamlet's "So excellent a king, that was to this / Hyperion to a satyr" (1. 2. 137-40.)

21. Clytemnestra's lover Aegisthus does not seem the main target of Goffe's Orestes' accusation, but a mere garnish to her crime.

22. Janet Adelman, *Suffocating Mothers: Fantasies of Maternal Origin in Shakespeare's Plays, Hamlet to The Tempest* (New York: Routledge, 1992), p. 14.

23. *Apollo*:
> The woman you call the mother of the child

> is not the parent, just a nurse to the seed,
> the new-sown seed that grows and swells inside her.
> The man is the source of life—the one who mounts.
> She, like a stranger for a stranger, keeps
> the shoot alive unless god hurts the roots.   (666-671)

24. For example,

> *Don Pedro* I think this is your daughter.
> *Leonarto* Her mother hath many times told me so.
>   (*Much Ado About Nothing*, 1. 1. 99-100)

> *Prospero* Thy mother was a piece of virtue, and
> She said thou wast my daughter; . . .
>   (*The Tempest*, 1. 2. 56-7)

25. F. L. Lucas, *Euripides and His Influence* (New York: Cooper Square Publishers, 1963), p. 100.

26. O'Donnell, pp. xxviii, cxiv-cxv.

The First and the Second Parts of Henry IV: Some Thoughts on the Origins of Shakespearean Gentleness

SHIGEKI TAKADA

IT WOULD GO without saying that the most important thing for a king is to hold his own country under firm reign. If we take kingship as a symbol of human existence in general, then the king's task would be to comprehend his situation in the manner most satisfactory to him and reform it to suit his own ideals. Moreover, if we were to regard kingship as a figure representing a dramatist, his task as "a king" would be to control his dramatic world with his own view of the theater in such a way as to thoroughly express his vision. For a king, however, the task of ruling the country will never be attained completely, no matter what means he resorts to; similarly, the will of a man or a dramatist for a totality, for a perfect mastery of his situation or a complete expression of his vision is always more or less doomed to failure.

Such an almost omnipresent issue seems to have a special thematic significance in the two parts of *Henry IV*, because Henry IV is a usurper whose kingship lacks from the outset an aura of the divine sanction bestowed upon a legitimate heir to a royal throne. This king, who lacks any semblance of legitimacy, claims to the throne by his own acts. Every one of these is exposed to the severe judgment of the people

The task imposed on Henry IV and his son, Prince Henry (Hal) may be said to be precisely the achievement of this firm rule. How do they carry it out? What do their methods of achieving this goal have in common with each other? Where do they differ? On what points can their aim be said to succeed and where do they fail? And in what sense is such a problem relevant to the concerns of Shakespeare the dramatist? The latter half of the 1590s when the second tetralogy of which these two plays are the central parts was written was the period in which the Lord Chamberlain's Men gradually exceeded and eclipsed the Lord

Admiral's Men. It was also the time when Shakespeare went on to establish his position unshakably within the company. The task of a literal "king" in the plays is thus subtly connected with that of "a king" as a central being in the dramatic company, and at the same time it draws our attention persistently and disturbingly to the universal issue of how human beings grapple with their situations.

The prince expresses his plan early in *The First Part*:

> I know you all, and will awhile uphold
> The unyok'd humour of your idleness.
> Yet herein will I imitate the sun,
> Who doth permit the base contagious clouds
> To smother up his beauty from the world,
> That, when he please again to be himself,
> Being wanted he may be more wonder'd at
> By breaking through the foul and ugly mists
> Of vapours that did seem to strangle him.
> If all the year were playing holidays,
> To sport would be as tedious as to work;
> But when they seldom come, they wish'd-for come,
> And nothing pleaseth but rare accidents:
> So when this loose behaviour I throw off,
> And pay the debt I never promised,
> By how much better than my word I am,
> By so much shall I falsify men's hopes;
> And like bright metal on a sullen ground,
> My reformation, glitt'ring o'er my fault,
> Shall show more goodly, and attract more eyes
> Than that which hath no foil to set it off.
> I'll so offend, to make offence a skill,
> Redeeming time when men think least I will.   (1. 2. 190-212)[1]

However prodigal and dissolute he seems now, his behavior is a strategy for setting off his reformation and for heightening people's applause for his proper reign later.

Indeed, the prince's sense of his goal provides a framework for the two parts of the play as a whole; it directs the response of the audience, and gives a meaning to every act of the prince as a step towards this goal.

He shares this methodology to a large extent with his father, King Henry IV, who, ironically enough, keeps complaining about his son's behavior. In fact, the lesson he gives to his son in Act 3 Scene 2 is based on an idea so similar to the prince's that it looks like a variation of the plan expressed in his soliloquy:

> By being seldom seen, I could not stir
> But like a comet I was wonder'd at,
> That men would tell their children, "This is he!"
> Others would say "Where, which is Bolingbroke?"
> And then I stole all courtesy from heaven,
> And dress'd myself in such humility
> That I did pluck allegiance from men's hearts,
> Loud shouts and salutations from their mouths,
> Even in the presence of the crowned King.
> My presence, like a robe pontifical,
> Ne'er seen but wonder'd at, and so my state,
> Seldom, but sumptuous, show'd like a feast,
> And won by rareness such solemnity. (3. 2. 46-59)

Royal majesty as a theatrical act performed with utmost care for its effects on the onlookers is a way of being they characteristically developed out of necessity to compensate for a perceived lack of "substance" in their claim to the throne.

Although the prince's prodigality always hides such an intention, it would be too facile to think he dissipates himself only for this purpose. His conversation with the drowsy-eyed Falstaff makes a sharp contrast with the strained negotiations between the king and Hotspur and his friends in the previous scene.

> *Falstaff* Now, Hal, what time of day is it, lad?
> *Prince* Thou art so fat-witted with drinking of old sack, and unbuttoning thee after supper, and sleeping upon benches after noon, that thou hast forgotten to demand that truly which thou wouldst truly know. What a devil hast thou to do with the time of the day? Unless hours were cups of sack, and minutes capons, and clocks the tongues of bawds, and dials the signs of leaping-houses, and the blessed sun himself a fair hot wench in flame coloured taffeta, I see no reason why thou shouldst be so superfluous to demand the time of the day. (1. 2. 1-12)

There seem to be two sorts of time in *Henry IV*: historical time that advances ruthlessly towards a goal, and festive time in which there seems to be no change. The Falstaff of *The First Part* embodies the latter, and the prince, who is always conscious of historical time, is somehow able to move in and out of this festive time freely. What enlivens the world of *The First Part* is precisely such a mode of existence.

Falstaff's way of being owes a lot to the tradition of fools and festivity from the Middle Ages. If we examine them in detail there seems to be some essential difference between the two, but it cannot be denied that Falstaff embodies the tough tenacity of traditional fools as shown in, for example, the fact that he is driven to various kinds of 'predicaments' and always finds some ways out of them through his subterfuges. When, after robbing on the highway, he himself is robbed by Hal and Poince in disguise, he flees, and later he makes up a lie to Hal on how he fought upon the occasion. And, when given the lie, he retorts unashamedly that he knew all along that it was the prince and fled so that he would not injure him. Falstaff in these episodes reminds us of medieval fantastic bragging, and this is one of the major reasons for the long and wide popularity of these plays.

Such an atmosphere, however, also owes much to the way of being of Prince Hal. The prince and Hotspur are often compared long before the direct confrontation between the two on the battlefield, and the king himself complains that, in contrast to the reliability of Hotspur, his son's conduct is deplorable. But the audience's evaluation of them is somewhat different. This is partly due to the fact that Hal expresses his intentions in the monologue quoted above. But it also seems to owe much to the difference in attitude the two show to the lies and boasting of Falstaff and Owen Glendower. While the prince takes his license with Falstaff as a means towards his final aim of dramatic reformation and knows Falstaff's words to be blatant lies—and, for that matter, Falstaff also knows only too well that the prince does not believe his words—and yet the prince has magnanimity to enjoy these words and foolery for their own sake, Hotspur unnecessarily refutes each of Glendower's boastings and hurts his feelings. And his conduct leads indirectly to the accident that Glendower refuses to muster his soldiers on a pretext of sickness.

This striking contrast between their attitudes to others suggests how the part of the world which Hotspur can grasp and rule is actually rather small, while, on the other hand, it highlights the prince's generous disposition befitting to a king. The prince succeeds in captivating the audience and "ruling" it psychologically, not by his subtle stage-management as he intends, but by the magnanimity he shows in pursuing a goal closely connected to performance and stage-management.

Moreover, at the moment when his real value as the Prince of Wales is questioned he never forgets to carry out his role in a perfect manner. On the battlefield, Hal challenges Hotspur to single combat, praising the other's military exploits, in order to avoid the unnecessary bloodshed of many soldiers. This challenge is not accepted because Worcester, the envoy from the rebels, does not report it for reasons of self-interest and the battle breaks out. There the prince shows admirable bravery, and shields his father, who is about to be overpowered by Archibald, Earl of Douglas, and this serves to clear from his name the stigma of an unworthy son. By fighting with Hotspur and defeating him, he deprives Hotspur of the title of a brave warrior which Hotspur has laid exclusive claim to until then, and succeeds in ensuring symbolically the victory of his side and establishing the basis of the subjugation of the land.

Furthermore, at such a critical time, he firmly sets aside his usual foolery: he does not here accept Falstaff's joke when he appears with a bottle of sack on his side instead of a sword or pistol. Yet, when, after the battle is settled, Falstaff appears with the body of Hotspur, which he found already dead and stabbed anew, and, declaring it as his feat, asks for some reward, Hal tells him to declare it afterwards and thus again shows his generosity in accepting a joke.

Here we can still see the festive time within the relentlessly advancing historical time. In the subtle and precarious balance between the two times, we may note one achievement of *The First Part*, and we can also identify it as a "provisional" answer the prince gives to the task he inherits from his father. But these two ways of being are, as a matter of course, essentially incompatible with and are always prone to undermine and nullify each other.

The outrages of Falstaff and his friends, whose social harmfulness was, in the case of the robbery in Act 2, canceled by the prince's promise to return the money with interest later, begin to threaten the social order more substantially in the latter half of the play. Each of the acts of Falstaff, who takes the bribes from young men from wealthy families and exempts them from military service bringing instead useless vagabonds to the battlefield as "food for powder," or lies on the ground in the battlefield pretending to be dead and saves his life without fighting at all, is a serious threat to social order and justice.

Such a "transformation" of Falstaff is closely related to the change of the whole world of the play, especially the prince's way of being. Indeed, as the action develops, the social and political roles Hal must play become more and more realistic in relation to the changing circumstances such as the rising of the rebels, the actual battle and the illness of the king. In these circumstances Falstaff's ruffianism is tolerated in narrower and narrower terms.

While the rebellion as a real threat does not actually impress the audience as substantially harmful except as a worry that distresses the sickly king, the accomplishment of *The First Part*—the comparatively free coming and going between the worlds of politics and play, and the magnanimity of the prince as a human being and therefore as a future king there presented—threatens to break down eventually due to its own implicit contradiction and is handed over to *The Second Part*.

*

The failure of balance implied in *The First Part* is revealed as an irrefutable fact in *The Second Part*. One of the major themes developed through *The Second Part* is "aging": there are full descriptions of literal aging, but age also symbolizes losses that the passage of time unavoidably brings about. This theme becomes obvious as early as the confrontation between Falstaff and the Lord Chief Justice in Act 1 Scene 2. Trying to baffle the Lord, who insists on scolding him, Falstaff is severely and sarcastically talked down by the other.

> *Falstaff* You that are old consider not the capacities of us that are young; you do measure the heat of our livers with the bitterness of your galls; and we that are in the vaward of our youth, I must confess, are wags too.
> *Chief Justice* Do you set down your name in the scroll of youth, that are written down old with all the characters of age? Have you not a moist eye, a dry hand, a yellow cheek, a white beard, a decreasing leg, an increasing belly? (. . .) And will you yet call yourself young? Fie, fie, fie, Sir John!   (1. 2. 172-85)

Indeed, Falstaff's hardships are not limited to his negotiations with the Lord Chief Justice and others who view him more objectively and coldly from the outside; some privations force him to self-awareness from the inside. Left alone, he swears from the pain of the pox and the gout. Though he makes shows of courage, saying "'Tis no matter if I do halt; I have the wars for my color, and my pension shall seem the more reasonable. A good wit will make use of anything. I will turn the diseases to commodities," his actions fail to show that vigor we saw in him in *The First Part*.

As the action of the play advances, this theme of "aging" gradually covers the whole world of the play, through many variations. In the scene of his festivity with Doll, his favorite whore at the inn of Hostess Quickly in Act 2 Scene 4, the shadow of death is glimpsed even in this temporary gaiety.

> *Doll* Thou whoreson little tidy Bartholomew boar-pig, when wilt thou leave fighting a-days, and foining a-nights, and begin to patch up thine old body for heaven?
> *Falstaff* Peace, good Doll, do not speak like a death's-head; do not bid me remember mine end (. . .) I am old, I am old (. . .) A merry song! Come, it grows late, we'll to bed. Thou'lt forget me when I am gone.
> (2. 4. 227-74)

The fleeting merriment, all the dearer because it is tinged with such a shadow, reminds us, however, of the depth of the night's approaching darkness and, like a negative picture of the license of the days when they enjoyed life more straightforwardly, gives us a smarting impression that the feast is coming to an end or, rather, has already ended.

The theme of "aging" is presented even more clearly in the negotiations between Falstaff and Justice Shallow and his friends in Gloucestershire. The words of the old judges, who indulge themselves in thinking fondly of their reckless youth impress us less with the energy and vigor they were once filled with than the decrepit senility of those who have nothing to do but miss the things they lost long ago, and thus sound like a variation on the general theme of aging and loss. Seeing the state of his old schoolmates, Falstaff, who assumes himself to be young and tough, goes out of his way to return to the village after the end of the battle, intending to dupe them. But he too soon gives himself over to their hospitality; hearing the king has died, he believes that, as his Hal becomes the new king, he will get a high post in the new government, and, thinking that he can also appoint these old friends to good positions by way of payment for a debt, he brings them to London with him. Needless to say, this expectation is cruelly shattered, but Falstaff's expulsion itself is a settled matter from the outset from the audience's viewpoint, and what is more impressive is Falstaff's misrecognition of political reality, which sets off his piteous decrepitude.

But, as I suggested above, such "aging" is not limited to the literal age of an old man or those around him, but is inseparably related to and reflects the transformation of the play's entire world and especially the change of Prince Hal and the deep sense of loss it would have caused in him.

The reformation of the prince which has been planned from *The First Part* becomes more and more urgent in accordance with the changes of circumstance such as the worsening of the king's illness. The compatibility between historical time regulated by the political role and the time of festivity and license becomes more and more difficult to sustain. In fact, except for the scene of renunciation and expulsion on the way to the coronation, the prince only shares the stage with Falstaff for one moment in all of *The Second Part*: Act 2 Scene 4, when the prince teases Falstaff in the inn. And even here, when a messenger from the court appears to call for him, he immediately leaves Falstaff without hesitation.

The prince, who comes to court at the report of a sudden turn of the king's condition for the worse, contemplates his father's deadly sleep and determines to take the crown and do his best to keep it and hand it down to his posterity—even as he recognizes the restless cares it will impose on him (Act 4 Scene 5). Thus he identifies his whole being with the role and the responsibilities of a king. Apart from this address to the crown and the short words of curse he refers to in his apology to the king for taking away the crown while he slept, he never expresses his mind even to the audience as to what inner sacrifices it would force on him.

The play, however, illuminates the price of this political choice from another angle. Being driven by a great military disadvantage, the rebelling noblemen accept the offer of peace by Prince John, the Duke of Lancaster and disband their army on his assurance that the king will hear their complaints and will correct what should be corrected. But immediately after they are all arrested and sentenced to death, and their disarmed soldiers are also pursued and put down by the king's army. The Duke of Lancaster's words to the rebels that it was their shallow inadvertence to assume their own exculpation and pardon were included in the conditions for peace cannot help but give the audience an impression of cruelty and deception. But the principle of the Establishment with which he identifies wholeheartedly depends on such violent force of exclusion. However ruthless it may look, it is ultimately unavoidable that the state should rely on such a force if it is to be kept in order.

According to this logic, the banishment of Falstaff by the prince is quite natural and beyond question. But in the prince the audience has enjoyed their prospect of a king who would surpass the mere efficiency of a governor: unlike the chief justice and Lancaster, who have no doubts about their roles as Establishment watchdogs, the prince has kept a subtle balance between the political world around the court and the marginal world of playing and ruffianism. So this banishment seems to the audience to be too heartless a treatment, which in turn suggests some inner sacrifice has been forced on the new king.

If the audience understands on the level of politics or government that the banishment of Falstaff is necessary—no spectator would admit his bribe-taking or swindling in everyday life—yet still feels a sort of discontent or regret—as it must do—this suggests the ambivalent relationship between politics and "culture" in a narrow sense: a relationship in which the two depend on and yet try to keep a distance from each other.

One of the *topoi* that represent this ambivalence of the culture that is critical and, as it were, marginal to the political world on one hand and yet depends on it and even supports its central ideologies on the other is the playhouse.[2] Indeed, it is misleading to think in binary terms, of politics and culture, or the authorities and the theater. In the Elizabethan Age, as in many other periods, the relationship between the theater and the authorities is always complex and delicate, but is even more complicated and difficult to grasp because of the distinctively theatrical character of Elizabethan politics. Drama represents politics and defines and establishes itself through politics, and, at the same time, politics gropes for its own appropriate state and expresses itself through drama. Apparent relations like protections and regulations or compliments and satires are no more than the remains of such an intermingled process of mutual regulation and constitution after its articulations and differentiations.

In the two parts of *Henry IV*, Shakespeare has brought to the surface this mutually constitutive relationship between politics and culture, by way of the actions of Prince Hal and the audience's response to them; at the same time, he seems to be trying to ensure his status as a dramatist and make it firmer in the course of writing.[3] Let us consider these circumstances by examining the problem of "Falstaff's banishment" from a different viewpoint.

Some have supposed that in the first performances of these plays the part of Falstaff may have been played by William Kempe, one of the share-holding actors in the Lord Chamberlain's Men and a representative stage clown of the 1590s. But we cannot accept this opinion readily, since the role of Falstaff requires subtle nuances of sorrow and melancholy and does not seem to fit very well Kempe's reputation for vigorous and energetic performances, for his jigs, and extemporal wit.[4] What seems to be of more interest here is what might be called an inner parallel between the banishment of Falstaff in *Henry IV* and Kempe's retirement from the Lord Chamberlain's Men a few years after the first performances of the plays.

Henry IV and Prince Hal's ideas of staging themselves as kings are conceived in theatrical terms. The prince's reformation is received with surprise and admiration by his brothers and the Lord Chief Justice, and so his play, setting this reformation at its climax, may be said to have been successful to this extent. This success, however, does not look so great to the audience. As we have seen before, what made the prince so dear to the audience of the play was not his calculating sense of purpose but the liveliness he shows in his relations with Falstaff. True, in order to be a politically competent king, he must finally have done with them, yet this is also a matter for regret. Political success thus achieved, indispensable as it is, cannot be a fully satisfactory answer to a desire to "rule" completely over the world around him, a desire perhaps not made fully conscious and yet all the more insuppressible. In this sense, the success of his performance can be said to be built on the giving up of a greater success.

Shakespeare has often been admired as "myriad-minded," as the "poet of nature," or of "negative capability." There would be few objections to the view that these words are lauding his distinctive dramaturgical ability to dramatize various kinds of personalities very naturally and put them into his plays in an unlabored manner. Indeed, no other Renaissance dramatists described so many kinds of people in so lively a fashion. But I think the vigor and liveliness of these people in his plays are essentially different from the vigor as is seen, for example, in the arts of Richard Tarlton and William Kempe, who made their reputations by diverting from the plots of plays freely, and responding to the jeers and heckling from the audience with extemporal wit, producing a merry and bustling sense of unity between the stage and the ground. In Shakespeare's plays, apparently extemporal and witty words like Falstaff's are no more than what was determined by the dramatist in advance, and things like genuine extemporal wit must be excluded as the impurities which cannot but ruin the unity of the play.

It is true that the people described by him have a really lively and exuberant air as if they had just come from the actual countryside. But in the course of weaving such an element firmly into the dramatic action, Shakespeare's drama seems to have worked rather to stifle the naive and unconstrained—though crude, one may say—vigor that the theater as popular culture originally had. The university wits like Robert Greene and Thomas Nashe are usually thought to have seen themselves as a part of an elite and therefore had a warped feeling regarding the theater in the manner of self-ridiculing cheap writers, and in fact make us feel it in their works. But they seem to have been actually far more open than Shakespeare to the vulgar humors and gratuitous laughter of the people and the gay and lively vivacity surrounding the theater.

And here we cannot help but think of a similarity between Prince Hal's attitude to Falstaff and the methods with which Shakespeare assimilated popular elements into his plays. As we saw, the prince takes his association with Falstaff and others as a means to an end and still he can enjoy this intimate relation in itself. But when the occasion for a final choice visits him, he ruthlessly abandons his former companions as detestable. And seen from this vantage point, even when he seemed to take part in Falstaff's extravagances, it was only within the limit that they do not infringe upon the security of the land, and he has never missed his final aim.

Likewise, Shakespeare absorbed popular elements into his drama avidly and by this means he constructed an incomparably rich theatrical world. But these elements, which seem to be very natural at first sight and claim their own unique world without any regard to the passing of time, are actually set in almost unmovable places and bear unalterable functions in the developments of the dramatic actions, and are never allowed to upset the final "artistic" ends of plays like the explorations of the inner worlds of the persons or the inquiries into the meaning of existence.

Falstaff has been especially popular among Shakespeare's fools, and people usually think of him as a quite outstanding figure, but he seems to me to be almost wholly dependent on the prince for his existence, rather poorly autonomous in this sense. These considerations would enable us to understand why he must be so. The second half of the 1590s was, as we saw at the outset, the period when Shakespeare was establishing his dramaturgy, setting his scripts at its center, at the same time that the Lord Chamberlain's Men gradually overpowered the Lord Admiral's Men. At this critical point, in the course of describing the self-establishment of Hal as king, Shakespeare half unconsciously commits his own self-establishment as a dramatist to the figure of his hero. It would be totally out of the question for the playwright who was making utmost efforts to unite the actions of his plays organically to permit Falstaff to go too far out of the control of Hal.

Although he was to be called "our gentle Shakespeare," unlike the university wits he had not been regarded as a gentleman because he had not graduated from a university. For him, it was only through this act of writing his plays that he could establish his selfhood as a socially respectable being, in a way similar to the fact that King Henry IV and Prince Hal prove the rightness of their claim to kingship through their actions. I think Shakespeare suppressed elements of popular theater in order to produce unity of the action of his plays in spite of his deep sympathy for them because, within him, the creation of a united dramatic world was inseparably intertwined with the establishment of his social identity, while, on the other hand, the university wits were deeply committed to their acts of "writing" and yet they did not make them primary preconditions for the constitution of their selves. Surely, few university wits would have had a secure social selfhood as those of born gentlemen, either. But, though their means of self-confirmation as university graduates sometimes would have worked to their disadvantage, it seems nevertheless to have supported their minds as a sort of undoubted guarantee of their status and this gave them scope to accept popular culture as it was without any reserve. We cannot help glimpsing an ironical paradox between social background and self-identification in that Shakespeare, who was more familiar with these elements in terms of both social status and cultural background, should try to establish himself by suppressing them.

The retirement of Kempe would have to be considered in this context. We do not know for certain how Shakespeare regarded this issue. This is only a guess, but it would be understandable enough if Shakespeare should have thought that he must exclude his improvisational fooleries at any cost in order to establish his own "artistic" drama based on his scripts.[5] While he might have welcomed the retirement of this old-fashioned and now rather bothersome actor and even encouraged it, on one hand, Shakespeare must have seen off with a deep sense of regret the clown who had been his friend and great colleague, as he had learned many things from his art and assimilated it into his works. Or one might say that ever since Shakespeare began to see Kempe's art as irksome long before his retirement, he felt it so with regret. That all the prodigalities in this play are presented as what should be missed and regretted prefigures the prince's imminent reformation, but it also seems to be Shakespeare's tacit mourning of the transformations and losses that these elements go through inevitably in the course of being assimilated into his plays, or rather of the fact they can be assimilated only by being processed and transformed.

Thus Shakespeare produces a certain sense of distance from the ruthless realities of politics and by way of it he secures the place of the theater as a topos or site of the culture that is in mutual dependency and complementarity with politics, and at the same time establishes his firm rule over the playhouse and his own dramatic world.

When we take such characteristics of his plays into account, it seems quite natural that his works should have come to occupy the place of the central ideological canon within English culture in general. His dramaturgy that presents all kinds of people in so lively a fashion and yet which puts them unshakably into an unified action has a form very similar to that of the ethos of the ruling elite who want to accomplish a thorough centralized rule all over the country as a national state.

As the hidden regret which the prince is supposed to have felt at the banishment of Falstaff gives him a subtle touch of shadow and human depth lacking in the Duke of Lancaster, so Shakespeare's very sense of loss for what he could not help abandoning and rather positively stifled in the course of establishing his dramaturgy constitutes a strong motive in Shakespeare to recover what is lost again in his drama and in the vision it expresses, though only in a form restrained and controlled by the dramatic action. And, if one may speak a little ironically, his sort of ambivalent self-confidence that regrets the loss and still approves his own dramaturgy that goes on stifling it gives him a uniquely soft personality, a mask called Shakespearean gentleness. Similarly, the gesture of generosity that modern English culture likes to assume is, at least partially, backed with the sense of loss for the strange which it stifled in the course of its establishment and does not really want to restore, a sense of loss, as it were, that is enabled by its self-confident sense of its own dominance.

This firm complementary relation between culture and politics in Shakespearean drama does, however, provide an opportunity for him to get away from this relation precisely because of its establishment. In other words, having achieved his selfhood as the expression of an ambivalence between loss and confidence, Shakespeare tries to recall what has been excluded back into the "culture" in a narrow sense, the culture which is contained in the stable relationship with the political ideology that has been secured simultaneously with the achievement of that selfhood and yet seems to be independent and different in dimension from the politics, that is to say, into the drama as "art." While his sense of loss constitutes an overture to the tragedies and problem plays, his self-confidence, even insolence, the other side of the same sense of loss, insures that the exploration of the dark abyss thus revealed can be carried out under the control of his own dramaturgy. Of course, the power recalled has internalized and much amplified its destructive energy by such suppression, and sometimes overwhelms the dramatist's conscious control that has been supposedly secured and bring about unexpected tensions and ruptures in his dramatic world. But, that is another story.

Notes

1. All the quotations from *Henry the Fourth* are from A. R. Humphreys ed. *The First Part of King Henry IV,* The Arden Shakespeare, (London: Methuen, 1960) and A. R. Humphreys, ed. *The Second Part of King Henry IV,* The Arden Shakespeare, (London: Methuen, 1966).

2. As to the ambivalent role of the theater in culture, see Steven Mullaney, *The Place of the Stage: License, Play, and Power in Renaissance England* (Chicago: Univ. of Chicago Press, 1988), especially ch. 2 "The Place of the Stage."

3. As to the ways Shakespeare and Elizabethan Theater in general appropriate the political power, see the acute discussion of Stephen Greenblatt, "Invisible Bullets" in his *Shakespearean Negotiations* (Berkeley: University of California Press, 1988).

4. See, for example, David Wiles, *Shakespeare's Clown: Actor and Text in the Elizabethan Playhouse* (Cambridge: Cambridge Univ. Press, 1987).

5. I am much indebted to the late Professor Jiro Ozu's farewell lecture "Exit Kempe," now included in his *Shakespeare Writing His Last Will and Testament* (in Japanese, Tokyo: Iwanami Shoten Co. Ltd., 1989) for this point.

"Remember Saint Crispin":
Narrating the Nation in *Henry V*

Ted Motohashi

1

HOMI K. BHABHA, focusing upon the chronic instability of the binary relationships constructed in colonial discourses, insists not on the fixity of inversions and divisions between the colonizing and the colonized, between the West and the Rest, but on such psychic economy as ambivalence, disavowal, and movements of contradiction and resistance. These destabilized elements register themselves at the very moment of colonialist intervention, when the colonizing try to impose their authority upon native cultural activities. As the colonialist authority is disturbed by its own complex psyche of anxiety and ambivalence, the hybridity of colonial subjects subverts the monolithic framework that divides the inferior from the superior, through practices of acculturation in which those subjects "mimic" the colonizers. "Mimicry," creating moments not only of imitation but of menace, produces stereotypical figures of colonized others as uncanny, at once familiar and strange, the object of rejection and of fascination, as the others emerge forming a part of fetishistic fantasy based on the invention of origin, demonization of difference, and myth of an integrated whole.[1]

Bhabha utilizes these motifs in his consideration of modernity, especially of the ambivalent formation of modern nationhood as sociopolitico-cultural artefact. As in the case of the construction of colonial subjectivities, the nation, according to Bhabha, is an unstable site of contradictory and contending discourses, chronically subject to subversion and disjunction at the very moment of its attempts to contain the gaps created by the conflicting elements. "National" history or literature, as forms that narrate the mythical origin of naturalized nationhood or nationality, is invented as an authoritative imposition upon the people, who have so far not been familiar with any identity based upon the arbitrarily created pseudo-integrity of the "nation."

Benedict Anderson, to whom Bhabha refers, observes that in those pre-modern communities such as kingdoms and tribes the kinship among relatives or relationship between master and servant is extended into a larger communal sense of one-bodiedness. According to Anderson, the nation, by contrast, through the folkloric invention of national saga, the penetration of education, and publishing media based on one designated "national language," emerges as a distinct demarcated "imagined community"— "that special kind of contemporaneous community which language alone suggests," a public identification process which Anderson calls "unisonance,"—thus naturalizing a national bond tying together the people who know neither the names nor faces of each other.[2] Bhabha, however, argues that this apparently secure spatiality and temporality of the modern nation enclosed by socio-political apparatuses are also prone to ambivalence and transgression at its boundaries. The key idea Bhabha employs in this context is that of a "double narrative movement," a tension between a "pedagogical" authority and a "performative" strategy:

> The people are not simply historical events or parts of a patriotic body politic. They are also a complex rhetorical strategy of social reference: their claim to be representative provokes a crisis within the process of signification and discursive address. We then have a contested conceptual territory where the nation's people must be thought in double-time; the people are the historical "objects" of nationalist pedagogy, giving the discourse an authority that is based on the pre-given or constituted historical origin *in the past*; the people are also the "subjects" of a process of signification that must erase any prior or originary presence of the nation-people to demonstrate the prodigious, living principles of the people as contemporaneity: as that sign of the *present* through which national life is redeemed and iterated as a reproductive process.
>
> The scraps, patches and rags of daily life must be repeatedly turned into the sign of a coherent national culture, while the very act of the narrative performance interpellates a growing circle of national subjects. In the production of the nation as narration there is a split between the continuist, accumulative temporality of the pedagogical, and the repetitious, recursive strategy of the performative. It is through this process of splitting that the con-

ceptual ambivalence of modern society becomes the site of *writing the nation*.³

Then, the unisonant discourse of the national narrative produces its collective identification of the populace not as some transcendent national identity, but in a language of doubleness that arises from the ambivalent splitting of the pedagogical and the performative. And in that struggle which produces rhetorical fissures within the imaginative national community, those potentially transgressive day-to-day living cultural practices are constantly under pressure of containment by the integrated movement of national story-telling.

What I am trying to locate in this essay is those contending sites of enunciation which reveal splits between the "pedagogical" and the "performative" on the seeming monolith of the national narrative. In other words, this may be compared to an attempt to listen, without essentializing them, to the noises of the displaced and the marginalized, or to glimpse the silenced, whose fragile and obscure presence might help us detect evocative ambivalence in the process of subjectivization. It is an essay at tracing the possibility of history as a personal testimony rather than history as a national narrative. The text I choose for this sensitive task is Shakespeare's *Henry V*.

2

There have been a number of critical attempts to discern in *Henry V* powerful moments of constructing a modern nationhood as an "imagined community" and of consolidating its infrastructure—including a nascent form of male conscription, domestication of women, and vernacularism—and of resisting and subverting such unifying efforts.⁴ In this interpretive vein, Henry's execution of the three conspirators at Southampton and of Bardolph, for example, can be seen as an exercise in the absolutist measures of law and order of the early-modern nation-state apparatus. Henry's self-reflection on the night before Agincourt may be regarded as a consequence of the ambiguity inherent in the body politic of kinghood spearheading the national integration. Henry's military and political enterprises crowned with the accession of France would be translated as redrawing boundaries between a "united kingdom" that have already embraced the geographic, linguistic and cultural regions of England, Wales, and Ireland, and Scotland. This

Kingdom also overrides the class divisions between the noble and the common, between soldiers and citizens, in movements deeply involved with the creation of an "imagined national community." At the same time, such diverse and discordant voices which are sometimes articulated by the Chorus, "foreign" characters like Fluellen, "low" figures like Pistol and Bardolph, "female" personalities like Isabel and Catherine, and "common" soldiers like Bates and Williams offer, to a varying degree, instances of distancing and alienating that ideology of national unity.

However, critical attempts to analyze this impulse towards the imaginative nation building in *Henry V* in terms of the politics of memory, of the poetics of body and sexuality, and of the economy of reproduction are still few. Recently, though, at the 6th World Shakespeare Congress in Los Angeles, we were fortunate enough to be offered three excellent papers on the play that gave lucid accounts of the above motifs. Phyllis Rackin takes issue with Benedict Anderson who, according to Rackin, presupposes the male fraternity as the basis for his analysis of nationalism. Rackin, pointing out that the battle-scenes in *Henry V* significantly lack the elements of knightly chivalry which dominate the other plays of the Second Tetralogy, regards *Henry V* as a "prototype" of the narrative construction of modern nationhood. Focusing on the gendering process in that narrativization, she argues that modern citizenship based on the system of male-only conscription was concurrent with the exclusion of women—regardless of their class affiliations—from the public sphere, and with the enclosure of their bodies inside the family framework.[5] Henry's imperialist conquest of foreign lands and women requires, on one hand, rounding up the common people from Williams to Pistol to the battlefields, and, on the other hand, naturalizing Quickly and Catherine as wives within the "respectable" English family.

Jean E. Howard also regards the construction of masculine subjectivities as central to the site of writing the nation. Focusing on representations of sexuality in the play, she makes a detailed comparison between the two film versions, one by Laurence Olivier and the other by Kenneth Branagh. Her acute observations include a point that in Branagh's version the homoeroticism suggested in Shakespeare's text is largely displaced (with a few exceptions—Henry's treatment of Scroop, and York's ecstatic death penetrated by men's swords) by dramatic exhibition of masculine physicality especially on the battlefields.[6] Howard seems to suggest that the commercial success Branagh's film achieved depends partly on Branagh's strategy in foregrounding heterosexism as the key to conjugal and consequently national harmony, which appeals to a desire for "stable and normal" sexuality accordant with nationalistic sentiment. The nationalistic mentality that craves for a "strong masculine fatherhood" like Henry's is still prevalent in the present-day capitalistic world.

Jonathan Baldo, on the same occasion, referring to the paradigm of nationalism, highlights the process of excluding the nation's others through the linguistic violence of writing the nation that involves forced practices of oblivion and remembrance.[7] As the sixteenth century "new" historiographies, which Shakespeare relied on when writing his history plays, opened the ground in writing the "past," with a consciousness to interpret history as past events that must be narratively re-membered and re-ordered, memories that cannot be contained within these narratives were suppressed, and because of that very suppression they sometimes suddenly and hauntingly returned to life in a ghostly manner. The memory of King Richard II that haunts the Henrys symbolizes that shadow of past events which the succeeding kings have at once to suppress and appease. Remembrances of real violence and atrocities are erased in the process of writing the nation, but always there remain splitting sites of contending discourses which revive those suppressed memories.

Having been inspired by these insightful discussions briefly surveyed above, we are now ready to analyze the narrative construction of a nation in *Henry V*, mainly in terms of the policing and appropriation of the people's memories and bodies. Henry's speeches, particularly those on the battlefields, are suffused with trenchant bodily metaphors, and this tendency reaches its pinnacle at the "Saint Crispin's day" oration. Here, membership in English nationhood under Henry is secured through a homosocial ritual of "re-membering" the day when the "dis-membering" of other memories, particularly those of women and of dissident voices, is accomplished:

> It ernes me not if men my garments wear;
> Such outward things dwell not in my desires.
> But if it be a sin to covet honour
> I am the most offending soul alive . . . .
> That he which hath no *stomach* to this fight,
> Let him depart . . . .
> He that outlives this day, and comes safe home

> Will stand *a-tiptoe* when this day is named
> And rouse him at the name of Crispian....
> Then will he strip his sleeve and show his *scars*
> And say, 'These *wounds* I had on Crispin's day.'
> Old men forget; yet all shall be forgot,
> But he'll *remember* with advantages,
> What feats he did that day. Then shall our names,
> Familiar in his *mouth* as household words—
> Harry the king, Bedford and Exeter,
> Warwick and Talbot, Salisbury and Gloucester—
> Be in their flowing cups freshly *remember'd*.
> This story shall the good man teach his son,
> And Crispin Crispian shall ne'er go by
> From this day to the ending of the world
> But we in it shall be *remembered* ....   (4. 3. 26-59)[8]

The masculine tone and motifs of this speech are apparent (we may be reminded that "member" is connotative of the male genitalia), and its rhetorical sway represents the process of reassembling "dis-membered" parts of the male body at its reproductive centre, by "re-membering" the partial, individual memories of soldiers into one grand narrative about this national feat and feast. The resulting "story" that "the good man [shall] teach his son" is a blatantly male-only version of the united family descending from traditional yeomanry, which excludes any womanly influence. With a shade of the myth of parthenogenesis, the everlasting genealogy created only by fathers and sons perpetually eradicates the presence of women that make the lineage possible through their reproductive capabilities and their genes.

Nevertheless, this seemingly sweeping narrative of transcendent national identity also reveals a crack in temporal and spatial breaks between "the pedagogical" and "the performative" within Henry's very rhetoric of homogeneity and simultaneity. Henry categorically states that he craves for inward "honour" not such "outward things" as "gold" or "garments"; but the memories of diverse soldiers cannot be contained by the narrative of collective identification of the people without each person evoking the names—outward signs of the bodies—of the famous aristocratic war-leaders. The violent reality in which those anonymous common soldiers fought, got wounded and died with grudges[9]— "the performative time" with the "scraps, patches and rags of daily life"—are suppressed and turned into a coherent national narrative which constructs the memory of a nation only through registering the "outward" names of Harry the King, England, Saint George, Agincourt and Crispin. Under a promise that the day's fight "shall gentle his [the regular soldier's] condition" (l. 63), those glittering names contain dissident voices, and, by the act of renarrating, they acquire a mythological status to permeate into every English family and become a part of the "household words." Within the patriarchal family structure, through the appropriation of the male body and sexuality, along with the suppression and governing of the female reproductive power, the soldiers personal memories are, at the very site of a splitting between the pedagogical authority and the performative strategy, turned into a unified discourse of the nation.

One of the reasons why Kenneth Branagh's film version of the play has such a popular appeal for contemporary audiences, I think, is that Branagh succeeds in constructing an imagined community of the nation (which is not confined to Britain but can be applied to many countries) by stressing the "family" values at every opportunity. For instance, we hardly fail to be impressed by the intimacy among the English peers, by the people's memory of Falstaff, and by the ineffective paternal French King (played by Paul Scofield). The film emphasizes Williams' personal remembrance of his children left at home, the English soldiers' rage over the slaughtered boys. Branagh even shows a group of French women attacking Henry after the battle. And one of his master strokes is to make Burgundy's "fertile France" speech dissolve into a montage of the killed Constable, and the English dead including York, the Boy, Quickly, Nym, Bardolph, Scroop and Falstaff. Moreover, all of these are underlined by a real family feeling evoked by the ensemble acting of the ex-RSC, and the Renaissance Company actors, with the music conducted by Simon Rattle. At the end of the Agincourt battle, over the sound of "Non Nobis", with a powerful symbol of Henry carrying the dead body of the boy, the film tries to teach a lesson. The script describes the scene:

> He [Henry] gently lays the Boy down, kisses him gently on the head, and then stands up as the rest of the army gather round him as best they can. We cut close on his blood-stained and exhausted face, the dreadful price they have all had to pay for this so-called victory clearly etched into his whole being. His head drops as if in shame.[10]

At this performative site of Henry's "shame," is created an illusion of one universal Christian family embracing the English and the French, the noble and the common, men and women alike. In this sense, Branagh's film indicates ambivalence within the pedagogical authority supported by Henry's overtly masculine rhetoric that constantly turns the performative moments— "victory," "shame," "death," "violence," "blood"—into a sign of coherent national culture based on family values.[11]

These rhetorics for unifying a community through a masculine agenda reveal their violent aspects more plainly when Henry delivers a frightening speech at a parley before the gates of Harfleur. This linguistic violence, raw and ragged, which repetitiously assaults the female bodies of the town, also erupts from a fissure between the paternalistic logic of the pedagogical and the transgressive spontaneity of the performative. It is this sheer force of the speech (played with awesome force by Branagh's Henry in the film), rather than any reasonable prospect of the war, that yields the town:[12]

> . . . the fleshed soldier, rough and hard of heart,
> In liberty of bloody hand shall range
> With conscience wide as hell, mowing like grass
> Your fresh fair *virgins* and your flow'ring infants . . . .
> What is't me, when you yourselves are cause,
> If your pure *maidens* fall into the hand
> Of hot and forcing violation? . . .
> The blind and bloody soldier with foul hand
> Defile the locks of your shrill-shrieking *daughters*;
> (3. 3. 91-115; emphasis mine)

"Mowing, violation, defilement"—the motifs of rape and infanticide—are naturalized as anonymous soldiers' collective action against the town's femininity, although those whom Henry addresses and we see on the platform are *"men* of Harfleur" only. This binary opposition between the active, cruel hands of ordinary English soldiers and the passive, innocent bodies of French women betrays a process of constructing subjects in which, on one hand, the real physical atrocities of the war are ascribed to those unruly, unpredictable elements of the commonality, and, on the other, the ideal conquest of one nationality by another is accomplished by the authoritative manoeuvre of the commanding king. That command is manifestly a literary one, as Henry's model of the English language is a plain, practical and paternally masculine one, while it discriminates itself from the French language that is defined as embellished, maternal and feminine, spoken by feminized noblemen.[13] In this mutual and hegemonic process of cultural construction, English linguistic nationalism either suppresses and encloses its own women deep inside the household (as in the Crispin speech where there is little room for women's agency in constructing a national memory and history), or monolithically represents foreign women as helpless targets of physical abuse, largely because their men are depicted as impotent and helpless in defending them.

The linguistic construction of the national and the foreign is parodically reiterated in Catherine's English lesson (III. iv), which immediately follows the violent ejaculation of the Harfleur speech. Here relevant to my reading are three motifs—space, body, and language. First, this scene is unique in the play in that it takes place in a private room. In Branagh's film, the enclosed space is occupied by two women and by a huge white four-poster bed, and the room is so small that there is not enough space for Emma Thompson's Catherine to move around but only to jump about on the bed (by comparison, both Olivier's and BBC's set the scene in a garden). This intimate interiority is tinged with a sexual dimension of the prospective marriage, which is all the more significant immediately after the mass "rape" tropes of the Harfleur speech.

Secondly, this language lesson employs the tradition of the "blazon," investigated by Nancy Vickers[14], a trope that rhetorically controls and possesses the woman's body through dividing it into parts. Moreover, that body is a sexualized one as an object of male desire, as the ending of the lesson suggests: the last two words put into English by Alice, "*De foot*" and "*de cown*" sounds to Catherine like French *foutre* ("to fuck") and *con* ("cunt"). As Branagh's film shows, this bedroom of Catherine's is the private sphere where the women can freely banter and laugh over sex, but it is at the same time tightly policed and surrounded by the outside world of men who are angry and anxious about the French women who, according to the Dauphin "will give / Their bodies to the lust of English youth, / To new-store France with bastard warriors" (3. 5. 29-31).[15] The national history that should only include male bodies of the single nationality is disturbed by its own women's reproductive capacities which reveal splits in the narrative address of the nation. In various sites of writing the nation that include women's private chambers as well as men's public battlefields, the "performative" dimension of female sexuality contends with the "pedagogical" one of male language.

Thirdly, this lesson, taking the form of one-to-one translation of words, points to a way in which English nationality or masculinity (whether it is of "the good man" of the family or of "the blind and bloody soldier") is constructed by linguistic differentiation. National language, whether English or French, does not exist as an authentic entity, but is produced by discerning itself from other languages through translation and comparison. Catherine's final comments on English words with a distinct sense of difference between the two languages—"Ils sont les mots de son mauvais, corruptible, gros, et impudique, et non pour les dames d'honneur d'user. Je ne voudrais prononcer ces mots devant les seigneurs de France pour tout le monde." (3. 4. 47-51)—can be extended into a general feature of English national language, as it is constructed as "ignoble and gross" against other languages like French which are regarded as "noble and gentle."[16]

3

We have so far examined in three scenes of the play a process of constructing "English nationality" mainly in terms of memory constructed through language and body. The remaining task is to see whether we can locate other splits between "the pedagogical" and "the performative", sites of conflicting discourses that compel the narrating of a nation. Before we set about the task, we must enter two caveats. First, we should not regard Bhabha's division between the two temporalities— "double-time"—as a rigid and stable one. The moment of creating the national identity is an *ambivalent* one in which the "pedagogical" authority is pregnant with fragmentation and transgression caused by the "performative" strategy that undermines the very identity affirmed by that authority. The politics of memory that deals with the narrative identity of a nation should be considered in terms of shifting sites of enunciation, of cultural studies of location. Second, closely connected with the first point, in order to avoid an ideologically oversimplified model of contrasted discourses, we should be wary of relying on the dual scheme between domination/oppression/control (e.g. Henry, state, aristocracy, policing) and reversal/subversion/resistance (e.g. Williams, women, common people, carnivalesque.) We should then avoid a wishful identification of the "performative" with a particular person or scene, and a hasty interpretation of the "pedagogical" as a mere strategy employed by the governing power.

As we look further with these precautions in mind for instances in which the nationalist pedagogy is uncannily fissured by the living principles of the present, sustained through recurring memories and acts of witnessing, rather than by the masculinist and nationalist moments of "re-membering" the nation, we encounter traces of the unrepresentable—those of Falstaff and the Welsh women. They have one thing in common—they do not themselves appear in the text of *Henry V*. Despite the author's promise at the end of *2 Henry IV*, in *Henry V* Falstaff only emerges through various peoples' testimonies. Let us attend to one of the most memorable memories about Falstaff, namely a narrative reconstruction of his body by Hostess Quickly:

> So a bade me lay more clothes on his feet. I put my hand into the bed and felt them, and they were as cold as any stone. Then I felt to his knees, and so up'ard and up'ard, and all was as cold as any stone. (2. 3. 21-24)

This recollection may also parodically appropriate the tradition of "blazon", but if Quickly's gaze involves a desire for possessing Falstaff's body, it is mediated by her remebrance of its colour, heat, smell, breath, last words, and touch of his clothes that covered it. For, as in Peter Stallybrass' memorable words, "Cloth . . . tends to be powerfully associated with memory. Or, to put it more strongly, cloth is a kind of memory. When a person is absent or dies, cloth can absorb his or her absent presence."[17] In Branagh's film version, this scene is remarkably well executed with Quickly's central narrative (played by Judi Dench) that reminds us, as well as those characters on the scene with her, of Falstaff's living presence—his humour, habits, charms and propensities.[18] This shot with one family of people—Quickly, Pistol, Nym, Bardolph, the Boy—disconsolately sitting on wooden stairs of the Boar's Head Tavern is very impressive, because it shows a scrap of life suffused with memories of a displaced friend. In comparison with the first Tavern scene of the film, where a long flashback recalling the former merry days at the Tavern is inserted, the second one very briefly shows the dead Falstaff on the bed, upon whose face Quickly leans over showing no apparent emotion.[19] Here again the film underlines family values and their deprivation, as we witness a final remnant of the Tavern life in Quickly's quiet despair in seeing off her fellows.

Then, Falstaff as an absent and unrepresentable entity becomes "performatively present" through others' testimonies. There is, however, one person in the play who should preserve memories about Falstaff most and yet never in fact does so—Henry himself. Instead of Falstaff, Henry *re-members* Richard's "body" and "soul" with his own "contrite tears" (4. 1. 283-90). The prayer for pardon then can form a part of a dynastical myth that the "good son" redeems the father's sin, which action God approves by awarding the son with the miraculous victory at Agincourt. This myth, coupled with a tale of a prodigal son proving to be a true-bred king, is constructed, through the excision of his memory about Falstaff, into the national history.

In this respect, it is worth considering Branagh's directorial decision to stage Bardolph's execution, when Henry is visibly moved to tears at the sight of the hanged body of his friend.[20] The execution is not only exhibited at full scale in front of the whole band of soldiers but is accompanied by another flashback showing Bardolph at the Tavern, with his neck encircled in his friends' mock outrage, speaking Falstaff's line in *1 Henry IV*, "Do not, when thou are king, hang a thief." The bloody and frightened face of the old man Bardolph (played by Richard Briers) powerfully suggests that Henry is "banishing" the last of pseudo-father figures. Moreover, Bardolph's dead trunk hanging from a tree remains on the screen as long as this scene continues, as if it were a visible sign of the "performative" price Henry has to pay for his "pedagogical" purpose of disciplining the common soldiers against pillage. Building an imagined community among the "band of brothers" necessitates the sacrifice of another community probably closer to Henry's heart and more genuinely memorable. Branagh's film by extending this episode about Bardolph (as another Falstaffian figure) indicates an ambivalent site within the national history at the very moment of its construction.

If we want to focus on another splitting place in moments of writing the nation—the voices and bodies of the Welsh women—, we have to seek their traces outside *Henry V* itself. At the beginning of *1 Henry IV*, there is a report, told by Westmorland, from Wales, "loaden with heavy news" of "the noble Mortimer taken by "the rude hands of that Welshman [Glendower]":

> A thousand of his people butchered—
> Upon whose dead corpse there was such misuse,
> Such beastly shameless transformation

> By those Welshwomen done as may not be
> Without much shame retold or spoken of. (1. 1. 42-46)[21]

Whether this news is true or not, it contains those stereotypes of the "others" we frequently encounter in colonial discourses— "irregular and wild," "beastly shameless," rampant sexuality, and cannibalism. According to Homi Bhabha, it is the force of the "productive ambivalence of the object of colonial discourse—that 'otherness' which is at once an object of desire and derision, an articulation of difference contained within the fantasy of origin and identity"—that gives the colonial stereotype its currency.[22] His suggestion that the stereotype must always be in excess of what can be empirically proved or logically construed indicates an inevitable connection, in the colonial process of signification, between persistent stereotypes and the drive to repeatedly tell them within forms of national narratives:

> As a form of splitting and multiple belief, the stereotype requires, for its successful signification, a continual and repetitive chain of other stereotypes. The process by which the metaphoric "masking" is inscribed on a lack which must then be concealed gives the stereotype both its fixity and its phantasmatic quality—the same *old* stories of the Negro's animality, the Coolie's inscrutability or the stupidity of the Irish *must* be told (compulsively) again and afresh, and are differently gratifying and terrifying each time.[23]

The stereotype as the disavowal of difference is nevertheless always threatened by differences of culture, race, sexuality, and becomes a splitting scene of fantasy of origin and identity. In Westmorland's speech above, there emerges a contending site between the "pedagogical" and the "performative" in that by referring to the Welshwomen's beastly shamelessness as fixity, the English makes the stereotype as a primary site of subjectivization for the colonizers themselves as well as for the colonized Welsh.

In *1 Henry IV*, there is another scene that suggests productive ambivalence in the process of subject formation in terms of the "otherness" of the Welshwoman. In Act 3, Scene 1, after a quarrel between Glendower and Hotspur subsides, two young pairs of people—one English pair, Hotspur and Kate, the other pair half English and half Welsh, Mortimer and his wife—make memorable contrasts. As Mortimer's wife only speaks and sings in Welsh, Shakespeare's written text does not represent her words. Though we may be unable to understand exact meaning of her words, the "performative" dimension of her voice can create an ambivalent site of subjectivization. In a stark contrast to Catherine's English lesson in *Henry V*, this Welsh singing, which defies fragmentation and translation, presents a silent narrative that upholds living principles of "the scraps, patches and rags of daily life." Then, they are turned into a coherent sign of "Welshness", a historical object of the nationalist pedagogy (3. 1. 195-205). We may also note the way in which Hotspur's subjectivity is constructed. Disapproving Mortimer's submission to the Welsh language, Hotspur, instead of acquiescing to the beauty of the Welsh lady's singing, insists upon women's sexual passivity. In the mutually constructed process of subjectivization, the "English nationality" based on stereotypes of manliness and femininity is fissured by the voice of one Welshwoman. Memory of this voice may be fragile but can be lasting enough to resist that "pedagogical" authority— "a Welsh correction [that] teach[es] ... a good English condition" (*Henry V*, 5. 1. 71-72)—represented by Fluellen.[24]

4

As Marjorie Garber observes, what happens in the Epilogue is a kind of reversal of the time:

> ... in the epilogue the audience is invited, not to imagine, but to remember—and specifically to remember Shakespeare's *Henry VI* plays ("Which oft our stage hath shown") as well as the historical events contained in them. The Chorus' remarks are at the same time a prediction of the future and a memory of the past— the future in history, the past in theater.[25]

Then, in terms of the politics of memory we have been concerned with, that "past in theater" as "the future in history" presents itself as a collective and theatrical memory about others in a form of testimony which discloses ambivalent moments of "re-membering" the nation. Notice deliberate changes in the tense in the epilogue—from present perfect ("hath pursued") through past ("lived," "made," "achieved," etc.) back to present perfect ("hath shown"), then finally present ("let ... take")— that manipulates our desire for a coherent story of national conquest and loss, reconciliation and redemption that is ineradicable and enduring against the tide of time. In other words, these concluding words of the epilogue, gesturing towards a reaffirmation of the power of theatre, can be seen as an attempt to recontain splits between the "pedagogical" and "performative" that the writing of a nation always involves. Upon an audience's recollection of his or her own theatrical experience, the Chorus reminds the audience of the attempt to re-narrativize English national history. The politics of memory is exerted in this final attempt to "remember" an imagined community within the walls of the theatre.

When in the Crispin Crispianus speech Henry tries to construct the circle of nationalized subjects around the "band of brothers," the future that is evoked by the theatrical past of 1415 is both an affirmation and a denial, through the contradictory function of the politics of memory, of the empathic community at the Globe theatre of 1599—the year *Henry V* was first staged there, with its contemporary background of Essex's dismal failure in the Ireland invasion. If, furthermore, Olivier's 1944 and Branagh's 1989 film versions of the play respectively contribute to some formation of narrative identities of the English nation at the time, it is because this "star of England" is powerfully "re-membered" with the help of contemporary cinematic technology, against such contexts as the Second World War, and the Falklands Conflicts. "Remember Saint Crispin" is not only a memory of the past but a message for the present, repeatedly evoked at the nation's crisis. It reveals splitting sites of enunciation that at once teach a history of the nation and stage testimony of the individual.

Notes

1. Homi K. Bhabha, "Of mimicry and man" in *The Location of Culture* (London and New York: Routledge, 1994), p. 86.
2. Benedict Anderson, *Imagined Communities: Reflections on the Origin and Spread of Nationalism* (London: Verso, 1983), p. 132.
3. Bhabha, "DissemiNation" in *The Location of Culture*, pp. 145-46 (Bhabha's emphasis.)
4. Perhaps one of the most influential accounts of the play which emphasizes inconsistency and indeterminacy within the ideology of national unity is still the 1985 essay by Jonathan Dollimore and Alan Sinfield ("History and ideology: the instance of *Henry V*" in John Drakakis ed. *Alternative Shakespeare* [London and New York: Methuen, 1985], pp. 206-27), in which they argue,

"foreign war was the site of competing interests, material and ideological, and the assumption that the nation must unite against a common foe was shot through with conflict and contradiction" as "the play circles obsessively around the inseparable issues of unity and division, inclusion and exclusion" (pp. 215, 218.) The present paper's emphasis on the ambivalence or fissures between competing discourses owes as much to this Dollimore/Sinfield essay as to Bhabha. One of the best accounts of modern criticism of Shakespeare's history plays, which can be "devided conveniently into two main camps", the "Tudor myth school" and those who attack the Tudor myth theory, is Phyllis Rackin, *Stages of History: Shakespeare's English Chronicles* (London: Routledge, 1990), especially Chap. 2, pp. 40-85. Rackin's own conclusion, which I find broadly persuasive, is that the series of history plays "replaces the teleological, providential narrative of Tudor propaganda with a self-referential cycle that ends by interrogating [with a self-conscious and skeptical attitude] the entire project of historical mythmaking", as "the redemption depicted in Henry V is severely qualified" (pp. 60-61).

5. Phyllis Rackin, "Henry V as Prototype"; paper read at the 6th World Shakespeare Congress, 7-14 April, 1996, Los Angeles. Unpublished.

6. Jean E. Howard, "Gender and the National History Play, Now"; paper read at the 6th World Shakespeare Congress. Unpublished.

7. Jonathan Baldo, "Stages of Forgetfullness: Shakespeare's History Plays"; paper read at the 6th World Shakespeare Congress. Unpublished.

8. *Henry V*, The Oxford Shakespeare, ed. Gary Taylor (Oxford and New York: Oxford Univ. Press, 1984). Emphases are mine. Quotations from the play will refer to this edition, and will be henceforth indicated only by Act, Scene, Line number in the parentheses following citations.

9. Recall Williams' argument against Henry at the camp the night before Agincourt: ". . . all those legs and arms and heads chopped off in a battle shall join together at the latter day, and cry all, 'We died at such a place'—some swearing, some crying for a surgeon, some upon their wives left poor behind them, some upon the debts they owe, some upon their children rawly left" (4. 1. 130-35).

10. William Shakespeare, *Henry V by William Shakespeare*: A screen adaptation by Kenneth Branagh, (London: Chatto & Windus, 1989), p. 114.

11. Among other things, one striking contrast Olivier's film makes to Branagh's very bloody and muddy representation of the war is its bloodless depiction of the battle: Olivier's army scores an easy, swift victory (including a chivalric duel between Henry and the Constable) in an idyllic, green-meadow-like miniature battlefield. The unphysicality of the film represents the people mostly as a mass. If there is any drive towards nationalism in Olivier's version (dedicated famously to "the Commandos and Airborne Troops of Great Britain, the spirit of whose ancestors it has been humbly attempted to recapture"), it is largely due to a one-man crusade without any suggestion of ambivalent sites revealing fissures between the "pedagogical" and the "performative" in the discursive process in which the concept of the "people" emerge as the "double narrative movement."

12. It is well-known that Olivier's film version cuts the speech so short that the Governor of Harfleur submits to Henry without any ado. Even the BBC version (directed by David Giles in 1979) which is supposed to be "faithful" to Shakespeare's text cuts most violent parts of the speech.

13. In Branagh's film, their "feminine" aspects are stressed as idle and patrician—civilized in an uncivilized way—in contrast to the hard-working familial English soldiers.

14. Nancy Vickers, "'The blazon of sweet beauty's best': Shakespeare's Lucrece" in Patricia Parker and Geoffrey Hartman, ed. *Shakespeare and the Question of Theory* (London: Methuen, 1985), pp. 95-115.

15. In this play, sex and language lesson is one. Recall Burgundy's caption when he saw Henry and Catherine together: "My royal cousin, teach you our princess English?"; to which Henry answers, "I would have her learn, my fair cousin, how perfectly I love her, and that is good English" (5. 2. 272-75).

16. In terms of the "language lesson" in this play, it is also important to take note of the marginalization not only of the "foreign tongues" within English, namely Welsh, Scottish and Irish, but of the language of the common populace of London. In Olivier's film, there is a disturbing scene in which the Irish captain Macmorris, played stereotypically as a dull, sentimental, almost womanish simpleton, is persistently harrassed by Fluellen and Jamy, with Gower the English captain observing this Irish bashing from a distance, which ironically reveals the hegemonic process of constructing the national language and character.

17. Peter Stallybrass, "Worn Worlds: Clothes, Mourning, and the Life of Things", *The Yale Review*, vol. 81, no. 2 (April 1993), 38 (emphasis original).

18. Dench's Quickly, while delivering the lines, sits absolutely still beside Pistol on the stairs, delineating the bodily memories of Falstaff by her words only. By contrast, in Olivier's version, Quickly (played by Freda Jackson), as she speaks, touches Pistol's body as if she restaged her tracing of Falstaff's body. This "female" gesture of demonstrating while telling a story seems to me to undermine the power of her testimony, because it tries to externalise her loss.

19. It may also be noted that her posture of leaning over Falstaff is almost an exact restaging of Branagh's Henry leaning over Scroop whom he condemns for treason in the immediately preceding scene. As Jean E. Howard points out in the paper aforementioned, Henry and Scroop, between whom a homoerotic relationship is suggested by the text, are in a position of sexual intercourse on a table, with their lips almost kissing each other's. (Henry, before accusing the three, is seen to touch playfully Scroop's cheek and chin as if they were the last signs of their fond memories.) Two leaning postures—one ferociously accusing his "bedfellow" of betrayal, the other silently mourning her best companion of life—embody the dearness of friendly ties and despair caused by their loss.

20. In Olivier's version, the execution is excised, along with other "disturbing" elements, such as Henry's indictment of the three traitors at Southampton, part of the Harfleur speech which contains the motifs of violation and rape,

and the references to Richard in Henry's prayer on the night before Agincourt.

21. William Shakespeare, *Henry IV, Part 1*, The Oxford Shakespeare, ed. David Bevington (Oxford: Oxford Univ. Press, 1987). Quotations from the play refer to this edition, and will henceforce be indicated by Act, Scene, Line number only in the parenthesis following citations.

22. Bhabha, "The other question" in *The Location of Culture*, pp. 66-67.

23. Bhabha, p. 77 (Bhabha's emphasis).

24. Terence Hawkes in a paper (titled "Bryn Glas") read at "Postcoloniality—Shakespeare—Johannesburg 1996" conference at Witwatersrand University in July 1996 argues that Fluellen as an ambivalent site of Welsh otherness presents a devastating critique of Henry's realpolitik when his "Welsh accent" independently signifies the absurdity of state legitimation of mass killings, bursting the boundaries between the noble and ignoble, English and Welsh, Alexander and the pig. I entirely agree with Hawkes that this is the "electrifying moment"; but in terms of the politics of memory, Fluellen does stand for a "pedagogical" time-scheme.

25. Marjorie Garber, "'What's Past Is Prologue': Temporality and Prophecy in Shakespeare's History Plays" in Barbara Kiefer Lewalski, ed., *Renaissance Genres: Essays on Theory, History, and Interpretation* (Cambridge, Mass.; London: Harvard Univ. Press, 1986), p. 324.

Tamburlaine's Prophetic Oratory and Protestant Militarism in the 1580s

Arata Ide

IN *TAMBURLAINE THE Great* we are required to approach two aspects of Tamburlaine's character: the one aspect as a divine hero who leads his army and a brave soldier famous for his military skill; and the other as a demonic tyrant who exterminates the enemies and boldly justifies his heinous deeds in the name of God. We are embarrassed by this two-facedness. It is, however, a noticeable fact that far from making a negative impression upon the Elizabethan audience, Tamburlaine could be regarded as a perfect heroic figure. Numerous contemporary references show admiration and enthusiasm for its hero.[1] What made the Elizabethan audience admire the protagonist in spite of defects too obvious to be ignored? It is very strange that we hardly hear of ethical outcries against Tamburlaine's atrocities, and yet it is possible that some dramatic mechanism was working to justify his cruelties. The play's pagan setting, which places Tamburlaine outside the Christian world of divine retribution, might function as a device to emphasize his heroic aspect; moreover, the characterization of Tamburlaine as a pagan defender of Christian Europe against Islam might contribute to the audience's admiration. A modern audience may well find that the repeated slaughters and atrocities limit or block admiration, yet it seems worth asking whether the first audiences found his fanatic genocide less offensive. Did their ethical responses resemble our own? I do not intend to maintain that they lacked moral sense, nor to deny that the play has an ingenious way of justifying his deeds. Rather, in this paper, I would like to stress the importance of focusing on the socio-religious milieu fostered by the dominant Protestant ideology, which promoted an ethical outlook rather different from ours and encouraged the audience to make light of Tamburlaine's moral flaws.

1

What makes a king a king? *Tamburlaine* gives a relatively definite answer to this question which has often raised delicate issues in Elizabethan drama. At the beginning of the play, we are presented with a regal misfit, Mycetes, who lacks eloquence. Cosroe, his brother having "a better wit," deplores the miserable state of Persia. One of the reasons he will not admit Mycetes as a king is that he cannot produce the kind of "great and thundering speech" that would captivate his subjects: wit and eloquence can give the true title and the authority of a king. Since a tongue-tied king who has no words has no swords, it is natural that the state of Persia is endangered. When raising his army against Cosroe, Mycetes arranges for Meander to make a proclamation speech, and on another occasion chooses Theridamas as his substitute: "Go, stout Theridamas, thy words are swords, / And with thy looks thou conquerest all thy foes" (*One* 1. 1. 74-5).[2] Indeed, in valuing wit and eloquence so highly, all the kings in *Tamburlaine* seem obsessed with the humanistic idea.[3] In this respect, Tamburlaine, a Scythian shepherd, is also a prospective king in spite of his low birth at the beginning of the play. This is confirmed by Theridamas when, in their first meeting, he is not only struck by his majestical looks but is also persuaded by Tamburlaine's eloquence to become his ally: "Not Hermes, prolocutor to the gods, / Could use persuasions more pathetical" (*One* 1. 2. 209-10). Tamburlaine is a match for Persian lords in oratory, as well as in looks and bravery. What then is it that makes Tamburlaine cut a conspicuous figure among the fluent candidates? What gives him the authority that makes Theridamas submit? The answer seems to lie in his "working words."

It is worth noticing that Tamburlaine alone regards his words as oracles or prophesies.[4] Just before his encounter with Bajazeth, he encourages his comrades: "Fight all courageously and be you kings: / I speak it, and my words are oracles" (*One* 3. 3. 101-2). He never doubts his supremacy, for he is assured of his election by the divine will. He claims to be chosen by God—like David, the King of Israel, who was once a shepherd. Meander reproaches him for hoping, "misled by dreaming prophecies, / To reign in Asia, and with barbarous arms / To make himself the monarch of the East" (*One* 1. 1. 41-3). The energy of Tamburlaine's "working words" originates not from his acquired faculty of speech, but from the fact that his words are divine "prophesies." Tamburlaine presents himself not only as a warrior and a monarch, but as a "prophet" in the Old Testamental sense: God's active agent who receives the word of God, delivers its contents to the people, and at times carries out the message by himself. This aspect of prophet can be found more or less in all prophets of the Old Testament; often, Israelite kings and judges also perform this prophetic function.[5] By receiving the divine oracle from God, Tamburlaine obtains an absolute licence to fulfill it, and by accomplishing his mission, he gives his/God's vision substance. Hence, "Will and Shall best fitteth Tamburlaine." Neil Rhodes has correctly pointed out that "the oracular power of which he speaks comprises not only the supremely persuasive eloquence of the Humanist orator, but also the destructive fury of the divine Word itself."[6] Tamburlaine's uttered words have reality and substance even before they are carried out. As he asserts that "Nor are Apollo's oracles more true / Than thou shalt find my vaunts substantial" (*One* 1. 2. 211-12), his words have a great potential for destructive power.

If his *word* is literally, as well as homophonically, *sword*, Tamburlaine's divine word also corresponds to his divine sword. As can be discerned in the prologue which tells us the outline of the play, his marvellous language is organically linked to his heroic conquests. At the beginning, we are informed that Tamburlaine is threatening the neighbouring countries with his word and sword.

> Where you shall hear the Scythian Tamburlaine
> Threat'ning the world with high astounding terms
> And scourging kingdoms with his conquering sword.
> (*One* The Prologue, 4-6)

The last two lines are close parallels, not only in meaning, but also in Tamburlaine's divine role as "the scourge of God" gaining supremacy over other nations with his word/sword. His divine word is in line with his holy war against the enemies. He describes the nature of his conquests in relation to his sacred words as follows:

> For fates and oracles of heaven have sworn
> To royalise the deeds of Tamburlaine
> And make them blest that share in his attempts. (*One* 1. 2. 7-9)

By God's authorization of him as a prophet, he comes to be an agent who embodies His word, and Tamburlaine's warfare becomes a holy war to fulfill His will. There is an interesting scene in which Tamburlaine and Bajazeth meet face to face just before the encounter, and vow their own victory over each other. On the one hand Bajazeth swears by his religious authority, Mahomet's sepulchre and the Koran. Against him, on the other hand, Tamburlaine swears by his sword. This is not because he believes in his arms only and denies all other religious authorities. Rather, his attitude shows that he regards his word/sword as the absolute truth revealed by God himself. Just after this scene, Tamburlaine defeats Bajazeth "with a wondrous ease," proving his word's infallibility and demonstrating that he is invested with full authority of His absolute power.

His bold confidence, almost indistinguishable from devout zeal, makes him profess that the battle with Cosroe "will prove a pretty jest" and that "the chiefest God" "will sooner burn the glorious frame of heaven than it should so conspire my overthrow." Una Ellis-Fermor comments that "his tone recalls less the boasting of some Scandinavian thane than the fervour of religious fanaticism."[7] His standard of judgment on warfare transcends human experience, but he challenges his followers to judge by his standard, just as he ironically challenges Theridamas: "Judge by thyself, Theridamas, not me." Thus the God's prophet, through his provocative speech, presses his followers to share his privileged point of view. It may seem surprising that the Elizabethan audience liberally praised such a coercive protagonist. Yet they were also Tamburlaine's followers who fell into his way of thinking, while admiring his prophesies and transcendental power.

2

The prophetic mode of Tamburlaine gives us an important clue in considering the dramatic device of justififying his deeds. Kocher succinctly describes the nature of God in the play: "desire for power, unchecked by morality, is characteristic of the deity. God is a God of Force."[8] By the oracles of the God, Tamburlaine's extermination is legitimatized, and the code of ethics is cancelled. Kocher comments that Tamburlaine "speaks like a prior incarnation of Nietzsche," but it is not necessary to look for such a God of force outside the Elizabethan world. Marlowe must have been able to find that God in the Old Testament. The God Tamburlaine serves has absolute authority to exterminate the enemy, like Jehovah, who commands Saul to "destroye ye all that perteineth vnto them, and haue no compassion on them, but slay bothe man and woman, bothe infant and suckeling, bothe oxe, and shepe, bothe camel, and asse."[9] The Old Testament is scattered with episodes of genocide by Jehovah's command. When Israel laid siege to cities or fought against neighbouring enemies, the leaders were given oracles through prophets and sometimes even functioned as prophets themselves. They declared the enemy to be *herem*, that is, in "the status of that which is separated from common use or contact" "because it is proscribed as an abomination to God," and exterminated the enemy as an act of devotion or profession to God. Jehovah sanctified Israel by killing all the uncircumcised people and seizing their land.[10] In this respect, the prophetic leaders of Israel are the scourge of God for the suffering gentiles, but Battenhouse's definition is not applicable here, as they are not doomed to fatal judgment in the end.[11] They make a holy war as the commanders of a crusade, so they can win God's favour and be even more blessed through genocide. In *Tamburlaine*, this vision of the holy war of Israel is clearly described by a Christian character, Frederick the lord of Buda:

> As fell to Saul, to Balaam and the rest
> That would not kill and curse at God's command,
> So surely will the vengeance of the Highest,
> And jealous anger of His fearful arm,
> Be poured with rigour on our sinful heads
> If we neglect this offered victory.   (*Two* 2. 1. 54-59)

Here he refers to Saul, the king of Israel, who failed to complete God's command to exterminate "those sinners the Amalekites." He was, consequently, compelled to abdicate his throne because he had "cast away the worde of the Lord." Frederick mentions Balaam as well, and Marlowe bears in mind here the episode of the prophet who, blinded by his selfish interest, hesitates to give blessing to Israel and to prophesy their stamping out other nations.[12] These characters in the Old Testament are notorious for their disobedience as those who do not follow God's command to extirpate the enemy, and Frederick invokes them to encourage Sigismond to assail the Turks.

The framework that a prophet destroys the neighbouring nations by God's command, found in the episodes of the Old Testament, has *Tamburlaine* as its counterpart. Tamburlaine, who tells oracles and fulfills them in the name of God, almost comes to be an Israelite hero. His violence and slaughterings are sanctified by God, and he does not draw divine wrath on himself.[13]

> But since I exercise a greater name
> The scourge of God and terror of the world,
> I must apply myself to fit those terms,
> In war, in blood, in death, in cruelty,
> And plague such peasants as resist in me
> The power of heaven's eternal majesty. (*Two* 4. 1. 153-158)

In this speech we cannot find any conscience-stricken hesitation nor palliative timidity, only a fanatic assurance. Tamburlaine maintains that heaven's majesty should be displayed in war, blood, death, cruelty as if "he implies that his divine role requires him to be more vicious than he might."[14] The tone of his speech is, however, not sarcastic but devotional. His argument is supported by the concept of receiving God's blessing by exterminating His, that is, the nation's enemy and he never deviates from its pivotal logic by suffering from a guilty conscience in the manner of some tyrants.[15] He is in this respect a unique figure in Elizabethan tyrant plays.

Tamburlaine defeats the invincible Turkish army in spite of his inferiority in strength, and immediately afterwards, at the beginning of Act 4, he brings Bajazeth in a cage and takes him out to be his footstool. The scene is the climax of the first part and Tamburlaine is at the zenith of his powers. There he declares as follows:

> Now clear the triple region of the air
> And let the majesty of heaven behold
> Their scourge and terror tread on emperors....
> So shall our swords, our lances, and our shot
> Fill all the air with fiery meteors;
> Then, when the sky shall wax as red as blood,
> It shall be said I made it red myself
> To make me think of naught but blood and war.
>   (*One* 4. 2. 30-32, 51-55)

It is important here to notice how his warfare overlaps with the Last Judgment through apocalyptic images. His making Bajazeth the footstool recalls Psalm 110, "I make thine enemies thy fotestole", that is, David's prophetic song on Messiah who "shal wounde Kings in the daie of his wrath" and "shal fil all with dead bodies, and smite the head ouer great countreis." His "blood and war" may also remind us of the eschatological terror, such as described in Joel. According to Sims, Marlowe tends to make effective use of biblical allusions based on his knowledge of its context.[16] We may fairly suppose that, in Tamburlaine as well as Marlowe's other plays, biblical allusions are deliberately used to mould Tamburlaine's character. But what character? If we regard *Tamburlaine* as a tyrannical scourge upon whom Heaven inflicts vengeance in the end, eschatological allusions should naturally link up with his Antichrist-like character.[17] A close examination of biblical allusions, however, makes it clear that Tamburlaine is not necessarily a variant of the Antichrist. Feasey interestingly concludes as follows:

> The Biblical passages on which Marlowe draws are not only those where a cruel enemy is sent by God to plague His people for their sins; he draws equally from passages where the people of God are themselves the avengers. Sometimes Tamburlaine appears to be not so much the Wrath of God, as the God of Wrath himself, who at the head of the armies of heaven shall 'smite the nations' with his conquering sword. Sometimes, indeed, he appears to stand for the God of the Final Judgment.[18]

Feasey's conclusion can be more or less supported by some historical evidence. It has been demonstrated that the ultimate source of the sequence of white, red and black colours leading to death is from the chapter 6 of Revelation, where the coming of "the great day of his wrath" is heralded through the symbolic white, red, black and pale horses, and their riders.[19] This sequence is clearly analogous to Tamburlaine's colour pattern and his attitude towards the enemy. Actually the sequence left a vivid impression upon Thomas Nashe:

> When neither the White-flag or the Red which Tamburlaine aduaunced at the siedge of any City, would be accepted of, the Blacke-flag was sette vp, which signified there was no mercy to be looked for; and that the miserie marching towardes them was so great, that their enemy himselfe (which was to execute it) mournd for it. Christ, hauing offered the Iewes the White-flagge of forgiuenesse and remission, and the Red-flag of shedding his Blood for them, when these two might not take effect nor work any yeelding remorse in them, the Black-flagge of confusion and desolation was to succeede for the obiect of their obduration.[20]

As we see here clearly, he compares Tamburlaine with Christ. If

Tamburlaine had been negatively characterized and regarded as an undesirable apocalyptic figure, Nashe's comparison would have been entirely irrelevant. Tamburlaine must have reminded the audience of the Messianic apocalyptic agent, described as being "clothed with a garment dipte in blood, and his name is called, THE WORDE OF GOD. And the warriers which were in heauen, folowed him vpon white horses, clothed with fine linen white and pure. And out of his mouth went out a sharpe sworde, that with it he shulde smite the heathen" (Rev. 19:13-15). Thus, the apocalyptic imagery gives the depth to his heroic grandeur, and draws the audience to regard him as a commander of God's army against the Antichrist. His battles and sieges, through his prophetic discourse, assume the aspect of wars of extermination in the Old Testament, while the eschatological analogy reinforces the prophet's self-sanction.

Let us now consider Tamburlaine's self-sanction from a different angle to examine the whole design of the play, for his prophetic discourse is involved in the politico-religious aim of the Elizabethan Establishment and interlocks with the religious sentiments of Elizabethan society.

3

The year 1585 was a turning point in Elizabeth's reign, when she decided to send troops under the command of Leicester to the Low Countries. When peace could no longer be maintained by her indecisive diplomacy with Spain and France, there were hurried preparations for war.[21] Walsingham, who had earnestly promoted his nationalistic bellicose policy, probably took the lead in the Privy Council in devising and executing not only the scheme of dispatching troops but also the national defence program. The whole nation was thus rushed into war with Spain and Roman Catholicism. The Privy Council found it necessary to muster a great number of soldiers, as well as to supply military expenses. As we can see in the papers of the Privy Council, they began to demand that each county or city recruit a definite number of soldiers from 1585.[22] The number of Englishmen who served in overseas expeditions conspicuously increased, and, according to Cruickshank, "from that year to the end of the reign annual recruitment for foreign service was well over 5000."[23] Naturally enough, levying the army during this national crisis was closely linked with the effort to encourage warlike attitudes on the part of those expected to serve as soldiers. This was because keeping the public bellicose was necessary in order to secure the necessary manpower and win full devotion to the national cause.

Though many attempts had been made before 1585 to stir up animosity against Roman Catholicism through pulpits and publications, open criticism against foreign nations was rigorously restricted, for there were fears that public criticism would upset the balance of the political status quo. However, once the country was actively at war with Philip II and the Pope, anti-Spanish and anti-Catholic discourse was openly allowed and welcomed. It was necessary for the anti-Spanish/Catholic campaign to be reinforced by provocative propaganda, a discourse which appeals not to reason but to emotions, so that people may regard war from the government's viewpoint and be inflamed with "righteous" indignation. The most effective means of propaganda was the pulpit.[24] The Church's systematic organization allowed the dissemination of the Establishment ideology on a large scale. Moreover, the pulpit made full use of eloquence to inspire the "spirit" of the audience. Stephen Gosson, reminding readers that preaching is compared in Revelation to thunder, explains that preaching is, as it were, a thunderbolt which inflames the heart of the audience. The preacher's words, charged by "the motion and agitation of the minde," hit and move them.[25] This oratorical power of the pulpit to grasp and manipulate people's minds played an important role in raising morale. While their hostility was heightened by the full output of provocative oratory, the biblical analogy interwoven with it endorsed the cause of justice. In *A Sermon profitably preached in the church within her Maiesties honourable Tower, neere the Citie of London* (London, 1586), Anthony Anderson, presumably patronized by Walsingham, spurs the audience:

> Wherefore our true English hartes, doe not feare at all your Romaine force. Goe to then Abner thou Abington, and all the broode of Sathan, for our God for his Dauid *Elizabeth*, is encamped against thee, & watcheth for the further protection, of our English *Israell*, whose holy name be blessed for euer, and euer Amen.[26]

He attempts in his sermon to legitimatize the anti-Spanish war from a theological perspective. His discourse is founded on biblical analogy invented by the Established Church, that makes such equivalence as Elizabeth/David or England/Israel possible. This analogy, which appears quite frequently in contemporary sermons, can validate the application of the concept of the holy war in the Old Testament to the case of "English Israel."[27]

Considering the intensity of morale-building by the pulpit, it is no wonder we frequently find this idea of the holy war in the pamphlets prepared for soldier readers.[28] There are many examples, but let us focus on a typical excerpt from Simon Harward's *The Solace for the Souldier and Saylour* (London, 1592). This pamphlet, dedicated to Archbishop Whitgift, vindicates "the lawfulnes of warre and force of armes agaynst the professed enemies of Gods truth" and the following passage is worth quoting at length:

> Howsoeuer the Spaniards beare the name of Christians, they are nothing lesse then what they pretend, they may be in the Church, but they are not of the Church, and they are so much worse then the heathen Infidels, as a rebell and traytor within the walles is more pernicious then a forraine or outward enemie: whatsoeuer punishment then may be inflicted on our professed foes, the same or much greater may iustly be layd on them: although indeede there is no more professed foe to the kingdome of our Sauiour Christ, then they which by all meanes vpholde that man of sinne, that sonne of perdition, which doth sit in the Temple of GOD as God, boasting himselfe that hee is God: that Babylonian strumpet, which sitting on the City that hath seuen hilles doe giue all nations to drinke of the cup of the wrath of her fornication, which therefore beareth the name of Antichrist, as the most bitter and professed enemy of the kingdome of Christ, chalenging to himselfe all those offices which of right and duety do onely appertaine to our Sauiour Christ.   (sig. C1^v-C2^r)

In this book, Harward, as well as other writers, often refers to the episodes in the Old Testament to arrive at the same conclusion. He directly denounces Spain and the Pope, and moreover, identifies them as the Antichrist and the Babylonian strumpet. Here he attempts to bring the apocalyptic vision into his argument in order to fortify the framework of self-legitimation, as well as to brand them as the deadly foes of Christ. This sort of argument is not, of course, uncommon. The author is simply following Protestant apologists who believe that Revelation tells them about the contemporary politico-religious situation of Europe and construe the text to suit their purpose. I would like to emphasize that the eschatological idea was the core of Protestant ideology in backing up the national cause in the critical stages of war. George Gifford declares in *Sermons upon the whole booke of the Revelation* (London, 1596) that "in this last battaile of Christ against the beast, there shall be not onely a spirituall slaughter, but also a killing of their bodies here upon earth with the sworde in warres."[29] In this manner, images and episodes in the Scripture, which by themselves allow various interpretations, were politicized under the bias toward nationalism in order to raise the morale of the public.

Thus, British Israelitism and nationalist apocalypticism, which involved the political aims of the Establishment, were disseminated throughout England from the pulpit. By arousing public attention to England's engagement in the same kind of war aided by God's miraculous powers, the enthusiastic oratory of the English prophets gives mimetic stimulus to the audience to follow the Israelite heroes in fighting an apocalyptic enemy. In the midst of this blind enthusiasm, the usual moral code naturally came to be modified and even nullified. The concept of the holy war set up a different code which encouraged the public to kill the Catholic/Antichristian enemies *herem*.[30] England was "armed with the lawfull authority of the sworde" by the working words of the prophets.

4

Incensed by effeminate Calyphas, who will not take up arms, Tamburlaine admonishes his sons to fight courageously as soldiers and not to be afraid of being injured. Then, he cuts his arm with his sword and says, "Come, boys, and with your fingers search my wound," as if Christ has told Thomas of the resurrection by his wounds, to demonstrate in practice that brave soldiers should take pride in shedding their blood. Showing the bleeding wound in his arm, he maintains that "Blood is the god of war's rich livery," and compares it to gold and jewels of India:

> Now look I like a soldier, and this wound
> As great a grace and majesty to me
> As if a chair of gold enamelled
> Enchased with diamonds, sapphires, rubies,
> And fairest pearl of wealthy India
> Were mounted here under a canopy,
> And I sat down, clothed with the massy robe
> That late adorned the Afric potentate

> Whom I brought bound unto Damascus' walls.   (*Two* 3. 2. 117-125)

The preciousness of soldiers' blood is extolled in this speech, reminding us of Faustus' praise for the power of black magic in which he compares it to the precious metal and stones of India. This high admiration for wounds shows the morale-inspiring purpose of the play. Just after the speech, Tamburlaine himself gives a reason not only for displaying his wound, but also for destroying the cities and using "high astounding terms":

> And let the burning of Larissa walls,
> My speech of war, and this my wound you see,
> Teach you my boys to bear courageous minds
> Fit for the followers of great Tamburlaine.   (*Two* 3. 2. 141-44)

He is a master who teaches his sons and comrades to be courageous enough to follow him, while his disciples, enchanted by his majestic prophesy, fashion themselves into his likeness.[31] This mimetic desire must have been shared also among the audience. The play evokes their sympathy to Tamburlaine's heroic oratory and exploits. By allowing the imagination its full play, the audience becomes one with Tamburlaine's invincible army and becomes trained to have "courageous minds" befitting his disciples. This training is not done through rational arguments, but through listening to their master's fanatical moving oratory. The public theatre was an educational institution where they underwent such mental training.

In *Playes Confuted in fiue Actions* (London, 1582), Gosson detects the dangerous mimetic effect of drama, and elsewhere gives warning against its powerful sensual appeal to passions of the common people. As he says that "*Tragedies* and *Comedies* stirre vp affections, and affections are naturally planted in that part of the minde that is common to vs with brute beastes" (sig. F1ʳ), the theatre came to have an instigative power to arouse the audience's enthusiasm and to manipulate their minds. He perceived that the emotional function the Church had monopolized to stir up religious sentiments might be usurped by the theatre and modified to a debased function to stir up brutal emotions.[32] Moreover, he declares that playwrights are learning how to agitate and manipulate the "affections" of the audience:

> But the *Poetes* that write playes, and they that present them vpon

the Stage, studie to make our affections ouerflow, whereby they draw the bridle from that parte of the mind, that should euer be curbed, from runninge on heade: which is manifest treason to our soules, and deliuereth them captiue to the deuill.

(sig. F1^v)

What drives Gosson's antitheatrical campaign is his sense of a crisis in which the public theatre comes to obtain the same power of oratory to reshape the feelings of the common people. Inspired words that control their passions are attributed to both poets and preachers. These words transmit the exuberant imagination of playwrights to the audience in the theatre, as well as the religious fervour of preachers from the pulpit to the congregation. The eloquent speech of playwrights is also charged "in the motion and agitation of the minde," "catches fire" then "hittes and mooues" the audience. Gosson's conversion to the ministry seems to have been a *volte-face*, but, in respect of his quest for a mass-manipulating oratory, he still remained a poet.

As stated before, in the 1580s, Walsingham took an active part in the anti-Catholic/Spanish campaign, utilizing to the fullest such influential media as the pulpit. When Privy Councillors were urged, at national crisis, to mould public opinion, it is quite probable that they placed this responsibility upon the theatre as well.[33] Richard Verstegan, a militant Catholic, slanders Burghley, Leicester and Walsingham in *A Declaration of the trve cavses of the great trovbles, presvpposed to be intended against the realme of England* (n.p., 1592), and there he asserts that the public theatre was employed for the campaign:

> But this cours of proceeding lyked not him [Cecil], that had designed his plots vnto other purposes, and that rather sought to woork some speciall domage to the king of Spaine, then to haue the potencie of the Turck diminished. And therefore for an introduction thereunto, to make him odious vnto the people, certaine players were permitted to scof and iest at him, vpon their comon stages.   (sig. B2^v)

Here he definitely implies that the public stage began participating in the creation of hostility against Spain more directly and powerfully than ever before. Marlowe, having been employed "in matters touching the benefitt of his Countrie" under the supervision of the Privy Council, was probably under the strong influence of Walsingham when he wrote the two Tamburlaine plays, which are usually assumed to have been written in 1587-8.[34] They speak of Marlowe in the highest terms of praise that "in all his acc*i*ons he had behaued him selfe orderlie and discreetlie wherebie he had done her Ma*j*estie good service, & deserued to be rewarded for his faithfull dealinge."[35] It is natural to think that, while Marlowe gained strong protection and support, the dynamics of patronage compelled him to endorse and promote his masters' ideological stance through his discourse.

When Marlowe came to London, the public theatre could give full scope to its potential to appeal to the emotions of the audience. Like Gosson, he must have been well versed in the provocativeness of drama, the traits of the Elizabethan audience, and the power of the public theatre in society and politics. Gosson, an ex-dramatist, urges that the theatre should be deprived of its social power to seize "affections", but Marlowe, who was once a Parker scholar inclined to take holy orders, goes in the opposite direction and exploits its power to the full. The theatre staging *Tamburlaine* shares the mass-manipulating oratory of the pulpit and the self-justifying logic of the holy war to declare the triumph of English Israel. I do not mean, however, that both institutions addressed the audience in the same way. They had their own range of influence. In the pulpit, there are too many restrictions to be able to urge the audience to act on their hostile and aggressive impulses. Even if it is fortified with the extermination theory, its capacity to encourage slaughter by force or to let their hatred loose is considerably smaller. The public theatre was the most suitable institution "to make our affections ouerflow." It was, so to speak, a debased version of the Church. Retaining the same goal as religious exhortations in the pulpit, dramatic agitations were directed at militarizing the audience by appealing to their brutal emotions. *Tamburlaine* is, as it were, a theatrical sermon which delivers the same morale-building message as that of the pulpit, using a different vehicle. The play, it seems, had a great success as an art of dramatic agitation to stir up the "affections" of the audience.

5

In concluding this essay, I would like to make a brief examination of the relationship between Marlowe and the ideology promoted by the Establishment, for I have left his attitude toward it untouched.

It has often been argued that Marlowe wrote the two parts to constitute a single action.[36] This kind of argument may support his ingenuity in giving them organic unity, but not the assumption that he wrote the first part planning a continuation up to Tamburlaine's death. Some evidences show that he had no intention to write a second part. For instance, Marlowe consumed his historical sources in the first part and did not distribute them appropriately to each part. Moreover, he says "The general welcomes Tamburlaine received / When he arrived last upon our stage / Hath made our poet pen his second part" (*Two* The Prologue, 1-3), and there is no reason to doubt the authenticity of this speech. We had better consider, not one, but two Tamburlaine plays.[37] When we take the separate design into account and consider the self-justifying logic of each play, it becomes obvious that there is a difference in how Marlowe handles it. In the first part, Tamburlaine's self-justifying logic works so latently through his prophetic oratory that his discourse compelling self-justification in the name of God wipes out all criticism. In the latter part, however, Marlowe seems to call our attention to the legitimacy of the logic itself.

The second part has many more scenes in which characters swear by their religious authorities, and this tendency is so conspicuous that it looks as if swearing and swaggering were the main theme of the play. In fact, almost all the political manoeuvres and military actions are legitimatized by the name of Christ or Mahomet. The most palpable case can be seen when Orcanes, the Turkish leader, enters into the peace treaty with Sigismond of Hungary, the representative of European Christians:

> *Orcanes.* But, Sigismond, confirm it with an oath,
>   And swear in sight of heaven and by thy Christ.
> *Sigismond.* By him that made the world and saved my soul,
>   Thy son of God and issue of a maid,
>   Sweet Jesus Christ, I solemnly protest
>   And vow to keep this peace inviolable.
> *Orcanes.* By sacred Mahomet, the friend of God,
>   Whose holy Alcaron remains with us,
>   Whose glorious body, when he left the world
>   Closed in a coffin, mounted up the air
>   And hung on stately Mecca's temple roof,
>   I swear to keep this truce inviolable. (*Two* 1. 1. 131-142)

They are always conscious of and alluding to their religious authorities. Shortly after, when this oath of truce is nullified by Sigismond's betrayal, the name of Christ is used to justify their breach of faith. His followers, Frederick and Baldwin, remind him of the Turks' "cruel slaughter of our Christian bloods," and assert that the holy laws of Christendom cannot impose restrictions on them since their enemies are infidels "in whom no faith nor true religion rests." Then, based upon the idea of the holy war of the Old Testament, Frederick urges Sigismond to destroy the pagan troops lest they should draw divine wrath upon themselves as Saul or Balaam did. Sigismond is persuaded and decides to fight. These Christians appear to us as plain Machiavellians employing religion for their political aims. In this respect, Orcanes is akin to them. After the battle, he comments on the triumph over Sigismond that "Now lie the Christians bathing in their bloods, / And Christ or Mahomet hath been my friend" (*Two* 2. 3. 10-11). Orcanes who began hostilities in the name of Mahomet does not care who supported him, once he secures the victory. Christ and Mahomet are interchangeable. It is, however, worth noticing that, though their actions are certainly grounded on Machiavellian principles, they do not realize that they *are* employing religion for their own convenience. They are too blindly devoted to understand that their "policy hath fram'd religion." Sigismond asks his followers "what motion is it that inflames your thoughts / And stirs your valours to such sudden arms?" "Revenge upon these infidels" is Frederick's answer. He demonstrates that they should not miss the opportunity God has given to "*scourge* their foul blasphemous paganism" (Italics mine). What drives them to the war is not so much their political artifice as their fervent warring spirit, which is in line with Tamburlaine's zealous devotion as "the scourge of God."

The historical battle of Varna was fought in 1444, some forty years after Timur's death, between Amurath II and Vladislaus of Poland and Hungary. Sigismond, a contemporary of Tamburlaine, is a Hungarian leader defeated by Bajazeth.[38] Marlowe anachronistically transfers the event to the age of Tamburlaine by exchanging the name Vladislaus for Sigismond. It is reasonable to think that the transposing of episodes originated from Marlowe's design of the play and not from his exhaustion of historical sources. Using the account of Varna, he depicts Christian characters who are filled with zeal in the cause of Christ and abuse the concept of the holy war. There is little possibility that the treachery of the Christians was regarded as subversive by the Protestant Establishment, since Sigismond and his comrades are Catholics of the fifteenth century who have no direct relation to Elizabethan England. It is interesting to note, however, that their discursive pattern bears close resemblance to that of Tamburlaine. By displaying their fanatically-motivated military actions on the stage, Marlowe spotlights the mechanism of divine legitimation, which was scarcely disclosed in the first part. He obliquely stains Tamburlaine with a fault common to the Christians in the play, who with religious enthusiasm employ God's name for their military actions, and suggests that Tamburlaine might be "a second (non-Christian) Sigismond, setting himself up in God's name as an avenger."[39] Marlowe is not so much interested in censuring and blackening the hero as displaying intelligibly the workings of the self-justifying logic, which is also the core of the religious discourse of the Establishment itself. Once the mechanism is analysed, both Tamburlaine's and the Establishment's discourses of holy war are relativized.

Thus, Marlowe shows a perfect understanding of the function of religious discourse and casts doubt on its legitimacy, even as he observes the Privy Council's request "orderlie and discreetelie." By the time he wrote the second part of *Tamburlaine*, it seems, his understanding of the delicate social dynamics between the Establishment, the public and the playwright can be observed in his mastery over the mass-manipulating power of the theatre and in his oblique comment on the hero. It is in this respect that we can discern a spark of his "excellent wit" as a dramatist.

Notes

1. Richard Levin has collected a variety of contemporary references to *Tamburlaine* and concludes that the perception of Tamburlaine's mightiness is evident in many allusions, as well as free of any negative qualifications. See his important article, "The Contemporary Perception of Marlowe's Tamburlaine" in J. Leeds Barroll, ed. *Medieval and Renaissance Drama in England*, 1 (New York: AMS, 1984): 51-70.
2. All the lines and quotations from *Tamburlaine* come from *Tamburlaine the Great* in The Revels Plays, ed. J. S. Cunningham (Manchester: Manchester Univ. Press, 1981).
3. On the humanistic eloquence and wit, see G. K. Hunter, *John Lyly: The Humanist as Courtier* (London: Routledge and Kegan Paul, 1962), chap. 1, and Neil Rhodes, *The Power of Eloquence and English Renaissance Literature* (Hemel Hempstead: Harvester Wheatsheaf, 1992).
4. The importance of prophecy in *Tamburlaine* has been pointed out in Regina

B. Reed, "Rebellion, Prophesy and Power in Four Works of the English Renaissance," State Univ. of New York at Buffalo Ph.D. thesis, 1970, pp. 66ff, and Johannes H. Birringer, *Marlowe's* Doctor Faustus *and* Tamburlaine (Frankfurt am Main: Verlag Peter Lang, 1984), pp. 97ff.

5. David, for instance, who receives God's messages directly, proclaims them, and sometimes puts them into action according to God's will, can be regarded as a prophet in this sense. Luke himself considers him as a sort of prophet in Acts 2:30.

6. Rhodes, p. 91.

7. U. M. Ellis-Fermor, *Christopher Marlowe* (London: Methuen, 1927), p. 27.

8. Paul H. Kocher, *Christopher Marlowe: A Study of His Thought, Learning, and Character* (1946; New York: Russell & Russell, 1974), p. 71.

9. 1 Samuel 15:3. All the quotations from the Bible are from *The Geneva Bible: A Facsimile of the 1560 Edition*, intro. Lloyd E. Berry (Madison: Univ. of Wisconsin Press, 1969).

10. Cecil Roth, et al. ed. *Encyclopaedia Judaica* (Jerusalem: Keter Publishing House, 1972), vol. 8, "herem." For instance, see Deuteronomy 7:23-24: "The Lord thy god shal giue them before thee, and shal destroy them with a mighty destruction, vntil they be brought to noght. And he shal deliuer their Kings into thine hand, and thou shalt destroy their name from vnder heauen: there shal no man be able to stand before thee, vntil thou hast destroied them."

11. Roy W. Battenhouse, *Marlowe's Tamburlaine: A Study in Renaissance Moral Philosophy* (1941; Vanderbilt: Vanderbilt Univ. Press, 1964).

12. As for these episode on Saul and Balaam, see 1 Samuel, chap. 15, Numbers, chaps. 22-23. Ellis-Fermor comments on this passage that "Marlowe's scriptural knowledge is not so sound as his knowledge of Ovid, for Balaam's position is the converse of Sigismund's." The New Testament is not, however, favourable to Balaam, for he "put a stumbling blocke before the children of Israel" (Rev. 2:14) and "loued the wages of vnrighteousnes" (2 Peter 2:15). Hence, it is quite natural that Saul and Balaam are referred in parallel here as those who did not follow God's command faithfully, and the passage is far from convincing as proof of Marlowe's little biblical knowledge. Cf. U. M. Ellis-Fermor, ed. *Tamburlaine the Great* (1930; New York: Gordian Press, 1966), p. 207.

13. Tamburlaine's speech in *Two* 5. 1. 178ff. has often been taken as his defiance not only to Mahomet but also to a God of moral law including the Christian deity. But he ridicules Mahomet as an antithesis to the true God. The audience recognizes that he has already been associated with "God alone, and none but he." So Tamburlaine, by deriding and blaspheming "superstitious" religious authority in such a provocative way as burning books in public, exalts "the chiefest God" and affirms his loyalty to Him. At the same time, Marlowe creates the impression of Tamburlaine's death as the result of physical exhaustion.

14. Alan Sinfield, *Literature in Protestant England 1560-1660* (London: Croom Helm, 1983), p. 111.

15. This aspect of Tamburlaine is correctly pointed out by Birringer as "self-

mythologization" which "works almost exclusively in terms of its aggressive rhetoric (p. 108). "As for the conscience syndrome of tyrants, see Robert Rentoul Reed, *Crime and God's Judgment in Shakespeare* (Lexington: Univ. Press of Kentucky, 1984), especially the chapters on *Richard III* and *Macbeth*.

16. Cf. James H. Sims, *Dramatic Uses of Biblical Allusions in Marlowe and Shakespeare* (Gainesville: Univ. of Florida Press, 1966), chap. 2. The most important study on Marlowe's use of biblical allusions in *Tamburlaine* is Lynette and Eveline Feasey, "Marlowe and the Prophetic Dooms," *Notes & Queries*, 195 (1950): 356-359, 404-407, 419-421.

17. This tendency can be seen, for instance, in Battenhouse, pp. 171-77; J. P. Cutts, *The Left Hand of God: A Critical Interpretation of the Plays of Christopher Marlowe* (Haddonfield: Haddonfield House, 1973), pp. 54-55, 100-107; John N. King, *English Reformation Literature: The Tudor Origins of the Protestant Tradition* (Princeton: Princeton Univ. Press, 1982), p. 196.

18. Feasey, 420.

19. J. P. Cutts, "The Ultimate Source of Tamburlaine's White, Red, Black and Death?" *Notes & Queries*, 203 (1958): 146-147.

20. Thomas Nashe, *Christs Teares over Iervsalem*, in *The Works of Thomas Nashe*, ed. Ronald B. McKerrow and F. P. Wilson (1957; Oxford: Basil Blackwell, 1966), vol. 2, p. 20.

21. Preparations of military forces in the 1580s are well documented in Lindsay Boynton, *The Elizabethan Militia 1558-1638* (London: RKP, 1967), chap. 5. See also Conyers Read, *Mr. Secretary Walsingham and the Policy of Queen Elizabeth* (1925; New York: AMS, 1978), vol. 3, chap. 13.

22. In the Acts of Privy Council their urgent demands can be seen, e.g. for recruits for the low countries, *APC* 14: pp. 55, 62, 65, 70, 80, 82, 107, 110, 115, 119, *APC* 15: p. 118, etc.; for the defence of the Realm, *APC* 15: pp. 252ff, 296; for 10000 men to be raised in London, *APC* 15: pp. 414, 428. The fact that the Privy Council ordered the recruitment of masterless men to reinforce troops (as well as to rid cities of vagrants) shows how desperately they were in need of soldiers. In 1585, rogues and vagabonds formed part of the first official expedition to the Low Countries. See also J. E. Neale, "Elizabeth and the Netherlands, 1586-7," *English Historical Review*, 45 (1930): 373-396.

23. C. G. Cruickshank, *Elizabeth's Army* (1946; Oxford: Oxford Univ. Press, 1966), p. 283 and Appendix No. 1.

24. Maclure has pointed out that "Nationalism and Protestant piety found united expression in fulminations against Spain. The war with Spain was a great gift to the preachers, for England was fighting a holy war, and the bloody pennos which waved over the flats of Flanders and the splintered decks of English privateers were the banners of the Church militant." Millar MacLure, *The Paul's Cross Sermons 1534-1642* (Toronto: Univ. of Toronto Press, 1958), p. 70. As for the strategy of Elizabethan propaganda, see Gladys Jenkins, "Ways and Means in Elizabethan Propaganda," *History*, 26 (1941): 105-114. On propaganda through the pulpit before the coming of the Armada, see also Boynton, pp. 151-152.

25. Stephen Gosson, *The Trumpet of Warre: A Sermon preached at Paules Crosse*

the seuenth of Maie 1598 (London, 1598), sig. A3^r.

26. Sig. F1^r. Anderson seems to have been in Walsingham's patronage, for he writes in "The Epistle dedicatorie" that "to whose [Walsingham's] goodnes I am not smally bounde, for that benefite, which earst by your honourable meanes I did attaine (sig. A2^v)."

27. The same analogical idea can be seen in William Grauet's *A Sermon Preached at Pavles Cross on the XXV day of June Ann. Dom. 1587* (London, 1587). He refers to several champions for justice in the Old Testament, and compares England's situation to the miraculous episode that "Gedeon accompanied with three hundred men onely fought against Madian, and Amalec, and the east people which were gathered togither like a multitude of locusts, and ouercame them." His conclusion is a prayer that "his mercifull power may alwaies protect, saue, and defend our most noble and gratious soueraigne, Queene *Elizabeth*, and this our realm of England, from all craftie and cruell assaults of our enimies" (pp. 73-4). Here, his conviction of England's triumph over idolatrous Catholics, parallel to Gideon's over idolatrous Baalites, is demonstrated. There is an excellent chapter on the analogy in Patrick Collinson, *The Birthpangs of Protestant England: Religious and Cultural Change in the Sixteenth and Seventeenth Centuries* (London: Macmillan, 1988), chap. 1. The important role of religion in the anti-Spanish campaign is pointed out by E. I. Kouri, in "For True Faith or National Interest?: Queen Elizabeth I and the Protestant Powers," in E. I. Kouri and Tom Scott, ed. *Politics and Society in Reformation Europe: Essays for Sir Geoffrey Elton on His Sixty-Fifth Birthday* (London: Macmillan, 1987), pp. 411-436.

28. Paul A. Jorgensen's article is valuable when considering the morale building of Elizabethan soldiers on a religious level. See his "Moral Guidance and Religious Encouragement for the Elizabethan Soldier," *Huntington Library Quarterly*, 13 (1950): 241-259.

29. Cited by Richard Bauckham, in *Tudor Apocalypse* (Oxford: The Sutton Courtenay Press, 1978), p. 175. He has elucidated that the Protestant interpretation of the Antichrist in Revelation was employed to legitimate the use of armed forces against Spain.

30. These psychological conditions are closely akin to those of religious riots. As to Catholic and Protestant legitimations of violence and their concern to destroy poluting elements in religious riots, see Natalie Zemon Davis, *Society and Culture in Early Modern France* (1965; Cambridge: Polity Press, 1987), chap. 6.

31. This sort of morale-building technique can be seen in plays under the strong influence of *Tamburlaine* such as *Four Prentices* or *Locrine*. Cf. Mark Thornton Burnett, "Marlovian Imitation and Interpretation in Heywood's *The Four Prentices of London*," *Cahiers Elisabethains*, 32 (1987): 75-78. Peter Berek, "*Locrine* Revised, *Selimus*, and Early Responses to *Tamburlaine*," *Research Opportunities in Renaissance Drama*, 23 (1980): 33-54.

32. Cf. Stephen S. Hilliard, "Stephen Gosson and the Elizabethan Distrust of the Effects of Drama," *English Literary Renaissance*, 9 (1979): 225-239.

33 An example of this is the hiring of playwrights and players to strike back at Martin Marprelate when he criticized the Established Church successfully

with surreptitious pamphlets. Cf. Chambers, *ES*, vol. 4, pp. 229-233. William Pierce's account in *An Historical Introduction to the Marprelate Tracts* (London: Archibald Constable, 1908) is still informative. See particularly, pp. 196-241. Interestingly enough, *Playes Confuted in fiue Actions* was dedicated to Sir Francis Walsingham. Some critics assume Walsingham's sympathy toward Puritanism may have motivated Gosson to choose him as a patron, but actually Gosson himself had a bias in favour of the Established Church and can never be identified as a Puritan. Walsingham was also, as Read admits, "very far from sharing the dour Puritan attitude towards pleasures of a similar character" (Read, vol. 3, p. 437). Hence it is not Walsingham's religious tendency, it seems, but rather the fact that he had a strong voice in regulating and patronizing the stage that made Gosson dedicate his pamphlet to him. There is no knowing Walsingham's personal views on the theatre. He did not treat Gosson or Maliverny Catlyn, another devotee of antitheatricalism, coldly, yet he was not necessarily hostile to the stage. He was instrumental in the organization of the Queen Elizabeth's men in 1583, and, in spite of the Lord Mayor's attack, he looked after the interests of the company so that they could continue to give performances. He may naturally have been in contact with actors, for Richard Tarlton, the leading comedian of the company, wrote from his death-bed to ask him to protect the interests of his wife, "a silly old widow of fourscore years," and "his son being six years of age" (*CSPD*, 1588, pp. 541-2). It may be that, though Walsingham's influence over the control of the stage drew antitheatrically-biased people around him, he neither positively suppressed nor openly supported it. This irresolute attitude seems to imply not his indifference but his political judgment. Having admitted what they claimed, he did not find any reason to abolish the public theatre. In other words, he was very much aware of its usefulness.

34. Almost all the biographers are unanimous, it seems, in thinking that Marlowe was probably engaged in Francis Walsingham's espionage activities. Recently, several studies on the Elizabethan secret service were published and Marlowe has been spotlighted in connection with Walsingham's spy network more than ever before: Charles Nicholl, *The Reckoning: The Murder of Christopher Marlowe* (London: Jonathan Cape, 1992); Alan Haynes, *Invisible Power: The Elizabethan Secret Services 1570-1603* (Stroud, Glous.: Alan Sutton, 1992); Roy Kendall, "Richard Baines and Christopher Marlowe's Milieu," *English Literary Renaissance*, 24 (1994): 507-552, and also see my article, "Christopher Marlowe and the Kentish Connection," *Studies in English Literature*, published by the English Literary Society of Japan (English Number, 1996): 17-35. The first part of *Tamburlaine* is usually assumed to have been written during the winter of 1587, and the second part immediately afterwards in 1588. This date is based on the preface to Greene's *Perimedes the Blacke Smith*, which was registered on 29 March, 1588. The reference is too obscure to decide whether he refers to the first or the second part, but "it has long seemed reasonable to assume that Greene has in mind the climactic incident in the second part, when Tamburlaine orders the burning of the 'superstitious books' of Mohammedan scripture (Cunningham, p. 22)." There is another convincing clue, if conjectual, to fix the

date earlier. Philip Gawdy, an esquire of Norfolk, reported in a letter to his father dated on 16 Nov. 1587 an accident during a play by the Admiral's men, the scene of which, some critics including Chambers have suggested, had a close resemblance to that of the execution of the Governor of Babylon in the last act of the second part. According to these critics, we can date the first part earlier to Marlowe's collegiate days, even to the year 1586, and the second part to the autumn or winter of 1587.

35. Cf. J. Leslie Hotson, *The Death of Christopher Marlowe* (1925; New York: Russell & Russell, 1967), pp. 57-64.

36. For instance, see Battenhouse and E. M. Waith, *The Herculean Hero in Marlowe, Chapman, Shakespeare and Dryden* (London: Chatto and Windus, 1962).

37. Cf. Kocher, pp. 69-70. G. I. Duthie persuasively shows how the first part of Tamburlaine has its own unity and theme. See his "The Dramatic Structure of Marlowe's *Tamburlaine the Great, Parts One and Two*," *English Studies*, 1 (1948): 101-126.

38. On the historical events and sources of the Sigismond episode, see Ellis-Fermor (1930), pp. 41-43.

39. Cunningham, p. 77. It is interesting to note that Tamburlaine, who regarded his sword as the religious authority when he meets Bajazeth face to face in the first part, no longer swears by his sword in the second part. He turns to Mahomet instead and often makes such an oath as "I have sworn by sacred Mahomet." It seems strange for him to swear by his name, for, though the historical Timur was a devout Mahommedan, this kind of swearing cannot be found in the first part. Moreover, Mahomet is ridiculed when Tamburlaine with his comrades persecutes Bajazeth at the banquet scene. This may not be due to Marlowe's opportunism, but his tacit design to interrelate his swearing by Mahomet with his burning of the Koran. In the name of Mahomet, Tamburlaine makes war against the Turks, kills his effeminate son Calyphas, and suddenly, at the end of the play, pulls Mahomet down from heaven. It seems that Marlowe uses Tamburlaine's defiance to Mahomet to propel the audience into enthusiasm, while he casts a backhanded lustre over Tamburlaine's heroic figure.

On the Margins of a Civilization: The Representation of the Scythians in Elizabethan Texts

ATSUHIKO HIROTA

IRELAND AND ITS inhabitants were one of the chief problems for Elizabethan England. Although Elizabeth I inherited the title of the queen of Ireland,[1] the English attempts to colonize Ireland were never completely successful. As a result, although Ireland was officially part of Elizabeth I's realm, English rule was effective only in limited areas and Ireland's population was regarded as a hostile "other."[2] The Irish fiercely resisted the English and the Elizabethan period records several Irish rebellions and their violent suppression. Ireland was dependent upon, yet separate from, England.

The Elizabethan Englishmen extended their interest in historiography to the history of Ireland and its inhabitants. For example, Edmund Campion wrote *A Historie of Ireland* in 1571 and Richard Stanyhurst used it as the basis when he wrote *The Description of Ireland* for Holinshed's *Chronicles*. These histories of Ireland owe much to myth and legend.[3] As Andrew Hadfield observes, however, growing scepticism about the sources characterizes early modern historiography.[4] Edmund Spenser's *A View of the Present State of Ireland* (c.1596) clearly reflects this new scepticism. In this treatise Eudoxus dismisses Irish chronicles as "most fabulous and forged." Irenius agrees but says: "But yet under these tales ye may in a manner see the truth lurk."[5] In this conversation we see the aspiration of the new historiography to seek for the truth lurking under unreliable sources.

In *A View* Irenius is engaged in the new historian's project of probing the true origin of the Irish people. He argues for their Scythian ancestry using as evidence Irish customs which he claims to have originated with the Scythians. In his insistence on the Scythian ancestry of the Irish, Irenius represents Spenser's view as he does in many other matters. Spenser's attempt to stress the Scythian origin of the Irish has drawn the attention of recent critics. For instance, Hadfield observes that Spenser is keen to stress the Scythian roots of the Irish rather than to confirm the British claim to Ireland.[6] Ann Rosalind Jones and Peter Stallybrass say that Spenser is intent to show that "the chiefest which have first possessed and inhabited" Ireland were the Scythians. Jones and Stallybrass also point out one of the difficulties Spenser confronted: the Scythians were, on the one hand, barbarous nomadic vagrants with the custom of cannibalism; on the other hand, early history records their military glory.[7] This dual character of the Scythians makes Spenser's treatment of the Irish in his treatise ambivalent.

In this essay I will argue the importance of the Scythian associations for Elizabethan culture. The Scythian descent of the Irish alone establishes the Scythians as this culture's important element, but the writers of the time present this barbarous nomadic tribe in other contexts, too. Among them I will discuss Marlowe's Tamburlaine and the Amazons in Spenser's *The Faerie Queene* and in Sir Walter Raleigh's *The Discouerie of the Large, Rich, and Bewtiful Empyre of Guiana*. In these texts the Scythians and their associates are presented as the entities which pose serious threats from the margins. Since the Elizabethan period was the time of the establishment of English identity as a civilized nation, the Scythians play a role in presenting its "other" in various contexts. By presenting the story of a Scythian nomad who begins as a shepherd and establishes a great empire extending from Asia to Africa, Marlowe explores in *Tamburlaine* images of the Scythians both as nomads and as fighters. Spenser and Raleigh probe another significant association of the Scythians: the one with the Amazons whom classical writers alleged to have originated in that region. We will see that the Scythians gained a new association in the New World via the images of the Amazons. The examination of the Scythian images in Elizabethan England will lead us from the Elizabethan underworld of the vagabonds to Ireland, and from Asia to America. This wide range of their distribution reflects the deep-rootedness of the Scythians as an "other" of which the Elizabethan writers took full advantage.

1

The Scythians and the Irish share common characteristics. Like their alleged ancestors, the Irish were both barbarous savages and good sol-

On the Margins of a Civilization

diers. Irenius observes this duality in the "galloglass and kerne." He stresses their savagery on the one hand:

> They spoil as well the subject as the enemy, they steal, they are cruel and bloody, full of revenge, and delight in deadly execution, licentious swearers and blasphemers, common ravishers of women, and murderers of children.

On the other hand, he admits that they are good soldiers:

> Yet sure they are very valiant and hardy, for the most part great endurers of the cold, labour, hunger, and all hardness, very active, and strong of hand, very swift of foot, very vigilant and circumspect in their enterprises, very present in perils, very great scorners of death.[8]

The repetition of the word "very" in this speech highlights that even Irenius cannot but praise his barbarous enemies. The emphasis on the Scythian origin of the Irish leads Irenius to an argument about contemporary problems. In the extensive description of the Irish customs allegedly derived from the Scythians, Irenius observes the custom of "Bollyng" first and foremost. When Eudoxus asks what is wrong with this custom, Irenius cites its three vices: firstly, "outlaws and loose people" will find rescue among the "Bollies"; secondly, cattle thieves are able to sell the stolen cattle to them; and thirdly, people who live in

> Bollies grow thereby the more barbarous and live more licentiously than they could in towns . . . for there they think themselves half exempted from law and obedience, and having once tasted freedom do . . . grudge and repine ever after to come under rule again.[9]

In short, "bollyng" permits those who practice it to taste the joy of freedom. It allows them to think themselves half out of the law's constraints and eventually to live "barbarously" and "licentiously." In the process of exploring the Scythian ancestry of the Irish, Irenius finds a reason why the Irish are nomadic and barbarous.

The vagrancy, the thieving, and the licentiousness provide us with a link to connect the Irish to the problem of vagrancy, another important problem for Elizabethan England. The authorities declared that the Irish constituted no small part of the vagrant population in England. "An Acte for the Punishment of Vacabondes, and for Relief of the Poore and

Impotent" (1572) includes sections prohibiting the import of vagabonds from Ireland and the Isle of Man and commanding them to be deported.[10] "A Proclamation for suppressing of the multitude of idle Vagabonds, and avoyding of certaine mischieuous dangerous persons from her Maiesties Court" (21 February 1594), which announces the threat of the Irish "traitors" to the queen herself, orders all the Irish vagabonds without licence to be sent back to Ireland on the ground that "the discouerie of these Irish traitours can hardly bee made, where there are also many other like vagrant persons of that Nation that haunt about the Court . . . ."[11] The vagrancy problem had haunted the reign of Elizabeth for a long time.[12] Particularly in the mid-1590s, there was a strong fear during the worsening crises in Ireland that Irishmen, who had been fighting against the queen, aimed at her life while hiding among vagabonds.

The proliferation of the rogue pamphlets in the late Elizabethan period reflects this official concern about vagrancy.[13] Among them Thomas Harman's *Caueat for Commen Cvrsetors Vvlgarly Called Vagabones*, . . . (1567) refers to Irish vagabonds in two places.[14] The Elizabethan playhouses were not indifferent to this problem, either. For instance, Anthony Munday and his collaborators presented on the public stage a murderous Irish highwayman in *The First Part of Sir John Oldcastle*.[15] If *Sir John Oldcastle* was, as the title page of the 1600 edition announces, performed by the Lord Admiral's Men, the same company had earlier presented another vagrant in Christopher Marlowe's *Tamburlaine the Great*. In this two-part play about the Scythian conqueror Marlowe presents the vagrancy problem on a grand scale. He employs various images which circulated around the Scythians in order to produce his empire-building Scythian vagabond. In *Tamburlaine* Marlowe refers to the images of the Scythians as nomads, warriors, and magicians. These images are also used by Spenser when he stresses the Scythian ancestry of the Irish in *A View*. The Scythians provide these Elizabethan writers with the bases upon which they explore contemporary problems.

Stephen Greenblatt points out Marlowe's fascination with the idea of limitless and unvarying physical movement.[16] In his first successful play Marlowe reveals this fascination in the forms of Tamburlaine's wandering and conquests which only his death can stop. The very first image of Tamburlaine in the play defines him as a wandering thief. Meander says to Mycetes, king of Persia:

> Oft have I heard your majesty complain
> Of Tamburlaine, *that sturdy Scythian thief,*
> That robs your merchants of Persepolis,
> Treading by land unto the Western Isles,
> And in your confines with his *lawless train,*
> Daily commits incivil outrages .... (Part 1: 1. 1. 35-40, italics mine)[17]

According to the official Persian view, Tamburlaine is a "sturdy thief" leading his "lawless train" on roads. Throughout the play his enemies repeatedly call Tamburlaine and his followers thieves: Ortygius calls Tamburlaine "a devilish thief" (2. 6. 20); Bajazeth "the Tartars and the eastern thieves" (3. 1. 2); Zabina "the great Tartarian thief" and "[i]njurious villains, thieves, runagates" (3. 3. 171 and 225); and Soldan the "rogue of Volga" with "a troop of thieves and vagabonds" and a "sturdy felon and a base-born thief" (4. 1. 4 and 6, and 4. 3. 12). All these names given to Tamburlaine and his troop are the same terms the Elizabethan authorities used for vagabonds. The Scythian Tamburlaine is a theatrical representation of Elizabethan vagabonds.

Mark Thornton Burnett provides three points in which Tamburlaine is associated with vagabonds: a freedom of movement, contempt of religion, and predisposition to theft.[18] These three points are exactly applicable to the Irish whom Spenser pictures in *A View*. As we have seen, Spenser points out that the Irish custom of "bollying" connects Irishmen to the freedom of movement and predisposition to theft. Furthermore, Spenser observes that the Irish were not only Roman Catholic, which was outrageous in itself, but also notorious for their superstitiousness. We find remarkable similarities between Tamburlaine and the Irish of *A View*. The wandering lawlessness inspired by shepherding links Tamburlaine to the Irish. Burnett also observes Marlowe's irony about the vagabond problem. He points out that Marlowe, by putting the attacks of Tamburlaine's vagrancy in his weak enemies' mouths, creates a discrepancy between the audience's opinion and these attacks.[19] We have seen that the Scythian origin makes the image of the Irish ambivalent for Spenser. Tamburlaine shares this ambivalence. Although his weak enemies repeatedly call him "thief" and "slave," and although his first appearance is as a shepherd, Tamburlaine is invincible.[20] Marlowe creates his hero on the ambivalence surrounding the Scythians.

2

We find another characteristic which links Marlowe's Scythian hero to the Irish in his ability to persuade Theridamas to join his wandering army. When Theridamas first appears as a Persian general being sent to suppress Tamburlaine, he says:

> Before the moon renew her borrowed light,
> Doubt not my lord and gracious sovereign,
> But Tamburlaine, and that Tartarian rout,
> Shall either perish by our warlike hands,
> Or plead for mercy at your highness' feet. (1. 1. 69-73)

He takes the official view of Tamburlaine's force being a "Tartarian rout" and vows to destroy it. Theridamas, however, betrays the Persian court and joins Tamburlaine's force. When Theridamas's army approaches, Techelles and Usumcasane insist on fighting, but Tamburlaine is aware that his enemy is stronger than his own force. He says: "A thousand horsemen? We five hundred foot? / An odds too great for us to stand against" (1. 2. 121-22). He proposes a parley and persuades Theridamas to betray the Persian king with a grand promise of sharing his glory. Theridamas says: "What strong *enchantments* tice my yielding soul? / Ah, these resolved *noble Scythians*!" (224-25, italics mine) and "Won with thy words, and conquered with thy looks" (228).[21] Theridamas now calls Tamburlaine and his followers "noble Scythians." The change from the "Tartarian rout" in his earlier speech to the "noble Scythians" is remarkable, but the ambivalence surrounding the Scythians may well have made this shift easy.

Theridamas's word "enchantments" reminds us of another classical image of Scythia which critics have not discussed fully in association with Tamburlaine, namely the image of the land of sorcery. Book Seven of Ovid's *Metamorphoses* presents Medea as a sorceress of Colchis. In Arthur Golding's translation we find that Scythia is her homeland: "To haue killde / This worthie knight [Theseus], Medea had a Goblet readie fillde / With iuice of flintwoort venemous the which she long ago / Had out of *Scythie* with hir brought."[22] Medea the Scythian sorceress provides Scythia with a strong association with a dark borderland of threatening female magical power.[23] Marlowe's interest in classical literature is obvious. He, however, was not the only playwright of the time who explored the classical association of Scythia with sorcery. In *The Tempest* Shakespeare produces another witch whose connection with Scythia introduces various related problems. Critics have agreed that the characterization of Sycorax owes much to Ovid's presentation of Medea. For instance, Stephen Orgel observes that the name Sycorax, although it has never been adequately explained, sounds like an epithet for Ovid's Medea, the Scythian raven. Orgel also points out the possible connection between the traditional Scythian cannibalism and Sycorax's son Caliban.[24] The Scythian association with sorcery was a cutural property of the time and both Marlowe and Shakespeare used it in their plays.[25]

The Scythian association with sorcery provides another link between the Scythians and the Irish. The Irish were readily associated with sorcery because of their Roman Catholic faith and their superstitiousness. Gamini Salgado points out that the medieval Catholic Church laid claims to many powerful kinds of magic, including confession and absolution, conjuration and consecration, and exorcism and healing.[26] After the Reformation the Church of England took the magic out of Christianity. The Protestant Church not only expelled magic from Christianity but also called magic a Catholic superstition. Keith Thomas observes that in the reign of Elizabeth I the term "conjuror" became a synonym for recusant priest and that a Puritan manifesto described the Church of Rome as the source of "all wicked sorcery."[27] The Protestant Church strategically called the Roman Catholic Church superstitious in order to destroy its authority. The Irish people's faith in Catholicism was one of the problems which irritated and worried the English authorities, especially during the war with Spain.

The Irish, in addition, were notorious for their pre-Christian superstitions.[28] About Irish superstitiousness Irenius says: "It is no cause of wonder at all, for it is the manner of all barbarous nations to be very superstitious and diligent observers of old customs and antiquities...."[29] Irenius has even harsher words:

> the fault which I find in religion is but one, but the same universal throughout all that country, that is that they are all Papists by their profession, but in the same so blindly and brutishly informed, for the most part as that you would rather think them atheists or infidels .... [30]

The Irish, according to Irenius, were Papists, which was offensive enough. Worse still, their ignorance made them "atheists and infidels." Both of these allegations—their Catholic faith and their superstitiousness—associate the Irish with sorcery. The Scythians and the Irish again come together in the Elizabethan association with sorcery.

3

One of the reasons why the Elizabethan Englishmen loathed the Irish so much lies in their power of absorbing English settlers into Irish culture. The Irish were the conquered nation with the implication that they were inferior to the conquering English in terms of culture. The Irish were barbaric and the English were civilized. The Irish, however, resisted the civilized English way and instead the English settlers became like the barbarous Irish. Irenius expresses his indignation at those who have become "almost as lewd as the Irish" and "as very patchocks as the wild Irish."[31] These Anglo-Irish settlers are particularly annoying for Irenius not only because they have given up "civility," but also because they have become hostile to English rule. Irenius says: "the most part of them are degenerated and grown almost mere Irish, yea and more malicious to the English than the very Irish themselves," and "the chiefest abuses which are now in that realm [Ireland] are grown from the English, and the English that were are now much more lawless and licentious than the very wild Irish . . . ."[32] Eudoxus finds it difficult to believe that an Englishman can choose to live like the Irish. In his speech the contrast between civilized England and barbarous Ireland is apparent:

> What hear I? And is it possible that an Englishman brought up naturally in such sweet civility as England affords could find such liking in that barbarous rudeness that he should forget his own nature and forgo his own nation?[33]

Eudoxus notes that England's "sweet civility" becomes an Englishman's own "nature." For him it is unnatural that an Englishman likes the "barbarous rudeness." These remarks reflect the exasperation of the Elizabethan colonizers including Spenser himself that the Anglo-Irish were a great hindrance to their enterprise.

Irenius provides an analysis of the causes of these English settlers' "degeneration." He is particularly indignant at their use of Irish names and the Irish language.[34] He then insists that there are two causes for the English settlers' embracement of the Irish language: their use of Irish nurses and their marriage with Irish women.[35] Irenius observes that English settlers' Irish nurses and Irish wives are responsible for their and their descendants' "degeneration." Irish women resist English colonization by assimilating the settlers just as Irish men resist by rebellions.

For Irenius the female threat can be more troublesome than rebellions. He has a master plan to extinguish military rebellions. He asserts that from the experience in Munster the use of famine is effective (and inexpensive):

> Although there should none of them fall by the sword, nor be slain by the soldier, yet thus being kept from manurance, and their cattle from running abroad by this hard restraint, they would quickly consume themselves and devour one another.[36]

Irenius, however, admits that he cannot stop the process of the "degeneration." To Eudoxus, who asks whether there is no law against it, he answers: "Yes, I think there be, but as good never a whit as never the better. For what do statutes avail without penalties, or laws without charge or execution?"[37] By observing the seriousness of the assimilation, Irenius emphasizes the role of women in the Irish resistance against English colonization. The threat from Irish women at least partly cancels the seriousness of the military threat from Irish men. Irenius first refers to Irish women as "wandering women" in mantles called "Monashut" in his argument about the use of mantles being one of the Scythian customs. He says that an Irish woman uses her mantle for "a coverlet for her lewd exercise" and that "under it she can hide both her burden and her blame."[38] From the beginning Irenius presents Irish women in terms of sexuality. Irenius's feminization of the Irish threat, however, does not contradict with the traditional representation of Ireland as a female to be conquered by male (English) conquerors.[39]

The feminine threat of Ireland reminds us of an Elizabethan reference to another classical sorceress. Ireland is compared to Circe in Holinshed's *Chronicles*. The last paragraph of *The Description of Ireland* begins: "Againe, the verie English of birth, conuersant with the sauage sort of that people become degenerat, and as though they had tasted of Circes poisoned cup, are quite altered."[40] We have already seen that

Scythia has a traditional link to sorcery through Medea. And according to Apollonius Rhodius, Medea is a niece of Circe who is notorious for transforming men into pigs.[41] In Holinshed the English settlers who are absorbed into Irish savagery are compared to those who drank Circe's cup and were transformed into pigs. Ireland itself is represented as a threatening female.

In the discourse of conquest it is not only Ireland which Elizabethan texts feminized. For instance, in *The Discouerie of the Large, Rich, and Bewtiful Empyre of Guiana* Sir Walter Raleigh writes about the "Maydenhead" of Peru and Guiana.[42] Although sexual conquest was a frequently employed analogy, it is not the only way of feminization for a male-centered culture to deal with the "other." The Scythians have a long tradition of feminization in the form of the Amazons as well as of sorceresses. In Greek mythology Scythia is the land of the Amazons. This association with the female warriors who put a serious challenge to the accepted male norm occurred because Scythia was on the borderland of Greek civilization. The image of the Amazons had undergone a significant development by the sixteenth century. It had expanded geographically corresponding to the expansion of the European world view. As Louis Adrian Montrose observes, the Amazons are relocated just beyond the receding boundary of *terra incognita*.[43] Just as Scythia had formed a boundary for ancient Greek civilization, the New World became a boundary for early modern European civilization. Both of these boundaries were regarded as Amazons' land.

Elizabethan texts abound with references to the Amazons. With the virgin queen as the supreme ruler, the image of the Amazons for the Elizabethans could not remain only in the exotic, newly found geographical margins. Although the linking of the Amazons to the queen was a sensitive matter, we find examples of such an association in the works of Raleigh and Spenser. Raleigh, introducing the Amazons in the neighboring region of Guiana, suggests that Elizabeth I should subjugate them along with Guiana.[44] This suggestion, according to Montrose, insinuates that the queen can be like an Amazon and that she can cleanse herself from contamination by the Amazons if she sanctions their subjugation. Montrose further observes that Elizabeth's conquest of the Amazons is analogous to Britomart's conquest of Radigund's Amazonarchy in Spenser's *The Faerie Queene*, Book V.[45]

Spenser's presentations of Amazons in *The Faerie Queene* not only deal with their association with the queen but also explore the confrontation of a civilization with a barbarous "other." Spenser, who manifestly supports Raleigh's project of the colonization of Guiana, writes:

> And that huge Riuer, which doth beare his name
> Of warlike Amazons, which doe possesse the same.
>
> Ioy on those warlike women, which so long
> Can from all men so rich a kingdome hold;
> And shame on you, ô men, which boast your strong
> And valiant hearts, in thoughts lesse hard and bold,
> Yet quaile in conquest of that land of gold.   (4. 11. 21-22)[46]

He encourages the male conquest of the Amazon's land in the New World. This conquest is a metaphor of the English conquest of the wealth of the New World, and the conquerors must be men. In Book 2 Spenser already compares Belphoebe—one of his poetic characterizations of Elizabeth I—to the classical Amazon queen Penthesilea. She is like "that famous Queene / Of *Amazons*, whom *Pyrrhus* did destroy" (2. 3. 31).[47] This association of Belphoebe-Elizabeth I with Penthesilea, particularly with reference to her death by the hand of Pyrrhus, reflects the problematic status of a female monarch in a patriarchal state: a queen is at the center of the state's power structure, but since she is a woman, she is always under the threat of being subjugated by males.[48]

Critics have read the episode of Britomart's victory over Radigund in *The Faerie Queene* Book 5 as a contrast between the acceptable and the threatening warrior women. As a story of the chaste Britomart's victory over the lascivious Radigund, it authenticates the established order. It is also possible, as Philippa Berry suggests, to read this episode as a political allegory of Elizabeth I's execution of Mary Queen of Scots, the incident which Spenser retells later in the same book as the trial and execution of Duessa.[49] The central mission of Book 5, however, is Artegall's rescuing of Irena (Ireland) from Grantorto (Catholicism). This book also refers to the Irish rebel: it has been pointed out that Malengin in canto 9 is an allegorical representation of the Irish kern.[50] When we read the episode of Radigund in the light of these episodes as well as in the light of the associations surrounding the Amazons, the Scythians, and the Irish, I think that yet another reading is possible. As an Amazon queen, Radigund is associated with Scythia and barbarism. Britomart's experience in the temple of Isis, the Egyptian goddess, underscores these associations.[51] Scythia is cold, nomadic, and barbarous; in contrast, Egypt is hot, settled, and civilized.[52] Radigund, the lascivious subjugator of men, and Britomart, who gained an association with Egypt, respectively represent each of these sets. Their combat is an allegorical representation of a civilization's struggle to conquer a barbarous "other"—similar to the attempt being practiced in Ireland by Elizabethan Englishmen including Spenser himself.[53]

I propose a reading of the combat between Britomart and Radigund as an allegorical representation of the conflict between civilized England and barbarous Ireland. The victory of Britomart confirms the victory of England and its civilization, and the destruction of the Amazonarchy suggests the destruction of the native Irish culture. In this reading it is noteworthy that Britomart's victory comes after Artegall's defeat and humiliating emasculation. Radigund's subjugation of Artegall reminds us of the "degeneration" which Irish women inflict upon English settlers. In the poem Britomart comes to rescue Artegall and assists him in achieving his mission of releasing Irena from Grantorto. Artegall's success doubly confirms the final success of the English colonizing project in Ireland together with Britomart's victory over Radigund.

*

Elizabethan texts present the Scythians and their descendants—vagrants, witches, cannibals, the Amazons, and the Irish—as an important "other." Although their appearances in these texts are often witnessed in the obscure margins of the Elizabethan world (with a remarkable exception of the association of the Amazons with the queen, which suggests the queen's sensitive position), the frequency and complexity of their associations with the wide variety of marginal entities paradoxically attests that the images of the Scythians and their derivatives have a place near the center of Elizabethan culture because the center always demands the margins.

The Scythians appear from the very beginning of British history as an enemy. Holinshed's *Chronicles* describes the invasion of Humber into Britain in the time of the Trojan Brute's three sons:

> While this Locrinus gouerned Logiers, his brother Albanact ruled in Albania, where in fine he was slaine in a battell by a king of the Hunnes or Scythians, called Humber, who inuaded that part

of Britaine ....⁵⁴

Although Locrinus and Camber defeat Humber, Locrinus falls in love with the Scythian Estrild and forsakes his wife Guendolonea. Guendolonea wages a war against her husband for revenge, kills him in defeat, and rules Britain as regent of her son. In this story of the first British encounter with the Scythians all the important characters of the Scythian threats are present. They are both military and sexual and jeopardize Britain's patriarchal power structure. This quotation from Holinshed's *Chronicles* demonstrates uncertainty about the origin of Humber: he was "a king of the Hunnes or Scythians." Geoffrey of Monmouth's *The History of the Kings of Britain* records no such reservation. Geoffrey calls Humber "the King of the Huns."⁵⁵ Holinshed's uncertainty apparently influenced the story of Humber's invasion in *The Faerie Queene*. In *Briton moniments*, which Arthur reads in Alma's castle in Book 2, Spenser writes that after the division of Britain by the three sons of Brute, they ruled each portion peacefully:

> Vntill a nation straung, with visage swart,
> And courage fierce, that all men did affray,
> Which through the world then swarmd in euery part,
> And ouerflow'd all countries farre away,
> Like *Noyes* great flood, with their importune sway,
> The land inuaded with like violence ...   (2. 10. 15)

Spenser does not specify the name of the invaders. He only provides their characteristics of dark complexion, fierce courage, and large scale conquests. In *Locrine*, an anonymous play first published in 1595, the uncertainty disappears. In it Humber calls himself "the *Scithian* Emperour" (2. 2. 472).⁵⁶ The change of Humber's tribe from the Huns in Geoffrey of Monmouth to the Scythians in *Locrine* through the uncertainty in Holinshed and Spenser suggests that the Scythians were becoming the general name for the belligerent Asian tribe in the late sixteenth century.

The Scythian and its derivative images are relevant to the important problems of Elizabethan England: the Scythians are the alleged ancestors of the Irish; the Scythian Tamburlaine is a dramatic representation of the vagrants; the Scythian association with sorcery connects them to Catholicism (especially applicable to the Irish); and the Amazons deal with the problem of a female monarch as well as they refer to the New

World expansion. All these are important matters in the establishment of English identity. Just as the ancient Scythians had been essential for the determination of Greek identity as the center of civilization, the Scythians and their derivatives were crucial in the formation of English identity as a civilized nation. Since the Scythian images were essential for Elizabethan England, it was natural that the Irish—the most important "other" for the English—were linked to the Scythians.[57] It was also inevitable that these Scythian images scattered all over the world in the time when England started geographical expansion. The Elizabethan writers presented the Scythian "other" in the tradition of European civilization. They also attached new significance to their images in the new context of the time. The abundance and the variety of the images surrounding the Scythians prove the strength of their incorporation as an "other" in European civilization. They also suggest the essentiality of the existence of an "other" for a civilization.

Notes

1. The proclamation of 17 November 1558 (1 Elizabeth I) defines the title of Elizabeth as: "Elizabeth by the grace of God Queen of England, France, and Ireland, defender of the faith, etc." *Tudor Royal Proclamations*, vol. II, ed. Paul L. Hughes and James F. Larkin (New Haven: Yale Univ. Press, 1969) p. 99.

2. For a discussion on the status of Ireland under the Tudors, see, for example, M. Perceval-Maxwell, "Ireland and the Monarchy in the Early Stuart Multiple Kingdom," *The Historical Journal*, 34 (1991): 279-95, especially, 279-85. Debora Shuger's intriguing article on the association between the Irish and Elizabethan aristocrats appeared as my article was in press (Debora Shuger, "Irishmen, Aristocrats, and Other White Barbarians," *Renaissance Quarterly*, 50 (1997): 494-525).

3. Edmund Campion, *A Historie of Ireland* (1571; New York: Scholars' Facsimiles & Reprints, 1940) p. 20. *Holinshed's Chronicles England, Scotland, and Ireland*, Vol. VI (1808; New York: AMS Press, 1965), p. 73.

4. Andrew Hadfield, "Briton and Scythian: Tudor Representations of Irish Origins" *Irish Historical Studies*, 28 (1993): 390.

5. Edmund Spenser, *A View of the Present State of Ireland*, ed. W. L. Renwick (Oxford: Clarendon Press, 1970), pp. 39, 43. All subsequent quotations from *A View* are taken from this edition.

6. Hadfield, 400.

7. Ann Rosalind Jones and Peter Stallybrass, "Dismantling Irena: The Sexualizing of Ireland in Early Modern England," *Nationalisms & Sexualities*, ed. Andrew Parker, et al. (New York: Routledge, 1992), p. 159.

8. Spenser, *A View*, p. 72.
Irenius also mentions Irishmen's horsemanship:

> ... I have heard some great warriors say that in all the services which they had seen abroad in foreign countries they never saw a more comely horseman than the Irishman, nor that cometh on more bravely in his charge .... (p. 70)

9. Spenser, *A View*, pp. 49-50.
10. 14 Eliz. c. 5. *The Statutes of the Realm*. Vol. IV, pt. 1. (1817; London: 1963), p. 596.
11. "A Proclamation for suppressing of the multitude of idle Vagabondes, and avoyding of certaine mischieuous dangerous persons from her Maiesties Court." (London: 1594). STC 8236.
12. For the recent studies of the vagrancy problem in early modern England, see, for instance, A. L. Beier, *Masterless Men: The Vagrancy Problem in England 1560-1640* (London: Methuen, 1985), J. A. Sharpe, *Crime in Early Modern England 1550-1750* (London: Longman, 1984), pp. 99-103, *Early Modern England: A Social History 1550-1760* (London: Edward Arnold, 1987), pp. 216-20, and Paul Slack, *Poverty and Policy in Tudor and Stuart England* (London: Longman, 1988), pp. 91-112. About the English policy against the Irish travelling on roads, see David Beers Quinn, *The Elizabethans and the Irish* (Ithaca: Cornell Univ. Press, 1966), Chapter X.
13. For discussions about the vagrancy problem and the rogue literature, see Beier, chapter 1 and Gamini Salgado, *The Elizabethan Underworld* (1977; Stroud, Gloucestershire: Alan Sutton, 1992), Chapter 6.
14. Thomas Harman, *A Caueat for Commen Cvrsetors Vvlgarely Called Vagabones*, ... (London: 1567). STC 12787. Folios 14^v, 20^r.
15. *The first part of the true and honorable historie, of the life of Sir John Old-castle, the good Lord Cobham. The Shakespeare Apocrypha*, ed. C. F. Tucker Brooke (Oxford: Clarendon Press, 1908), 5. 2-10.
16. Stephen Greenblatt, *Renaissance Self-Fashioning: From More to Shakespeare* (Chicago: Univ. of Chicago Press, 1980), p. 194.
17. Christopher Marlowe, *Tamburlaine*, ed. J. W. Harper (1971; A & C Black; New York: W. W. Norton, 1984). All subsequent quotations from *Tamburlaine* are taken from this edition.
18. Mark Thornton Burnett, "Tamburlaine: An Elizabethan Vagabond" *Studies in Philology*, 84 (1987): 310.
19. Burnett, p. 321.
20. The association of the Scythian Tamburlaine with a slave may have come from the Elizabethan association of the Russians with slavery. About this association, see, for instance, the phrase "slave-borne Muscovite" in Sir Philip Sidney's *Astrophil and Stella*, Sonnet 2.
21. This extraordinary rhetorical power of the Scythian Tamburlaine, whose barbaric origin takes him out of the tradition of rhetorical skill, suggests an irony on the part of Marlowe. For the rhetorical tradition and Renaissance

humanist emphasis on rhetoric, see, for instance, Isabel Rivers, *Classical and Christian Ideas in English Renaissance Poetry: A Students' Guide* 2nd ed. (London: Routledge, 1994) chapter 9 and Robert Weimann, *Authority and Representation in Early Modern Discourse*. trans. David Hillman (Baltimore: The Johns Hopkins Univ. Press, 1996), Chapter 7.

22. *The. xv. Bookes of P. Ouidius Naso, entytled Metamorphosis, translated oute of Latin into English meeter, by Arthur Golding Gentleman*, . . . (London: 1567) STC 18956, folio 87r.

23. For the association of borderlands with female threats, see Jeanne Addison Roberts *The Shakespearean Wild: Geography, Genus, and Gender* (Lincoln: Univ. of Nebraska Press, 1991), p. 97.

24. Stephen Orgel, Introduction, *The Tempest*, by William Shakespeare (Oxford: Oxford Univ. Press, 1987), p. 19. The possible connection between Caliban and the Scythians extends to their communalism of women as sexual objects.

25. Marlowe's interest in sorcery and physical movement is also apparent in *Doctor Faustus*. "Juglers," who were part of the vagrants subject to punishment by the 1572 act, leave their traces in the stage productions of *Tamburlaine* and *Faustus*.

26. Salgado, pp. 72-73.

27. Keith Thomas, *Religion and the Decline of Magic* (New York: Charles Scribner's Sons, 1971), p. 68.

28. For a discussion about the Irish superstitiousness, see Quinn, chapter VII.

29. Spenser, *A View*, p. 60.

30. Spenser, *A View*, p. 84.

31. Spenser, *A View*, p. 64.

32. Spenser, *A View*, pp. 48, 63.

33. Spenser, *A View*, p. 48.

34. Jones and Stallybrass observe that at the root of the "transformation" of colonizers there was the question of language. pp. 163-64.

35. For a discussion of the problem of the intermarriage, see Patricia Parker, *Shakespeare from the Margins: Language, Culture, Context* (Chicago: Univ. of Chicago Press, 1996), p. 172.

36. Spenser, *A View*, p. 104.

37. Spenser, *A View*, p. 68.

38. Spenser, *A View*, p. 53. For a discussion of English writers' use of women as exemplary models of Irish treachery, see Sheila T. Cavanagh, "'The Fatal Destiny of That Land': Elizabethan Views of Ireland," *Representing Ireland: Literature and the Origins of Conflict, 1534-1660*, ed. Brendan Bradshaw, Andrew Hadfield, and Willy Maley (Cambridge: Cambridge Univ. Press, 1993), pp. 123-5.

39. Jones and Stallybrass, p. 164.

40. Holinshed's *Chronicles*, vol. VI, p. 69.

41. Judith Yarnall, *Transformations of Circe: The History of an Enchantress*. (Urbana: Univ. of Illinois Press, 1994), p. 80.

42. Sir Walter Raleigh, *The Discouerie of the Large, Rich, and Bewtiful Empyre of*

Guiana (1596; Leeds, England: The Scolar Press, 1967) folios 3^v, 96^r.

43. Louis Adrian Montrose, "'Shaping Fantasies': Figurations of Gender and Power in Elizabethan Culture" *Representing the English Renaissance,* ed. Stephen Greenblatt (Berkeley: Univ. of California Press, 1988), p. 36.

44. Raleigh, fols. 100-101.

45. Montrose, p. 46. See also Elizabeth D. Harvey, *Ventriloquized Voices: Feminist Theory and English Renaissance Texts* (London: Routledge, 1992), p. 42.

46. Edmund Spenser, *The Faerie Queene* ed. Thomas P. Roche, Jr. (Harmondsworth, Middlesex: Penguin, 1978). All subsequent quotations from *The Faerie Queene* are taken from this edition.

47. For the figuration of Belphoebe, see Philippa Berry, *Of Chastity and Power: Elizabethan Literature and the Unmarried Queen* (London: Routledge, 1989), p. 160.

48. See Berry, p. 68, where she quotes John Knox's *The First Blast of the Trumpet against the Monstrous Regiment of Women.* Knox uses the references to Amazons and Circe in order to support his argument against the female ruler. For a discussion of the controversy about the Tudor queens, see Constance Jordan, *Renaissance Feminism: Literary Texts and Political Models* (Ithaca: Cornell Univ. Press, 1990), pp. 116-33.

49. Berry, p. 162.

50. Sheila T. Cavanagh points out that Malengin personifies the duplicity and the elusiveness of the kern in addition to many physical similarities: "Malengin's magical metamorphoses and his ability to elude his pursuers also recall the reputation of the Irish soldiers." ("'Such Was Irena's Countenance': Ireland in Spenser's Prose and Poetry," *Texas Studies in Literature and Language,* 28 (1986): 38.)

51. Spenser, *The Faerie Queene,* 5. 7. 1-24.

52. F. G. Butler refers to this paradigm in his article about the Scythian associations in *King Lear.* ("The Barbarous Scythian in 'King Lear'," *English Studies in Africa,* 28 (1985): 75.)

53. Another argument for linking Radigund to Ireland is that the historical Radegund was a founder of monastery for women. Berry observes: "Britomart's dismantling of the Amazonarchy is also used to make a less direct attack on Catholic monasticism . . . " (p. 162).

54. Holinshed's *Chronicles,* vol. I, p. 444.

55. Geoffrey of Monmouth, *The History of the Kings of Britain,* trans. Lewis Thorpe (Harmondsworth, Middlesex: Penguin, 1966), p. 75.

56. *The Tragedy of Locrine,* ed. Ronald B. McKerrow (Oxford: The Malone Society Reprints, 1908).

57. For an extensive discussion of the role of the Irish in determination of English identity, especially in Shakespeare's history plays, see Michael Neill, "Broken English and Broken Irish: Nation, Language, and the Optic Power in Shakespeare's Histories," *Shakespeare Quarterly,* 45 (1994) 1-32.

The Masque of Queens: Between Sight and Sound

Yumiko Yamada

THE MASQUE OF *Queens* (1609), Jonson's third masque commissioned by Queen Anne, has been interpreted exclusively from the Neoplatonic point of view, along with its predecessors, *The Masque of Blackness* (1605) and *The Masque of Beauty* (1608).[1] Jonson, having dealt with "Beauty" in the first two masques, then turned to the theme of "Good" or "Virtue"; just as the "foul" complexions of twelve Negro nymphs were blanched by the mystic Sun of Britannia, so twelve witches who threaten the ideal universe are conquered by twelve queens who embody their antithetic virtues. The subject of the witch-purge has also been taken as propaganda for James I's policy against sorcery. On his accession to the throne in 1603, the king reissued his *Daemonology* (first published in 1597) and ordered Reginald Scot's sceptical book *The Discoverie of Witchcraft* (1584) to be publicly burned; in the following year he stiffened the law against practising sorcery, in accordance with the canon against expelling devils without the licence of bishops. In the year before the performance of the masque, the trial of Dr. Simon Reade, the suspected necromancer, took place, which would have made this grand spectacle, on which Inigo Jones collaborated, all the more opportune in the eyes of the king and queen, as well as a galaxy of their guests both at home and abroad.

However, to follow the king's policy and write a masque against sorcery involves a public acknowledgment of the existence of devils and the effects of magical art. What cannot be overlooked here is the fact that this kind of commitment seems to contradict the attitude Jonson adopted around the period, expressly in his three comedies. Both in *Volpone* (1606) and in *The Alchemist* (1610) Jonson is consistently sceptical about, or derisive of, Neoplatonic thought on the occult, whether concerning the transmigration of the soul or alchemical processes; likewise in *Epicoene* (1609), the "Amazons" are no longer allowed to retain any vestige of the Platonic Virtue or Beauty of their counterparts in the masque. As regards to this apparent disparity between the comedies and the masques, critics have accounted for it with reference to the difference in genre, asserting that, in his masques, Jonson put aside his usual spirit of burlesque altogether, to create a region of the ideal and of courtly elegance.[2] But in the history of ideas, realism and idealism are rarely reconciled. Had Jonson been an adherent of the latter, he would have produced, in the field of comedy, romantic pieces like those of Shakespeare, rather than burlesque satires. It is true that masque writing involves Neoplatonic conventions and flattering eulogies to the sponsor, yet we are not altogether without clues as to the shifts that Jonson can be argued to have made in order to maintain his own standpoint under these constraints. It may be worthwhile to reexamine how far the author of *Volpone*, *The Alchemist*, and *Epicoene* committed himself to the ideal world he depicted in his most "Platonic" court spectacle.

1

After the performance of *The Masque of Queens*, Jonson dedicated a text with a detailed commentary to the fifteen-year old Prince Henry, instead of to Henry's mother, the queen, who was honoured in the masque:

> *Poetry*, my Lord, is not borne wth euery man; Nor euery day: And, in her generall right, it is now my minute to thanke yor Highnesse, who not only do honor her wth yor eare, but are curious to examine her wth yor eye, and inquire into her beauties, and strengths. Where, though it hath prou'd a worke of some diffculty to mee to retriue the particular *authorities* (according to yor gracious command, and a desire borne out of iudgment) to those things, wch I writt ovt of fullnesse, and memory of my former readings; Yet, now I haue ouercome it, the reward that meetes mee is double to one act: wch is, that therby, yor excellent vnderstanding will not only iustefie mee to yor owne knowledge, but decline the stiffnesse of others originall Ignorance, allready armd to censure.
> ("Dedication to Prince Henry," 27-41)[3]

Jonson, who in writing the masque had depended largely on his "fullnesse, and memory of my [his] former readings," spent nearly half

The Masque of Queens 257

a year checking all the sources anew to build up an elaborate commentary, at the request of the prince, who showed keen interest in the work.[4] Especially in the first half that deals with witches and magic arts, the inundation of words used in the commentary almost submerges the lines of the text. The commentary is drawn from dozens of ancient and modern "*authorities* . . . to those things," including James I's *Daemonology*. The whole task has been generally ascribed to Jonson's rather pedantic industry; it is said, for example, he strove to show "how a really learned poet managed these matters," by setting this work against Shakespeare's *Macbeth*, just as he had set *Sejanus* against *Julius Caesar*.[5]

This may be true to some extent, but we cannot altogether neglect the fact that Jonson on the other hand despised the pursuit of knowledge for its own sake:

> *I know* no disease of the *Soule*, but *Ignorance*; not of the Arts, and Sciences, but of it selfe: Yet relating to those, it is a pernicious *evill*: the darkner of mans life: the disturber of his *Reason*, and common Confounder of *Truth*: with which a man goes groping in the darke, no otherwise, then if hee were blind.
> (*Discoveries*, 801-6)

We may wonder what all the minute details concerning "the particular *authorities* . . . to those things [sorceries]" amount to, unless it was his ambition to educate the young prince to be a Dr Faustus.

In the text of the masque Jonson suggests that unlike "Porters, and Mechanicks," his courtly spectators should have "quick eares," "beside inquiring eyes," in order really to understand the spectacle (lines 105-10). Since the Platonic motif through which the twelve witches are conquered by the same number of virtuous twelve queens is as clear to "Porters, and Mechanicks" as to cultivated courtiers, it should seem more reasonable to suspect some ulterior motive behind his academic exertion that could be grasped only by "quick eares," in addition to "inquiring eyes."

In the passage quoted above from the "Dedication," he says "yor Highnesse . . . not only do honor her [*Poetry*; i.e. the masque] wth yor eare, but are curious to examine her wth yor eye"; most probably the prince, whose "quick eares" caught hold of some deeper meaning besides its visual message of simple didacticism, wished it to be confirmed in the written commentary. What he perceived is not made clear, but the phrase "a desire borne out of iudgment" implies it was not altogether off the point.

As regards the auditory factors of the masque, a number of disparities have been observed between the meaning that should be conveyed by the text and the nonliterary elements, such as rhythm, tune, and music that counterpoint it.

It has been pointed out, for example, that the lines containing "*Darknesse, Deuills, Night,* and *Hell*" spoken by the Dame when she flies into a rage (295-312) preserve a relative composure, marked by a graver and more temperate rhythm, while those of Heroic Virtue immediately after his triumph over the witches (368-75) are masculine but somewhat rude;[6] which is at odds with their respective positions as conquered and conqueror. Also, syntactical awkwardness has been observed in the full chorus of the final song "Who, *Virtue,* can thy power forget" (763-73), as if the poetry of statement were unwillingly contained by an alien, lyric mode; in the preceding song "When all the Ages of the earth" (742-48), Ferrabosco's music is said to fail to convey the meaning of the words.[7] The same thing can be said of the music in the Antimasque, where the hags fall into "a *magicall Daunce,* full of præposterous change, and gesticulation" (344-50); according to the text, the music should represent the uncanny disturbance of the peace, but it does not sufficiently fulfill its function; its F major melody sounds composed, even tranquil, rather than tumultuous.[8]

Here the question arises of whether these nonliterary disparities, which might have been perceived with "quick eares," are nothing but accident, or the result of a lack of skill on the part of Jonson or the composers. Our next step is to reexamine the literary elements with the help of the elaborate notes affixed by the author.

The vices embodied by the twelve witches are reported to be "faithfull Opposites / To *Fame,* & *Glory*" (132-33). The Dame introduces them in order, as one vice breeds another: Ignorance, Suspicion, Credulity, Falsehood, Murmur, Malice, Impudence, Slander, Execration, Bitterness, Rage, and lastly Mischief [*Ate*] embodied by herself (lines 117—31). Here again we may wonder why Jonson seized on these for his vices; if he had regarded witches as the agents of the devil according to the orthodoxy, he might have included seven deadly sins, or the "faithfull Opposites" to the seven cardinal virtues. Secondly, to have Ignorance as the initial of his vices may be taken as apostasy, when the original sin of man is said to derive from eating the forbidden fruit of the tree of knowledge. Also, Heroic Virtue, who expels the witches, is defined by Aristotle, the "father" of scholastic theology, as "superhuman" and "divine,"[9] but he does not need to be either of these to expel the twelve vices that are all of the earth, earthy.

What appears to be more important is that we see no effect of their magical art on stage, for all the following "particular *authorities*":

> Here the *Dame* put her selfe into the midst of them, and beganne her following invocation; wherein she tooke occasion to boast all the power attributed to witches by the *Antients*: of wch euery *Poet* (or the most) doth giue some. *Homer* to *Circe*, in the *Odyss*. *Theocritus* to *Simatha*, in *Pharmaceutria*. *Virgil* to *Alphesiboeus*, in his. *Ouid* to *Dipsas* in *Amor*. to *Medea*, & *Circe*, in *Metamorp*. *Tibullus* to *Saga*. *Horace* to *Canidia*, *Sagana*, *Veia*, *Folia*. *Seneca* to *Medea*, and the Nurse, in *Herc. OEte*. *Petr. Arbiter* to his *Saga*, in *Fragment*. And *Claud*. to his *Megaera lib. j. in Rufinum*: Who takes the habite of a Witch as these doe, and supplies that *historicall* part in the *Poëme*, beside her *morall* person of a *Fury*.
> (*The Masque of Queens*, 205-17)

The Dame, who boasts of "all the power attributed to witches by the *Antients*," attempts to disturb the peace and solemnity of the world of the masque, using the ingredients and charms recorded by these authorities. But the action of her followers reveals that they are not so skillful or competent as their seeming weirdness suggests:

> These eleuen Witches begiñing to daunce . . . on the sodayne one of them miss'd they^r *Cheife*, and interrupted the rest, wth this Speach.
> Sisters, stay; we want o^r *Dame*.
> (*The Masque of Queens*, 43-48)

It is inconceivable that the eleven witches should begin their magical dance without noticing the absence of their own chief, unless the scene is intended as comical and ludicrous. Sure enough, they have "neuer a starre yett shot" (263), to the grief of the Dame:

> [DAME.] Stay; All our *Charmes* do nothing winne
> Vpon the night; Ou^r Labor dies!
> (*The Masque of Queens*, 284-85)

With a blast of loud music, she and her followers vanish along with their Hell, in place of which appears the magnificent House of Fame. There is no confrontation between evil and good which would make the scene dramatic; it is as if Jonson persistently refuses to exploit the dramatic possibilities. This has been explained as serving to evoke the impossibility of confrontation between the absolutes,[10] but still we are not altogether satisfied.

2

At the beginning of the written text, Jonson, after a lengthy account of how he came to choose the theme of "Fame" to honour the ladies at the request of the queen, slips in a statement that he has composed the masque according to the "rule of the best *Artist*":

> It encreasing now, to the third time of my being vs'd in these seruices to her Maties personall presentatio's, wth the Ladyes whome she pleaseth to honor; it was my first, and speciall reguard, to see that the Nobilyty of the Invention should be answerable to the dignity of they^r persons. For wch reason, I chose the Argument, to be, *A Celebration of honorable, & true Fame, bred out of Vertue*: obseruing that rule of the best *Artist*, to suffer no object of delight to passe wthout his mixture of profit, & example. (*The Masque of Queens*, 1-9)

Jonson affixes a note on "the best *Artist*," pointing out that this refers to Horace, who wrote the *Ars poetica*, in which he refused to give delight "w^thout his mixture of profit, & example." But what "profit, & example" are we to draw from Jonson's masque? After seeing the helpless stupidity of the witches, we are unlikely to be able to satisfy ourselves with the naive moral of poetic justice.

Among the group of ancient writers from Homer to Claudius that is cited above as the *"authorities"* for the Dame's art, we find the name of Horace. We may notice that in the clause "all the power attributed to the witches by the *Antients*: of wch euery *Poet* (or the most) doth giue some" (207-8), "(or the most)" modifies or furtively negates "euery *Poet*" with very good reason, for among those cited by Jonson, only Horace refuses to acknowledge the power of his witches.

If we examine the flood of quotations and citations that threaten to submerge the text, we find it sparsely dotted with the name of the poet. Though reference to Horace is neither frequent nor conspicuous, Jonson refers to his witches at crucial points, such as during the description of the Hell, their rites, and their appearance.

> [3. CHARME.] The Ditch is made, and or nayles the spade,
> Wth pictures full, of waxe, and of wooll;
> Theyr liuers I stick, wth needles quick
> There lackes but the blood, to make vp the flood.
> (*The Masque of Queens*, 83-86)

In the massive note of twenty-seven lines affixed to this passage for Prince Henry, Jonson again slips in a mention of Horace, this time of his eighth satire in Book 1, burying it, as if to guard it from "inquisitive eyes," between the references to Bodin, Remy, Delrio, cited as a proof that the method is still in use, and those to Ovid, Homer and the recent examples in England.

Jonson also affixed a note that the Dame, who appears nine lines below the passage, is modelled on Canidia in Horace's same satire and the fifth epode.

> At this, the *Dame* enterd to them, naked arm'd, bare-footed, her frock tucked, her hayre knotted, and folded wth vipers . . .
> (*The Masque of Queens*, 95-97)

In his satire Horace depicts how a pair of witches, Canidia and Sagana, steals into a garden, which was once used as a common burial place, to perform their black rite designed to vex human souls; like Jonson's Dame, Canidia walks with black robe tucked up, and her feet bare (23-24), and like Jonson's witches, they dig a ditch with their nails, fill it with pictures of wax and wool (30-33), and prepare the blood of lamb to pour into it (27-28).[11] When they begin chanting a spell to invoke the spirit of darkness and the rite is about to reach a climax, the wooden statue of the garden god Priapus suddenly cracks with the noise of an explosion. The two hags are so frightened at this that they run away into town, where they make themselves a laughingstock of the people; Canidia's teeth and Sagana's high wig, and the herbs and enchanted love-knots from their arms, have come tumbling down (48-50). These witches also appear in the fifth epode of Horace, where they victimize a youth to make a philtre, in conspiracy with Veia and Folia, another pair of hags referred to in the extract above (*The Masque of Queens*, 205-17).

It is quite probable that those who had "quick eares" would have been reminded of Horace's satire on hearing lines 83-86, and the allusion would have been confirmed when they saw the Dame enter nine lines below. Prince Henry, who is reported in Jonson's dedication to have done "honor her [i.e. the masque] wth yor [his] eare," had no doubt perceived the allusion, and requested him to build up a commentary on it, being "curious to examine her [the masque] wth yor [his] eye."

The eighth satire in the first book of Horace was known as a parody of the eleventh book of the *Odyssey*, where Circe performs a rite to conjure up the spirits of the dead from Erebus.[12] Jonson's desire to remind the reader of the Horatian scheme is unmistakable when he refers to this allusion in his note to lines 83-86 of his masque. Jonson called Horace "the best Artist" precisely because he thus tactfully disclosed the inefficacy of the black art; by so calling him Jonson declared his own disbelief in "those things."

Interestingly enough, John Selden, who was always on friendly terms with Jonson, and was respected by him, was also a sceptic about the matter, and in his confidential talk with his mates criticized the law against witches as unreasonable:

> The Law against Witches does not prove that there bee any, but it punishes the malice of those people, that use such meanes to take away mens liues. If one should profess that hee could by turning his hatt thrice & crying Buz! take away a mans life (though in truth hee could doe nothing) yet this were a just Law made by the State, That whosoever shall turne his hatt thrice and cry Buz! with an Intention to take away a mans life, shall bee putt to Death. (*Table Talk*, "Witches")[13]

It would appear that in the self-same spirit Jonson tried to undermine the king's policy in his very presence, by means of the magnificent spectacles on which were lavished no small part of the royal expenditure as well as the talents of the best of the artists, for the purpose of impressing leading figures both at home and abroad with the power and dignity of the British monarchy. Considering this came shortly after the public burning of Scot's *The Discoverie of Witchcraft*, we may realize how audacious was Jonson's endeavour; it was an age when Francis Bacon, the father of modern science, remained still hesitant to deny the power of occult arts, such as alchemy and astrology, and when, across the Channel, Nicholas Remy, an ardent promoter of witch-hunting in succession to Jean Bodin, Scot's "champion of witchmoongers"—both are repeatedly cited as authorities of witchcraft in Jonson's masque—boasted of condemning nine hundred "witches."[14]

3

Since the magical power of the witches is proved thus incompetent to cause actual harm, we may reasonably wonder how we should evaluate the achievement of Heroic Virtue in overthrowing them. This father of Fame announces the appearance of the House of Fame as the symbol of the triumph of good, in the place of the Hell that has just vanished. What might be noticed here is that "Fame" is a notion with too much ambiguity and precariousness to have a fixed standard of value. Jonson presents Fame, the daughter of Heroic Virtue, according to the fourth book of Virgil's *Aeneid*, where she is depicted as a dreadful and enormous monster of scandal that has innumerable eyes, mouths, tongues and ears; not a few of the audience might have been reminded of the first scene of the fifth act of Jonson's *Poetaster* (1601), where he makes Virgil recite the self-same passage, likening a gang of informers to this monster.

It also seems to be frequently overlooked that the virtuous queens who have been immortalized in the House of Fame act, like the statues and figures that decorate the magnificent building, to remind us of dire chronicles of slaughter and sacrifices.

> First for the lower Columnes, he [Inigo Jones] chose the *statues* of the most excellent *Poëts*, as *Homer, Virgil, Lucan,* &c. as beeing the substantiall supporters of *Fame*. For the vpper, *Achilles, Æneas, Caesar,* and those great *Heroës,* wch those *Poets* had celebrated. All wch stood, as in massy gold. Betwene the Pillars, vnderneath, were figur'd *Land-Battayles, Sea-Fights, Triumphes, Loues, Sacrifices,* and all magnificent Subiects of Honor: In brasse, and heightend, wth siluer.   (*The Masque of Queens*, 683-91)

As is implied in the last two lines of the description of the House, "Honor" is a thing bestowed in compensation for the blood which is shed in battles, loves, sacrifices, and other grim acts sung in epics. The female warriors, who drag in triumph the witches that can do no harm, in fact symbolize bloodshed that does no good. Jonson is thus revealing that the "Honor" or "Fame" Queen Anne desires to be accorded to the ladies has another face—one smeared with blood.

It is also implied that the primary cause of the tragedy is Ignorance, the first of the deadly vices embodied by the witches. In the line 41 of the "Dedication to Prince Henry" quoted above, Jonson uses the phrase "originall Ignorance," making a pun on the theological concept of "original sin." Unlike those who follow the doctrine and regard knowledge as the root of man's misfortune, Jonson believed that knowledge is benevolent. From this point of view, virtue can be no less harmful than vice, when it is idealistically sublimed into an absolute concept; it comes to have an absolute power by turning its adversary into an absolute, and thus forbidding man to make any further investigation. If Jonson was tempted to follow Horace in mixing "profit, & example," it would have been not so much a warning against the harm that sorcery was believed to cause as against that of "Ignorance," or blind acceptance of what might be called supernatural power, whether good or evil.

In the course of portraying man's ruin, beginning in Ignorance, Suspicion, Credulity, &c. and ending in Mischief, Jonson notes that he took the last of the vices from the first book of Homer's *Iliad*, "where he makes her swift to hurt Mankind" (note on 95). Homer deifies the root evil of all misfortunes of the parties concerned as "Ate," or Mischief, which deprives man of reason and drives him to inhuman acts; in the epic he sings how this goddess incurred the wrath of Achilles and sent countless brave souls hurrying down to Hades.

What the discerning audience is expected to observe in *The Masque of Queens* is not that supernatural or absolute vice is replaced by its opposite, virtue, but that a seemingly foul "Mischief" is replaced by another seemingly fair "Mischief." The human being who is possessed with "Mischief" stiffens his or her own judgement into absolute self-righteousness. All the heroic achievements that were immortalized by "the most excellent *Poëts*" and now shaped and painted by the great designer Inigo Jones to adorn the House of Fame are, if we listen to "the best Artist" with Jonson, reduced in the final analysis to as many monuments of man's disaster, brought about by the conflict between self-righteous causes that blindly believe themselves to be "absolute."

Sometimes the subject of who it was that Jonson sided with—the queen, the king, or the prince &c.—has come under investigation,[15] yet let us satisfy ourselves with thinking that Jonson remained free and neutral, as many humanists did, from any faction in the court. To Queen Anne he reveals the grim reality of Honour or Fame; as for James I, he criticizes his "Ignorance" in asserting his divine right and prohibiting the practice of sorcery—both in all seriousness, although Jonson was not reluctant on the whole to appreciate the king's peace-making policy.

And he tries to admonish Prince Henry, the warlike standard-bearer of Protestantism, that he should not fall into his father's fallacy, by flattering him about his outstanding intelligence:

> For, whether it be y^t a diuine soule, being to come into a body, first chooseth a Palace fit for it selfe; or being come, doth make it so, or that *Nature* be ambitious to haue her worke æquall; I know not: But, what is lawfull for me to vnderstand, & speake, that I dare; w^{c}h is, that both yor vertue, & yor forme did deserue yor fortune. The one claym'd, that you should be borne a Prince; the other makes that you do become it.... Amongst the rest, Yo^r fauor to letters, and these gentler studies, that goe vnder the title of Humanitye, is not the least honor of yor wreath. For, if once the worthy Professors of these learn-ings shall come (as heretofore they were) to be the care of Princes, the Crownes they^r *Soueraignes* weare will not more adorne they^r Temples; nor they^r stamps liue longer in they^r *Medalls*, than in such Subiects labors.
> ("Dedication to Prince Henry," 7-27)

We can see that by pretending "I know not," Jonson avoids ascribing Henry's royal birth to divine providence; rather, by asserting "both yor vertue, & yor forme did deserue yor fortune," he underscores that it was by a mere chance that he was "borne a Prince" and with princely "vertue" and "forme." And, to use his fortune reverently, he advises him to be most careful to encourage "letters, and these gentler studies, that goe vnder the title of Humanitye," which could expel "Ignorance," the mortal enemy of man. Here, too, Jonson succeeds in expressing "lawfully" what he really means, by mixing "profit, & example" in a pleasant eulogy, after the manner of "the best *Artist*."

Thus *The Masque of Queens* warns those who have ears to hear against the danger of the idealism that pursues virtues such as truth, good and beauty in their absolute state, advising instead that they be limited within the compass of human experience and understanding. If we are to reexamine its "Platonic" predecessor *The Masque of Blackness and Beauty* in the same light, we may find that the author reveals the absurdity of striving to turn blackness into white and ascribing this "miracle" to the mortal human king, by undermining the work's seeming grace with a vulgar proverb— "To blanch an ÆTHIOPE, and reuiue a *Cor's*" (*The Masque of Blackness*, 255)—and laughing at the "Ignorance" of the spectators who stand amazed at the fantasy materialized in the old Banqueting House.

The Masque of Queens must have dazzled the eyes of the spectators who knew no better than to see the magnificent settings and wondrous machines of Inigo Jones which impressed them with the triumph of absolute virtue over absolute vice. But it allowed the audience with an "excellent vnderstanding" to make the most of their ears along with their eyes to recognize thereby the very limit and self-destruction of Platonic idealism. By thus turning the subtle gap between the two senses to his own advantage, Jonson has succeeded in incorporating in his humanistic project his earlier masques as well as other genres.

Notes

This is the revised version of the paper read at the general meeting of the English Literary Society of Japan, held at the University of Tokyo in 1993.

  1. For this account see especially Stephen Orgel, *The Jonsonian Masque* (1965; New York: Columbia Univ. Press, 1981), p. 138.

  2. See, for example, *Ben Jonson*, ed. C. H. Herford, Percy and Evelyn Simpson, 11 vols. (Oxford: Clarendon Press, 1925-52), II, p. 279; John C. Meagher, *Method and Meaning in Jonson's Masques* (Notre Dame, Indiana: Univ. of Notre Dame Press, 1966), p. 152; Alexander Leggatt, *Ben Jonson: His Vision and His Art* (London: Methuen, 1981), p. 163.

  3. All the quotations from Jonson are taken from *Ben Jonson*, ed. Herford and Simpson; further citations will appear as "H & S." As regards *The Masque of Queens*, I also referred to the facsimile of the holograph in the King's Printer's edition (London, 1930), which has been reproduced from the original preserved in the King's Library at the British Museum.

  4. Rosalind Miles, *Ben Jonson: His Craft and Art* (London: Routledge, 1990), p. 127.

  5. H & S, vol.II, pp. 279-80.

  6. H & S, vol.II, pp. 280, 282.

  7. Orgel, p. 146; Mary Chan, *Music in the Theatre of Ben Jonson* (Oxford: Clarendon Press, 1980), p. 230.

  8. Orgel, p. 146; Chan, p. 209.

  9. *Nicomachean Ethics*, bk.7, ch.1. The quotation is taken from *Aristotle: Nicomachean Ethics*, ed. and trans. H. Rackham (1926; Cambridge, Mass.: Harvard Univ. Press, 1990).

  10. Orgel, p. 138.

  11. The citation from *Satires* is taken from *Horace: Satires, Epistles and Ars Poetica*, ed. and trans. H. Rushton Faircloth (Cambridge, Mass.: Harvard Univ. Press, 1978), and that from *Epodes* are from *Horace: Odes and Epodes*, ed. and trans. C. E. Bennett (1914; Cambridge, Mass.: Harvard Univ. Press, 1988).

  12. Faircloth, ed., *Horace: Satires, Epistles and Ars Poetica*, p. 98n.

13. *Table Talk of John Selden*, ed. Frederick Pollock and Edward Fry (London: The Selden Society, 1927), p. 140.

14. Robert E. Knoll, *Ben Jonson's Plays: An Introduction* (Lincoln: Univ. of Nebraska Press, 1964), pp. 126, 131; Reginald Scot, *The Discoverie of Witchcraft* (1584), ed. Montague Summers (London: John Rodker, 1930), p. 11.

15. See, for example, John Pitcher, "'In Those Figures which they seeme': Samuel Daniel's *Tethus' Festival*," *The Court Masque*, ed. David Lindley (Manchester: Manchester Univ. Press, 1984).

Contextualizing Shakespeare:
The Renaissance Debate on the Nature of Slavery

Sergio Mazzarelli

TO INTRODUCE THE Renaissance debate on slavery, I would like to refer to an unduly neglected Elizabethan treatise on statecraft, the *Sphaera civitatis*.[1] Published in 1588, the *Sphaera civitatis* was used as a university manual in Oxford and in other Northern European universities until the 1630s, and therefore deserves to be considered as one of the most influential Elizabethan political works. The *Sphaera civitatis* was written by an Oxford scholar and educator, John Case, and published by Joseph Barnes, printer to the University of Oxford.[2] Although the woodcut prefaced to the *Sphaera civitatis* (Fig. 1) has attracted considerable scholarly attention for its depiction of Elizabeth I in a position analogous to that occupied by God in a Ptolemaic diagram of the universe, no in-depth study of the treatise itself has yet been published.[3]

The *Sphaera civitatis* is written in Latin, the international language of Renaissance culture, and its title can be translated as "The Sphere of the Commonwealth." It is a very substantial work, containing about a quarter of a million words. The *Sphaera civitatis* is divided into eight books, and consists of 225 questions on political matters, such as: "Is it lawful and just to wage war against neighbouring countries to expand one's own country?"; "Are there slaves by nature?"; "Is it dangerous for a country to accept immigrants?" These questions are answered according to Case's interpretation of Aristotle's thought. Aristotle is therefore heavily quoted, but Case also refers his readers to all sorts of ancient and modern philosophers, poets, historians, orators, religious reformers, jurists, and so on. From Augustine to Beza, from Thucydides to Contarini, from Plato to Bodin, from Cicero to Bartolus of Sassoferrato, from Virgil to Sebastian Brant, a whole range of authorities is used by Case to support his theses.

[269]

Several commendatory poems are prefaced to the *Sphaera civitatis*. They were written by the Vice-Chancellor of the University, the dean and the bishop of Winchester, and many other distinguished figures, including the poet John Lyly. In the dedication to the Lord Chancellor of England, Sir Christopher Hatton, Case stated that he had been encouraged to write the *Sphaera civitatis* by the Lord Treasurer, Robert Cecil, and by Sir Henry Unton, the ambassador. Case's enterprise certainly did not lack supporters. It did not lack reward, either, for in 1589 Case was appointed by the Queen to a sinecure worth around 20 pounds a year.[4]

I have been able to ascertain that a special presentation copy of the *Sphaera civitatis* was prepared for the Archbishop of Canterbury, John Whitgift.[5] This copy, which is kept in Lambeth Palace Library, bound in vellum with the arms of the Archbishop in gold tooling, has an extra leaf placed before the title-page.[6] The recto of this leaf is blank, but on the verso, facing the title-page, one can read a printed dedication, "Reverendissimo Primati Archiepiscopo Cantuar. &c" ("To the Most Reverend Primate Archbishop of Canterbury"). This is followed by two Latin verses that translate: "If you had not blessed what we shall give you with your holy fairness, / This gift could not shine."[7] In Latin, the word I translated as "fairness" means both "candour" and "whiteness," so that there is a pun on the name of the Archbishop, which means "white gift." One of the offices of the Archbishop of Canterbury was to license books for printing, and therefore these lines are probably to be seen as an expression of gratitude to Whitgift for allowing the book to be printed.[8] Such an unusual dedication reminds us of the importance of censorship in Elizabethan England.

It is not without significance that a book like the *Sphaera civitatis*, published by a prominent academic with the backing of political and religious authorities, contained a defence of the Aristotelian theory of natural slavery. This theory had recently been attacked by the great French political theorist, Jean Bodin, who, in his *Six Books of a Commonwealth*, had stated:

> Aristotle is of opinion that the seruitude of slaues is of right naturall: and to proue the same, We see (saith he) some naturally made to serue and obey, and others to commaund and gouerne. But Lawyers, who measure law not by the discourses or decrees of Philosophers, but according to the common sense

and capacitie of the people, hold seruitude to be directly contrarie vnto nature; and do what they can to maintaine libertie, still interpreting such things as are obscure and doubtfull (whether it be in the lawes, or in testaments, in couenants, or iudgements) so in fauor of libertie, as that they giue no way either to lawes or testaments: And if so be that the force of the lawes be so great and so plaine as they may not swarue from them: yet do they protest that bitternesse of the lawes to displease them, calling it hard and cruell.[9]

Bodin regretted that slavery, after having as he thought virtually disappeared from the "Christian Commonweale," had now reappeared in Spanish and Portuguese territories and was spreading quickly all over Europe.[10] It is important to stress that Bodin denounced all slavery, not just American Indian slavery, and explicitly mentioned the plight of the "Neigros."[11] Oddly enough, Bodin was convinced, like the Aristotelians, that the climate and geography of each country made its inhabitants different from those of any other country. In fact, he developed an analysis of the characters of the different nations that was unprecedented in scope and detail. From this he derived what we would call a sociological theory of legal differences and has therefore been hailed as an anticipator of eighteenth-century empiricism.[12] In other words, Bodin's hostility to slavery certainly did not spring from the belief that there were no important differences between the peoples of the world. It could be argued that he was one of the forerunners of that project which, by providing essentialist representations of "other" cultures, would eventually serve the interests of more sophisticated forms of imperialism, such as the ones described by Edward Said in his *Orientalism*.[13] However, the fact that Bodin took into consideration non-European legal traditions in order to establish the most workable principles of law was truly remarkable for his time.[14] Bodin was one of the founders of comparative jurisprudence, and his work had great resonance all over Europe. We know that, when Bodin accompanied the duke of Alençon to England, he found to his surprise that his *Six Books of a Commonwealth* was being studied at London and Cambridge.[15] At that time, Bodin had not yet translated this work from French into Latin, but the English had prepared a Latin translation of their own, which Bodin found unsatisfactory.[16] Bodin's fame is also attested by Gabriel Harvey who, in the 1580s, observed that one could not enter a scholar's study without the chances being ten to one that he would be found studying either Le Roy's commentary on Aristotle's *Politics* or Bodin's *Six Books*.[17] John Case himself certainly knew not only the *Six Books*, but also the *Method for the Easy Comprehension of History*, the other major work by Bodin, since he quoted both books in notes to the *Sphaera civitatis*.[18] It is clear that Case was also reacting to Bodin's statements when he tried to refute objections to the theory of natural slavery.

A major obstacle for those who supported the cause of slavery was that in France and England this institution had fallen into disuse by the end of the Middle Ages. According to Bodin,

> In Fraunce, although there be some remembrance of old seruitude, yet it is not lawfull there to make any slaue, or to buy any of others: Insomuch that the slaues of strangers so soone as they set their foot within Fraunce become franke and free; as was by an old decree of the court of Paris determined against an ambassador of Spain, who had brought a slaue with him to Fraunce.[19]

A similar opinion was expressed with regard to England by William Harrison in his *Description of England* (1577):

> As for slaves and bondmen, we have none; nay, such is the privilege of our country by the especial grace of God and bounty of our princes that if any come hither from other realms, so soon as they set foot on land they become so free of condition as their masters, whereby all note of servile bondage is utterly removed from them, wherein we resemble (not the Germans, who had slaves also, though such as in respects of the slaves of other countries might well be reputed free, but) the old Indians and the Taprobanes [Ceylonese], who supposed it a great injury to Nature to make or suffer them to be bond whom she in her wanted course doth product and bring forth free."[20]

However, Bodin did not draw his conclusions merely from custom, and therefore did not think that they applied only to his country. He brought a fundamental principle of Roman law to its logical consequence. It was probably under the influence of Stoic philosophy that the great Roman jurist, Florentinus (second century AD), had explicitly defined slavery as "an institution of the law of nations whereby one man is, contrary to nature, subject to the dominion of another."[21] This definition was later incorporated in Justinian's *Institutes* and *Digest* (sixth century AD) and through it, after the rediscovery of Roman Law in the late eleventh century, transmitted to generations of medieval and Renaissance lawyers. The *Institutions* stated that "through force of circumstances and human needs, peoples have developed certain measures for themselves: wars have arisen with subsequent captivity and slavery—which is contrary to natural law (for, by natural law, all men were born free)."[22] In other words, legal thought had sanctioned the existence of slavery while admitting that it was contrary to nature. From this premise, it should not have been difficult to conclude that slavery must be abolished. Yet almost nobody in the ancient world seems to have found it possible to imagine how society could work without this institution. Even when thousands of slaves courageously rebelled against the cruelty of their masters, they just wanted to be free themselves, and not to abolish slavery altogether.[23] We only know of two small Jewish sects, the Essenes and the Therapeutae, which forbade their members to own slaves.[24] Mainstream Judaism, Christianity and, later, Islam all accepted slavery.[25] At the same time, it must be said that none of these religions saw slavery as a good in itself. Therefore, when social organization (or economic exploitation) in Europe took forms that did not require the existence of slaves, it is not surprising that a Christian intellectual such as Bodin actually found it impossible to justify its existence anywhere in the world. The necessity of having slaves could not be taken for granted any more, as there were societies that worked without them.

Unfortunately, very few thinkers followed Bodin's path. On the contrary, the so-called discovery of the New World led to the revival of the Aristotelian theory of natural slavery. Aristotle had argued that Greeks were a superior race and that non-Greeks were to be their slaves. We know from Plutarch that Aristotle was very disappointed when his former pupil, Alexander the Great, recognized equal rights to all freeborn Greeks and non-Greeks and encouraged intermarriage between Greeks and Persians. If we read the *Politics*, we can see why. For Aristotle, "Barbarians have no class of natural rulers . . . . Hence the saying of the poets: 'Tis meet that Greeks should rule barbarians,' implying that barbarian and slave are the same in nature."[26] Aristotle claimed that, because the barbarians were born inferior, they would actually benefit from being ruled by the more rational Greeks. It must be noted that this theory did not find many followers. Although slavery remained one of the pillars of ancient society, post-Aristotelian philosophers, such as the Epicureans, the Cynics, and the Stoics denied any difference in nature between masters and slaves. For centuries nobody tried to identify the natural slaves or barbarians mentioned by Aristotle with any specific human population. In the Mediterranean, where slavery continued to exist throughout the Middle Ages, it was seen as a consequence of war.

The Renaissance was a crucial moment in the history of slavery. The great geographical discoveries of the fifteenth century opened new lands to European colonization. The inhabitants of these lands could not be portrayed as aggressors or invaders by whom the Christian Europeans had felt threatened, like the Moslems or the pagan tribes of Eastern Europe. Yet the Europeans needed an ideological justification for their ruthless behaviour, which included slaughter and enslavement on an unprecedented scale, and would eventually change the face of the earth. The first to look back to Aristotle to find a justification for European imperialism was John Major (1469-1550), a Scottish historian and scholastic divine who taught at the University of Paris. In his *Commentary on the Four Books of Peter Lombard's "Sentences,"* which he published in Paris between 1509 and 1517,[27] he first invoked a religious justification for the aggression against the Indian kingdoms in America: the Indians must be converted to Christianity, and they would not accept preachers if they were not forced to do so. Of course, Major explained, this is a very expensive undertaking, and can only be made possible if the riches of the pagan Indian kings are taken to cover the costs. This argument, although incredibly hypocritical, was still a religious one. However, later on Major adduced a different reason to justify Spanish colonialism. He quoted Ptolemy to the effect that people who live near the equator and the poles were beastly, and concluded:

> The reason why their first invader has the right to rule them [i.e. the Indians] is that they are slaves by nature, as is evident. In the third and fourth chapter of the first book of the Politics, the philosopher says: "It is manifest that some people are slaves and others freemen by nature."[28]

This was racism pure and simple, and it soon caused reactions.[29] The Spanish theologian and jurist, Francisco de Vitoria (1483?-1546), explicitly denied that the Indians were natural slaves, however barbarous their customs may be. Officially, Spain's monarchs repeatedly forbade the enslavement of the Indians, but such orders were never seriously enforced. Pope Paul III's bull, *Sublimis Deus* (1537), stating that

"Indians and all other nations which come to the knowledge of Christians in the future must not be deprived of their freedom and the ownership of their property," also went unheeded.[30] In 1547, the President of the Council of the Indies encouraged the Aristotelian scholar, Juan Ginés de Sepúlveda (1490-1573), to write *Democrates alter*, a treatise arguing that the Indians were natural slaves and that the wars waged against them were just. Sepúlveda, a distinguished humanist, had just returned to Spain after spending twenty years in Italy, where he had studied under the direction of Pietro Pomponazzi. He was completing a masterly Latin translation of Aristotle's *Politics* which would be published at Paris the following year. However, Bartolomé de Las Casas (1474-1576), a Dominican friar who had spent almost half a century in America defending the cause of the Indians, managed to block the publication of Sepúlveda's racist treatise on the grounds that it was doctrinally unsound. Las Casas's lobbying in favour of the Indians continued until, on 16 April 1550 Charles V, King of Spain and Holy Roman Emperor, ordered that all conquests in the New World be suspended until a special commission of theologians and counsellors had listened to Sepúlveda and Las Casas.[31] The commission was in the end unable to decide whether it was just or not for the king to wage war against the Indians. On their part, the two contestants kept arguing at a distance for years. Spanish tracts written by Las Casas in defence of the Indians were translated in many languages, including English. *The Spanish colonie, or briefe chronicle of the acts of the Spaniardes in the West Indies*, was printed in London by Thomas Dawson for William Brome in 1583.[32]

John Case lists Sepúlveda among the authorities he consulted in order to write the *Sphaera civitatis*. The Catholic church suppressed Sepúlveda's most virulent tract, *Democrates alter*, and I think that Case's own advocacy of the theory of natural slavery may be one of the reasons why the *Sphaera civitatis* was included in the *Index librorum prohibitorum* published under Clemens VIII in 1596.[33] Case dedicated many pages to refuting the arguments of those who denied the existence of natural slaves. For example, he argued that to wage war against barbarians is proven to be lawful and natural: "By the example of nature, which teaches men to hunt wild beasts. But the barbarians are like wild beasts, and are unwilling to submit to authority unless they are forced to do so."[34] To the objection that it is wrong to use violence against other human beings and that nature's commandment is, "Do not do unto others what you do not wish to be done unto you," Case replies

"To wage war against barbarians is neither to use violence nor do injustice. As a judge is neither said to use violence nor to commit injustice, when he condemns criminals to receive punishment, so those who wage war against savage barbarians are said not to exercise violence or injustice, but to carry out nature's prescription."[35] Case also makes specific reference to the deeds of the Iberian monarchies in the New World: "Even if I am not pleased to hear of the excessive severity exercised against the Indians by Spaniards and Portuguese during their memorable voyages, nevertheless it is necessary to force barbarians into the orderly rule which the law of nature commands. Therefore, although the infidels, insofar as they are hostile to the Christian faith, must not be forced into conversion, they must nonetheless be drawn to civil life by the force of arms."[36] Case was undoubtedly one of the first theorists of English imperialism.

Although in Case's time England did not yet have a colonial empire, it was already present as an imperialist power in Ireland. Moreover, in the 1560s the Crown had supported the attempts by John Hawkins to involve English ships in the lucrative slave trade between Africa and the New World.[37] After one expedition produced a sixty percent profit, Hawkins was awarded a singular coat of arms: its crest showed "a demi-Moor proper bound captive, with annulets on his arms and ears" (Fig. 2).[38] Hawkins's slaving expeditions were eventually discontinued because of the deterioration of relationships with Spain. This put a premium upon good relationships with the Portuguese, who had vigorously complained about the English interference in Africa that violated their monopoly of slave trading with the Spanish colonies.[39] However, a seed had been sown which would later bear fruit. In the meantime, a number of black slaves started being brought to England. The fear of unrest among the poor, who were prone to riot against any foreigners who deprived them of their jobs, apparently led the Privy Council to order the deportation of such slaves in 1596, and again in 1601.[40] It is interesting that the *Sphaera civitatis*, while justifying slavery, openly opposed the presence of foreigners in England. Case pithily observed that "nothing infects the human body faster than the union of pestilential vapours with inborn humours. Likewise, nothing corrupts the state faster than the acceptance of foreigners, which hides contamination and poison."[41] Case's passionate xenophobia is a product of the same racism that allowed him to justify slavery. He compares letting foreigners settle in the state to nourishing snakes in one's bosom. He says that aliens are to the state what locusts are to crops. There is no point in integrating them because, "even if they are branches of the same plant, they do not draw wholesome sap from the root, but venom, and the whole plant eventually dies poisoned by it."[42] Case then concludes by voicing his approval for the expulsion of the Jews from Spain.[43]

On the whole, the *Sphaera civitatis* helps us to trace the historical development of racist ideology in Elizabethan England. It proves that the spread of racial prejudice was closely interconnected with religious intolerance and a growing nationalism. I would now like to give a few examples of how a knowledge of the racist ideology used by Elizabethan intellectuals to justify slavery may affect our reading of Shakespeare.

First of all, I suspect that there may be some significance in the fact that in the Shakespearean canon the word "slave" appears 131 times, which means it has the same frequency of terms such as "mouth" and "wonder." This without considering the plural "slaves" (thirty-eight occurrences), and the genitive "slave's" (two occurrences). "Slavery" appears five times, "slavish" seven, and "slave-like" once.[44] Other semantically related terms include "bondage" (twenty-one occurrences), "bondmaid" (one occurrence), "bondman/men" (fourteen occurrences), "bondslave(s)" (three occurrences), "servile" (eleven occurrences), "servility" (one occurrence), "servilely" (one occurrence), and "servitude" (four occurrences). It may be objected that Shakespeare often uses the word "slave" simply as a term of abuse. But then should we not ask ourselves how the word "slave" could ever become a term of abuse? In a society that considers slavery to be wrong, it would be unthinkable to insult people by calling them slaves.

A look at the *OED* will show that it was in the Tudor period that "slave" came to be used as an insult. The first recorded example of such usage occurs in a state-paper, written in 1537, which describes the galloglasses, foreign troops maintained by Irish chiefs. Other figurative uses of the word "slave," such as "one who submits in a servile manner to the authority or dictation of others," or "one who is completely under the domination of, or subject to, a specific influence" also came into fashion in the Tudor period. Indeed, Shakespeare may even have contributed to make them popular. Before the Tudors, "slave" only meant "one who is the property of another person." It appears that the imaginations of Renaissance Englishmen were much more fired by slaves than those of their medieval predecessors, although the latter actually owned many more slaves than the former. It would be strange if this had nothing to do with an awareness of Europe's ongoing colonial expansion.

Moreover, the contemptuous term "slave"—as used by Shakespeare's characters—often displays connotations that are compatible with the ideological assumptions about slaves found in the *Sphaera civitatis*. Just to take an example, one of the characteristics of the natural slave, according to Aristotle and Case, was that he lacked spirit.[45] In other words, the slave was generally a coward by nature. In *1 Henry IV*, when Prince Harry reproaches Falstaff for his cowardice at Gadshill, he says, "What a slave art thou, to hack thy sword as thou hast done, and then say it was in fight!" (2. 5. 264-65). In *Cymbeline*, when Posthumus describes how the Romans were ignominiously defeated by the Britons, we find these words, "A rout, confusion thick; forthwith they fly / Chickens the way which they stooped eagles; slaves" (5. 5. 41-42).

For Case, slaves were such by birth, and therefore those who issued from noble loins could not have the characteristics of slaves. In *1 Henry VI*, when John Talbot refuses to flee before the enemy, he says to his father,

> O, if you love my mother,
> Dishonour not her honourable name
> To make a bastard and a slave of me.
> The world will say he is not of Talbot's blood
> That basely fled when noble Talbot stood. (4. 5. 13-17)

Slaves are cowards, and a cowardly John Talbot would be thought a bastard, since his father was a paragon of courage.

In *Othello*, Brabanzio declares to be sure that the council will punish Othello for having married Desdemona, "For if such actions may have passage free, / Bondslaves and pagans shall our statesmen be" (1. 2. 99-100). He is implying that Moors like Othello are natural bondslaves, i.e. slaves, of the Venetians. They should not be allowed to mix their blood with that of their masters. The word "pagans" is also important. The Spaniards despised and persecuted all Christian Moors living among them, after those who refused conversion were expelled from the country (1502). Religious and racial prejudice were entwined, as in the case of the Jews.

However, Elizabethan English was capable of an even more disturbing usage of the word "slave." In the last scene of *Othello*, when Montano and Lodovico wish to sum up Iago's nature, the word that comes to their lips is "slave" (5. 2. 250; 298; 341). In other words, by his actions Iago has proven that he does not deserve to belong to the category of freemen and that his constitution is that of a slave. Slaves were believed to be tainted with evil because either they themselves or their ancestors had been God's enemies. Therefore, it is perfectly fitting that in the same scene where he is repeatedly called "slave," Iago should also be referred to as a "devil," a "demi-devil," and a "hellish villain" (5. 2. 293; 307; 378).[46] Paradoxically, a similar mechanism seems to be at work in *King Lear*, a play set in pagan times, when Lear says to the dead Cordelia, "I killed the slave that was a-hanging thee" (Quarto, Sc. 24. 270; Folio, 5. 3. 249). Again, a monstrous action transforms its perpetrator, in this case a captain, into a slave. If Lear has learned humility on the heath, here the in-built metaphors of his language do not allow him to renounce racial pride.

Finally, there is a passage in *The Merchant of Venice* where Shylock talks about slaves in a way that appears very effective to modern audiences. He says to the Venetians:

> You have among you many a purchased slave
> Which, like your asses and your dogs and mules,
> You use in abject and slavish parts
> Because you bought them. Shall I say to you
> 'Let them be free, marry them to your heirs.
> Why sweat they under burdens? Let their beds
> Be made as soft as yours, and let their palates
> Be seasoned with such viands.' You will answer
> 'The slaves are ours.' So do I answer you.
> The pound of flesh which I demand of him
> Is dearly bought. 'Tis mine, and I will have it.   (4. 1. 89-99)

Shylock is saying that the socially acceptable cruelty involved in the ownership of slaves, based on the principle that property acquired by legal purchase may be used as the purchaser desires, compares with and justifies his legal demand for a pound of Antonio's flesh. This speech strikes at the heart of the Renaissance debate on slavery that I have tried to summarize in this paper. If one accepted John Case's version of Aristotle's argument, there was nothing wrong in using slaves "in abject and slavish parts." That was what slaves were for. Nature had produced them for that purpose and, since they were intellectually inferior to their masters, they actually benefited from being ruled. One can imagine the Venetian ruling classes, just like the Elizabethan ones, clinging to this doctrine. However, Shylock's speech definitely implies that slaves are not such by nature, and that their masters have a right to own them only because they paid money for them. At that time, this was likely to be considered by many as an extremist and dangerous opinion, although compatible with the traditional tenet of Roman law according to which men were born equal, and slavery was legal, but unnatural. It was dangerous as someone like Case would probably say because it could lead to the conclusion that one should dispense with slavery altogether, a most detestable idea entertained by that rash critic of Aristotle, Bodin, and by such arrant knaves as the Anabaptists, enemies of God-given social hierarchy (and of the theatre as well).

In Shakespeare's source for Shylock's speech, Alexander Silvayn's *The Orator*, the Jew remarks on the cruelty of slavery *as a penalty for failure to pay debts*, and quotes an ancient Roman law that prescribed such penalty.[47] His potential victim can then easily answer that this law was abolished by the Romans themselves. Shakespeare changed this innocuous hint into an indictment of slavery in general. We may wonder whether he was undermining the assumptions of Elizabethan ideology, or he was actually discrediting a subversive opinion by attributing it to someone who, as Stanley Wells puts it, "is in many ways a repellent figure."[48] After all, Shylock is not asking the Venetians to abolish slavery, but to let him have his revenge. Yet among the reasons why Shylock wants to revenge himself on Antonio there is the fact that Antonio treats him like a slave, a non-person. On his very first appearance on stage Shylock makes it clear that he will never talk to Antonio "in a bondman's key" (1. 3. 122), although Antonio expects just that. In this respect, it is worth noting that Antonio is not an eccentric: in the Renaissance some Christian authors considered the Jews as a special category of slaves. For example, the Elizabethan statesman and scholar, Sir Thomas Smith, stated in his discussion of slavery in *De republica anglorum* that, "amongst all people Jewes be holden as it were in common servitude."[49] Moreover, James Shapiro has shown that sometimes Jews were said to be black. He has also observed that Shylock's "countryman," Cush (mentioned in *The Merchant of Venice* 3. 2. 283), was named after the biblical progenitor of Black Africans.[50] Therefore, I think that Shylock may well have been seen by an Elizabethan audience as a slave who tries to revenge himself on a member of the master race. Those who shared the prejudices exemplified by John Case's theories probably thought that *The Merchant of Venice* showed the just punishment of an evil slave. However, if there were any people among the audience who agreed with Bodin's condemnation of slavery, these people are likely to have sympathized with Shylock's rebellion.

Notes

This is a revised version of the paper I read at the 35th General Meeting of the Shakespeare Society of Japan held at Ritsumeikan University in October 1996. All quotations from Shakespeare's texts are from *The Complete Works*, ed. Stanley Wells and Gary Taylor, Compact Edition (Oxford: Clarendon Press, 1988). Unless otherwise indicated, all translations from Latin are mine.

1. John Case, *Sphaera civitatis* (Oxford: Joseph Barnes, 1588). STC 4761. Five more editions of this work were printed in Germany. See M. A. Shaaber, *Checklist of Works of British Authors Printed Abroad, in Languages other than English, to 1641* (New York: Bibliographical Society of America, 1975). All my references are to the first edition.

2. Almost nothing is known of Case's life until 1564, when he entered St John's College, Oxford. By the summer of 1572, he had become a fellow of the same college. He subsequently resigned from his fellowship in order to marry the widow Elizabeth Dobson, but kept teaching as a private tutor in Oxford, and held various offices that allowed him to play an important role in the administration of the University. From 1584 to 1599 he published nine philosophical manuals that gave him considerable fame at home and abroad. The *Sphaera civitatis* was one of them. In 1589, Case was licensed as a medical doctor and thereafter he practised medicine with a certain success. John Case died in 1600, leaving substantial assets to his wife and stepson-in-law. On Case's life see Charles B. Schmitt, *John Case and Aristotelianism in Renaissance England* (Kingston: McGill-Queen's Univ. Press, 1983), pp. 77-105. See also J. W. Binns, *Intellectual Culture in Elizabethan and Jacobean England: The Latin Writings of the Age* (Leeds: Cairns, 1990), pp. 366-77.

3. Therefore, this paper draws on my "Aspects of Hierarchy and Order in John Case's *Sphaera civitatis* (1588)," Diss. Birmingham 1996. On the woodcut see Roy Strong, *Gloriana: The Portraits of Queen Elizabeth I* (London: Thames, 1987), pp. 131-33. The woodcut is also reproduced in Allardyce Nicoll, *The Elizabethans* (Cambridge: Cambridge Univ. Press, 1957), p. 21 ; *The Riverside Shakespeare*, ed. G. Blakemore Evans (Boston: Houghton, 1974), plate 18; Frances A. Yates, *Astraea: The Imperial Theme in the Sixteenth Century* (London: Routledge, 1975), plate 9c; Ian Maclean, *The Renaissance Notion of Woman: A Study in the Fortunes of Scholasticism and Medieval Science in European Intellectual Life* (Cam-

bridge: Cambridge Univ. Press, 1980), on the jacket; Philippa Berry, *Of Chastity and Power: Elizabethan Literature and the Unmarried Queen* (London: Routledge, 1989), plate 8.

4. Schmitt, pp. 90-91,

5. To the best of my knowledge, the existence of this dedication has never been reported in print. There is no mention of it in Franklin B. Williams, Jr, *Index of Dedications and Commendatory Verses in English Books Before 1641* (London: Bibliographical Society, 1962), and in the same author's "Dedications and Verses through 1640: Addenda," *The Library*, 5th series 30: 1 (1975), Supplement 1-20.

6. I wish to thank the Assistant Librarian of Lambeth Palace Library, Christina Mackwell, first for answering my request for bibliographical information concerning this copy (classmarked 1588. 16), and then for allowing me to examine it personally.

7. "Tu nisi quod dabimus SACRO CANDORE beâris, / Nullus in hoc DONO CANDOR inesse potest" (sig. π^v).

8. On 23 June 1586 a Star Chamber Decree stated that all books "must be first seen and perused by the Archbishop of CANTERBURY and the bishop of LONDON for the tyme beinge or any one of them." See Edward Arber, *A Transcript of the Registers of the Company of Stationers of London, 1554-1640*, vol. 2 (New York: Smith, 1950), p. 810.

9. Jean Bodin, *The Six Bookes of a Commonweale*, trans. Richard Knolles (London: G. Bishop, 1606), sig. $D5^r$.

10. Bodin, sig. $E3^v$-$E4^v$.

11. Bodin, sig. $E4^r$.

12. See Julian H. Franklin, *Jean Bodin and the Sixteenth Century Revolution in the Methodology of Law and History* (New York: Columbia Univ. Press, 1963), pp. 78-79.

13. Edward W. Said, *Orientalism* (1978; Harmondsworth: Penguin Books, 1995).

14. Franklin, pp. 68-74.

15. See *Biographie Universelle*, ed. L. G. Michaud, 2nd edn, vol. 4 (Paris: Desplaces; Leipzig: Brockhaus, 1854-65), p. 65.

16. The official Latin translation was eventually published at Basle in 1586.

17. Quentin Skinner, *The Foundations of Modern Political Thought*, vol. 2 (Cambridge: Cambridge Univ. Press, 1978), p. 300.

18. *Sphaera civitatis*, sig. $V8^r$ (*Six Books*), $Ii8^r$ (*Method*).

19. Bodin, sig. $E3^v$.

20. William Harrison, *The Description of England*, ed. G. Edelen (Ithaca, NY: Cornell Univ. Press, 1968), p. 118. Harrison (1534-93) was a graduate of Christ Church, Oxford. His *Description of England* was not published as a self-standing volume, but as an introduction to Raphael Holinshed's *Chronicles* (1st ed. 1577; 2nd ed. 1587).

21. "Servitus autem est constitutio iuris gentium, qua quis dominio alieno contra naturam subicitur" (Justinian, *The Institutes of Justinian: Text, Translation and Commentary*, ed. J. A. C. Thomas [Amsterdam: North-Holland, 1975], 1. 3.

2). Thomas's translation. This legal opinion is attributed to Florentinus in *Digest* 1. 5. 4. 1.

22. "Usu exigente et humanis necessitatibus gentes humanae quaedam sibi constituerunt: bella etenim orta sunt et captivitates secutae et servitutes, quae sunt iuri naturali contrariae (iure enim naturali ab initio omnes homines liberi nascebantur)" (Justinian, *Institutes* 1. 2. 2). Thomas's translation.

23. See *The Oxford Classical Dictionary*, 2nd ed. (Oxford: Clarendon Press, 1970), p. 996.

24. Milton Meltzer, *Slavery: A World History*, updated ed., vol. 1 (New York: Da Capo, 1993), p. 44.

25. On Jewish slave legislation see Salo Wittmaker Baron, *A Social and Religious History of the Jews*, 2nd ed., vol. 1 (New York: Columbia Univ. Press, 1952), p. 70. On slavery in the Muslim world see *The Cambridge History of Islam*, ed. P. M. Holt, Ann K. Lambton, and Bernard Lewis, vol. 2 (Cambridge: Cambridge Univ. Press, 1970), pp. 515-16, 524.

26. Aristotle, *Politics*, trans. H. Rackam (1932; London: Heinemann; Cambridge, MA: Harvard Univ. Press, 1990) I. 1. 1252 b. On Aristotle's disappointment with Alexander's policies see Aristotle, *Politique*, ed. Jean Aubonnet, vol. 1 (Paris: Les Belles Lettres, 1960), pp. lxxxviii-xcv. For a different view on the whole question see Roberto Andreotti, (Per una critica dell'ideologia di Alessandro Magno,' *Historia*, 5 (1956): 257-302.

27. My exposition of Major's thought is indebted to Pedro Leturia, "Maior y Vitoria ante la conquista de America," *Estudios Eclesiásticos* (1932): 44-82, although at times I depart from his interpretation.

28. "Quare primus eos occupans iuste eis imperat, quia natura sunt servi, ut patet. Primo Politicorum tertio et quarto dicit Philosophus: quod sunt alii natura servi alii liberi, manifestum est" (John Major, *In secundum librum sententiarum*, 2nd ed. (Paris: I. Gräion, 1519), fol. clxxxvii^v, col. 2).

29. I am aware of the fact that, according to some scholars, one should not talk of racism before the eighteenth century. However, I think that their definition of racism is too narrow. In my opinion, one can already find racist doctrines in Hippocrates, the founder of Western medicine, who lived in the fifth century BC.

30. Quoted by Tzvetan Todorov, *The Conquest of America*, trans. Richard Howard (New York: Harper, 1985), pp. 162-63.

31. Lewis Hanke, *Aristotle and the American Indians: A Study in Race Prejudice in the Modern World* (London: Hollis, 1959), pp. 36-37.

32. STC 4739. For a modern translation of the same work see Bartolomé de Las Casas, *A Short Account of the Destruction of the Indies*, ed. and trans. Nigel Griffin (Harmondsworth: Penguin, 1992).

33. See Heinrich Reusch, *Die* Indices Librorum Prohibitorum *Des Sechzehnten Jahrhunderts* (1886; Neeuwkoop: De Graaf, 1961), p. 559. In the following year the *Sphaera civitatis* also appeared in a Portuguese Index of forbidden books. See *Índices dos Livros Proibidos em Portugal no Século XVI: Apresentação, Estudo Introdutório e Reprodução Fac-similada dos Índices*, ed. Artur Moreira de Sá (Lisbon: Instituto Nacional de Investigação Científica, 1983), p. 787.

34. "Ex imitatione et exemplo naturae, quae homines persequi feras venando docuit. Sed barbari sunt quasi ferae, qui subiici et obtemperare imperio nisi coacti nolunt" (*Sphaera civitatis*, sig. D8^r).

35. "Bellum barbaris indicere, nec est vim inferre, nec est iniuriam facere. Nam ut iudex nec vim inferre, nec iniuriam facere dicatur, cum in supplicium reos sceleris condemnat, ita qui in homines immanitate barbaros bellum gerunt, non vim sed imperium, non iniuriam sed praescriptum naturae exequi et exercere dicuntur" (*Sphaera civitatis*, sig. D8^r-8^v).

36. "Etsi libenter non audio nimiam Hispanorum et Portugalensium in Indos severitatem, quam in memorabili sua peregrinatione exercuerunt, barbaros tamen ad ordinem et imperium (quod ratio naturae iussit) pellere et coercere oportet. Quare licet infideles ut sunt a fide alieni, non sint cogendi ad fidem, ad amplexum tamen studiumque civilis vitae vi et armis sunt pertrahendi" (*Sphaera civitatis*, sig. D8^r-D8^v).

37. Accounts of Hawkins's slaving expeditions were published in the first edition of Richard Hakluyt's *Principall Navigations, Voyages and Discoveries of the English Nation* (1589; Cambridge: Cambridge Univ. Press, 1965), pp. 521-22, 523-43, 553-57. It is very striking for a modern reader to see that there is not a word in these accounts to suggest that the slavers had any human feelings towards the human beings they captured and sold.

38. Bernard Burke, *The General Armoury of England, Scotland, Ireland and Wales* (London: Harrison, 1884), p. 469. Peter Fryer, *Staying Power: The History of Black People in Britain* (London: Pluto, 1984), p. 8, adds that "three black men shackled with slave collars were displayed on the coat of arms itself." However, there is no mention of such men in Burke. Fryer probably misinterprets the drawing in Mary S. Hawkins, *Plymouth Armada Heroes: The Hawkins Family* (Plymouth: Brendon, 1888), p. 67 (reproduced here as Fig. 2.) There, the arms of Sir John Hawkins are impaled with those of his two wives, Katherine Gonson and Margaret Vaughan. The coat of arms of the Vaughan family (Burke, p. 1050) included three boys' heads with snakes wrapped around their necks.

39. J. Holland Rose, A. P. Newton, and E. A. Benians, ed. *The Cambridge History of the British Empire*, vol. 1 (Cambridge: Cambridge Univ. Press, 1929-36), p. 50.

40. Fryer, p. 9.

41. "Nam ut nihil citius corpus humanum inficit quam pestilentium vaporum cum innatis humoribus copulatio, ita nihil velocius corrumpit civitatem quam peregrinorum hominum admissio, in qua contagio et venenum latet" (*Sphaera civitatis*, sig. Ee2^r).

42. "Quippe etsi rami sint eiusdem plantae, a radice tamen non salutare succum sed venenum hauriunt, quo tandem infecta tota planta cadit" (*Sphaera civitatis*, sig. Ee3^v). For the comparisons of foreigners to snakes and locusts see sig. Ee3^r.

43. *Sphaera civitatis*, sig. Ee3^v.

44. I derived these figures from Marvin Spevack, *A Complete and Systematic Concordance to the Works of Shakespeare*, 9 vols (Hildesheim: Olms, 1968-80).

45. *Politics* VII. 6. 1327 b. See also Case's statement that natural slaves do

not rebel because their nature is timid in *Sphaera civitatis*, sig. Ss3^r.

46. Likewise, when Othello envisages burning in hell for having murdered the innocent Desdemona, he calls himself a "cursèd slave" (5. 2. 283). However, Othello's racial identity adds special connotations to his words, which could be interpreted as validating Brabanzio's racist assessment of his son-in-law's nature.

47. See William Shakespeare, *The Merchant of Venice*, ed. John Russell Brown, 7th ed. (London: Methuen, 1959), pp. 168-72.

48. Stanley Wells, *Shakespeare: A Dramatic Life* (London: Sinclair, 1994), p. 159.

49. Sir Thomas Smith, *De Republica Anglorum*, ed. Mary Dewar (Cambridge: Cambridge Univ. Press, 1982), p. 138.

50. James Shapiro, *Shakespeare and the Jews* (New York: Columbia Univ. Press, 1996), pp. 170-72.

51. Shapiro, p. 172. In the Bible, Cushites are the people of the upper Nile River. Jeremiah 13. 23 argues that Judah can no more change its tendency to sin than a Cushite (translated as "an Ethiopian" in the King James Version) can change skin colour. Genesis 10.6 says that Cush was a son of Ham. According to a tradition, Noah had commanded his sons, Ham, Shem and Japhet, not to copulate with their wives while staying in the Ark. Believing that the first child born after the Flood would inherit the earth, Ham disobeyed his father's command. In order to punish Ham, God decided that his son, Cush, and all his descendants would be born black. This tradition was well-known in the Renaissance and an account of it can be found, for example, in Richard Hakluyt, *The Principal Navigations, Voyages, Traffiques, and Discoveries of the English Nation*, vol. 7 (Glasgow: Maclehose, 1904), pp. 263-64. In Genesis 9. 21-26 Ham's sin is that he saw his father naked, and the punishment indicted on his descendants is perpetual slavery. See Virginia Mason Vaughan, *Othello: A Contextual History* (Cambridge: Cambridge Univ. Press, 1994), pp. 53-54.

Fig. 1. ¶1ᵛ of John Case, *Sphaera civitatis* (Oxford: Joseph Barnes, 1588). By permission of the British Library. Shelfmark 8006.b.8.

Fig. 2. The Arms of Sir John Hawkins, in Mary S. Hawkins, *Plymouth Armada Heroes: The Hawkins Family* (Plymouth: Brendon, 1888), p. 67. By permission of the Bodleian Library, University of Oxford, Shelfmark 22853 d. 2.

ARMS OF SIR JOHN HAWKINS,
Impaling Gonson and Vaughan.

Notes on Contributors

YASUNARI TAKAHASHI, the former President of the Shakespeare Society of Japan, is a professor of English at Showa Women's University, Tokyo. His publications include *The Literature of the Fool* (1977)*, "Towards a Theatrical Body: Notes on Hamlet" (1992), translations of Shakespeare and Beckett, and comparative studies of these dramatists vis-à-vis Noh and Kyogen. He is also the author of *The Braggart Samurai* (1991)*, a Kyogen adaptation of *The Merry Wives of Windsor*.

MAMI ADACHI is an associate professor of English at the University of the Sacred Heart, Tokyo. Her publications on early modern drama include "Song as Device: Ben Jonson's Use of Seduction Songs in *Volpone* and *The Devil is an Ass*" (1989), "'My Brain the Stage': Margaret Cavendish's Self-fashioning" (1996)* and "'Our court shall be a little academe': Representations of the Single-Sex Academy in Tennyson, Cavendish and Shakespeare" (1997). Japanese representative of the Board of the Margaret Cavendish Society, she is currently working on the eponymous woman-writer in 17th-century philosophical and literary contexts.

EMI HAMANA is a professor of English at Rikkyo Jogakuin Junior College, Tokyo. She has published articles including "A Stylistic Approach to the Use of Tense-Mixing in Shakespeare's *Venus and Adonis*" (1981), "Sexual Politics / Politics of Interpretation: A Reading of *Antony and Cleopatra*" (1994)*, "Whose Body Is It, Anyway?: A Re-reading of Ophelia" (1995) and "A New Politics of Pornography" (1997)*. She is working on Shakespeare criticism and contemporary cultural criticism.

ATSUHIKO HIROTA is a research fellow at the University of Tokyo, Komaba. His publications include an article, "Single Combats in Shakespeare's History Plays" (1995). His current interest is in the relationship between historiography and literature in early modern nationalism, and he is completing his Ph.D. dissertation, "The Romanticization of a British Past: Early Modern Nationalism and the Literary Representations of Wales."

MARIKO ICHIKAWA is an associate professor of English at Ibaraki University. She is working on the original staging of Shakespeare and his contemporaries. Her publications include "A Note on Shakespeare's Stage Direction" (1985) and "Time Allowed for Exits in Shakespeare's Plays" (forthcoming). She is currently completing a book jointly with Andrew Gurr on staging in Shakespeare's theatres.

ARATA IDE is an associate professor of English at Toyo Eiwa Women's University, Yokohama. He has published articles including "Christopher Marlowe and the Kentish Connection" (1996). "Christopher Marlowe and the Stationer: On the Publication of *Tamburlaine the Great*" (1996)* and "Protestantism, Stationers, and Hack Writers: On News Pamphlets of Anthony Munday" (1997)*. He is currently working on a biographical study of Marlowe.

SOJI IWASAKI is a professor of English at Tokai Women's College, Gifu. He is the author of *The Sword and the Word: Shakespeare's Tragic Sense of Time* (1973), *Nature Triumphant: Approach to* The Winter's Tale (1984, 1991) and *Icons in English Renaissance Drama* (1992). His articles include *"Veritas filia temporis* and Shakespeare" (1973), "Relative Values in Medieval and Renaissance Drama" (1992), and "Hamlet and Melancholy: An Iconographical Approach" (1995). He is preparing a book on "Shakespeare and Early Modern Europe."

MITSURU KAMACHI is an associate professor of English at Kyoto University. Her articles on Elizabethan drama include "The Anamorphic Box: Sonnet 24 and the Portrait of Edward VI" (1996)*, "What's in a Name?: Hermione and the Hermetic Tradition in *The Winter's Tale*" (1994), "'Lente Currite Noctis Equi': *Doctor Faustus* and Its Audience" (1985) and "Vindice Vindicatus: The Hidden Trickster in *The Revenger's Tragedy*" (1981). She is currently working on a book entitled *The Forest of Anamorphoses: Perspectives on Elizabethan Drama*.

SHOICHIRO KAWAI is an associate professor at the University of Tokyo, Komaba. His publications include "The Four Basic Dramatic Functions of Characters in Shakespeare's Comedies" (1989), "Disguise in Shakespeare / Shakespeare in Disguise" (1993), "Hamlet's Imagination" (1995), and "John Lowin as Iago" (1996). He has just submitted a Ph.D. thesis, "Disguise in Renaissance Drama," to the University of Tokyo. His current interest is in the relationship of text and performance in Elizabethan drama.

Notes on Contributors

TETSUO KISHI is a professor of English at Kyoto University. His publications include *Shakespeare in the Theatre* (1991)* and an annotated edition of *The Merchant of Venice* (1996). His essays appear in *English Criticism in Japan* (1972), *Images of Shakespeare* (1988), *Reading Plays* (1991), and *Shakespeare and Cultural Traditions* (1994), which he edited with Roger Pringle and Stanley Wells. He is currently writing *Shakespeare in Japan* with Graham Bradshaw. He has translated works by Jan Kott, Peter Brook, George Steiner and Kenneth Branagh as well as plays by Harold Pinter.

MISAKO MATSUDA is a part-time lecturer in English at Japan Women's University, Tokyo. Her articles include "The Renaissance Concept of Opportunity and *Richard II*" (1992), "Fiction and Astrology: A Study on the 'Venus Tragedie' in Robert Greene's *Planetomachia* (1585)" (1994)*, and "The Grotesque Viewpoint in the Renaissance Mythological Paintings and the English Renaissance Literature" (1997)*. She is currently working on Renaissance devotional emblem books and Shakespeare.

SERGIO MAZZARELLI teaches English at Kwassui Women's College, Nagasaki. He is particularly interested in Elizabethan writings in Latin and their relationships with the vernacular literature of the period. His unpublished doctoral dissertation, "Aspects of Hierarchy and Order in John Case's *Sphaera civitatis* (1588)" (Birmingham Univ., 1996), analyses the ideas on slavery, women, Machiavelli, and astrology contained in the only university textbook on political theory written by an Elizabethan.

AYA MIMURA is a lecturer of English at Meiji University, Tokyo. Her articles include "Myth Transfiguration: Three Tragedies on the Legend of Phaidra" (1992)*, "'Edgar I Nothing Am': Body Presence in *King Lear*" (1994)* and "The Absent Reader: Tension in Fulke Greville's Prose and Tragedy" (1996). She is currently working on the adaptation of classical myths and legends in Renaissance England.

TED MOTOHASHI is an associate professor of English at Tokyo Metropolitan University. His recent articles include "Body Politic and Political Body in *Coriolanus*" (1994), "'The play's the thing ... of nothing': Writing and 'the liberty' in *Hamlet*" (1995), "Cannibal and Caliban: *The Tempest* and the Discourse of Cannibalism" (forthcoming), and "The Discourse of Cannibalism in Early Modern Travel Writing" (forthcoming).

KOICHI MURANUSHI is an associate professor of English at Nagoya University. His published articles on Shakespeare and related topics include "Weapons Encircled with Written Words: Literacy and Orality in *Titus Andronicus*" (1993)*, "Gory Recipe, Pregnancy, and Revenge in *Titus Andronicus*" (1994)*, "Multiplied Twins in *The Duchess of Malfi*" (1977)*, and "Patriarchal Control and Sexual Revenge in *Hamlet*" (1997)*. The present essay forms part of a book-in-progress tentatively entitled *Shakespeare's Tragedies and the Body*.*

SHIGEKI TAKADA is an associate professor of English at Kanazawa University. His articles include "Calls and Silence: Style of Distance in *Julius Caesar*" (1986), "*Othello*: The Plot of Complicity" (1990)* and "Prospero Returning Home" (1995)*. He has also translated Stephen Greenblatt's *Renaissance Self-Fashioning: From More to Shakespeare* into Japanese (1992). He is currently working on how the subjects of Elizabethan poets and playwrights were constituted in the process of writing.

YOKO TAKAKUWA is a part-time lecturer in English at Chuo University, Tokyo. Her research is concerned with a theory of gendered subjectivity in the Shakespearean and Kabuki theatres, within which field she completed her doctoral thesis and has published articles in *Women: A Cultural Review* (1994), *Q/W/E/R/T/Y* (1995), *New Literary History* and *Il Confronto Letterario* (1996). Her most recent essay is "The Performance of Gendered Identity in Shakespeare and Kabuki" (forthcoming). She is currently working on the paradox of courtly love as rhetorical performance in Shakespeare's plays and sonnets.

YUMIKO YAMADA is an associate professor of English at Osaka City University. Her publications on Renaissance literature include "Classics That Revolt: Modernizing Factors in *Sejanus*, *Epicoene* and *Catiline*" (1988) and "*The Staple of News*: Kings and Kingdoms" (1990), *Ben Jonson and Cervantes: Tilting at the Chivalric Romance** (1995), "Ben Jonson and Censorship: Mainly on *Sejanus*" (1996)* and "Hamlet Remodelled into Iago: The Other Aspect of *Othello*" (1996)*. She is currently working on a sequel to *Ben Jonson and Cervantes*.

The publications marked with asterisks are written in Japanese.

Index

Adelman, Janet 125, 177
Aeschylus 169, 176; *Eumenides* 177; *Libation Bearers, The* 169
Alciati, Andrea *Emblematum Liber* 135, 136
Alexander the Great 275
Amadas, Philip 39
Anderson, Anthony *Sermon profitably preached in the church within Tower, A* 223
Anderson, Benedict 198, 200
Aristotle 258, 269, 273, 274, 275, 278, 279, 280 *Poetics* 271; *Politics* 273, 275
Augustine, St 269

Bacon, Francis 262
Bainham, James 126
Baldo, Jonathan 201
Barlowe, Arthur 39
Barnes, Barnabe *Devil's Charter, The* vii
Barnes, Joseph 269
Bartolus of Sassoferrato 269
Bate, Jonathan 132
Becherman, Bernard 150, 151
Berry, Phillipa 40, 247
Beza, Theodore 269
Bhabha, Homi K. 197, 198, 206, 209
Blackfriars, The 155
Bodin, Jean 262, 269, 270, 271, 273, 280, 281; *Method for the Easy Comprehension of History* 272; *Six Books of a Commonwealth* 270
Botticelli, Sandro *Tragedy of Lucretia, The* 131; *Venus and Mars* 138
Branagh, Kenneth 200, 203, 204, 205, 207, 208, 211
Brant, Sebastian 269
Brome, William 275
Brooke, Arthur 97
Bruck, Jacob à *Emblemata Moralia et Bellica* 136
Burghley, Lord 39
Burke, Kenneth 127
Burnett, Mark Thornton 241
Bush, Douglas 132

Camerarius, Joachim 136
Camino, Mercedes M. 132
Campion, Edmund 237
Campion, Edmund
  Historie of Ireland, A 237
Cary, Elizabeth *Tragedie of Mariam, The* 63
Case, John 269, 270, 272, 275, 276, 277, 278, 279, 280; *Sphaera civitatis* 269, 270, 272, 275, 276, 277, 278

Castillo, Bernal Diàz del *Conquest of New Mexico, The* 48
Cats, Jacob *Emblemata Moralia et Aeconomica* 135
Cavell, Stanley 125, 127
Cavendish, Charles 71
Cavendish, Margaret 3, 69, 70, 71, 72, 73, 74, 75, 76, 77, 78, 80, 81, 82; *Female Academy, The* 81; *Loves Adventures* 72; *Natures three Daughters Beauty, Love and Wit* 79; *Philosophical Fancies* 71; *Poems and Fancies* 71; *Religious, The* 81; *World's Olio, The* 82; *Youths Glory and Deaths Banquet* 79
Cavendish, Willaim 72, 73, 74, 75
Cecil, Robert 270
Chapman, George *Monsieur d'Olive* 55
Charleton, Walter 78
Chaucer, Geoffrey 133
Cicero 269
Clark, Sandra 61
Claudius 260
Cockpit Company, The 151
Columbus, Christopher 40
Contarini 269
Corinthians 123
Cranach, Lucas *Lucretia* 131; *Lucretia and Judith* 131
Crane, Ralph 153
Cruickshank, C. G. 222

Daly, P. M. 135
Dante Alighieri 121 *Divine Comedy, The* 117, 121
Dare, Virginia 38
Dawson, Thomas 275
Derrida, Jacques 19, 20, 26, 27, 32 *Spurs* 26
Descartes, René 72, 78
Domitianus 138
Drake, Francis 40
Dryden, John 53, 107
Durling, Robert M. 121, 125, 127

Eliot, T. S. *Waste Land, The* 103
Elizabeth I 3, 37, 39, 45, 46, 47, 48, 49, 168, 172, 173, 174, 222, 223, 237, 243, 246, 247, 269
Ellis-Fermor, Una 218
Elyot, Thomas *Boke Named the Governour, The* 132
Euripides *Electra* 169
Fletcher, John 3, 53, 55, 56, 57, 60, 61, 62, 63; *Bonduca* 62; *Cupid's Revenge* 59; *Custom of the Country, The* 60; *False One, The*

60; *Humorous Lieutenant, The* 63; *Night Walker, The* 55; *Sea Voyage, The* 62; *Tragedy of Valentinian, The* 58; *Wild-Goose Chase, The* 53, 54, 55, 57, 58, 60, 61; *Woman's Prize, or The Tamer Tamed, The* 57, 62,
Ford, John *Laws of Candy, The* 60
Francis, Duke of Alençon 38
Frazer, James G. *Folk-lore in the Old Testament* 118
Freud, Sigmund 19

Garber, Marjorie 210
Garrick, David 97, 99
Gassendi, Pierre 78
Genesis 118, 119
Geoffrey of Monmouth *History of the Kings of Britain, The* 249
Ghismonda 151
Gifford, George *Sermons upon the whole booke of the Revelation* 224
Gilbert, Humphrey 39
Ginzburg, Carlo 126, 127
Glanville, Joseph 78
Globe Company, The 150
Globe, The 155, 157, 211
Goffe, Thomas 167, 173, 174, 175, 176, 177; *Tragedy of Orestes, The* 167, 173, 178
Goldberg, Jonathan 172
Golding, Arthur 242
Gosson, Stephen 223, 226, 227, 228; *Playes Confuted in fiue Actions* 226
Greenblatt, Stephen 240; *Marvelous Possessions* 48; *Renaissance Self-Fashioning* 126; *Sir Water Ralegh* 43
Greene, Robert 38, 193

Hadfield, Andrew 237, 238
Haec-Vir: Or The Womanish-Man 62
Hakluyt, Richard 38, 39, 40, 41, 45, 48; *Principal Navigations* 38, 39, 41
Hamlet and Japan 3
Hamlin, William M. 46
Hammerton, Stephen 60
Harman, Thomas *Caueat for Common Cvrsetors Vvlgarly Called Vagabones* 240
Harrison, Willaim *Description of England* 272
Harvey, Gabriel 271
Harward, Simon *Solace for the Souldier and Saylour, The* 224
Hatton, Christopher 270
Hawkins, John 276
Helmont, Johannes Van 78

Heywood, Thomas *Captives* 151
Hic Mulier: Or, The Man-Woman 62
Hobbes, Thomas 78
Holinshed 248; *Chronicles* 132, 237, 245, 248, 249
Homer 260, 261; *Iliad* 264; *Odyssey* 262
Horace 260, 261, 262, 264; *Ars poetica* 260
Horapollo *Hieroglyphica* 136
Howard, Jean E. 200
Hoy, Cyrus 61
Hulme, Peter *Colonial Encounters* 38
Hyll, Thomas 136; *Proffitable Arte of Gardeing* 136; *Proffitable Instructions of the Perfite Ordering of Bees* 136

Isaiah 120

James I 44, 46, 47, 138, 167, 168, 172, 174, 175, 255, 257, 264; *Daemonology* 255, 257
Jeremiah 120
Johnson, S. F. 119
Johnson, Samuel 54
Jones, Ann Rosalind 238
Jones, Inigo 255, 264, 266
Jonson, Ben 4, 53, 75, 76, 102, 255, 256, 257, 258, 259, 260, 261, 262, 263, 264, 265, 266; *Alchemist, The* 58, 255; *Epicoene* 256; *Masque of Beauty, The* 255, 265; *Masque of Blackness, The* 255, 265; *Masque of Queens, The* 255, 256, 261, 264, 265; *Poetaster* 263; *Sejanus* 257; *Volpone* 255

Kahn, Coppélia 16
Kawakami, Otojiro 2
Kempe, William 192
Kennedy, Andrew K. 89, 92, 94; *Dramatic Dialogue* 89
King Leir 61
King's Men, The 53
Knapp, Jeffrey 40
Kurosawa, Akira *Kumonosu-jo* (*Throne of Blood*) vii

Lacan, Jacques 19, 31
Las Casas, Bartolomé de *Spanish colonie, The* 275
Lee, Henry 138
Leech, Clifford 53
Leigh, Dorothy *Mothers blessing, The* 60
Livy 131, 132, 140, 141; *History of Rome, The* 131
Locrine 249
Lord Admiral's Men, The 184, 194, 240
Lord Chamberlain's Men, The 183, 192, 194

Index

Lucas, Elizabeth 71
Lucas, John 72
Lydgate, John *Fall of Princes, The* 118; *Serpent of Division, The* 132
Lyly, John 270

Machiavelli, Niccolò 140
Major, John *Commentary on the Four Books of Peter Lombard's "Sentences"* 274
Maria, Henrietta 71
Markham, Gervase *English Huswife, The* 60
Marlowe, Christopher 3, 218, 221, 227, 228, 229, 230, 231, 238, 240, 242, 243; *Tamburlaine the Great* 215, 219, 221, 225, 226, 228, 229, 231, 238, 240, 241
Marston, John *Antonio and Mellida* 151; *Antonio's Revenge* 173
Marvell, Andrew 7, 15
Massinger, Philip *Maid of Honour, The* 61
Mazotta, Guiseppe 117
Middleton, Thomas *Revenger's Tragedy, The* 173, 175; *Women Beware Women* 61, 173
Montrose, Louis 38, 40, 246
More, Sir Thomas 126
Munday, Anthony 240

Nashe, Thomas 193, 221, 222
Newton, Issac 78
Ninagawa, Yukio *Macbeth* viii

O'Donnell, Norbert F. 173
Old Vic, The 91
Olivier, Laurence 200, 205
Onions, C. T. 14
Orestes plays 3
Orgel, Stephen 8, 9, 38, 243; *Impersonations* 8
Otway, Thomas 93, 94, 96, 97, 99; *History and Fall of Caius Marius, The* 93
Ovid 131, 132, 140, 141, 242, 243, 261; *Fasti* 131, 140 ; *Metamorphoses* 242

Painter, William *Palace of Pleasure, The* 132
Partridge, Eric *Shakespeare's Bawdy* 12
Paster, Grail Kern 8
Paul III, Pope *Sublimis Deus* 274
Peacham, Henry *Basilikon Doron* 138; *Minerva Britanna* 15, 139
Peele, George 137
Philip II (of Spain) 38
Pickering, John 169, 170, 171, 173, 174; *History of Horestes, The* 168; *Newe Enterlude of Vice* 167
Plato 269

Platt, Hugh *Delightes for ladies* 60
Plutarch 273
Pomponazzi, Pietro 275
Porter, Henry *Two Angry Women of Abington, The* 59
Ptolemy 274
Purchas, Samuel 38, 45, 46, 47, 48, 49; *Hakluytus Posthumus, or Purchas His Pilgrimes* 38, 45

Quint, David 119

Rakin, Phyllis 200
Ralegh (Raleigh), Walter 38, 39, 40, 41, 42, 43, 44, 45, 46, 48, 238, 246, 247; *Discoverie of the Large, Rich, and Bewtiful Empyre of Guiana, The* 38, 40, 41, 44, 45, 246
Reade, Simon 255
Remy, Nicholas 262
Revelation 120
Rhodes, Neil 217
Rose, The 155
Rowley, William *Maid in the Mill, The* 58; *Woman Never Vext, A* 58
Rubinstein, Frankie 7, 11, 14

Said, Edward *Orientalism* 271
Saito, Takeshi *Shakespeare: His Life and Art* 2
Salgado, Gamini 243
Scofield, Paul 203
Scot, Reginald *Discoverie of Witchcraft, The* 255, 262
Selden, John 262
Seneca 167, 173, 174, 176
Sepúlveda, Juan Ginés de *Democrates alter* 275
Shakespeare, William
  Antony and Cleopatra 9, 145, 155, 156; *As You Like It* 1; *Comedy of Errors, The* 62; *Coriolanus* 3, 115, 118, 120, 121, 126; *Cymbeline* 19, 20, 30, 63, 152, 153, 278; *Hamlet* 1, 2, 148, 149, 157, 173, 175; *Henry IV* 3, 183, 184, 185, 186, 187, 188, 189, 190, 191, 192, 207, 208, 209, 278; *Henry V* 3, 137,197, 199, 200, 201, 207, 208, 210, 211; *Henry VI* 278; *Julius Caesar* vii,1, 257; *King Lear* 1, 146, 278; *Macbeth* 25, 61, 108, 173, 257; *Measure for Measure* 152, 153; *Merchant of Venice, The* 1, 63, 278, 280, 281; *Merry Wives of Windsor, The* 19, 20, 25, 33, 147; *Midsummer Night's Dream, A* 99, 153, 158; *Much Ado About Nothing* 93; *Othello* 2, 3, 19, 20, 23, 145, 278; *Pericles*

104, 109; *Rape of Lucrece, The* 3, 140; *Richard II* 156; *Richard III* 104, 107, 110, 111; *Romeo and Juliet* 1, 3, 5, 8, 9, 15, 16, 55,58, 89, 93, 96, 145; *Taming of the Shrew, The* 57; *Tempest, The* vii, 103, 106, 109, 111, 155, 243; *Titus Andronicus* 155; *Troilus and Cressida*104, 105, 107, 137; *Twelfth Night* 11; *Two Gentlemen of Verona, The* 134; *Two Noble Kinsmen, The* 58; *Winter's Tale, The* 19, 20, 22
Shapiro, James 280
Sharp, Richard 60
Silvayn, Alexander *Orator, The* 280
Smith, Thomas *De republica anglorum* 280
Southampton, Earl of 132
Spenser, Edmund ii, 237, 238, 240, 241, 244, 246, 247, 248, 249; *Faerie Queene, The* 238, 246, 247, 249; *View of the Present State of Ireland, A* 237, 240, 241
Stallybrass, Peter 207, 238
Stanyhurst, Richard *Description of Ireland, The* 237
Stone, Lawrence 11
Strachey, William vii

Suzuki, Tadashi *Tale of Lear* viii

Takahashi, Yasunari *Braggart Samurai, The* viii
Tarlton, Richard 192
Taylor, Gary 108, 158
Theatre, The 155, 156, 157
Theocritus 135,
Thomas, Keith 243
Throckmorton, Elizabeth 42
Thucydides 269
Tourneur, Cyril 102
Tsubouchi, Shoyo 1; *Notes on the Study of Shakespeare* 2

Unton, Henry 270

Vavell, Stanley 125
Veronese 131
Verstegan, Richard *Declaration of the trve cavses* 227
Vickers, Nancy 205
Virgil 269; *Aeneid* 263
Vitoria, Francisco de 274
Walsingham, Francis 222, 227
Watts, Cedric 11
Webster, John *Duchess of Malfi, The* 61, 173
Wells, Stanley 280
White, John 42

Whitgift, John 270
Whitney, Geoffrey *Choice of Emblemes, A* 15, 136
Wilson, John Dover 108
Wiseman, Susan 77
Wither, George *Collection of Emblemes* 138
Woolf, Virginia 70
Wright, Thomas *Passions of the Mind* 8

Yeager, R. F. 124

Zeffirelli, Franco 91